New York City
April 2007

CLOSING

BALANCES

CLOSING BALANCES

Business Obituaries

FROM

The Daily Telegraph

EDITED BY
Martin Vander Weyer

INTRODUCTION BY
Hugh Massingberd

First published in Great Britain
2006 by Aurum Press Limited,
25 Bedford Avenue,
London WC1B 3AT

A catalogue record for this book is available from the British Library.

ISBN-10: 1 84513 204 1
ISBN-13: 978 1 84513 204 0

1 3 5 7 9 10 8 6 4 2
2006 2008 2010 2009 2007

Printed and bound in Great Britain by MPG Books Ltd, Bodmin, Cornwall

⇻ CONTENTS ⇺

INTRODUCTION
Hugh Massingberd
VII

EDITOR'S NOTE
Martin Vander Weyer
XI

⇢⟹ INTRODUCTION ⟸⇠

BY

Hugh Massingberd

As in the City of London, the 'Big Bang' in the world of obituaries occurred in the mid-1980s, though it took several years before much attention was paid to the transformation of what had always been regarded as an obscure backwater of journalism. An article in the Christmas 1994 issue of *The Economist* – written, like most obituaries, anonymously – reflected, 'In the mid-1980s, when a general, structural upheaval overtook the British quality press, provoking sharp new competition for market share and a search for editorial edge, the unexpected potential of obituaries was recognised, and the obituaries came into their own.'

A wider recognition that, as *The Economist* put it, obituaries had become 'a source of daily fascination and delight', proved something of a mixed blessing as far as I was concerned on the obits desk of the *Daily Telegraph*. When I started the new section in 1986 – hitherto no set space had been allocated for obituaries, which just had to take their chance with other 'news' stories – I was largely left to my own devices and happy to be ignored by the hard-nosed hacks who regarded obits as a worthless dead end. But by the early 1990s our little corner of Siberia was beginning to be noticed and suddenly I found myself under fire.

At some sort of management conference in a hotel – to which, naturally, I was not invited – a fashionable *bien-pensant* figure had been hired to tell the assembled editorial executives what was wrong with the paper. (As one wag remarked, if it was insult therapy that you were looking for, it would have been cheaper to go to Soho.) Apparently the speaker took particular exception to the plethora of brigadiers, bishops and backwoods baronets on the obits page which she considered to resemble a parody of 'the old *Torygraph*'. (In fact, it was the one feature that the old paper *didn't* have.) How could we hope to attract bright new readers with this sort of dead wood? What we needed were thrusting achievers from New Britain.

This message was duly conveyed to me by a junior management nark. He solemnly showed me a pie chart that he had prepared illustrating the unhealthy percentage of old colonels and clergymen currently covered. Then, without a hint of irony, he urged me to concentrate more on, say, bright, young businesswomen. Perhaps, I wondered, I was now expected to carry a Kalashnikov through the City on my way to the *Telegraph* offices in Docklands in order to supply myself with suitable subject matter.

Yet, such absurdities aside, a raw nerve had been exposed. I was acutely conscious that the City and commercial world were closed books to me. Although my maternal grandfather had been a stockjobber (whatever that was), I was virtually innumerate and my attempts at becoming a solicitor in an earlier incarnation had foundered on my having, as my principal put it, 'no head for business'. But the City and its arcane rituals had always held a certain fascination; and as I perched on a stool in Sweetings, the century-old fish restaurant in Queen Victoria Street, guzzling oysters and swigging Black Velvet from a tankard, I wondered whether I would ever be initiated into its mysteries. As an obits fancier from an early age, I used to enjoy the euphemisms used in *The Times*, which recorded how a thumping crook had 'perhaps not always upheld the highest ethical traditions of the City of London'.

It was high time to take the plunge. I went to consult the oracle, Christopher Fildes, the wise and witty *doyen* of the *Telegraph*'s City pages whose company I had enjoyed on the Turf. Would he himself possibly take on the role of City and business obituarist? He replied that he did enough anonymous journalism ('leaders', and so forth) already, but mentioned that, by chance, the son of an old friend of his in the City had recently left the 'Big Bang' investment banking firm of Barclays de Zoete Wedd and was now thinking of trying his hand at journalism. Why not give him a go?

And so it came to pass that I had lunch with the editor and principal author of this book, Martin Vander Weyer, whose masterly potted biographies of City figures and businessmen were to play such a major part in enhancing the reputation of the *Telegraph*'s obituary page. We lunched not at Sweetings but on a rather ropey boat in Docklands, a far cry from the floating junks in Hong Kong's Aberdeen area in which Martin had been accustomed to eat as a budding Taipan in his previous career. A delightfully gentle, sympathetic, thoughtful, observant and humorous man, with a passion for the theatre (joyously expressed at Helmsley Arts Centre in his North Yorkshire hometown), Martin told me of his journalistic ambitions, which were to be realised remarkably swiftly on the *Spectator* and elsewhere.

From the word go, it was abundantly clear that Martin was 'a natural' – a consummate obituarist and, above all, an excellent writer with the rare gift of making his specialist subject not only comprehensible but enjoyable for the ordinary reader. Indeed he immediately established an honoured place among the handful of contributors to the obituaries page whose copy did not need to be tweaked. The Vander Weyer texts exemplified the style of obituary writing defined by *The Economist* as 'anecdotal, discursive, yet elegantly concise; learned, touching, and, in a kindly way, often extraordinarily funny'. One sensed, to quote *The Economist* again, that like a true obituarist, 'his greatest pleasure is more likely to derive from simple but satisfactory storytelling – the giving of a decent send-off to someone who has had a worthy, useful life, or has added a dash of colour to the passing pageant, but of whom no biography is ever likely to follow'.

It is a particular pleasure to welcome this collection of some of Martin Vander Weyer's greatest hits (plus a few gems by other contributors) between hard covers. There is no shortage of fun to be found in these pages – from a stockbroker's party trick of 'setting light to his own chest hair' to a dodgy tycoon's penchant for 'leather-clad lesbian chauffeuses'. The author has an acute eye for character, and a sharp ear for the telling 'quote' and City dictum. I particularly relished the following: 'the better the lunch, the worse the advice'; 'Bob [Maxwell] was squeaky-clean with me'; 'only two things in life really matter – friends and flowers'; 'leadership is something you just have – like spots'; 'everyone over sixty is entitled to a Rolls – under sixty you look a jerk'; and 'the chairman is twice as clever as he looks, but only half as clever as he thinks'. Among the feast of anecdotes to be truffled out are the story of Monty's ADC who had his hat eaten by an elephant ('which swiftly chewed it up, spitting out only the 12th Lancers badge'); the future property magnate who ran Hitler over in Munich in 1931; and the 26-stone squash player, the colourful 'Sir

Cumference', who 'would position himself in the centre of the court and, by playing ambidextrously, would make it impossible for an opponent to get past him to score a point'.

Through reading this book I have overcome much of my ignorance about City lore, and the secrets of sheltered institutions like 'the Uncles' at Warburgs, as well as learning the background of such celebrated business concerns as Patak Spices, Guinness, Sainsbury's, Marks & Spencer, ASDA, GKN, Viyella, Eurotunnel, McKinsey, Pilkington Glass, Fiat, Tetra Pak, Sony, Berni Inns and many more – not forgetting Mars, whose tyrannical old chairman used to order his son 'to kneel and pray for the company'.

In the best traditions of the *Telegraph* obituary, Martin Vander Weyer has a nice line in understatement. For example, he refers to the 'combative style' of Kenneth Keith, founder of Hill Samuel – which was originally to be called 'the Samuel Hill Investment Trust' until it was pointed out that this would have 'unattractive acronymic possibilities'. As ever, the deadpan presentation of biographical details often achieves the most effect. Thus we learn that 'Tiny' Rowland (with his 'threat of menace') was once a porter at Paddington station and a waiter at the Cumberland Hotel; Victor Matthews, the future proprietor of the *Daily Express*, used to deliver papers as a boy in north London; Sir Michael Clapham of ICI and the CBI designed his wife's clothes; and Lord Cowdray had a penchant for cottage pie. Mrs Edmond Safra described going to bed with her husband as 'like a board meeting'. I could happily go on citing the gems within, but – '*That's enough – Ed*'.

Although there are some famous, or infamous, names among the lives celebrated so skilfully here – Jimmy Goldsmith, Bernie Cornfeld, J.K. Galbraith, but not, alas, Robert Maxwell, who somehow escaped our clutches – the special strength of the book is the light it throws on the illustrious obscure. To quote yet again from *The Economist*: 'we remind ourselves that our world is shaped and coloured not only by the actions of great leaders and the interplay of economic forces, but by countless lesser contributors'. Finally, as the *Telegraph*'s City and Business obituarist has now blown his cover, I feel inclined to make public my own hunch that the author of the anonymous analysis of 'The Obituarist's Art: Lives After Death' in *The Economist* was none other than Martin Vander Weyer himself. Like all good obituaries, it was plainly an inside job.

BY

Martin Vander Weyer

Hugh Massingberd has identified me as the principal author of many – though by no means all – of the obituaries in this book. But there is not a single item here that was not improved by the editorial process introduced by Hugh, in which the stories of business lives are seamlessly woven together with telling and colourful passages contributed by specialist writers on military history, racing, cricket, genealogy, architecture and much else besides.

A great part of the credit for this book must therefore go to Hugh himself and to his successors – David Jones, Kate Summerscale, Christopher Howse and Andrew McKie. They have been ably assisted at various times by Jay Iliff, George Ireland, Georgia Powell, Katharine Ramsay and David Twiston-Davies. Among the brotherhood of obituary writers whose work has contributed to this collection I should also mention David Bowman, Robert Gray and the late Chaim Bermant. David Twiston-Davies and Teresa Moore, the long-serving and admirable secretary of the Obituaries Desk, have both been particularly helpful to me in the preparation of *Closing Balances*. On the home front I owe huge thanks to my multi-talented helper Erica Zarb.

Each one of these obituaries is, I hope, a gripping tale of personal endeavour and imagination, of risk and reward, of fortunes made and lost. But each one is also part of a larger jigsaw depicting a panorama of economic and social change, in Britain and around the world, in the second half of the twentieth century. Through individual life stories we can understand how the City of London changed from a club-like enclave of top-hatted gentlemen to a multinational centre of global securities trading; how old industries have declined and new ones grown up; how consumer tastes and shopping habits have been shaped by the bold notions of entrepreneurs; and how money made in the business world has been converted into stately mansions, fine art collections and great acts of philanthropy as it passes down the generations.

The way this jigsaw of the business world fits together day by day has never lost its fascination for me. I hope readers will share that feeling, and find this collection both instructive and richly entertaining.

~⊃ PART ONE ⊂~

CITY CHAPS

MICHAEL BELMONT – *eccentric stockbroker*
CHRISTOPHER CASTLEMAN – *dynamic head of Hill Samuel*
HILTON CLARKE – *the Bank of England's money market man*
THE EARL OF CROMER – *aristocratic Bank of England governor*
SIR PETER DANIELL – *top-hatted government broker*
SIR SEYMOUR EGERTON – *bachelor chairman of Coutts & Co*
JOCELYN HAMBRO – *jazz-loving merchant banker of the old school*
JOHNNY HENDERSON – *stockbroker who was Monty's ADC*
MARTIN LAMPARD – *lawyer who resorted to 'vulgar abuse'*
SIR MICHAEL RICHARDSON – *Margaret Thatcher's favourite banker*
SIR PHILIP SHELBOURNE – *irascible takeover adviser*
A.G.C. 'TONY' TROLLOPE – *colourful head of the City Building Society*

Michael Belmont

⊷▰▱▰ 1930–1996 ▰▱▰↢

Eccentric Stockbroker

Michael Belmont was a stockbroker who played a bold entrepreneurial role in the development of North Sea oil. He was a partner of Cazenove & Co, the most blue-blooded of City houses, from 1957 to 1990, but his ebullient personality and adventurous approach to business were in contrast to the subfusc style usually associated with the firm.

A big, handsome man with a booming voice, he enjoyed life to the full and threw himself wholeheartedly into every assignment. Through a brief meeting in 1964 with a Canadian oil prospector, Jack Pierce of Ranger Oil, Belmont developed a fascination with the possibilities of North Sea exploration. Together with another Cazenove partner, Peter Smith, he persuaded institutions in London and Edinburgh to invest first in Ranger, then in a joint venture called Scottish Canadian Oil & Transportation (SCOT), and finally in London and Scottish Marine Oil (LASMO), which was incorporated in 1971. Three years later the Ninian oilfield was discovered, with some 30 per cent of it in the North Sea block shared by LASMO, Ranger and BP.

This was a formidable challenge for a fledgling venture hobbled by the industrial policies of Tony Benn and in competition with giant multinationals. But Belmont set about raising the huge sums of capital required to develop the Ninian find, including in 1976 the largest private sector loan stock issue made in London up to that date. SCOT and LASMO merged to form Britain's fourth largest oil company, created in only six years, but in August 1977 Belmont was told by his bankers that he could not go on. Searching for new sources of funds, he discovered by chance that the vice-chairman of Midland Bank, Sir David Barran, was himself a former oilman: a last-gasp rescue by Midland was duly arranged. The company survived to see oil begin to flow in December 1978 and became a major name in the industry.

Michael Jeremy Kindersley Belmont was born in London on 26 February 1930. His father Algy (known as 'Electric Whiskers' on account of his fierce moustaches and short temper) became a partner of Cazenove in 1925, and developed the firm's first significant dealings in New York during the 1930s. Algy was in line to become senior partner, but was killed in 1944 in a motor accident while inspecting anti-aircraft batteries in Hyde Park during the blackout.

Young Michael was educated at Eton. After his father's death he spent a good deal of time at the home of his maternal grandfather, the 1st Lord Kindersley, a City grandee who founded the National Savings movement, and it was there that Michael learned to mix easily with distinguished people in all walks of life.

After national service as a second lieutenant in the 10th Royal Hussars, Belmont joined Cazenove in 1951. Antony Hornby, the pre-eminent Cazenove partner of the postwar era, took him under his wing, despatching him to travel round Britain re-establishing relations with a list of 100 industrial companies with which the firm had lost contact because of the war. Provincial hotel accommodation was austere in that era, but a Kindersley uncle was chairman of the Trust House hotel chain and Belmont – having taken to heart Hornby's maxim that business should always be fun – rarely failed to arrange lavish hospitality for himself and his colleagues.

He also took a hand in the firm's South African business, and became the first Cazenove man to make an international telephone call, having ignored a ruling that two partners should be present to authorise such a radical use of technology. In 1957 Belmont was sent to New York for three months' attachment to the Wall Street firm of Kidder Peabody, where his ebullience, his willingness to learn and his knack for making friends at all levels made him a brilliant success. Over the years his circle of American acquaintance embraced everyone from Walt Disney to Muhammad Ali and Richard Nixon. The latter, while vice-president, was entertained to lunch at Cazenove's offices in Tokenhouse Yard, and once witnessed Belmont's most celebrated party trick, which involved setting light to his own chest hair. Belmont became one of only two British participants in Bohemian Grove, the elite annual summer camp in the redwood forests of California.

He returned from New York to join the partnership and

establish Cazenove's first foreign department. He found new opportunities in Japan, which he first visited in 1963, and in Australia, but he made a particular speciality of California, a rapidly expanding economy then virtually unknown to British investors. In 1967, Cazenove bought a seat on the Pacific Coast stock exchange, becoming the first European member of any US bourse.

In 1974 Belmont yielded responsibility for the international side in order to concentrate on corporate finance, and particularly on his oil ventures. The strain of keeping LASMO afloat took a toll on him, not least in sharpening his heroic thirst for strong drink, but he remained a respected and hugely popular City figure. His retirement party at Claridges, at which the centrepiece was an ice sculpture in the shape of an oil rig, was attended by all 56 living partners of Cazenove, out of a total of 111 since the firm began in 1823. He remained a non-executive director of LASMO. Observing that its market capitalisation had grown to £1.8 billion, he liked to recall that at the time of its formation he had briefly owned half of the company.

In retirement Michael Belmont devoted his time to improving his Oxfordshire garden and to shooting.

He married, in 1953, Virginia Tate, known to social columnists of the 1950s as 'Miss Cube' by virtue of being the daughter of the sugar magnate Vernon Tate; her mother, Eva Carrington, had been one of the original Gibson Girls of the Edwardian stage. They had two sons and a daughter.

12 December 1996

Christopher Castleman

⊷⇛ 1941–2006 ⇚⊶

Dynamic head of Hill Samuel

Christopher Castleman was one of the most dynamic merchant bankers of his generation. Chief executive of Hill Samuel, and subsequently a director of Standard Chartered and a senior adviser to UBS Investment Bank, Castleman was widely admired in the financial world for his straightforwardness, his ability to motivate those who worked with him, and his formidable intellect and stamina. A chain-smoker in his younger days, he had an apparently inexhaustible appetite for nightlife as well as business. He favoured tumblers of iced kümmel at the end of the evening – but never allowed his wits to be dulled, and left nothing until tomorrow that could be done today. If he was sometimes prone to tempestuous decisions, his particular gift as a corporate financier was to be able to listen to a client's problems and instantly dictate, with near-perfect fluency, a detailed memorandum of solutions. In negotiation he could be tough, but he always kept his word.

At Hill Samuel, the merchant bank built up in the 1960s and '70s by Lord Keith, Castleman made his name running the Australian and South African arms of the business before being appointed group chief executive in 1980, aged 38, in a reshuffle which followed the abrupt departure of Keith, who had failed to persuade his colleagues of the merit of selling Hill Samuel to Merrill Lynch.

In the period leading up to the 1986 'Big Bang' reforms which allowed banks to venture into securities trading, Castleman was reluctant to follow his City competitors in expensive acquisitions of stockbrokers and jobbers, and it was somewhat against his better judgement that Hill Samuel took a stake in the broking firm Wood Mackenzie.

He described as 'lunacy' the idea of trying to compete with the giants of Wall Street, and resisted the fashion for hiring star performers from other banks at inflated salaries, preferring to get the best out of his own team – who were in turn devoted to him.

Hill Samuel under Castleman was successful on several fronts, including investment and insurance as well as corporate finance, but was limited by lack of capital and inevitably became the subject of takeover attention. When an approach arrived from Union Bank of Switzerland in July 1987, Castleman opposed a merger but a majority of his board disagreed with him, leaving him no choice but to resign: six weeks later UBS withdrew, and Hill Samuel was bought by Trustee Savings Bank.

Next, Castleman became chief executive of Blue Arrow, a fast-growing employment agency group which became the focus of controversy over a mishandled share issue at the time of the October 1987 stock market crash. Castleman was untouched by the scandal but uncomfortable with the way the company was run, and resigned after three months.

He went on to head an investment business, Johnson Fry, and to operate as an independent consultant until he was invited in 1991 to become an executive director of Standard Chartered, which was going through an extensive restructuring. He took responsibility for its acquisitions and disposals – of which he oversaw more than a hundred, small and large, over the following decade, helping to refocus the bank on its core regions of Asia, Africa and the Middle East and reduce its exposure in Europe.

Christopher Norman Anthony Phillips was born at Beaconsfield on 23 June 1941 and adopted his stepfather's surname, Castleman, when he was 12 – his own father, an RAF pilot, having died in an accident at the end of the Second World War. He was educated at Harrow and Clare College, Cambridge, where he gained a First in law. He began his City career in 1963 by joining M. Samuel & Co, a small bank controlled by the family which founded the Shell oil company. Two years later, Samuel merged with Philip Hill Higginson to form Hill Samuel. Castleman's abilities were swiftly recognised, and in 1970 he was posted as the firm's first representative in Australia, returning to London in 1972 to become a director. He served a stint in New York and was posted in 1978 to South Africa, where he ran a flourishing business before being called back to London to take command of the group.

Castleman was also at various times a director of Macquarie Bank of Australia (the successor of the Hill Samuel business he had set up) and Consolidated Goldfields, as well as chairman of National Investment Holdings. After retiring from Standard Chartered's board in 2001 he remained an adviser there and also at UBS Investment Bank, formerly UBS Warburgs, where he was much valued for his international contacts and his ability to win the trust of senior clients.

Away from work, Christopher Castleman was passionate about sport. He ran marathons for charity, and played cricket until the last summer before he died: he was a wicketkeeper who did not believe in under-appealing, and an opening batsman who never thought it necessary to play himself in. He was happiest with his children and grandchildren, and took particular joy in the family's holiday home in South Africa.

He was diagnosed with leukaemia in 2003, and suffered the trauma of a serious fire on New Year's Eve 2004 at his 17th-century Bedfordshire manor house, in which his baby granddaughter had to be rescued from the smoke. A ceiling painting by James Whistler was destroyed in the fire. But he remained active and positive, and was working until a few days before his death.

Christopher Castleman married first in 1965, Victoria Stockdale, who died in 1979; they had a son and a daughter. He married secondly, in 1980, Caroline Westcott (dissolved 1990), a South African with whom he had two daughters; and thirdly, in 1990, Suzy Diamond, also South African, with whom he had another son and daughter.

26 April 2006

Hilton Clarke

⊷⇒ 1909–1995 ⇐⊶

The Bank of England's money market man

Hilton Clarke was Principal of the Discount Office of the Bank of England. The Discount Office controlled the money markets through day-to-day dealing with discount and accepting houses, and watched over the creditworthiness of all banks in the City of London. As its Principal from 1953 to 1967, Clarke was, in effect, the eyes and ears of the Governor of the day. In his disciplinary role, which he executed with wisdom and good humour, he was the personification of 'the Governor's eyebrows'.

Clarke's breadth of acquaintance and his ability to gather City intelligence were legendary. A master of the calculated indiscretion, he would appear to let slip confidential snippets, whilst at the same time extracting far more information from his interlocutors than they ever intended to reveal. Tall, dapper and resplendent in his silk hat, he controlled the discount market by the force of his presence. He liked to assume a mildly roguish air – insisting, for example, that the prettiest girls should be posted to his department – but was in fact a man of the highest principles. His firmness was never resented. When a young bill broker asked for the customary seven-day loan to cover a cash shortage, Clarke replied that the Bank would lend to him for nine days, and at a punitive rate. As the supplicant protested, Clarke cut him short: 'And it'll be eleven days in a moment.'

He was also a skilled diplomat, who did much to improve communications between the Bank and the City. Each Friday morning, by tradition, he would escort representatives of the discount houses to call on the Governor. When one broker ill-advisedly made jocular remarks about interest-rate rises, the aloof and humourless Governor Cobbold announced that no more money market men were to be allowed into his presence. But Clarke was able to negotiate a suitable apology, and weekly meetings resumed.

The mid-1960s was an unsettling period, as sterling endured a series of crises leading up to the 1967 devaluation and lending was strictly controlled by the Labour government. But Clarke was never defensive and was always ready to accept change in the City. The many foreign banks attracted to London by the development of Euro-currency markets found him welcoming and helpful: his mastery of his job enhanced the Bank's special esteem in the financial world.

The son of a timber salesman, Hilton Swift Clarke was born on 1 April 1909 and educated at Highgate School. He entered the Bank of England, where his elder brother was already a clerk, shortly after his 18th birthday. The official who interviewed him for the post recorded him as 'an exceedingly nice fellow, with good appearance and manners'.

Good reports continued as Clarke rose steadily through the ranks. In 1938 he was attached to Governor Montagu Norman's private office, and at the outbreak of war in 1939 he played a part in setting up the Bank's Exchange Control system – it was his task to persuade City foreign-exchange dealers, whose trade had been suddenly curtailed, to join the Bank as staff of the new department. In 1942 he became assistant principal of the Dealing & Accounts Office. After the war Clarke was expected to succeed, in due course, as head of foreign-exchange dealing; his appointment as deputy principal of the Discount Office in 1950 was in preparation for that role. But in 1953 the incumbent principal resigned suddenly, and Clarke took his place.

The Discount Office had (despite its broad supervisory duties) a tiny staff, but ambitious younger officials were always keen to be trained by Clarke. Several of his protégés rose to the highest levels of the Bank.

Having retired from Threadneedle Street after forty years' service, Clarke remained active in the City until his late seventies. He was chairman of the merchant bankers Charterhouse Japhet, of Atlantic International Bank and of the money brokers Astley & Pearce. He was also a director of United Dominions Trust and the plantations group Guthrie, and a member of the London board of the Bank of Scotland.

He was appointed CBE in 1984.

He married first in 1934, Sibyl Salter, who died in 1975; they had a son. He married secondly in 1984, Ann Marchant, a former colleague at the Bank of England.

6 December 1995

The Earl of Cromer

-»═ 1918–1991 ═«-

Aristocratic Bank of England Governor

The 3rd Earl of Cromer became managing director of Baring Brothers, the merchant bank, almost by force of destiny but his rare abilities also secured him high public office as Governor of the Bank of England and Ambassador to Washington.

When 'Rowley' Cromer was appointed Governor of the Bank of

England in 1961, one cynical Labour MP, Woodrow Wyatt, demanded to know how such an office could have been bestowed upon a man with whom the Prime Minister had only a tenuous family connection.

'He is a young man, which is said to be not a bad thing,' Harold Macmillan drawled in reply. Cromer was indeed young, at only 42 the youngest Governor for two centuries, but there was more to it than that. 'He is very intelligent. He agrees with me,' the Prime Minister recorded in his diary in June 1962.

In fact, faced with the task of rejuvenating the Old Lady of Threadneedle Street, Cromer proved a notably independent governor. The bank was in low water at the time. The Parker tribunal into the supposed 'bank raid leak' had found no leak, but showed up the bank's methods as amateurish. And the Radcliffe Committee on the working of the monetary system had concluded that the bank depended too much on its conservative instincts and not enough on modern economics.

The Governor, Lord Cobbold, had served 12 years and wanted to retire. The succession was contested between supporters of Sir Oliver Franks, then chairman of Lloyds Bank, and Lord Harcourt of Morgan Grenfell. Finally, the Chancellor of the Exchequer, Selwyn Lloyd called Cromer back from Washington, where he was working as economic minister at the British Embassy, and offered him the governorship on the spot. Cromer accepted the post and at once began to shake up the bank, bringing in a stream of young talent from outside. Two of his choices, Jeremy Morse and Kit McMahon, were later the knighted chairmen of high-street banks.

Cromer had to contend with increasing pressure on sterling, which came to a head in 1964 with the return of a Labour government. From then on, he had to fight on two fronts – with the markets and with ministers. In November of that year there was a serious run on the pound, and it seemed possible that the reserves might be entirely exhausted. Cromer, after some preliminary calculations on the back of an envelope, prevented both an enforced devaluation and a potential international economic crisis with a few hours of hectic telephoning, which raised credits of more than £1 billion from other central banks. But a series of sterling crises followed, and although Cromer arranged international credits to get the pound through them, ministers saw their plans for growth frustrated by his caution.

Cromer had frequent disagreements with the Prime Minister, Harold Wilson. It was said that at a Buckingham Palace lunch the two men sat opposite each other without uttering a word. Cromer thought that Wilson counted too much on a supposed friendship with President Lyndon Johnson, and on the belief that the Americans would always bail Britain out. Wilson, for his part, felt cornered by Cromer's conservative instincts and on one occasion turned on him with the question: 'Who is Prime Minister of this country, Mr Governor, you or me?' He even threatened an election on the issue of who should run Britain – the elected government, or the financiers who so disliked high spending on social policies.

Cromer, though, was shrewd enough to point out that a government victory in such a contest would only intensify the pressure upon the pound, and continued to voice public criticism of Labour's policies. In February 1965 he warned that the credits which he had negotiated were 'no more guarantees of our future than Dunkirk presaged swift victory in 1940'. He went on to urge the absolute necessity of cuts in public expenditure. The speech precipitated a furore among left-wing MPs, who demanded the governor's resignation. Cromer, however, remained in office until June 1966, the end of his five-year term, when Wilson, to no one's surprise, advised the Queen to appoint another governor.

Now a Privy Councillor, Cromer returned to Barings as senior partner, but his public work continued. He produced a report for the Board of Trade on the financing of major overseas capital projects and went to Stockholm to advocate the creation of a European Monetary Board to restore public confidence in money and international exchanges.

In 1968 he was chairman of a working party set up to investigate the operations of the insurance market at Lloyd's – the first time in two centuries that this institution had been subjected to scrutiny from the outside.

Meanwhile his criticism of Wilson's government persisted.

While the Prime Minister was assuring television viewers, after the devaluation of 1967, that the pound in their pockets retained its value, Cromer was referring to 'this default of 2s 10d in the pound'. Many thought that he turned the tide in the 1970 general election campaign, when, in an interview on *Panorama*, he cast doubt upon Labour's optimistic assessment of the state of the economy and referred to £1.5 billion of outstanding debts. In November of that year the triumphant Edward Heath rewarded Cromer by naming him as the successor to John Freeman as British Ambassador in Washington. There were family precedents for this appointment: Alexander Baring, a distant kinsman, had been in Washington in 1842 to negotiate the boundary between the United States and Canada.

Heath, however, was activated less by the force of history than by the need to have an expert in international finance in Washington at a time when he was pursuing negotiations for joining the Common Market. The new ambassador was required to convince the Americans that Britain's new economic alignment would spur, rather than impede, the development of commerce between the old world and the new.

Cromer had the misfortune to arrive in Washington in the aftermath of the Rolls-Royce bankruptcy, which called into question not only the American Lockheed Tristar aircraft project, for which Rolls was producing the RB-211 engine, but also the whole future of British defence sales to America.

In Britain the Labour opposition attacked Cromer for his impassioned defence of the Heath government, and complained that the ambassador was acting like a spokesman for the Conservative Party. Through no fault of Cromer's, the interchanges between Heath's government and Nixon's administration were not a high point of the 'special relationship'. Henry Kissinger, in particular, was given to fulminations against the 'pygmy' governments of Europe who presumed to distance themselves from American policies.

There was particular bitterness in the autumn of 1973 over Britain's comparative lack of enthusiasm for the Israeli cause in the Yom Kippur war: 'The most consulted were the least co-operative,' Dr Kissinger complained.

'I take it, Henry, you were referring to the Russians?' Cromer discreetly enquired.

George Rowland Stanley Baring was born on 28 July 1918, the only son of the second Earl, who was then assistant private secretary to King George V and later became Lord Chamberlain of the Royal Household. His grandfather, Sir Evelyn 'Over' Baring, 1st Earl of Cromer, was the virtual ruler of Egypt at the turn of the century.

The Barings were the most successful of the families of the mercantile aristocracy which entered the peerage during the 19th century. They were originally Lutherans from North Germany, who settled in Exeter in the early 18th century. In 1818 the Duc de Richelieu was said to have remarked: 'There are six great powers in Europe: England, France, Prussia, Austria and the Baring Brothers.' In 1890, as a result of imprudent commitments in South America, the family bank was in serious difficulties and had to be baled out by the Bank of England. Barings was reconstituted as a joint stock company and made a fairly speedy recovery: four years later the advance made to the company from the guarantee fund set up to avert a catastrophe had been repaid. By 1900 there were four Baring peerages and today there are five.

Rowley's mother, a daughter of the 4th Earl of Minto, the Viceroy of India, observed that, as the sign of the cross was made on the boy's brow at his christening, he 'raised higher and higher a little up-stretched hand'.

But the 3rd Earl was never impressed by this anecdote: 'My mother was very poetic. I have not inherited that.'

Rowley, who was styled Viscount Errington until succeeding his father in the earldom in 1953, became a page of honour first to his godfather, King George V, and then, in 1937, to Queen Mary at the coronation of George VI, when he was employed for the purpose of handing Princesses Elizabeth and Margaret their coronets.

He was educated at Eton and spent eight months at Grenoble University, where he learnt French. In 1937 he entered Trinity College, Cambridge to read law, but found the subject less than enthralling, and left after a year.

In later life Lord Cromer claimed that he had always known that he would have to work for a living. The Baring fortune was not what people believed, he would explain; and his grandfather had been the eighth of ten children. As for the Mintos, the daughters never inherited anything. So Rowley Baring started work at a salary of £100 a year in the postal department of Baring Brothers. But it must be added that before undertaking this lowly employment, he spent a summer acting as private secretary to the Marquess of Willingdon, whom he accompanied on an official tour of Argentina, Uruguay and Brazil.

The outbreak of the Second World War found Baring in service with the Grenadier Guards, though the Army granted him leave of absence early in 1940 so that he could undertake another journey with Lord Willingdon, this time to New Zealand by flying-boat.

In 1944 he saw action with the Guards' Armoured Division in Normandy; subsequently his division was among the first Allied troops to reach Brussels. Baring was mentioned in despatches and appointed MBE – more, he would say, for administrative work than for military heroism – and was demobilised at the age of 27 as a lieutenant colonel.

In 1947 Baring Brothers sent him to New York to study American banking practice. Thus qualified, he returned next year to London as managing director of Barings. Other directorships followed, notably of the Royal Insurance Company, the Liverpool London and Globe Insurance Company, and the Daily Mail and General Trust.

Three years after succeeding to the earldom, in 1956, during the first Suez crisis, he made his first speech – on the iniquities of Nasser – in the House of Lords, resplendent in the uniform of a lieutenant colonel of the Grenadier Guards.

Cromer's career changed direction in 1958, when, unconsciously foreshadowing his future eminence, he became economic minister at the British Embassy in Washington. He served in this post for three years, combining it with several other functions. These included the running of the UK Treasury and Supply Delegation, and a stint as executive director for Britain on the International Monetary Fund.

From 1967 to 1970, and again from 1974 to 1979, Cromer was chairman of IBM (UK). He was a director, variously, of Union Carbide Corporation of New York, Imperial Group, the P&O Steam

Navigation Company, Shell Transport and Trading, and the Compagnie Financière de Suez.

Lord Cromer was appointed MBE in 1945, KCMG in 1971, GCMG in 1974, and sworn into the Privy Council in 1966. In 1977 he was installed as a Knight of the Garter. He was appointed one of HM lieutenants for the City of London in 1961 and made a deputy lieutenant for Kent in 1968.

He married, in 1942, Esmé Mary Gabrielle Harmsworth, younger daughter of the 2nd Viscount Rothermere and a Lady of the Bedchamber to the Queen from 1967 to 1971. They had two sons, and a daughter who died in 1974. The elder son, Evelyn Rowland Esmond Baring, styled Viscount Errington, born in 1946, succeeded to the earldom.

16 March 1991

Sir Peter Daniell

⋅➤≡◑ 1909–2002 ◐≡➤⋅

Top-hatted Government Broker

Sir Peter Daniell was an influential City figure as the senior Government Broker, responsible for conducting the government's business in the gilt-edged market. Daniell was senior partner from 1963 to 1973 of Mullens & Co, the stockbroking firm, founded in 1786, which provided a link between the Bank of England, the Commissioners for the Reduction of the National Debt and the gilt-edged market in the London stock exchange. He was the fourth generation of his family in the firm, his great-grandfather having started work there in around 1840.

The role of the Government Broker – now obsolete – was to raise new money and maintain an orderly market in gilt-edged stocks; 'lengthening the debt' by issuing long-dated paper and buying in shorter issues. He was also required to attend the Bank of England on a Thursday morning to be told of any change in Bank Rate, which he would then communicate to the stock exchange.

A handsome figure in the Government Broker's traditional black silk top hat, Daniell had an easy-going manner but demanded high professional standards from his staff and handled his own duties with the utmost discretion and tact. On his visits to the Bank he was accompanied by a Mullens waiter, or messenger, who was instructed that, if Daniell was run over on the way back, the Bank Rate would be found on a piece of paper in his pocket, which the waiter should deliver to the Exchange.

Soon after he became senior partner, Harold Wilson's government came into office, and Daniell was surprised to receive a telephone call from the new Chancellor, James Callaghan, who said that he did not in the least understand what the Government Broker did and would like to learn more. Daniell invited him to lunch, and found him both willing to learn and excellent company. But two days later, Callaghan made a speech in Cardiff in which he lambasted the City, and in particular the gilts market. Daniell rang Downing Street and asked whether anything had been misunderstood during their lunch conversation. Callaghan replied that he had understood very well, but that the speech was 'just politics'.

The latter half of the 1960s was a period of turmoil for the gilts market, including the repercussions of the 1967 devaluation, the nationalisation of the steel industry and the imposition and subsequent removal of capital gains tax on gilts. After the advent of the Heath government and the adoption of liberalisation measures set out in the policy paper known as *Competition and Credit Control*, Daniell worked closely with Governor O'Brien to oversee major changes in the Bank of England's gilts operations. By the time he retired in 1973, the annual volume of new gilts issues had risen in a decade from £100 million to £1 billion.

Peter Averell Daniell was born in London on 8 December 1909. His father, the eldest of ten children, married late in life; Peter was an only child but had a great many cousins. He was educated at Eton and Trinity College, Oxford where he read history, enjoyed himself enormously and took what he called 'a ropey degree'. Having spent childhood holidays in Switzerland to cure asthma he became a passionate mountaineer, scaling many Alpine peaks in his student days.

Peter's father had been reluctant to follow his own father into

Mullens (known after a merger in the late 1920s as Mullens, Marshall, Steer, Lawford & Co) and did not oppose Peter's first ambition to pursue a military career. While at Oxford he was offered a commission in the Rifle Brigade but he did not relish the prospect of a long posting in India, and in 1932 he decided after all to go into Mullens, where he served his time as a clerk before becoming a dealer on the stock exchange floor.

When war became imminent he joined the Queen's Westminster territorials, which in due course became the 11th Battalion Kings Royal Rifle Corps. Taking up the commission he had been offered at Oxford, he was quickly promoted to captain in 1939 and became a steadying influence on younger men in his unit, which was sent to Suez and took part in the battle of El Alamein. He went on to serve in Syria and Italy before returning as a major and second in command of a depot battalion in Yorkshire. He received the Territorial Decoration in 1950.

On demobilisation he returned to Mullens & Co to join the partnership, becoming deputy senior partner to Derrick Mullens in 1953. It was a time of many developments in the gilt market, including the introduction of 'tap' stocks, which proved highly effective in regulating market flows. Though the two men were the same age, Derrick Mullens stepped aside in 1963 to allow Daniell to take the top job.

Mullens & Co was also broker to a number of colonial and Commonwealth governments. Daniell travelled to New Zealand and was a regular visitor to Rhodesia until declared *persona non grata* as an agent of the British authorities by Ian Smith. At an earlier stage Daniell had also proposed to the Bank of England that he should spend time with the US Federal Reserve learning how the American government raised money. The answer came back from Washington that the Fed never took in brokers. 'You'll take mine,' replied Governor Cobbold imperiously, and Daniell duly spent six weeks there.

Daniell was a City traditionalist who did not always like change, though he coped professionally with a great deal of it over four decades. In 1970 he was asked by an interviewer whether the fact that Mullens had found a place in its partnership for the son of a senior official might be 'rather frowned on these days'; he replied that modern, meritocratic attitudes were 'damned stupid, I think. Doesn't do any harm at all'.

He was knighted in 1971. He was master of the Drapers Company in 1980–81 and was on the council of the King Edward VII Hospital for Officers. He was also chairman of the 1930 Fund for District Nurses. In later years he was a prominent figure in his home village of Buckland in Surrey, looked after his family farm at Chelsham, played golf at the New Zealand club at West Byfleet, and entertained generously at his holiday house in France. He was appointed deputy lieutenant of Surrey in 1976.

Peter Daniell married, in 1935, Leonie Harrison, the sister of a friend at Oxford; she died in 1997. They had a daughter and two sons, of whom the elder, Roger, became the fifth generation in the Mullens partnership.

27 May 2002

Sir Seymour Egerton

⟿ 1915–1998 ⟿

Bachelor chairman of Coutts & Co

Sir Seymour Egerton was a long-serving chairman of Coutts & Co. Founded in 1692, Coutts traditionally holds the monarch's bank accounts. Though in Egerton's era it was a subsidiary of what is now NatWest, Coutts preserved its own distinctive style, characterised by the black frock coats worn by its male staff. Many of the bank's aristocratic customers were also Egerton's friends. He and his fellow directors sat side-by-side in an open office accessible to customers and staff alike – though Egerton kept a private smoking room nearby – and their working day followed an orderly, long-established pattern: administration matters at 10.30 a.m., loans at 11, trustee business at noon, and onward to lunch.

A jovial, self-deprecating man, 'Timmy' Egerton was no intellectual, but he was astute in business and skilful in his handling of people: he made everyone feel at ease, and possessed a gift for friendship.

His royal duties were undemanding, but carried out with the utmost courtesy and discretion; he was particularly close to the Queen Mother's household. He preserved Coutts' traditions to the full, but his 25-year chairmanship, which began in 1951, was also a period of growth and modernisation.

Staff numbers tripled to around 1,200 and a bold modernisation was commissioned for the bank's Strand headquarters, an elegant 1830s building which forms part of a scheme by John Nash. Computerisation was introduced for the first time to an organisation more attuned to hand-written ledgers. 'Isn't it a hoot!' Egerton confided to Coutts' historian, Edna Healey, 'I didn't understand it.'

Interviewed in old age by Healey, Egerton gave credit for Coutts' progress to his fellow director deputy chairman, the 7th Earl of Harrowby, saying, 'He's the wonderful fellow who did the whole thing', whilst describing himself as 'the chap with the oil can, pouring oil on troubled waters' – a skill particularly needed during the merger of Coutts' parent company, National Provincial, with Westminster Bank to form NatWest. Egerton's modesty disguised his achievement in preserving the soul of Coutts & Co during an era of change. In doing so he created a model for success in private banking which many competitors later sought to imitate.

Descended from an old Cheshire family, Seymour John Louis Egerton, always known as Timmy, was born on 24 September 1915. His paternal grandparents were courtiers in the household of the Duke of Connaught. His childhood was rather lonely: his father, Captain Louis Egerton, was killed in France in 1917. Seymour and his brother Francis (born after his father's death and later chairman of Malletts, the Mayfair antique dealers) were brought up apart, Seymour remaining with his mother, who remarried; she was a daughter of the Rev. Lord Victor Seymour and granddaughter of the 5th Marquess of Hertford.

Young Seymour was educated at Eton, and embarked on a tour of India before entering the City as a trainee bill broker. At the outbreak of the Second World War he was commissioned in the Grenadier Guards, serving in France and later in North Africa and

Italy. On leaving the Army in 1945 he was recommended to Coutts by a relation, who wrote to the directors emphasising his soundness and reliability: 'There never seems to be any trouble around Timmy.'

Having lost several senior directors through retirement or death during the war, the bank was in need of fresh blood, and Egerton himself was surprised by the speed at which he became a director in 1947. He protested that he could not be a director because he 'didn't know the first thing about taxes' but was reassured that this was no barrier to promotion.

In 1951 the then chairman, Sir Jasper Ridley, died suddenly, and Egerton – still only 36 – was chosen to succeed him. He remained as chairman until 1976 and as a director of the bank until 1985. He was also a director of Phoenix Assurance and Alexanders Discount Co, and of *The Times* in the last years of its ownership by the Astor family.

He was a governor of St George's Hospital and the Peabody Trust; treasurer of Church House, Westminster, the Royal College of Music and the Boy Scouts Association, and a benefactor of the Union Jack clubs for members of the Services.

He was appointed KCVO in 1970, and advanced to GCVO in 1977.

Egerton inherited a late 17th-century house in Kensington Square, in which Talleyrand had once stayed, but later moved to a garden flat in Eaton Square. A bachelor, he was a familiar figure in Boodles and Pratt's, a keen fisherman in Devon and Scotland and an adventurous traveller, especially in Africa.

26 May 1998

Jocelyn Hambro

⟿ 1919–1994 ⟿

Jazz-loving merchant banker of the old school

Jocelyn Hambro was an elegant and entrepreneurial City figure from the sixth generation of the Hambro banking dynasty. He was chairman of Hambro's Bank and later of JO Hambro & Co, a private investment house formed with his three sons.

The Hambros had established themselves as traders in Copenhagen in the late eighteenth century and Jocelyn's great-grandfather Carl Joachim began a banking business in London in 1839. Jocelyn inherited a sharp eye and a gambler's instinct for risk, disguised by an urbane, insouciant style: an American visitor to the bank in 1960 noted 'a charming, handsome Englishman of thirty-one, who talked about horses and jazz'. (He also inherited Wilton's restaurant, famous for its oysters, which his father had bought during the Blitz).

Jocelyn's chairmanship of the bank, from 1965, was an era of expansion after a relatively conservative post-war period. Among his successes was Hambro Life Assurance, a venture launched with Mark Weinburg in the early 1970s in which an initial stake of £1 million was eventually multiplied almost two-hundredfold.

Having retired from the bank in 1983, Jocelyn joined with his three sons, Rupert, Richard and James, in forming JO Hambro, a family-owned business in the field of investment management and acquisitions advice. This reversion to the private partnership format of earlier generations – as opposed to the large-scale public company which Hambro's Bank had become – was one of the most successful 'boutique' businesses to emerge in the reshaped City of the late 1980s.

Jocelyn Olaf Hambro was born on 7 March 1919, the only son of Ronald Olaf Hambro, who chaired the bank from 1932 to 1961. In 1931, on the day before Jocelyn was due to go to Eton, the family was involved in a boating tragedy on Loch Ness in which Jocelyn's mother Winifred drowned as she swam for the shore behind him; no trace was ever found of her body.

After Eton, Jocelyn studied first at Heidelberg, where the arrival of weekly parcels of butter sent by his father's butler (prompted by Goering's famous dictum about the German preference for guns) caused him to be accused by the Gestapo of insulting the Third Reich. Unscathed, he went on to study at Trinity College, Cambridge, but was called up in 1939 before completing his degree.

Commissioned in the Coldstream Guards, Hambro commanded

a tank squadron in the Normandy landings. On 1 July 1944 he was ordered to advance without infantry support on Caumont Hill, a strongly held German position. Hambro's tanks rushed forward and held the hill until infantry came up behind, drawing favourable comment from General Montgomery. Hambro was awarded the Military Cross. Six weeks later, an officers' conference in which he was participating suffered a direct hit by a German shell. Hambro lost a leg, and was invalided out of the army, 'What a day to be shot, August the 12th,' he noted cheerfully, some years later. He recovered to play good tennis and enjoy field sports.

Jocelyn entered Hambro's Bank in 1945. After early training with Brown Brothers Harriman, the oldest private bank on Wall Street, he was given the task of building export trade with the United States to help reduce Britain's war debt. This he did by establishing a trading company in Dallas through which he had considerable success in selling MG sports cars and James motorcycles, appointing jukebox and radio salesmen as dealers in order to circumvent the obstacles of the American motor trade. Attempts to deal in Scottish kippers (which rotted on the quay) and jars of honey (which exploded in the heat) proved less successful.

Jocelyn's influence brought dynamism and innovation to Hambro's conventional business of trade finance in the 1950s and '60s. He was instrumental in forging a link with the bullion-trading house of Mocatta & Goldsmid and quick to see the potential of the growing Eurodollar market. He developed new contacts in Italy, France and North America as well as building on traditional links with Scandinavia.

He was also chairman of Phoenix Assurance and Charter Consolidated.

Hambro's chief pastime was the Turf. He bought his first horse, Courier, in 1950, and later became a successful breeder, first at Redenham in Hampshire and later at Waverton Stud in Gloucestershire (formerly owned by the bookmaker William Hill) where he commissioned a Palladian mansion by Quinlan Terry. He became a member of the Jockey Club in 1959 and a steward in 1976, serving on numerous other racing committees and boards.

Hambro's first and second wives both died of cancer, and he

became very active in support of cancer charities, forming the Joint British Cancer Charities committee in an attempt to reduce friction between competing bodies in that field. He was also chairman of Smith's Charity, the South Kensington landlord, and a governor of the Peabody Foundation.

Jocelyn Hambro married first in 1942, Silvia Muir, who died in 1972; they had three sons. Secondly in 1976 he married Elizabeth, widow of the 9th Duke of Roxburgh, who died in 1983; and thirdly, in 1988, he married Margaret, former wife of the 7th Earl Fortescue.

19 June 1994

Johnny Henderson

⊸⇒ 1920–2003 ⇐⇷

Stockbroker who was Monty's ADC

Johnny Henderson was a long-serving ADC to Field Marshal Montgomery, and later a popular and respected figure on the Turf and in the City. Henderson was a 22-year-old captain in the 12th Royal Lancers when he was chosen to join Monty's staff in the North African desert in November 1942. After a few days he had doubts, and asked to be returned to his regiment, but he was told to stay until a replacement could be found, and to accompany Monty to Cairo for the thanksgiving service for the victory at El Alamein.

While there, Henderson took time to visit the zoo with a friend, who offered Henderson's hat to an elephant – which swiftly chewed it up, spitting out only the 12th Lancers badge. Henderson, bareheaded, had to lurk in the distance at the guard of honour for their departure back to the desert next morning.

When Monty asked why he had no hat, Henderson explained that it had been eaten by an elephant. 'If you feel as bad as that,' came the brusque reply, 'you had better go inside and lie down.'

Somehow the incident cemented their relationship, and Henderson stayed on, through the Italian campaign and the advance from Normandy to the German surrender, and finally for a year with Montgomery as Chief of the Imperial General Staff in London. The ADC role proved a good deal more congenial than Monty's martinet reputation had led Henderson to expect. The great commander liked to be surrounded by lively young officers, treated them generously, and expected them to speak frankly to him. A degree of jocularity was generally encouraged – though Monty was not amused to be told, in France, that Henderson had been plying him with flasks of hot coffee in order to win a bet as to how often he would relieve himself during the day.

Among Henderson's many other duties was to find King George VI a seat for his thunderbox – preferably one which had not been freshly painted, it was intimated – during a royal visit to the desert, and to entertain Winston Churchill late into the night while Monty stuck to his rigid habit of retiring to bed shortly after 9 p.m. A less welcome assignment was to fly in the glass nose of the B17 Flying Fortress bomber which was Monty's preferred means of transport during the Sicilian campaign, not least as a form of one-upmanship over his American rival General George Patton. Landing at Palermo to visit Patton's HQ, they found the runway significantly too short for the lumbering plane, leaving the pilot no option but to swing around at the last moment and crash sideways into a hangar. It was, said Henderson, 'the most frightening thing that ever happened to me'. But he remained devoted to Montgomery throughout their time together, and was in friendly contact with him until his death in 1976.

In the racing world, Johnny Henderson was well known as an owner, a former amateur jockey and the father of the leading National Hunt trainer Nicky Henderson. But his great contribution to the sport was as the financial brain behind the creation of Racecourse Holdings Trust (RHT), a non-profit-making body which stepped in to save a number of struggling courses in an era before broadcasting revenues made them more viable.

The venture had its origins at Cheltenham, where in response to a threatened takeover by property developers, Henderson brought together a group of investors to buy the course for £240,000 in 1963. RHT was set up the following year, and a decade later Henderson and his fellow subscribers gave their shares in it to the Jockey Club at a nominal price, ensuring that all RHT's revenues would be ploughed back into racing. Over the years RHT became the owner of Wincanton, Nottingham, Warwick, Market Rasen, Haydock, Newmarket and Aintree – where Henderson joined the pantheon of racing figures who can claim over the years to have rescued the Grand National.

From 1973 to 1985 he was also a trustee of Ascot, which was still suffering the financial burden of its 1960s redevelopment: Henderson initiated a sinking fund which became the foundation for the rebuilding in 2005.

John Ronald Henderson, always known as Johnny, was born on 6 May 1920. His grandfather Harry was the younger brother and right-hand man of Alexander Henderson, the 1st Lord Faringdon, who made a fortune financing railways across Argentina and Spain. Johnny was brought up by his mother – a Garrard of the jewellery family – after his father abandoned them, and was also much influenced by his housemaster's wife at Eton, the celebrated Grizel Hartley, whose letters he later helped to publish. He went on to read history at Trinity College, Cambridge, and might have pursued a career as a jeweller if war had not intervened.

After leaving the Army as a major in 1946, Henderson joined Cazenove & Co, the blue-blooded stockbroking house into which a family firm, Greenwood Henderson, had been merged in 1932. He became a partner in 1954, bringing to the business not only his valuable range of social contacts, but a very shrewd judgement of investments and people: the firm's historian described him as 'deceptively hard-working'.

As the pension fund industry grew in the 1950s and '60s, Henderson built relationships with fund managers which gave Cazenove its formidable 'placing power' for share issues. Internally, he was one of the partners responsible for selections, nurturing the subfusc professional style and quasi-regimental *esprit de corps* for which the firm was universally admired. He also made frequent entries in the partners' wagers book, whether betting on elections, cricket scores or the number of cherry stones left by a fellow partner on his lunch plate.

He retired from Cazenove at the end of 1982 to become chairman of Henderson Administration, the fund management group originally established in the 1930s to look after his grandfather's and great-uncle's holdings. He was also a director of Barclays Bank – where he was one of a minority of board members who voted against severing the bank's ties with South Africa in 1986 – and the chairman of its trust company.

Johnny Henderson was appointed MBE in 1945, and OBE and CVO in 1985. In all his activities – he was also Lord Lieutenant of Berkshire, and chairman of White's club – he was cheerful, loyal, gregarious and genuinely interested in everyone he met, whatever their station. He loved good company and funny stories, and was happiest among the people of West Woodhay, the estate near Newbury which he inherited from his Henderson grandfather, or on the racecourse.

He had had the pleasure of seeing his horse Mighty Strong, trained by Nicky, win three times at Newbury in the last few weeks before his death.

He married, in 1949, Sarah Beckwith-Smith, by whom he had two sons and a daughter. Sarah died in a hunting accident in 1972 and he married secondly, in 1976, Catherine Christian, who had a son and two daughters by a previous marriage.

16 December 2003

Martin Lampard

⋆☞ 1926–2000 ☜⋆

Lawyer who resorted to 'vulgar abuse'

Martin Lampard was a City solicitor with a formidable reputation for integrity, aggression and cunning. He was senior partner of Ashurst Morris Crisp & Co, where he developed a hugely successful practice in corporate takeover work. His name carried such clout that merchant banks would hasten to instruct him on their side of a hostile bid rather than leave him available to the other side.

One reason for this success was that he dispensed with conventional niceties by which, for example, the defence side would first emphasise the qualities of its own business, then highlight the inadequacies of the bidder, and only then, if still under siege, resort to what lawyers call 'vulgar abuse'.

Lampard went for vulgar abuse right from the start, often in the most imaginative terms. He was entirely his own man, scared of no one. He swore like a trooper and cared not at all what anyone thought of him. He was a better lawyer, in a technical sense, than he pretended to be; his advice was often unconventional but always robust, and he had a knack of getting out of what seemed to be indefensible positions.

Unpredictable and easily bored, he was quite capable of cutting short an important meeting and announcing that he was going to the pub instead. Though he was fiercely loyal to his clients, he could also be devastatingly rude to them: when one of them, who had been called an idiot during a conference with learned counsel, protested that he saw no reason to sit there and be gratuitously insulted, Lampard replied: 'I can assure you this is not gratuitous. It is very expensive.'

Lampard's client list ranged from Paul McCartney – for whom he acted in the dissolution of the Beatles business partnership in 1970, though he had difficulty persuading McCartney to wear a tie in court – to business dynasties such as the Rothschilds and the Keswicks of Jardine Matheson.

One of his most important City allies was Philip (later Sir Philip) Shelbourne, a schoolfriend who became a leading tax barrister, a partner with Rothschilds and finally chairman of Samuel Montagu. The two worked together on behalf of numerous clients, including the Showering family, the West Country cider-makers and inventors of Babycham who took control of Allied Breweries and eventually created the Allied-Lyons conglomerate – of which Lampard was a non-executive director.

He was also on close terms with the eminent banker Sir Siegmund Warburg, one of many people over the years who tried to poach Lampard to work for his company. Another, bizarrely, was Robert Maxwell – of whom Lampard proudly counted himself a longstanding adversary, having acted for the American company Leasco in its 1969 bid for Maxwell's Pergamon Press, in the course of which fraud was discovered in Pergamon's accounts. The two had a series of encounters, and after one particularly hard-fought day in court, found themselves sharing a lift. 'You're a f***ing liar, Bob,' Lampard said with characteristic directness.

'I know, but I always get away with it,' Maxwell chuckled.

When Lampard retired as senior partner of Ashursts, Maxwell – as was his wont – telephoned to offer him a sumptuous office in the Mirror building; needless to say, Lampard declined.

Martin Robert Lampard was born in London on 21 February 1926, and brought up in Kent, where his childhood was devoted to ferreting, beagling and shooting. His grandfather had made a fortune developing Malayan rubber plantations, but by the 1930s the money had largely been lost or spent. Young Martin was educated at Radley and volunteered for the RNVR in 1943, before his 18th birthday. He served in the North Atlantic and, after the end of the war, in Palestine.

After demobilisation Lampard talked his way into Christ Church, Oxford, to read law; he claimed to have been the only commoner in an intake of brilliant scholars whose studies had been deferred because of the war, and proceeded to secure a Third.

Neither his tutors nor his contemporaries thought him likely to prosper in the profession, but he went on to take articles with Wilde Collins & Crosse and moved in 1954 to the old-established City firm of Ashurst Morris Crisp, then going through something of a lull in its fortunes.

He became a partner three years later and set out to raise the firm's profile in corporate work, advancing to senior partner in 1974. Juniors in the firm thrived if they met his demanding and sometimes eccentric standards, but did not last long if they did not. He introduced a rule obliging partners to retire at 60 to make way for new blood, and in 1986 he cheerfully applied the rule to himself.

In his youth Lampard was a keen ocean racer, crewing for Myles Wyatt on *Bloodhound* and *Tiger*, yachts that were subsequently sailed by Prince Philip. Lampard kept his own boat for some years at Aldeburgh.

In 1966 he bought a large house in Suffolk, where he farmed Simmental cattle and ran a very informal shoot. It was a happy, chaotic home, in which drink and conversation flowed generously, but pomposity and small talk were never tolerated. Lampard himself was a heroic drinker and smoker; his suits were made with special pockets to accommodate large packs of untipped Benson & Hedges.

Martin Lampard married, in 1957, Felice MacLean, whose Scots ancestors had migrated to Germany; they had three daughters.

25 April 2000

Sir Michael Richardson

⤙⤏ 1925–2003 ⤜⤐

Margaret Thatcher's favourite banker

Sir Michael Richardson, the investment banker, was a tireless City dealmaker and networker. As a senior executive first of the stock-brokers Cazenove & Co and then of NM Rothschild, Richardson had a hand in innumerable headline-making transactions of the 1970s and '80s, including a large portion of the Conservative government's privatisation programme.

But his choice of clients was not always wise: he was a long-standing adviser to Robert Maxwell, and a connection with another financier of questionable standing brought his career to a humiliating close when, in his mid-70s, he was banned from office by the City authorities.

Richardson dramatically raised the profile of NM Rothschild after joining in 1981 as head of corporate finance. He was particularly well placed to win privatisation mandates, having befriended Margaret Thatcher when their sons played cricket together at Harrow a decade earlier, and having helped introduce her to the City when she became leader of her party.

He had also known Nigel Lawson since the latter was a City editor in the 1960s. 'While at first sight too suave and smooth to be true,' Lawson wrote in his memoirs, 'Richardson's unfailing charm, courtesy and good manners disarmed all who came into contact with him. Like Siegmund Warburg, although from a very different background, he owed his considerable success to manipulating people rather than money.'

Richardson was at pains to deny that his personal connections made a difference, but his competitors certainly believed he had an edge that helped Rothschilds to win leading roles in the sale of state interests in Britoil, British Gas, British Petroleum, Rolls-Royce, the technology group Amersham International and the entire water and electricity industries. In total Rothschilds had a hand in raising some £35 billion for the government through share sales.

The transaction which most tested Richardson's sinuous skills was the £7 billion sale (at the time, the world's largest) in October 1987 of the Treasury's residual stake in BP. Between the opening and closing of the public offer came the Black Monday stock market crash. Richardson had arranged the underwriting of the issue by an international syndicate at £3.30 a share, but the market price fell far below that. Subscriptions were negligible and the underwriters faced huge losses. Though his official role was as adviser to the government, Richardson now had to represent the views of fellow underwriters – particularly the Wall Street investment banks – who wanted the BP sale cancelled. He had some success in persuading the Bank of England of their case, but met a stony response from Lawson who, with the prime minister's support, decided in the taxpayers' interest that the sale should go ahead, supported by a low-priced, buy-back offer to prevent the share price from collapsing altogether.

Richardson said later he felt like 'the nut in the nutcracker' in these discussions, but the sale was completed, the underwriters' losses eventually diminished, and his reputation survived.

It was more difficult for him to shake off his association with the Mirror publisher Robert Maxwell, for whom he had first acted in the 1960s during his earlier career with the stockbrokers Panmure

Gordon. Richardson made a glowing speech at Maxwell's 65th birthday party and went on to play a key role in the flotation of Mirror Group Newspapers in 1991. Even after Maxwell's mysterious death later that year, when his fraudulent empire began to unravel, Richardson declared that 'Bob was squeaky-clean with me'.

Michael John de Rougemont Richardson was born in London on 9 April 1925. His father was a City insurance broker and his mother's family, who were of Huguenot descent, were associated with Lloyd's of London.

Michael was educated at Harrow and Kent School, Connecticut. In 1943 he joined the Irish Guards. He was wounded in action in the Netherlands, and by the end of the war, still only 20, he was adjutant of his battalion. He was posted to Palestine, but before he left a brother officer introduced him to John King, a young entrepreneur who was building up a ball-bearing business in Yorkshire.

The intention was that Richardson should become King's personal assistant, but by the time he returned from the Middle East the job had gone. King (later Lord King of Wartnaby) nevertheless became a close friend and in due course, as chairman of British Airways, an important client. It was through King that Richardson met another Yorkshire entrepreneur and future Rothschild client, James (later Lord) Hanson.

On leaving the Army Richardson went up to Cambridge, but found university life dull and did not linger. Instead he found work in the City with Harley Drayton, an idiosyncratic financier who held sway over a large number of companies through a network of investment trusts.

After this apprenticeship, Richardson joined Panmure Gordon as a junior partner in 1952, and began to develop a corporate finance practice. Among other notable deals, he acted alongside Warburgs in the City's first real contested takeover bid, by Tube Investments and Reynolds for British Aluminium in 1959.

On Maxwell's behalf he acted in the 1964 flotation of Pergamon Press, and in 1968 he travelled to Australia to try to spike Rupert Murdoch's acquisition of the *News of the World*.

Richardson eventually fell out with his Panmure partners and was invited to join Cazenove – together with his distant cousin David Mayhew, whom he had brought into Panmure, and who in due course became Cazenove's senior partner. Richardson's relentless glad-handing and deal-chasing – even, it was said, his habit of taking copious notes in meetings – caused some consternation among his new partners.

There was never any doubt about his effectiveness in winning business and carrying it through – he played leading roles in the Grand Metropolitan takeover of Watneys, the first BP share sale by the Callaghan government and House of Fraser's defence against Lonrho. But there were mixed feelings about his rise towards the top, and he was passed over for senior partner in 1980.

The following year, he accepted an invitation from Evelyn de Rothschild to join NM Rothschild, filling the considerable gap left by the departure of Evelyn's cousin Jacob (later Lord) Rothschild. One City competitor, Sir David Scholey of Warburg, called Richardson's appointment at Rothschild the worst news he had received all year.

Meanwhile, Richardson was for twenty years a director of the Savoy hotels group, and one of the most regular customers of the Savoy's River Restaurant, where he habitually occupied a window table overlooking the Thames. He played a leading part both in the long-running defence of Savoy against the takeover ambitions of Lord Forte, and in the 1989 settlement which finally persuaded the warring parties to co-operate with each other.

In that year Richardson stepped down from his executive role at Rothschilds to become a vice-chairman of the bank and non-executive chairman of Smith New Court, the securities trading house in which Rothschilds held a stake. He retired from both these roles in 1995. But still eager to do deals, he became a full-time vice-chairman of JO Hambro Magan, a 'boutique' corporate finance house which offered him the close-knit partnership style he most enjoyed. The firm was bought by NatWest and became Hawkpoint Partners, but Richardson's tenure was to end in ignominy, following what appeared to be a bizarre lapse of judgement.

In 1998 and 1999, he wrote a series of letters on Hawkpoint stationery to an American-based acquaintance, Alan Shephard, confirming that Shephard had several hundred million dollars of loan funds available to him. It transpired this information had come from Shephard – a former bankrupt who had faced fraud allegations – and had not been verified by Richardson, who continued writing the letters despite warnings from NatWest that it did not wish to do business with Shephard.

Two independent tribunals into the affair found Richardson 'no longer fit and proper to be registered with the Securities & Futures Authority', effectively ending his City career. Richardson declared that he would rather be judged on 'fifty years of decent hard work' than on the SFA's 'very harsh view of a small error', but contributed £85,000 to the SFA's costs.

Richardson was often named as a senior Freemason, though he said that he had 'never combined Masonry with business in any way'. For some years he was chairman of the Royal Masonic Hospital in Hammersmith. He was knighted in 1990.

Away from the City, Michael Richardson's passion was hunting: 'I love the moment when the horse and I sail over the fence,' he observed. 'Then, if we're still in one piece, we look for the next one.' He rode fearlessly despite punishing falls, and was master of the Crawley & Horsham Foxhounds until he was seventy. In the summer he raced Redwing sailing boats off the Isle of Wight.

He married, in 1949, Octavia 'Paddy' Mayhew who died in 1999; they had a son and two daughters.

12 May 2003

Sir Philip Shelbourne

⊷══◑ 1924–1993 ◐══⊶

Irascible takeover adviser

Sir Philip Shelbourne, the merchant banker and former chairman of Britoil, was a City grandee of strong opinions and fastidious tastes who provoked – and returned – affection in some quarters but animosity in others.

Shelbourne came to prominence first as a brilliant young barrister and then as a leading City takeover adviser of the 1960s. In his later career he played a central role in the privatisation of North Sea oil.

The British National Oil Corporation (BNOC), established by the Labour government in 1976, was a prime target for privatisation in the first Thatcher administration. But its chairman, Lord Kearton, and managing director Alastair Morton (later chairman of Eurotunnel) were opposed to any sell-off or break-up. When Kearton stood down, no suitable name from the oil industry could be found to replace him. The choice fell instead on Philip Shelbourne, who was then chairman of the merchant bank Samuel Montagu.

Although he had been advising the Conservatives on this and other privatisation possibilities since before the 1979 election, Shelbourne's appointment in May 1980 caused a storm; criticism centred on his lack of industrial experience. Morton, who had previously worked with Shelbourne, immediately resigned.

Hostile reactions were not unusual with Shelbourne. His intellect was as quick as it was powerful; he was always demanding, often intolerant, sometimes supercilious. A very private man, he could be cold on first acquaintance. But to those close to him he was generous and fiercely loyal.

Shelbourne interfered little in operational matters at BNOC, concentrating his meticulous attention on the details of the forthcoming share sale, the biggest of its kind in that era. He initially opposed the government's plan to split BNOC into its oil production and trading components, but in due course he moved across to be chairman of Britoil, which offered 51 per cent of its shares to the public in November 1982. Last-minute nervousness in the oil market undermined the issue, which (through no fault of Shelbourne's, the government having chosen the method and price) was largely spurned by the investing public.

Shelbourne's declared strategy was to internationalise Britoil, diversifying its assets beyond the North Sea. This he did with limited success. Although the balance of the government's shares were sold to the public in 1985 without further hitch, the stock market's lukewarm view of Britoil's prospects left the company vulnerable to takeover bids.

In late 1987 a bid was forthcoming from BP. Shelbourne preferred a rescue deal offered by an American group, Atlantic Richfield (ARCO). But the government still held a 'golden share' in Britoil, and the symbolic importance of North Sea oil as a national treasure militated in favour of a British bid. ARCO withdrew; Britoil fell to BP and Shelbourne retired.

In the course of the takeover the terms of his contract with Britoil had been made public, revealing unusually lavish retirement benefits which were swiftly curtailed by the new owners. Befitting a habitué of the Savoy Grill with a famously sweet tooth and a deep knowledge of wine, the package had included a lunch allowance equivalent to £92 per day.

Philip Shelbourne was born on 15 June 1924, the only child of Leslie Shelbourne, a director of the Runciman shipping line. Philip's mother having died in childbirth, his upbringing was largely entrusted to aunts. He was schooled at Radley.

Commissioned in the Royal Gloucestershire Hussars, Shelbourne was a troop leader in the 11th Armoured Division in northwest Europe in 1944–45. He returned to complete his education at Corpus Christi College, Oxford, and Harvard Law School.

In 1951 he was called to the Bar by Inner Temple. There he built a reputation as the outstanding tax lawyer of his generation – inventive, concise in his opinions, and businesslike in his organisation. Unusually for a young barrister, he arrived at his chambers by chauffeur-driven Rolls-Royce – a luxury acquired on tax-efficient terms from a grateful client. But Shelbourne did not take Silk, and never wanted to be a judge; a strong commercial instinct drew him to the business world.

In 1962 the ideal career opportunity was offered by another of his legal clients, the merchant banking house of NM Rothschild. He became, at 38, only the third non-member of the Rothschild family to join the partnership. Together with Jacob Rothschild, he set out to build up the bank's nascent corporate finance business. He specialised in takeover bids, in which he was a formidable tactician.

Among numerous successes, he helped the property group MEPC to fight off Commercial Union. He advised on the merger, forced by the Labour government in 1969, of the ball-bearing companies that formed Ransomes Hoffman Pollard. He also secured Harveys of Bristol for Showerings (later Allied Breweries, then Allied-Lyons), which had failed in an earlier bid for the same target before taking Shelbourne's advice. In 1971 he moved to become chief executive of the Drayton investment group, which had been rudderless since the death in 1968 of its founder, the financier Harley Drayton. Shelbourne gave the business a dynamic new lead, expanding into corporate finance and property lending.

In 1974 he arranged the sale of Drayton to Midland Bank, which merged Drayton with its own merchant bank, Samuel Montagu. This was both a convenient match and a shrewd precaution against the coming property crash. Shelbourne himself emerged as chairman and chief executive of Montagu. Although he fought for Montagu's autonomy within Midland, he aspired to the chairmanship of the Midland itself and was disappointed when the former civil servant Lord Armstrong of Sanderstead was preferred. Shelbourne remained at Montagu until he was summoned to BNOC.

In 1976 Shelbourne had also become a non-executive director of Allied Breweries, his former Rothschild client. Five years earlier he had advised Lord Crowther, chairman of Trust House Forte (THF), during Allied's bid for THF – which was supported by Crowther but vehemently, and in the end successfully, opposed by Lord Forte.

After leaving Britoil, Shelbourne was chairman of the merchant bankers Henry Ansbacher. He was also deputy chairman of the Panel on Takeovers and Mergers, a member of the Securities & Investment Board and one of the 'three wise men' appointed to the Council of Lloyds.

Shelbourne was knighted in 1984 and became an honorary bencher of the Inner Temple in the same year.

A lifelong bachelor, Shelbourne lived for many years in a Victorian house in Highbury, north London, in which he collected antiques and installed a complete Indonesian sitting room. In 1985 he acquired, and exquisitely restored, a Queen Anne mansion in

Salisbury Cathedral close, former home of the historian Sir Arthur
Bryant.

Sir Philip Shelbourne was passionately interested in classical
music and opera. He also liked dogs. A Boston terrier called
Montagu commemorated a successful Samuel Montagu venture in
the United States; later a mongrel called Brit, found in Green Park,
slumbered under the chairman's desk at Britoil.

15 April 1993

A.G.C. 'Tony' Trollope

⟶▭ 1914–2003 ▭⟵

Colourful head of the City Building Society

Tony Trollope was the colourful and long-serving head of the City
of London Building Society after an early career as a railway
manager and wartime transport officer; he was also the father of the
novelist Joanna Trollope.

Trollope was in charge of transport for the National Coal Board
in 1952 when he was headhunted – through Oxford connections,
and on the strength of his classical education rather than his
expertise in logistics – to become general manager of the Fourth
City Building Society, a small institution that had fallen into some
difficulties. He knew alarmingly little about finance, but was
successful in putting the business back on an even keel.

It was renamed the City of London Building Society, and
Trollope became well known in the money markets as a shrewd
and benign individualist, of high integrity, who ran his business
entirely according to his own rules – and invariably wore scarlet
socks. He took little notice of anything said by the Building
Societies Association or the larger societies which dominated it,
against which he had no wish to compete for conventional, off-
the-peg mortgages: he was happier lending to impecunious
architects and conservationists to buy dilapidated Georgian
houses on the City's fringes.

A manager in the frugal, disciplined style of an earlier era, he opened all the post himself every morning and was proud to have the lowest operating costs of any comparable society; but his staff were completely devoted to him. He remained chief executive until 1980, when he was 66, and was president of the society until it merged into the Chelsea Building Society three years later.

Arthur George Cecil Trollope was born on 30 April 1914, one of six children of a prep school headmaster at Seaford, Sussex. The Trollopes descended from a line of Lincolnshire squires, and the novelist Anthony was his distant cousin – he shared his famous relative's broad forehead and square jaw and was known by the nickname Tony, though his mother called him Cecil.

Tony was educated at Charterhouse and Trinity College, Oxford, where he read Greats and played hockey. On graduation he was recruited as a management cadet by the London North Eastern Railway (LNER). He also joined the Territorial Army, and was sent to France as a transport officer with the Royal Engineers supplementary reserve before the outbreak of war in 1939.

When the order came to withdraw in May 1940, Trollope was one of the last to find out. He burned his papers at the Gare St Lazare and made his way to the coast after the main evacuation from Dunkirk had already been completed, but was rescued by one of a convoy of three small fishing boats from Falmouth. The other two were sunk during the homeward crossing, and Trollope was so seasick that he often said afterwards he had hoped his would be sunk too.

He worked at the War Office for a time, and married in 1941 the artist Rosemary Hodson, daughter of the vicar of Minchinhampton in the Cotswolds. Tony was due to be sent to the Far East but was given a deferral after the death in infancy of their first child, a daughter. When he finally sailed for India in 1943, he did not know that Rosemary was pregnant with Joanna – the future bestselling author, who was born in her grandparents' rectory and did not meet her father until she was four.

In India and Burma, Trollope supervised movements of troops and supplies, even to the extent of finding quantities of ice cream for

American units. He was promoted to full colonel – the youngest in the Indian army at the time.

On demobilisation Trollope returned to LNER at York, where he was responsible for dealing with train breakdowns at all hours of the day and night. Many young railway managers who had gone off to the war returned to find themselves back at the bottom of the pecking order below those, often less able, who had stayed behind. In Trollope's case, this frustration was coupled with bitter living conditions for his family in the winter of 1947, when they were sustained chiefly by pounds of Gloucestershire sausages sent through the post by his mother-in-law.

He left LNER to become transport manager for the newly formed National Coal Board, based at Stourbridge – where he remained for five years, though he found the nationalised body far too bureaucratic for his liking.

Tony Trollope was a devout churchman, with a passionate interest in ecclesiastical architecture and an encyclopaedic knowledge of City churches in particular. He was a churchwarden of St Margaret Lothbury (the 1686 Wren church which includes the Bank of England in its parish) where his family had long connections. He was a regular lunchtime speaker at St Lawrence Jewry in Gresham Street.

He also loved sacred music. As a singer and amateur organist, he claimed to have chosen where to live during his City career and retirement years – at Reigate, then at Overton in Hampshire – by first finding a decent choral society, then finding a house nearby. When he travelled on the continent he relied on antique Baedeker guidebooks, and spoke Latin to make himself understood.

But Trollope was by no means a fuddy-duddy. At his club, the Gresham in Abchurch Lane – where he was instantly recognisable, even when hidden behind a newspaper, by his socks – he pressed vigorously for the admission of women as members. His wife made him a gold waistcoat for their golden wedding anniversary, prompting one grandson to comment that this could be taken to signify that the family was rich; at his memorial service four of his grandsons wore red ties in his memory.

Tony Trollope was appointed MBE in 1992. He was a freeman

of the City of London, a fellow of the Royal Society of Arts and a member of MCC. He took a close interest in country houses and was secretary of the Jane Austen Society.

He was survived by his wife, two daughters – Joanna and Victoria, an archivist – and a son, Andrew, a QC.

22 September 2003

PART TWO

MAVERICKS, MONSTERS AND ROGUES

Octav Botnar – *Nissan car dealer and fugitive from justice*
Sir Kenneth Butt – *participant in the 1936 Budget leak scandal*
Peter Cadbury – *argumentative entrepreneur*
Bernie Cornfeld – *the man behind the IOS scandal*
Matthew Harding – *controversial Lloyd's broker*
Bill Harrison – *'Attila the Brum'*
Sir Julian Hodge – *'the usurer of the Valleys'*
Lord Keith of Castleacre – *ruthless financier*
Ephraim Margulies – *secretive commodities trader*
Forrest Mars – *misanthropic head of the confectionery empire*
Gerry Parish – *Queensway Carpets founder*
Tiny Rowland – *'the unacceptable face of capitalism'*
Lord Spens – *Guinness trial defendant*
Edouard Stern – *banker murdered in a sado-masochistic ritual*

Octav Botnar

⊷⟾ 1913–1998 ⟾⊶

Nissan car dealer and fugitive from justice

Octav Botnar arrived in Britain as a refugee from communist Romania in 1966 and built up a multimillion-pound business as the controller of Nissan car sales, only to end his life in self-imposed exile in Switzerland, locked in legal wranglings with the Inland Revenue.

Nissan UK developed from small beginnings to become hugely lucrative, and Botnar channelled a substantial portion of the dividends – more than £80 million – into charitable causes. The Great Ormond Street Children's Hospital was a notable beneficiary. But his company's contract with the Japanese car-maker was acrimoniously terminated in 1991, and Botnar himself was accused of massive tax fraud.

When Botnar first acquired the Nissan franchise in 1970, the cheaply produced cars, sold under the Datsun marque, were ridiculed by discerning motorists. But, as quality and reputation improved, Botnar was able to build up a 6 per cent share of the United Kingdom car market. He controlled more than 200 Nissan retail dealerships as well as the central distribution.

Secretive, unconventional and ruthlessly autocratic, Botnar never enjoyed warm relations with his Japanese counterparts or with the business press. After Nissan built its first factory in Britain in 1984, there were rows over the pricing of the Bluebird model, and it was evident that the Japanese saw Botnar as an obstacle to expansion in Europe. Development of the Primera range at the new Nissan plant in Sunderland brought matters to a head. The severance of Botnar's contract, at one year's notice, was accompanied by a storm of mutual recrimination.

The Japanese alleged that Botnar's company, Nissan UK, had violated the agreement by transferring ownership of car-dealing subsidiaries to another of Botnar's companies. They alleged that the charitable trusts which controlled Nissan UK were a sham, and that

Botnar was the real beneficial owner – which he vigorously denied. The Japanese also accused him of insulting behaviour, claiming that he had called them 'stupid' and 'small-brained'.

Botnar's version was that the Japanese simply wanted to gain control of his highly profitable dealership network. He believed that the British government was anxious to please Nissan, one of its most important overseas investors, and that the Inland Revenue's investigation of his tax affairs was provoked by Nissan in order to weaken his claim for massive damages in respect of the severed contract.

International arbitrators, sitting under Japanese commercial rules, found against Botnar in his dispute with Nissan – demolishing without compensation the main substance of his business empire. Botnar accused Nissan of the 'greatest act of treachery since Pearl Harbour'.

Meanwhile, in June 1991, an army of 135 tax inspectors had descended on Botnar's offices in Worthing and a dozen other locations. He was alleged to have defrauded the Inland Revenue of more than £100 million since 1983, by artificially inflating the cost of car freight from Japan in order to reduce declared profits in Britain. Correspondingly large sums were alleged to have been laundered into Swiss bank accounts.

Two of his British colleagues were jailed, but Botnar sent word from his chalet overlooking Lake Geneva that doctors had advised against the strains of a lengthy trial. There being no extradition treaty between Britain and Switzerland, he did not return. In 1996 the Inland Revenue's £250 million claim against Nissan UK was settled by a £59 million *ex gratia* payment from Botnar.

Botnar described the Revenue's tactics as 'bearing a striking similarity to those of the terror police in former communist countries of which I have had first-hand experience'. In 1997, the Inland Revenue dropped all criminal action against him on the grounds that he was too ill to stand trial. He was fighting a losing battle against cancer, but nevertheless announced his intention to sue the Revenue for malicious prosecution.

Octav Botnar was born on 21 October 1913 at Czernowitz, the German-speaking capital of Bukovina in the mountainous

Carpathian province of the Austro-Hungarian empire. Bukovina was annexed by Romania in 1919, and by the Soviet Union in 1940. It is now part of western Ukraine.

Botnar believed that his early life was 'nobody's business except my own', but revealed that during his school days he had been influenced by the communist youth movement, and that at 18 he was imprisoned for organising a demonstration. By his own account, he was released from prison in 1936, but then sentenced, in absentia, to seven years' imprisonment for trying to organise a group to fight in the Spanish Civil War. Evading the authorities, he made his way to France, en route to join the Republicans in Spain.

However, by the time he reached the Spanish border, he found it closed, and consequently the outbreak of the Second World War found him in France. He is thought to have enlisted in the French army, to have become a prisoner of war in 1940, and subsequently to have escaped and joined a Resistance network.

In 1946, he returned to Romania, where until 1960 he worked in various companies controlled by the Ministry of Foreign Trade. Then, he claimed, he was sentenced, for political reasons, to seven years' hard labour, including two years in solitary confinement. Under an amnesty for political prisoners in 1964, he was released early – from a forced-labour barge in the Danube delta. He and his wife and daughter were allowed to emigrate to Germany – although he denied Nissan's curious claim that he had once held East German citizenship.

He arrived in Britain in 1966 to reorganise the distribution of German NSU cars and motorcycles. NSU (which in 1970 was absorbed by Volkswagen) also owned the Datsun franchise and when they decided to drop the contract Botnar obtained it for his newly established Moorcrest Motors marketing group. Moorcrest would become Nissan UK.

Although based in Britain for 25 years, Botnar never became resident for tax purposes and owned no property here. He maintained luxurious homes in Switzerland, Paris and Monte Carlo. In 1974, Botnar transferred his ownership of Nissan UK to a Panamanian company controlled by charitable trusts. He protested against any suggestion that he remained the principal beneficiary of the company's accumulating profits, even taking legal steps to have his name removed from a published list of Britain's richest men.

Botnar sought no publicity for his philanthropy, which was directed especially towards children's charities. After the death in a car crash in 1973 of his only daughter Camelia, aged 21, he established the Camelia Botnar Foundation to provide a home and training facilities for difficult teenagers. He gave £1 million to the Royal Ballet School and to the then government's embarrassment, was revealed to be a substantial donor to the Conservative Party. Botnar's £8 million gift to Great Ormond Street at Christmas 1990 had prompted the former cabinet minister Lord Parkinson to describe him as 'truly one of our great philanthropists'.

In 1993, Botnar's wife Marcela officiated on the ailing fugitive's behalf at a contract-signing ceremony for the construction of the hospital's new pathology wing, the Camelia Botnar Laboratories.

11 July 1998

Sir Kenneth Butt

⋆⇒ 1908–1999 ⇐⋆

Participant in the 1936 Budget leak scandal

Sir Kenneth Butt, 2nd Bt, was a landowner, bloodstock breeder and Lloyd's underwriter who played a part in the 1936 'Budget leak' scandal that ended the political career of J.H. Thomas, Stanley Baldwin's Colonial Secretary.

At the time of the Budget, Butt was an up-and-coming under-writer with Gardner, Mountain & d'Abrumenil, a well-established firm of Lloyd's brokers. The Chancellor of the Exchequer, Neville Chamberlain, raised income tax by 3d – an unusual change, since the tax rate normally moved up or down by 6d. Rumours circulated soon afterwards that an exceptionally large amount of insurance had been placed at Lloyd's against both a 3d income-tax rise and a rise in tea duty, which also appeared in the Budget provisions. Such prescience clearly suggested a leak, which could only have come from a member of the Cabinet.

A tribunal chaired by Mr Justice Porter swiftly confirmed the culprit to be J.H. 'Jimmy' Thomas, the rumbustious former engine driver and favourite of King George V, who was one of the Labour members of the National Government. Thomas had leaked the vital information to two men, Alfred Bates – who had allegedly paid Thomas £20,000 in return for the right to publish his as-yet-unwritten autobiography in the *Leader* (a periodical largely devoted to competitions) – and Kenneth Butt's father, Sir Alfred Butt MP.

On Budget Day itself, a substantial volume of tea-duty insurance was arranged in Lloyd's by Kenneth Butt. When questioned by the chairman of his firm, Butt failed to reveal that the business had been placed on behalf of his own father. He later gave a full account of the transaction when interviewed by the Treasury's solicitors, and – whilst declaring that 'my conscience remains absolutely clear' – resigned from Gardner, Mountain & d'Abrumenil.

Both Sir Alfred and Thomas stood down as MPs and retired from public life in the aftermath of the scandal. The tribunal had called for Thomas's bookmakers' accounts in evidence; the Prime Minister, Stanley Baldwin, told a confidant that the disgraced minister was 'a terrific gambler' who 'most likely . . . let his tongue wag when he was in his cups . . . the two weaknesses of his class'.

The younger Butt, however, was able to return to Lloyd's after a brief interval, as an underwriter with the firm of Sir William Garthwaite, whose director declared: 'We think very highly of Mr Kenneth Butt.'

Alfred Kenneth Dudley Butt was born on 7 July 1908. His father rose to prominence as the managing director of a string of London and provincial theatres, including the Palace (where Pavlova and Maud Allen topped the bill), the Theatre Royal, Drury Lane and the Glasgow Alhambra. Alfred Butt was Unionist MP for Wandsworth, Balham and Tooting from 1922 until his resignation, and was created a baronet in 1929.

Young Kenneth was educated at Rugby and Brasenose College, Oxford, and entered Lloyd's in 1929. He was commissioned in the

Royal Artillery in 1939, and served throughout the Second World War, rising to the rank of major.

After the war he returned to the insurance business for some years as chairman of Parker Wakeling & Co; he remained a Name at Lloyd's until 1974.

Having acquired a 1000-acre estate near Royston in 1951 and inherited the Brook Stud near Newmarket on his father's death in 1962, Butt devoted himself in later life to farming and bloodstock. Among the Brook Stud's successes were the stallion Petition, which won the Eclipse and Gimcrack Stakes for Sir Alfred and was the sire of Petite Etoile and Pristina, and the mare, School for Scandal, which broke course records at Worcester and Wolverhampton and was the mother of Scholar Gypsy.

Kenneth Butt was chairman of the Thoroughbred Breeders Association in 1973. He was also a knowledgeable cattle-breeder, and the owner of a notable herd of Aberdeen Angus. He was president of the Aberdeen Angus Cattle Society in 1968–69.

He married first, in 1938, Kathleen Farmer; the marriage was dissolved in 1948 and he married secondly in that year Marie Josephine 'Joey' Birts, née Bain, the widow of Lt Col Ivor Watkins Birts, an artillery officer by whom she had two children. There were no children of either of Sir Kenneth Butt's marriages.

10 February 1999

Peter Cadbury

⟶⟦ 1918–2006 ⟧⟵

Argumentative entrepreneur

Peter Cadbury, the founder of Westward Television, was a maverick entrepreneur and social figure whose career was punctuated by heated rows with boardroom colleagues, wives, neighbours, motorists, the Conservative Party and the Devon & Cornwall Constabulary.

Cadbury was a scion of the Quaker chocolate-making dynasty,

but never worked for the family firm and was distinctly un-Quakerish in every aspect of his personal and business life. After an early career as a test pilot, barrister and head of the Keith Prowse theatre ticket agency, he was involved in 1959 in the establishment of Tyne Tees Television. Having perceived the moneymaking potential of the medium, he flew himself to Plymouth 'with a copy of *Who's Who* and a map, collected 200 shareholders and started Westward Television'.

He won the franchise against 11 competing bids. But within less than two years, the station was making serious losses, which Cadbury attributed to excessive tax demands, declaring that he himself was able to draw a salary of only £6 per week – 'less than half what I pay my gardener'.

The position improved and Westward gained a good reputation for programming. But Cadbury remained an outspoken critic of financial constraints imposed on independent broadcasters. This eventually brought him into conflict with his own board, who ousted him by a 5–2 vote in 1970, with one colleague telling the press that they were 'sick and tired of his wild statements'. Eight days later he was reinstated, the incident being officially described as a 'misunderstanding'.

Cadbury remained unrepentant. Westward prospered, but by 1980 – when the franchise was coming up for renewal, with rival bidders in the wings – he was at odds with his board once more. When he announced to the press on Westward notepaper that he was selling his Devon home and moving to Hampshire because of 'police persecution', the directors (led by former Labour minister Lord Harris of Greenwich, whom Cadbury had recruited) voted him out of office. Cadbury, who controlled 55 per cent of the company, promptly called a shareholder meeting, which voted overwhelmingly to remove Harris.

Confusion reigned until the Independent Broadcasting Authority intervened, threatening to take Westward off the air. The television scriptwriter Ted Willis, who was a founder shareholder of Westward, defended Cadbury as 'a buccaneer, a crazy fighter pilot, a man of impulses'. Cadbury's wife Janie, meanwhile, announced that she would 'have Harris's guts for garters'.

But Cadbury finally agreed to withdraw, and sold his share-holding. Westward lost its franchise, and Cadbury penned a 200,000-word account of the battle which proved too libellous to print. In later years the mention of Lord Harris made Cadbury think of 'sticking pins in wax effigies'.

Peter Egbert Cadbury was born on 6 February 1918, the elder son of Air Commodore Sir Egbert Cadbury DSC DFC, a First World War ace who shot down two zeppelins over the North Sea from his Sopwith Camel, and went on to become a managing director of Cadbury Bros, the predecessor of Cadbury Schweppes. Egbert was in turn a grandson of John Cadbury, a Quaker who had started business as a tea, coffee and cocoa merchant in Bull Street, Birmingham in 1824.

John's sons, Richard and George (Egbert's father), developed a formula for chocolate in 1866 and went on to build Bournville, the company village near Birmingham which pioneered decent work-ing and housing conditions for employees; Cadbury Bros became one of the world's largest confectioners. Peter recalled as a child being allowed to dip his fingers into vats of molten chocolate.

Young Peter was educated at Leighton Park, a Quaker school founded by his grandfather, and Trinity College, Cambridge. Having been taught to fly at 17 by his father, he joined the Fleet Air Arm in 1940 and was seconded to the Ministry of Aircraft Production as an experimental test pilot.

He became a member of the team which flew the first Meteor jet aircraft, surviving numerous crashes. Six of his close colleagues were killed, including one pilot who crashed on Minchinhampton golf course only minutes after Cadbury had handed over the plane to him. The legendary Spitfire pilot Douglas Bader was best man at Cadbury's first wedding.

At the end of the war, Cadbury was invited to become a parliamentary candidate for the Liberal Party, which his family had traditionally supported. He stood for Stroud, declaring at the end of his first public meeting 'Those are my views and if you don't like any of them I can change them, because I only learned them yesterday.' He took 30 per cent of the poll, splitting the Conservative vote and allowing Labour to win. Not long afterwards he became a Tory.

In 1946 he was called to the Bar, and (accompanying his godfather, the celebrated advocate Norman Birkett) appeared as a junior prosecutor in the Nuremburg trials. In the early 1950s he shared chambers in Lincolns Inn with the young Margaret Thatcher. 'An exceptionally talented girl,' he said later, 'I love her dearly.' But he saw no possibility of making a fortune in the courts, and left in 1954 to enter the business world.

As his first venture he borrowed £75,000 from his father to buy the Keith Prowse ticket agency. A keen theatre-goer, he could guarantee success for West End productions by placing huge block-bookings known as 'library deals'. His preferences were robustly middlebrow: he disliked anything experimental, gloomy or involving 'people being ill all over the stage', and revealed that he would back a show only when he felt his mother would like it. This provoked the dramatist John Osborne to fulminate: 'It's not a healthy situation when every play that opens in London has to depend on catching the fancy of a tasteless man's tasteless mother.'

Keith Prowse went public in 1960, and subsequently became a subsidiary of Westward. As ever, Cadbury battled with his board-room colleagues, who included the impresario Emile Littler and the 10th Duke of Rutland. He survived an attempted coup in 1964, remaining chairman and managing director until the agency was sold in the early 1970s.

Cadbury was associated with numerous other enterprises, including his own airline and travel businesses. Among the ventures that failed to take off were a bid to acquire the MG sports car business, and another, in partnership with the former boxer George Walker, to take over the Playboy Club in London. He was asked, but declined, to succeed his uncle Laurence Cadbury as chairman of the *News Chronicle*, a Liberal paper which was the last survivor of the so-called 'cocoa press'. He briefly rescued *Working Woman*, a glossy 1980s magazine, but closed it after its founding editor, Audrey Slaughter, resigned on finding that his ideas were diametrically opposed to hers.

Peter Cadbury's private life occupied at least as many column inches as the ups and downs of his business career. On more than one occasion he was involved in fisticuffs on the highway after incidents involving his Ferrari or his Bentley. In 1970 he was taken to court by a Berkshire neighbour who accused him of keeping pigs next to her cottage purely to annoy her.

He owned yachts, racehorses, properties in the West Indies and a succession of grand country mansions. The latter included Preston Candover in Hampshire, which boasted a mile-long airstrip and hangars for five aircraft. Having sold the estate to Sir John Sainsbury, he moved briefly to Lyneham House in Devon – but decided to move again on the grounds that 'police harassment' made his life there intolerable.

He had developed a particularly fierce animosity towards the chief constable of Devon and Cornwall, whose appearances on Westward news programmes he tried to censor. Among other brushes with the local force, Cadbury was charged with wasting police time in connection with an anonymous letter alleging local authority corruption in Plymouth, and of shooting protected geese.

At his last home, Upton Grey in Hampshire, he did battle with one neighbour over the use of automatic bird-scarers and with another over the spreading of manure. When the house was burgled in 1994, he announced the termination of his 45 years of support for the Conservative Party, in disgust at the failure of law-and-order policies. He also declared that he would 'shoot an intruder without hesitation. Shoot first, ask questions afterwards.'

Thieves broke into Cadbury's house again in 1999, and got away with his wallet, his wife's jewellery and much else – including the gun that Cadbury had kept by his bed for 40 years. Thereafter Cadbury armed himself with a crossbow, which, after the jailing of Tony Martin for shooting two burglars at his farmhouse in Norfolk in 2000, he robustly declared he was ready to use against a burglar who broke in late at night.

Cadbury's sympathies often lay more with animals than with people. As chairman of the George Cadbury Trust, he directed its funds chiefly towards animal charities. He kept a parrot and a Great Dane, adopted a Rwandan gorilla, and once observed: 'There's nothing I can do about Africans; I *can* do something about Irish horses.' He was, however, a trustee of Help the Aged and of Winchester Cathedral.

Peter Cadbury married first, in 1947, Benedicta Bruce, by whom he had a son and a daughter. The marriage was dissolved in 1968. Secondly, in 1970, he married Mrs Jennifer Morgan-Jones, 27 years his junior, whom he had known since her childhood and had employed as a junior at Keith Prowse. He credited her with steering him through the first of his Westward boardroom crises, and married her shortly afterwards. In due course she became (as Jennifer D'Abo, after her own third marriage) a formidable businesswoman in her own right. They had a son – Joel Cadbury, the restauranteur – and were divorced in 1976. 'The marriage broke up because she's a better entrepreneur than I am,' Cadbury observed. He married thirdly, in that year, Mrs Jane Mead, by whom he had two more sons.

'There are always difficulties living with an old sod like Peter,' the third Mrs Cadbury told a gossip columnist in 1982, but the marriage endured. Peter Cadbury was survived by his wife and five children.

17 April 2006

Bernie Cornfeld

⊷⊨⊙ 1927–1995 ⊙⊨⊷

The man behind the IOS scandal

Bernie Cornfeld was the founder of Investors Overseas Services (IOS), which precipitated one of the most spectacular financial scandals of the modern era. Through aggressive pyramid-selling of mutual fund (unit trust) investments, IOS grew in the 1960s at a breathtaking rate, attracting more than a million investors in 95 countries and amassing some $2.4 billion of savings, much of which was held in Cornfeld's notorious Fund of Funds, a vehicle which provided cover for reckless mismanagement and sharp practice.

Cornfeld was ousted after market confidence in his empire collapsed in 1970, but although his investors suffered massive losses, he was eventually acquitted of fraud charges.

On his way down, no less than on his way up, Cornfeld advertised the benefits of self-enrichment by maintaining a wildly flamboyant lifestyle. 'I deliberately went out and created an image I thought most people wanted to emulate. I had mansions all over the world. I threw extravagant parties. And I lived with 10 or 12 girls at a time. I know the average man couldn't carry it off – living with a harem. But I could. For me it was a lot less complicated to have a lot of pretty girls around than having just one ... I wanted casual, playful relationships.'

Among the many beautiful women who shared Cornfeld's 35-room mansion in Beverly Hills (the former home of Douglas Fairbanks); his house in West Halkin Street, Belgravia, and his chateaux in France and Switzerland was the actress Victoria Principal, later a star of *Dallas*, whose role in Bernie's ménage was described as that of 'backgammon teacher'. He also claimed to have 'discovered' Heidi Fleiss, the Hollywood madam, as a 19-year-old starlet; she explained that she had left him because 'he was not monogamous'.

Stocky and unprepossessing in appearance, Cornfeld's success with women, as with investors, was attributed to silken and manipulative powers of persuasion. On more than one occasion he was accused of beating up his girlfriends, and he espoused unreconstructed sexist views: 'A beautiful woman with a brain', he said in 1974, 'is like a beautiful woman with a club foot.'

Bernard Cornfeld was born in Istanbul on 17 August 1927. His father was a Romanian actor, impresario and film producer; his mother was of Russian Jewish origins. The family migrated to America in 1931, settling first in Providence, Rhode Island and later in Brooklyn, where young Bernie was educated at Abraham Lincoln High School.

After a two-year stint in the merchant navy, Cornfeld completed his education with a degree in psychology at Brooklyn College. There he developed left-wing political views, and was also influenced by the psychological theories of Alfred Adler (Freud's great rival), who believed that human beings were driven by 'goal-seeking', often towards 'superiority' in wealth and power.

Cornfeld's personal goal had already been formulated: 'to make a very great deal of money'. The catchphrase indelibly associated with him – 'Do you sincerely want to be rich?' – was a crude application of Adlerian analysis to the motivation of potential salesmen and investors.

After graduation Cornfeld returned briefly to sea, then began his financial career as a salesman for a mutual funds business. Mutual funds were praised by their proponents at that time as an instrument for social justice, bringing wide investment possibilities to small savers; in that context, selling them was not incompatible with Cornfeld's professed radicalism. Cornfeld also spent a brief period as a social worker for the Jewish philanthropic institution B'nai B'rith in Philadelphia, an interlude he later capitalised on shamelessly.

In 1955, with a few hundred dollars in his pocket, Cornfeld moved to Paris. The following year he established the nucleus of IOS, attracting salesmen from among the Bohemians and misfits of the expatriate American community and finding natural customers among the relatively well-paid American military community in Europe. In 1958, IOS moved its headquarters to Geneva, expanding its sales force and beginning to tap into a flow of offshore capital attracted by the secretive Swiss banking system.

IOS was initially an agent for the Dreyfus Fund, a New York investment house noted for having bought shares in the Polaroid camera company at $32 apiece that eventually rose to $6,372. From 1960, however, Cornfeld and his colleagues began to develop their own funds, beginning with the International Investment Trust, a loosely assembled vehicle, registered in Luxembourg, which eventually attracted $700 million of investors' cash.

Two years later, they launched their most famous investment idea: the Fund of Funds, a mutual fund which invested only in other high-performing mutual funds, thereby offering, according to the salesmen's logic, diversity of risk combined with the possibility of the highest performance of all. But the greatest beneficiary was in fact IOS itself which, by creating its own 'proprietary' funds for the Fund of Funds to invest in, was able to charge double slices of management commission and brokerage and to conceal a multitude of imprudent speculations.

IOS activities expanded to include banks and insurance companies (100,000 British investors signed up for 'Dover Plan' life insurance policies) as well as reckless ventures such as oil and gas exploration rights in the Canadian Arctic – the blatant over-valuation of which was to be a major factor in the eventual collapse. Many of IOS's investments proved to be unmarketable, having been made chiefly for the benefit of the firm's directors and their friends. In an era when offshore investment and currency trading were strictly controlled, rules were constantly infringed.

The growth of IOS funds was driven by a pyramid-selling system, in which salesmen (of whom at the zenith there were 16,000) were lavishly rewarded with commissions and stock options, and were often themselves heavy investors in IOS schemes. Cornfeld's personal wealth was estimated to have peaked at $150 million.

The collapse and disgrace of his empire began with a public offering of $110 million of IOS shares in September 1969. The prospectus indicated that the cash was to go towards further development of the business, but in fact a large portion of the shares sold were those which had already been issued to IOS employees under the stock option scheme. Some $30 million of the issue proceeds went straight to Cornfeld and 489 of his salesmen, many of whom became millionaires as a result. Cornfeld's own slice of the takings was $7.8 million.

Early in 1970, rumours of gross mismanagement and over-valuation abounded. Profits for 1969 turned out to be substantially less than the issue prospectus had forecast. Heavy selling of stocks in which IOS was known to be an investor hastened the decline, and caused panic on the London stock exchange. It was revealed that most of IOS's remaining cash had been lent to directors for their personal ventures, including, in Cornfeld's case, the purchase of a BAC 1-11 airliner fitted out to rival the Playboy chief Hugh Hefner's famous 'Black Bunny' jet.

Cornfeld was forced off the IOS board at an acrimonious meeting of shareholders. Expressing concern for investors and denying wrongdoing, he struggled briefly and unsuccessfully to regain control. After a three-year investigation by the Geneva State

Prosecutor, he was arrested and spent 11 months in 'preventive custody' before being granted bail of SFr5 million, the highest in Swiss legal history. At the trial in 1979, however, he was acquitted of fraud in relation to the share issue, other charges of dishonest management and incitement to speculation having been dropped.

IOS meanwhile, had passed into the hands of the financier Robert Vesco, who was initially welcomed as a white knight but in due course absconded to Puerto Rico with $225 million. Those IOS investors who could be traced eventually received a few cents in the dollar by way of refund.

Although describing himself as a 'professional defendant', Cornfeld continued to dabble in film production, real-estate development and other ventures, including the marketing of a range of vitamin pills claimed to be capable of doubling the average person's sex drive. Although his wealth had been decimated in the IOS collapse it still ran to several million dollars supporting luxurious homes and nubile girlfriends on both sides of the Atlantic.

His philandering was curtailed in the early 1980s by marriage to a model, Lorraine Armbruster, by whom he had a daughter, Jessica. After their separation, however, he returned to his sybaritic ways. In 1987 he was reported to be sharing his Californian home with eight women, and to have two more companions in London. Shortly before the heart attack which finally incapacitated him in 1994, he was sighted in his Rolls-Royce accompanied by 'two leather-clad, lesbian chauffeuses'.

27 February 1995

Matthew Harding

-✦=◎ 1953–1996 ◎=✦-

Controversial Lloyd's broker

Matthew Harding, who died in a helicopter crash, was a multimillionaire Lloyd's broker; he came to public prominence as a financial backer of both Chelsea Football Club and New Labour.

Diminutive, fast-talking and confident in his opinions, Harding was one of the Lloyd's insurance market's most single-mindedly successful operators, if not necessarily one of its best liked. He rose in little more than 15 years from tea boy to chairman and major shareholder of the Benfield reinsurance broking group, acquiring a personal fortune estimated at some £150 million.

Harding had been an ardent Chelsea fan since watching his first game as an eight-year-old in 1962. In the few years before he died he underpinned the club's fragile finances by buying the freehold of the Stamford Bridge ground for £16.5 million (receiving £1.5 million a year rent in return) as well as making interest-free loans of more than £10 million to complete the new North Stand and pay for player transfers. But he declined to convert his loans into shares in the club's holding company, Chelsea Village, and came into open conflict with the major shareholder, Ken Bates. Harding, who could recite the name of every Chelsea player in living memory, wanted to recapture the team's glory days of the 1970s, rather than concentrate resources on the redevelopment of the ground. He resigned from the Chelsea Village board in November 1995, denying that he nurtured aspirations to take over Bates's position, but remained vice-chairman of the football club itself.

In September 1996, the Labour Party announced that it had received the promise of a donation of £1 million from Harding, who said, 'What New Labour under Tony Blair's leadership is trying to do is the right thing at the right time. Labour has a far greater understanding of the enterprise economy than many people in the Tory Party do.'

This declaration came as a surprise to those who saw Harding as a typical self-made entrepreneur of the Thatcher era and a natural Tory; but he had in fact long been a staunch Labour supporter and was thought by some close observers to harbour political ambitions of his own. 'In America,' he pointed out, 'you can be fabulously wealthy and be a Democrat and nobody blinks an eyelid.'

The donation was trumpeted by Blairites as an indication that enlightened businessmen were turning towards Labour. But it was dismissed by another outspoken Chelsea fan, the Conservative MP David Mellor, as 'a freak'; Mellor regretted that the money had not been used to buy 'a chunk of Georgiou Kinkladze', the Manchester City midfield player.

The son of a successful Lloyd's cargo underwriter, Matthew Harding was born on 26 December 1953 and educated at Abingdon School. Though he achieved ten O Levels and an A Level in Latin he disliked life at public school, not least because he was forced to play rugby rather than soccer.

His City career began in 1971. He had spent short periods with two merchant banks when his father introduced him to Ted Benfield, a Lloyd's broker who was in the process of setting up a new company, Benfield, Lovick and Rees. Harding was taken on as the firm's most junior employee, responsible for the post and the coffee.

Over the following decade he learned the intricacies of the broking business and became a major contributor to the profits of the company, then a relatively small player in the market. His success was based partly on close relations with Richard Outhwaite, a powerful underwriter later to be sued by Names who found themselves disastrously overexposed to asbestosis claims.

In 1982 Harding is said to have demanded to know whether the directors of Benfield wanted him to work for them or with them. Their response was to offer him 10 per cent of the company and to invite him on to the board. Five years later he led a management buy-out, acquiring himself a 32 per cent holding for £160,000.

Stripped of its peripheral activities and focused on high-yielding, but sometimes controversial, reinsurance techniques, Benfield became phenomenally successful under Harding's leadership. Employing only 65 staff, it made profits of £32 million in 1994 and £29 million in 1995. Harding's earnings in salary and dividends surpassed £5 million a year.

Harding enjoyed the trappings of fortune, which included a well-publicised mistress, a convertible Ferrari and a mansion in Sussex complete with deer park and private football pitch. But he also retained the full style of a Chelsea devotee: although he carried a suit to change into when he reached the directors' box, he would set off to matches wearing a Blues shirt and a clip-on earring, joining denizens of the Shed (Stamford Bridge's most raucous stand) for Guinness in the Imperial Arms beforehand and a curry afterwards. His other passions were for Bob Dylan and Wagner.

Matthew Harding was survived by his wife Ruth and their four children.

22 October 1996

Bill Harrison

⤚⇒ 1948–2005 ⇐⤙

'Attila the Brum'

Bill Harrison was a hyperactive City financier who deployed an unpolished style, acquired in his Birmingham youth, which endeared him to industrial clients but attracted the nickname 'Attila the Brum'.

Harrison's rumbustious career took him to prominent positions in no less than seven banks, as well as two oil companies and his own corporate finance boutique. He left his mark on all of them, but perhaps the most colourful passage was his brief tenure as chief executive of Barclays de Zoete Wedd, the ill-fated investment banking arm of Barclays.

Harrison had been hired from Robert Fleming in June 1996 by Martin Taylor, Barclays' chief executive, with a mandate to bring together warring elements of BZW and Barclays and mould them into a global force to compete with the giants of Wall Street. He set to the task with gusto, presenting ambitious investment plans and presiding over a stampede of hirings and firings.

Taylor, however, had concluded by the autumn of 1997 that BZW was both unmanageable and unlikely ever to be sufficiently profitable; he decided to break it up, disposing of the corporate finance and equities businesses on which Harrison's energy was focused. Harrison departed with robust dignity, having collected a total of more than £4 million of remuneration for thirteen months' work: 'These things happen,' he said later. 'I didn't throw my toys out of the cot.'

Harrison always bounced back. Throughout his career he was as successful in selling himself to new employers as he was in broking mergers and acquisitions between corporate clients. After his high-profile exit from BZW, he joined Deutsche Morgan Grenfell as its vice-chairman, responsible for global corporate and institutional business, but soon found himself in another wasp's nest of internal politics – Deutsche was about to expunge the name of Morgan Grenfell and merge the remains of its business with Bankers Trust. He departed again after little more than a year – again collecting a large pay-off – to set up his own corporate finance boutique, Harrison Lovegrove, advising clients in the oil and gas sector.

More of a salesman than a manager at heart, Bill Harrison was once voted 'the London investment banker you'd most like to meet for a drink' in a City survey. One journalist observed that 'with his longish hair, curly moustache, big jaw, short legs, swelling paunch and Brummie accent, he might be a retired Aston Villa striker who had made it big in the motor trade'; but clients welcomed his straight-talking style and his relentless thirst to do deals.

William Robert Harrison was born in Birmingham on 5 October 1948. His childhood was tough: his father left when Bill was very young, leaving him to be brought up by his mother – who worked as a secretary in an engineering firm – and his grandparents. He was educated at George Dixon Grammar School in Edgbaston, where he captained the soccer team, and went on to the London School of Economics, where he gained an MSc with distinction in Economics.

He began his City career in 1971. If a lack of grooming or connections might have been an obstacle to joining any of the elite British merchant banks in that era, it recommended him to Manufacturers Hanover, one of several American firms which set out to recruit graduates who lacked social credentials but showed real hunger for business. Harrison was exactly that, and acquired a reputation as an unusually forceful young banker.

He moved in 1977 to British National Oil Corporation as a protégé of Alastair Morton (later, as Sir Alastair, the famously combative Eurotunnel chairman), who thought very highly of him.

Next he joined the London office of Lehman Brothers, the New York investment bank; then in 1981 he became finance director of another oil business, Tricentrol, where his brother-in-law, Graham Hearne, was chief executive.

In 1983 he became a director of Schroders, but after three years he returned to Lehman for an eight-year stint as head of European investment banking. This was by some distance his longest stay in any job, and perhaps his most successful. His client list included Courtaulds, British Aerospace and BAT, and it was at Lehman that Harrison coined his celebrated exhortation to junior executives – 'A weekend with the family is a missed marketing opportunity'. He could be exhausting and maddening to work for, but his team also regarded him with affection and respect. One of them recalled 'a real piece of work, a human dynamo with an incredible energy level, a great sense of humour and a very sharp brain'.

In 1993, Harrison moved to become head of investment banking at Robert Fleming, a very traditional, family-controlled City firm. His appointment inevitably attracted headlines such as 'Upstart in the patrician camp', but again he made a distinctive impact, extracting new value from the bank's international network and handling major deals such as the Glaxo takeover of Wellcome and the rescue of Barings by the Dutch institution ING. He favoured a 'transactional' approach – thinking up deals and taking them to companies rather than relying on established clients to provide a flow of activity – but this also brought criticism, as did the rapid turnover of executives in his department.

After successfully establishing Harrison Lovegrove, he took yet another new direction in 2002 as the London representative of a US investment firm, Compass Partners. Finally, in March 2005, he became chairman of the UK advisory board of ING, where his energies were reported to be undimmed. He was also a non-executive director of Pilkington, an adviser to the law firm Herbert Smith, a trustee of the Royal Botanic Gardens at Kew, and a former High Sheriff of Greater London.

In rare moments of relaxation, Harrison enjoyed reading, gardening, supporting Arsenal and taking safari holidays beyond the reach of a mobile phone.

He married, in 1970, Jacqueline Brown, whom he had first met at a school party when they were both 16; they had a son and a daughter.

15 November 2005

Sir Julian Hodge

-⭑⟾ 1904–2004 ⟾⭑-

'The usurer of the Valleys'

Sir Julian Hodge was Wales's leading financier and one of the principality's most active philanthropists, but his career was dogged by controversy.

Hodge was a formidable corporate operator who held director-ships, at various times, of 165 companies and built up a personal fortune of more than £60 million. His unconcealed hunger for success provoked mixed reactions. Though admired by many people in Wales for his patriotism, his puritanical business precepts and his charitable largesse, his relationship with the financial authorities in London was sometimes uneasy and he was regularly pilloried in *Private Eye* as 'the usurer of the Valleys'.

The core of his empire was a conglomerate of hire-purchase, secondary finance and property companies, built up in the 1950s and '60s. It was run from a tinted-glass tower – one of Cardiff's most prominent landmarks – where Hodge exercised power in irascible and idiosyncratic style – he forbade anyone but himself to use green ink on corporate paperwork, for example.

Just before the onset of the 'fringe bank' crisis, in which many finance businesses fell into trouble at the end of 1973, the Hodge Group was sold to Standard Chartered for £45 million. The timing of the deal was fortuitous; though the group might have survived the crisis, it would never have commanded such a price in the following years. 'I feel it must have been my guardian angel,' Hodge remarked.

By then he had a more grandiose project in hand. In 1972, he had founded the Commercial Bank of Wales. He had hoped to call it simply 'the Bank of Wales', but the Bank of England objected that it might be mistaken for a central bank. Nevertheless, he had high ambitions for it as a truly Welsh institution which would deploy local depositors' funds to finance much-needed industrial regeneration and turn Cardiff into a regional financial centre. The bank's founding directors included the Labour MPs James Callaghan (to whom Hodge was particularly close) and George Thomas (later Speaker of the House of Commons and Viscount Tonypandy) and the former ambassador Lord Harlech.

But the Commercial Bank did not achieve the progress and prestige that Hodge had hoped for. This was partly due to depressed economic conditions and partly because his own reputation was the subject of so much press comment. Shortly after its takeover by Standard Chartered, Hodge Group (of which Sir Julian remained chairman) was revealed to have lent money on second mortgages to 1000 West Indian investors to finance their participation in a pyramid-selling cosmetics franchise operation called Holiday Magic, which collapsed.

It was the Holiday Magic episode which particularly held the attention of *Private Eye*, but there were other accusations levelled against Hodge. In the House of Commons in 1973, it was said that his companies were charging up to 45 per cent interest on second mortgages for poor immigrants in Birmingham and Lancashire. His name was also connected with a dubious proposal by John Stonehouse – the former Labour minister who later faked his own drowning – to launch a bank to serve the Bangladeshi community in Britain.

When Hodge denied having supported the scheme, Stonehouse responded in the House of Commons in April 1976 by claiming that a proposal some years earlier by James Callaghan, then Chancellor, to make Hodge a director of the Bank of England, had been vetoed by senior civil servants. It was a speech that caused Stonehouse to be ejected from the House of Commons for disorderly conduct.

The authorities in London continued to view Hodge's enterprises with some caution. In 1978 – the year in which Hodge himself retired as chairman of the group – the Office of Fair Trading said that it was 'minded to refuse' to grant consumer credit licences to two Hodge companies, not least because of the harshness with which they chased debts. The Bank of England decided in 1981 not to grant full banking status (under the 1979 Banking Act) to the Commercial Bank of Wales, though it relented in response to Hodge's vociferous appeals some months later – a decision at which, Hodge declared, 'all Wales will rejoice'.

Julian Stephen Alfred Hodge was born in London on 15 October 1904, the son of a plumber. The family moved to South Wales in 1909, settling at Pontllanfraith where young Julian attended the council school. At 13 he was despatched to London to work in his aunt's chemists' shop in Holloway Road. On returning to Wales, he became a clerk on the Great Western Railway (GWR) at 30 shillings a week, and studied accountancy at Cardiff Technical College. When his father abandoned the family to return to London, Julian became the breadwinner for his mother and five younger brothers.

When he qualified in 1930 he put a brass plate – 'Julian S. Hodge, Certified Accountant' – on the door of his mother's terraced house and began to trawl the locality for small-business clients. Though still working for GWR – where he refused a promotion to manager that would have taken him out of the district – he also became a part-time life assurance salesman and ventured into running local cinemas.

By the time he finally resigned from the railway in 1941, Hodge had already established a portfolio of audit and insurance businesses, as well as taking over the management of the New Continental Restaurant in Cardiff on behalf of an interned family of Italian immigrants. After the war he branched out further, buying up local garages and selling cars by hire-purchase. He became a director of numerous other companies, and acquired a reputation in the 1950s as a combative shareholder and boardroom agitator. His own group went public in 1961 but remained an impenetrable financial maze that was only understood completely by Hodge himself. In the mid-1960s it hit problems of financial control, and had to be urgently restructured.

Hodge's other interests included the Avana bakery group – a supplier to Marks & Spencer – which he helped to steer from near bankruptcy to substantial profit. He was chairman of Avana from 1974 to 1980, and built up a £7 million personal stake. He also controlled the Reliant car company.

In 1962, guided by his friend the financier and philanthropist Sir Isaac Wolfson, Hodge established the Jane Hodge Foundation in honour of his mother who had died in 1946. The foundation provided funds for religious and educational causes as well as building children's and old people's homes. This and his own charitable trust became the beneficiaries of 80 per cent of the shares in his family holding company, distributing many millions of pounds – following Hodge's own preference, largely to causes that included an element of self-help.

He had little taste for the high life (it was said that he celebrated becoming a paper millionaire after the 1961 flotation by taking his wife to one of his own cinemas for the evening) but he enjoyed rubbing shoulders with the famous. In 1970 he instituted an annual Jane Hodge Memorial Lecture, bringing speakers to Cardiff who included the Governor of the Bank of England, the head of the IMF, Prince Philip and Sheikh Yamani of OPEC.

Hodge was chairman of the industrial sub-committee of the Aberfan Disaster Fund, president of the University of Wales Institute of Science & Technology (where he endowed the Julian S. Hodge Chair of banking and Finance) and a member of the Welsh Economic Council.

Though he considered himself a socialist for most of his life and provided financial support for a number of Labour MPs, Hodge became a backer of Sir James Goldsmith's Referendum Party. He also funded the 1997 Welsh anti-devolution campaign – with so many layers of elected officials, he declared, 'Wales is being democratised to the point of exhaustion'.

Hodge was a devout Roman Catholic and the holder of a papal knighthood in the order of St Gregory. In his retirement years he conceived an ambition to endow a new cathedral for Cardiff. When Pope John Paul II visited Wales in 1982, Hodge was instrumental in persuading him to bless a 'foundation stone' for the project, which Hodge insisted would be built in the grounds of Cardiff Castle. But worshippers remained fond of their existing cathedral, St David's, designed by Pugin and consecrated in 1887, and church officials were wary of the financier's motives. His declaration that he wanted to build a church because 'I've done everything else,' prompted one local priest to ask, 'Would it be a Roman Catholic cathedral he is proposing or a Hodge cathedral?' In a last attempt to launch the project in time for the Millennium, Hodge – by then living in Jersey – doubled his proffered donation to £3 million, but was politely turned away.

Julian Hodge, who was knighted in 1970, married, in 1951, Moira Thomas, who had been a ledger clerk in his Cardiff office. They had two sons and a daughter.

18 July 2004

Lord Keith of Castleacre

⋅⊷⊜ 1916–2004 ⊜⊷⋅

Ruthless financier

Lord Keith of Castleacre was one of the most aggressive and ambitious financiers in the postwar City; he created a major merchant bank, Hill Samuel, through a series of mergers marked by clashes with those who stood in his way. He was also a formidable chairman of Rolls-Royce, the aero engine-maker.

Physically imposing, forceful in his opinions and determined to succeed, Kenneth Keith first made his presence felt in the financial world as a young man with a good war record who revived the fortunes of the issuing house Philip Hill in the late 1940s. The firm operated in the West End rather than the City, and Keith was initially regarded as a bumptious outsider.

When he arranged in 1951 to merge with Higginson & Co, a modest but respectable merchant bank, and to move the combined operation to Moorgate, the Governor of the Bank of England remarked that he expected to see 'some changes in the sort of policy on issue business previously followed by Philip Hill'. Undeterred,

Keith was relentless in pursuit of new industrial clients to bring to the stock market. Profits quadrupled, Keith made his first million, and in 1959 Philip Hill Higginson was admitted to the exclusive Accepting Houses Committee.

Shortly after that, the acquisition of Erlanger & Co strengthened the banking side of the business, though Keith immediately fell out with its senior partner, Leo d'Erlanger, whom he would not accept as chairman of the combined firm. A Wall Street firm, Harriman Ripley, was also brought into the fold, but was sold again after another falling-out.

The next step of this process of agglomeration came in 1965, when Keith negotiated a merger with M Samuel, a family-owned bank whose founder had also created the Shell oil company. A Samuel descendant, Lord Bearsted, became chairman of the merged firm with Keith as chief executive, but that did not prevent friction with Bearsted's right-hand man Lord Melchett, who lost the tussle and (through the intervention of Roy Jenkins as Chancellor of the Exchequer) left to become chairman of British Steel Corporation.

'Samuel Hill' was touted as a name for the group, but the ultimate parent would then have been Samuel Hill Investment Trust, which as one commentator put it, had 'unattractive acronymic possibilities'; so 'Hill Samuel' won out. The business moved to Wood Street offices formerly occupied by the soup-maker Crosse & Blackwell, and the Keith approach prevailed in its business.

In the months that followed, the firm acted for Charles Clore in his controversial bid for Selfridges and for Allied Breweries in its bid for Showerings, the Babycham-maker, shortly after acting for Showerings in an unsuccessful bid for Harvey's of Bristol, the sherry firm.

Many executives from the Samuel side, accustomed to gentler ways of doing business, departed. The ripples caused by Keith's combative style prompted the Bank of England to insist on the appointment of a former Treasury official, Lord Sherfield, as an emollient chairman to follow Bearsted. Nevertheless, Keith (who followed Sherfield in 1970) was at the height of his powers and was now where he wanted to be: at the heart of the financial establishment. Though he made enemies easily, he also provoked loyalty and affection; his sense of humour was warm, and he could be engagingly contrite.

But he was still unashamedly hungry. In 1969 he had floated the idea of a merger with Siegmund Warburg's firm – again a potentially explosive mix of management styles. Though Warburg himself was ready to step aside, the stumbling block for the merger was his right-hand man, Henry Grunfeld, who (though already 67) had no intention of retiring, and indeed never did so. Keith recognised that he could not work with the cerebral, ultra-fastidious Grunfeld, and after much negotiation the deal fell away.

Keith had to content himself with buying a shipbroker, Lamberts, and an insurance broker, Noble Lowndes, turning Hill Samuel into more of a financial conglomerate than a traditional merchant bank. He failed in an attempt to take this concept forward by acquiring the property group MEPC, but in 1973 a far more significant merger prospect came into the frame: the fast-moving and controversial investment group Slater Walker.

This would have created a £1.5 billion investment bank – by some distance the biggest player in its field in the City. Jim Slater, the genius of Slater Walker, had health worries and seemed ready to let Keith take the lead, but as negotiations dragged on he had second thoughts. Finally, a Saturday-morning call from Keith berating Slater for not keeping Hill Samuel apprised of some share dealings brought matters to a head. 'I did not like being taken to task over my breakfast,' Slater wrote. 'By the time the telephone conversation had ended, so had our plans to merge.'

After taking on the Rolls-Royce chairmanship in 1972, Keith operated as non-executive chairman of Hill Samuel from a resplendent suite above the bank's branch in St James's Square, leaving his deputy Robert Clarke to run day-to-day business in Wood Street.

Keith still saw a need for consolidation to compete on a global scale, however, and in 1980 he tried to engineer a takeover of Hill Samuel by the Wall Street giant Merrill Lynch – without consulting his own board first. Merrill's bid was rejected and Keith stepped down as chairman, though he remained chairman of the holding company, Philip Hill Investment Trust, until 1987.

The son of a prosperous Norfolk farmer, Kenneth Alexander Keith was born on 30 August 1916, and was educated at Rugby, which he heartily disliked. On leaving school he took articles with the London accountancy firm of Peat Marwick & Mitchell, qualifying as a chartered accountant shortly before the outbreak of war in 1939.

He was commissioned in the Welsh Guards, saw action in North Africa and Italy, and was mentioned in despatches. For a time he was a POW, but in the later stages of the war he showed his mettle as a lieutenant colonel on the intelligence staff at Eisenhower's Supreme Allied Headquarters. He was awarded the French Croix de Guerre with Silver Star, and caught the attention of the head of intelligence, Major General Strong (later, as Sir Kenneth, a director of Philip Hill) who took Keith with him as his deputy when he took charge of the Foreign Office's political intelligence department in 1945.

Keith was eager to return to the financial world, however, and in April 1946 he joined Philip Hill – on the introduction of a fellow POW, Lt Col Brian Mountain, whose family controlled Eagle Star Insurance, which in turn controlled Hill. Keith and Harry Moore, a colleague from Peat Marwick who was at Keith's side throughout his City career, rapidly took command of the business and drove it forward.

Kenneth Keith was asked to take the chair of Rolls-Royce after its 1971 financial collapse and subsequent, highly controversial nationalisation by the Heath government. He took a fiercely independent view of his role, and his long experience of working with industrial clients gave him a good understanding of the challenges involved. He saw to completion the delivery of RB211 engines for the Lockheed Tristar aircraft which had been the cause of the collapse, and became a powerful high-level salesman for the Rolls-Royce name, particularly in the US market but also as far afield as Egypt (where he befriended President Sadat) and China. He resigned in 1980, when a further round of financial problems loomed.

He was also at various times chairman of Beecham, the pharmaceuticals group, and of Standard Telephones & Cables; vice-chairman of British European Airways; and a director of Eagle Star

Insurance, Times Newspapers, National Provincial Bank and the Bank of Nova Scotia.

He was a member of the National Economic Development Council from 1964 to 1971, a governor of the National Institute for Social & Economic Research, president of the British Standards Institution and the Royal Society for the Prevention of Accidents, and a governor of Manchester Business School.

He was knighted in 1969 and appointed a life peer, as Lord Keith of Castleacre, in 1980.

Shortly after the war, Keith had acquired an attractive country home at Castle Acre in his ancestral territory of north Norfolk, where he was a successful farmer, a generous host and a first-class shot. He was president of the Royal Norfolk Agricultural Association in 1989.

He married first, in 1946, Lady Ariel Baird, daughter of Viscount Stonehaven and the Countess of Kintore; they had twins, a son and a daughter. The marriage was dissolved in 1958 and he married secondly, in 1962, Mrs Nancy Hayward, a New Yorker. He married thirdly, in 1973, Mrs Marie Hanbury, and finally, in 2002, Mrs Penelope de Laszlo.

1 September 2004

Ephraim Margulies

◆⇒ 1924–1997 ⇐◆

Secretive commodities trader

Ephraim Margulies was a mercurial and secretive commodities trader who became known as 'the Fifth Man' in the Guinness share scandal. Known to the City as 'Marg', Margulies was chairman of S & W Berisford, a trading house which dealt in cocoa, metals and coffee and owned the British Sugar Corporation, a major producer of beet sugar.

He was a central player in the £100 million share-support operation co-ordinated by Guinness as part of the 1986 takeover of Distillers which it fought out against a rival bid from the Argyll grocery chain. Margulies bought £15 million worth of shares to help sustain Guinness's share price during the bid.

Enquiry later focused on whether he had asked for, or had been given, an illegal indemnity against losses on the holding. A secret payment of £1.9 million was made by Guinness to a Swiss-based Panamanian company allegedly associated with the Margulies family, and a further £1.5 million to a Berisford subsidiary. When pressed, Margulies claimed that the latter payment related to Third World barter trade arrangements for Guinness in Nigeria, and had nothing to do with share dealings. Nevertheless he paid it back.

Margulies had been introduced to Guinness by the stockbroker Anthony Parnes, who with Ernest Saunders and the property tycoon Gerald Ronson, served a jail sentence for his role in the bid, whilst a fourth defendant, Jack Lyons, was fined and stripped of his knighthood.

Parnes had family connections with Margulies – Parnes' grandfather had helped the Margulies family when they arrived in England as migrants from Hungary – but was said to have been 'terrified of Marg' and to have 'sobbed tearlessly' when giving evidence about him to the DTI. Parnes claimed that Margulies had threatened to frame him by making it seem that the Swiss payment had been destined for Parnes himself. Guinness finance director Olivier Roux later testified that bogus invoices for the controversial payments were produced to meet Margulies' demand that he be 'kept out of the picture'.

A meeting of DTI officials in January 1987 compiled a list of 'potential accused' which included the words 'Margulies (more in Ronson category)'. But there was no direct evidence that Margulies had asked for an indemnity and the full story of the Swiss payment proved impossible to unravel. Though Margulies was severely criticised in a leaked interim DTI report, no charges were ever brought against him. Publication of the final DTI report was still awaited at the time of his death.

Ephraim Solomon Margulies was born on 9 October 1924 into a family of poor Jewish immigrants in London's East End. As a schoolboy he added to the family income by buying and selling groceries. After service with the Royal Navy as a cook, he began his City career as a cocoa trader.

Margulies' first company, JH Rayner of Mincing Lane, emerged as a dynamic player in the booming markets of the 1960s. In 1969 he completed an audacious takeover of the much larger S & W Berisford, where he achieved explosive profit growth, from £2 million in 1970 to over £30 million by 1980.

Though he shunned publicity, he acquired an awesome reputation in London's commodity exchanges for his ability to exploit technical shortages. He lost money in the collapse of the tin market in the early 1980s, but consolidated Berisford's advance by the £280 million acquisition of British Sugar. Over the next five years, Berisford became a darling of the stock market and resisted no less than four takeover bids.

But Margulies was never comfortable with the constraints placed on him as chairman of a public company. Berisford's 1987 annual shareholders' meeting, at a time when both Tate & Lyle and an Italian group, Ferruzzi, were trying to gain control of the company, lasted all of 18 minutes; the chairman's address was clocked at 45 seconds.

'Marg' was by nature a solo operator, who relied on his trader's instinct. He maintained a homespun style, combined with ultra-orthodox religious observance, which belied his reputation as a ruthlessly brilliant predator. 'I like to keep my options open', was as much as he would give away about his strategy: 'We buy a little, we sell a little,' he once said, 'and with God's help we make a little.'

He also relied on personal relationships: the highest com-pliment for those he trusted was to be called 'a good boy'. One of his closest allies was Jay Pritzker, a Wall Street arbirtrageur who held a stake in Berisford. Pritzker was a player in the controversial mid-1980s battle for the troubled tobacco group RJR Nabisco.

Pritzker's team urgently needed an investor to take a $125 million stake in RJR, but it was Saturday, the Sabbath, and Margulies' New York colleagues could not be reached until after sunset. Nevertheless a meeting was arranged, and Pritzker's advisers were surprised to be met by Marg himself, softly whistling the theme tune from Alfred Hitchcock's 1950s television series; without his glasses, the squat and tubby Margulies bore a striking resemblance to Hitchcock.

Even more surprising was the fact that Margulies agreed within twenty minutes to put up the cash; his lieutenant drafted the necessary payment instructions on the flap of a pizza box. In the event, the money was never called for, as RJR fell to another bidder; but it would have been a very high-risk investment. 'Do these people have any idea what they're doing?' asked one participant in the meeting, 'Why should they do it?'

'Jay asked them to', was the only reply.

By 1990, however, Margulies's habit of treating Berisford as a personal fiefdom had brought the company to the brink of disaster and he was running out of friends. His resistance to issuing new shares that might dilute his own holding had pushed the group deep into debt, and he faced losses of more than £200 million on investments in Manhattan real estate.

Eventually, pressure from other shareholders forced him to resign, and (though he collected a £350,000 golden handshake) he lost an estimated £30 million as the company's share price tumbled.

Margulies and his family – including his son Ari, who was both a rabbinical scholar and a well-known Wall Street speculator – retired from public view.

2 September 1997

Forrest Mars

-⇌ 1904–1999 ⇌-

Misanthropic head of the confectionery empire

Forrest Mars developed the world-famous confectionery brand that bears his name, and established one of America's richest dynasties. He was a secretive, penny-pinching, foul-tempered bully, but his monstrous character proved no obstacle to his building up a family fortune estimated shortly before his death at £12.5 billion, making Forrest and his three children the eighth richest family in the world at that time.

Their privately owned company, Mars Inc, employed 28,000

people and was one of the world's most successful food con-glomerates, with a wide range of famous branded products (for pets as well as humans) besides the ubiquitous Mars Bar itself.

But Mars family and business affairs were always conducted in the utmost secrecy. According to a set of precepts laid down by Forrest before he handed over the reins in 1973, executives at the company's headquarters in Virginia clocked in each morning with punch cards, worked in sparse, open-plan offices, travelled economy class and never spoke to the press. They received bonuses for punctuality, but could be fired automatically if their sales fall below target. After Forrest's death, the family continued to control every aspect of the business.

Forrest himself ranked as one of monsters of American capitalism, alongside the likes of Armand Hammer, Howard Hughes and J Paul Getty Sr. He was notorious for his frugality, his obsessive attention to detail, his vicious temper and his merciless capacity to humiliate any Mars employee, including his own children, who displeased him.

Forrest Edward Mars was born on 21 March 1904. His father Frank was a wholesaler in Minneapolis of 'penny candies' such as lemon drops, peppermint sticks and liquorice. But Frank's business skills were poor, and several times the family found itself penniless. After his parents divorced, young Forrest was brought up by his maternal grandparents in Canada, where he attended Lethbridge High School in Alberta.

Frank eventually found success in the early 1920s with the Mar-O-Bar, a gooey combination of caramel, nuts and chocolate. By then Forrest was studying to become a mining engineer at the University of California, and had not seen his father for 15 years. But during his vacation, he worked as a salesman for Camel cigarettes in Chicago, and when he was arrested for flyposting Camel advertisements on shop windows and the case was reported in the local press, it was his father who came to bail him out.

According to Forrest's account, the reunited pair discussed ways of improving Frank's business and came up with the Milky Way, a chocolate-covered bar of malt-flavoured nougat, which achieved $800,000 of sales in its first year.

Forrest graduated in 1928 and joined the business – which was by then producing 20 million candy bars a year from a showpiece factory in Chicago. By 1932, turnover had reached $25 million and Mars was the second biggest confectioner in the United States. But father and son were on strained terms. Forrest demanded a one-third share of the company, and when his father declined, told him to 'stick his business up his ass'. But eventually, Frank (who died soon afterwards) gave Forrest $50,000 and the foreign rights to the Milky Way bar. Forrest set off via Switzerland, where he studied Swiss chocolate-making techniques, to make a new start in England.

He set up a small kitchen in Slough and produced his first Mars Bar in August 1933. The product, with its layer of very sweet caramel, appealed to the British taste, and sales took off. A larger factory was opened, and the business also expanded into what are now Pedigree Chum pet foods.

Forrest began to develop the management style for which he became notorious, demanding complete loyalty from staff and terrorising his own shop floor. But he also paid higher wages than his rivals, and linked the pay of every worker, including himself, to sales and profits. Mars swiftly became Britain's third largest chocolate-maker after the established leaders of the industry, Cadbury and Rowntree.

Forrest returned to America in 1939. His father's factory was for the time being in the hands of his stepmother's family, so again he branched out on his own. In 1940 he launched M&Ms – chocolate drops coated in coloured sugar candy which had the advantage of not melting on the fingers. (Mars Inc always denied that this idea was stolen from Rowntree in England, which had introduced Smarties a few years earlier.)

Forrest also launched Uncle Ben's Rice, and by the late 1940s he had built a substantial international empire. But despite repeated boardroom assaults he did not gain complete control of the original Mars business in Chicago (of which he inherited a large stake on his stepmother's death) until 1964, when he bought out the rest of the shareholders. The company's weaknesses and extravagances had enraged him for many years. On the day he took over, he summoned executives and sank to his knees in front of them, declaiming, 'I pray for Milky Way, I pray for Snickers . . .' He then proceeded to demolish the executive dining room, fire the French chef, sell the art collection and increase salaries by 30 per cent. Every Mars worker (or 'associate', as they were called) was henceforth expected to conform to Forrest's unbending rules.

The most long-suffering victims of Forrest's tyranny were his sons, Forrest Jr and John, who joined the business in the 1960s, and his daughter Jacqueline, who was later its vice-president. They had all endured a grim and austere childhood, despite Forrest's growing fortune. The boys would frequently be screamed at for the slightest flaw in performance and told in front of other staff they were unworthy of their inheritance. At a marketing meeting in Germany in 1964, the 29-year-old John was ordered to kneel and pray for the company, and was left on the floor for almost an hour as discussions continued around him.

Yet in 1973, Forrest suddenly handed over control to John and Forrest Jr, and withdrew from active involvement in the company. He retired to Las Vegas, where he set up another successful business (named Ethel M Chocolates, after his mother) making liqueur chocolates. He lived reclusively above his office, observing operations through two-way mirrors: staff referred to him as 'the phantom of the candy factory'. Forrest Mars re-emerged briefly in 1992, aged 88, to try to initiate a merger deal between Mars and Nestlé behind his sons' backs.

His wife Audrey died in 1989.

1 July 1999

Gerry Parish

⊶═ 1931–2002 ═⊷

Queensway Carpets founder

Gerry Parish was a maverick entrepreneur who pioneered the concept of out-of-town discount warehouses; but having made a modest fortune as the founder of the Queensway Carpet chain, he lost it on other ventures and devoted the rest of his life to medical research.

Parish was a mercurial and unconventional businessman who produced a constant flow of new ideas, some good and some less so. Visiting the United States in the mid-1960s he was inspired by the brash, cut-price home furnishing stores he saw there, and returned home to create the Queensway concept in a disused bonded warehouse in Queen's Road, Norwich. This was the first time that English provincial shoppers were able to buy carpet straight from the roll, tie it to their roof rack, and drive home with it – as opposed to choosing from a pattern book and waiting six weeks for delivery.

Boosted by bold advertising ('Save More Than You Spend' was the slogan for half-price offers) and free underlay, the business rapidly took off, becoming very profitable in the boom years of the early 1970s. It expanded into beds and furniture, and despite many difficulties with local planning authorities, grew into a chain of 38 outlets around the country.

Parish himself was an archetypal 'alternative' entrepreneur of the era, preferring flared velvet trousers to suits, expressing communist and CND sympathies, and distributing shares in the business to his staff. His flair for marketing was accompanied by a distinct lack of interest in mundane matters such as stock control, though his simple solution to the problem of customers who did not pay was to offer no credit at all.

At the height of his success, Parish was struck by a mystery illness which caused mood swings, memory loss and fatigue. He no longer felt able to run Queensway: having abandoned plans for a stock-market flotation, he sold the company in 1977 for a knockdown price of £2 million to the retail entrepreneur Philip Harris, now Lord Harris of Peckham. When Harris lost control of the business in a 1988 takeover battle, it was valued at £450 million; it fell on hard times in the 1990 recession, but survives today as Allied Carpets.

Anthony Royal Parish, always known as Gerry, was born in Norwich on 6 May 1931, the son of a bookkeeper. A dyslexic pupil, he attended many different schools, and was a wartime evacuee in Scotland; his formal education ended at 14 at Henderson secondary modern school in Norwich.

In his teenage years he worked in a dry-cleaning shop

before being called for national service as an orderly in the Royal Army Medical Corps in Egypt. After that, he made his living as a floor tiler and carpet fitter, latterly for Bonds of Norwich department store. In due course he and his brother Ronnie opened their own carpet shop, Parish Bros, and went on to launch Queensway.

Parish was also well known locally as a musician, playing blues and folk harmonica in Albert Cooper's band in gigs at Norwich's Mischief Inn and appearing on the television talent show *Opportunity Knocks*. He was a financial backer of the Jacquard folk club – a former pub where Cooper and his brother presented artistes such as Stefan Grapelli, George Melly and BB King.

At the height of his success, Parish lived in flamboyant style. He bought Woodlands, a 12-bedroomed Georgian-style mansion on the outskirts of Norwich, which was first his home and then his business headquarters. After the Queensway sale he converted the house into The Oasis health club – another idea that was well ahead of its time.

Having sold the club in 1978, his next venture was 'Pueblo Esparragos', a village of holiday apartments in Cala Llonga, Ibiza. He then moved to Florida in 1983 to try to recreate the success of Queensway. He set up a furniture warehouse called 'Forget' (pronounced as though it were French) but it floundered, and he lost the £300,000 he had invested.

He returned to England and retired from business to seek a cure for his continuing illness. Eventually an American doctor prescribed a drug that brought complete recovery, having diagnosed a brain condition that may have been caused by exposure to the solvent trichloroethylene when he worked in the dry-cleaning trade forty years earlier. Parish set out to prove this connection, compiling a detailed case which he pursued unsuccessfully against ICI, the makers of the solvent. He also investigated the side effects of Valium, which he had been prescribed for several years and which he believed was another trigger of his illness; his long-running lawsuit against the manufacturers, Roche, was still pending at the time of his death.

These researches led him into other areas of medical controversy. He offered his experience of exposure to drugs and chemicals as evidence in the debate over so-called Gulf War Syndrome, and developed a theory about cot death, or Sudden Infant Death Syndrome, which was related to the effect on the infant brain of anaesthetic drugs given to the mother during childbirth. His lack of academic qualifications meant that his work was often dismissed, but his findings were widely read on the Internet and were published in the journal *Medical Hypotheses*. He was a fellow of the New York Academy of Sciences.

Gerry Parish was a boundless optimist who always saw the funny side of his ups and downs, and identified particularly with the humour of Spike Milligan. He was increasingly interested in matters of spirituality as well as science.

He married first, in 1955, Marjorie Salisbury; they had two daughters and a son. He married secondly, in 1971, Cherry Wales, by whom he had two more sons. He briefly married and separated again in 1979, and married fourthly in 2001, Rema Navarro, who survived him.

16 December 2002

'Tiny' Rowland

⋆⇒ 1917–1998 ⇐⋆

'The unacceptable face of capitalism'

'Tiny' Rowland transformed Lonrho from a small mining company in Africa into a huge international conglomerate, but never achieved his ambition to own Harrods.

Secretive, ruthless and contemptuous of anything that smacked of 'Establishment hypocrisy', Rowland made few concessions to accepted principles of corporate governance, and none at all to public relations. It was in 1973 that his methods were rebuked by Prime Minister Edward Heath, as 'an unpleasant and unacceptable face of capitalism'. His later career was marked by a series of vendettas – most notably against the Fayed brothers – pursued with cold, obsessive fury.

But to an army of small shareholders, well satisfied with the dividends his methods produced, he was a hero, his reputation tarnished only by Lonrho's sharply declining financial performance in the early 1990s. And in black Africa he was held in barely less esteem than were the heads of state who were his friends and business allies there. He was, according to a colleague interviewed by government inspectors, 'a sort of tyrant, and part madman to boot, but a brilliant one'.

His association with Lonrho – originally the London & Rhodesia Mining and Land Co – began in 1961. Lonrho was then a modest and almost moribund enterprise. Angus Ogilvy, the husband of Princess Alexandra, who was a director, was asked by Harley Drayton, one of its major shareholders, to find someone to rejuvenate the company. Ogilvy suggested Rowland, who became joint managing director.

The business expanded aggressively, particularly in mining. It diversified out of Rhodesia, where Rowland, who had a special empathy with black Africans, disliked the racist tone of Ian Smith's regime. Rowland established from an early stage his habit of taking major investment decisions with little or no consultation in the Lonrho boardroom, but by 1970 the speed of expansion had begun to over-stretch the company's finances. At the same time, Lonrho executives in South Africa were accused of fraud. The accountants Peat Marwick were called in to report on the company.

As a result, Rowland was obliged to bring in a number of outside directors; these included, as chairman, the unmistakeably Establishment figure of Sir Basil Smallpiece, formerly of Cunard and BOAC, who wanted to change the company's strategy and to force Rowland to be more open in his methods. In 1972, Smallpiece – leading a cabal of directors known as the 'straight eight' – attempted to oust Rowland, accusing him of recklessness, intolerance, disloyalty and deceit. But 3000 shareholders who packed an extraordinary meeting at Central Hall, Westminster, in May 1973 voted overwhelmingly in Rowland's favour. Smallpiece and his group were jeered, and were themselves ejected from the board.

The findings of the subsequent DTI enquiry, which censured Lonrho for flouting Rhodesian sanctions, prompted Heath's famous condemnation. There was never again any effective suggestion that Rowland's power might be tempered by independent voices on his board – he once referred to non-executive directors as 'Christmas tree decorations'. From a drab and anonymous headquarters in Cheapside, surrounded by his loyal inner court, he presided as an autocrat over a conglomerate that grew to encompass some 800 businesses: in newspapers, vehicle distribution, textiles, mines, hotels and many other spheres. During its peak years in the late 1980s, his group's profits surpassed £270 million.

The core of Lonrho's success remained in Africa. Rowland often spent three weeks in every month there, crisscrossing the continent by private jet. His methods were robust – he employed a private army to protect plantations in Mozambique – and politically acute. He courted heads of state and, when he saw advantage, rebel leaders – Presidents Kaunda, Banda and later Mugabe were claimed as friends. Unita in Angola received his backing and Oliver Tambo of ANC had the use of his private plane.

Rowland relished backroom influence in high politics, and was thought to have close contacts with British and US intelligence services. His access to Anwar Sadat is thought to have helped open the way for the Camp David Agreement in 1978. He was rumoured to have had a hand in Lebanese hostage negotiations, and even in Falklands peace manoeuvres.

If Rowland was unrivalled in his grasp of African business and politics, his touch elsewhere was less sure. His long battle over the ownership of Harrods department store, for example, was felt by many to have been a damaging distraction of his energies and an unjustifiable cost (estimated at £20 million) to Lonrho. The Harrods saga began in 1977. Rowland had identified retailing as a potential boom sector, and some observers thought that ownership of the Knightsbridge store would provide a measure of respectability otherwise denied to him. Lonrho began buying shares in Scottish & Universal Trusts, the holding company of Sir Hugh Fraser's family interests and the holder of 29 per cent of the store group, House of Fraser, which owns Harrods. When the rest of Scottish & Universal was acquired by Lonrho the following year, City institutions closed ranks against Rowland. The subsequent bid battle for House of Fraser was ferocious. Rowland's anger was targeted particularly at the combative Fraser chairman, Professor Roland Smith, and the unfortunate Sir Hugh – who Rowland had initially courted as an ally, but who he later helped to ruin with revelations about gambling debts.

When victory seemed to be in sight for Lonrho, the Government blocked the takeover on grounds of national interest. Lonrho's shares were then, according to Rowland, 'parked' temporarily with the Fayeds. According to the Egyptian brothers, the shares had been sold to them outright, and they used them as a springboard to acquire the whole of House of Fraser before the government's decision against Lonrho could be reversed. Rowland responded with a campaign to discredit the Fayeds and their alleged backer, the Sultan of Brunei, conducted through the pages of the *Observer* Sunday newspaper, which Lonrho had acquired in 1981, and by long, trenchant letters to ministers and public figures.

In 1989 a secret DTI report highly critical of the Fayed takeover was leaked by the *Observer* in a special midweek edition headlined 'The Phoney Pharoah'. Rowland felt vindicated, but – despite a continuing barrage of litigation – control of the store eluded him. The defeat cast a bitter shadow over the last years of his career. Rowland's use of the *Observer* to conduct his campaigns was another source of criticism, but he made no bones about his proprietorial rights. When he fell out with Daniel arap Moi of Kenya, his paper ran exposés of corruption there which named the President. When reporting of atrocities in Matabeleland displeased Rowland, he threatened to sell the paper to Robert Maxwell until the editor backed down.

All Rowland's corporate battles had a dark personal edge. 'He's a very hard man. He's the sort of enemy no one wants to have,' the wife of one adversary remarked. His most merciless victory was over the Australian tycoon, Alan Bond, whom he at first befriended as a potential 'white knight' when Lonrho was being stalked by another predator, Asher Edelman. Bond bought out Edelman's stake, boasted of himself as Rowland's natural successor, and continued buying up shares. Rowland turned on him with savage intensity, publishing a 93-page document claiming that Bond, sustained by a fragile pyramid of borrowings, was technically insolvent. The Australian's bankers demanded their money back, fulfilling Rowland's prophecy; before long, Bond was bankrupt and in jail.

But in 1991 serious cracks began to appear in Lonrho's impenetrable facade: the dividend was cut, and the share price tumbled. A billion pounds of debt forced a shedding of assets. The lucrative Volkswagen Audi franchise had to be sold and, ever unpredictable, Rowland offered to sell part of his hotel interests to his arch-enemies, the Al-Fayeds. Most controversially, a £177 million stake in the Metropole Hotels group was sold to the Libyan government, just at the moment when the UN was considering sanctions against Libya connected with the Lockerbie bombing. 'To me, Gaddafi is a super friend,' Rowland explained. 'Don't talk to me about morality and proper behaviour. I pay my taxes here. Gaddafi and Lonrho are a perfect fit.'

But he continued at 75 to defy his critics. The arrangements he made in December 1992 for the eventual sale of his own 15 per cent stake in Lonrho – to a little-known German property developer, Dieter Bock, at a price substantially better than Rowland's loyal band of small investors could hope to obtain for their own Lonrho shares – provoked a storm of hostile comment. At the same time there was speculation as to whether Bock (whom Rowland had only recently met) was really his chosen successor, or was in some way being set up by Rowland to be, as one commentator put it, 'flayed alive' like Alan Bond.

This inscrutability and threat of menace were at the heart of the City's distrust of Tiny Rowland. He in turn trusted only his closest collaborators, to whom he could be fiercely loyal while they were with him – sometimes carrying dead wood – but utterly unforgiving if they jumped ship.

Although capable of charm – and of unexpected kindness to fallen tycoons such as Sir Freddie Laker – he had very few personal friends, suspecting venal motives in those who tried to get close to him. He eschewed the social trappings and foibles that his immense wealth (much of it hoarded in cash deposits) might have brought him. The intrigues of business and power, conducted according to his own uncompromising lights, occupied virtually the whole of his existence.

Rowland was born Roland Walter Fuhrhop on 27 November 1917, in a detention camp in India in which his German father, a successful merchant, and his Anglo-Dutch mother, were held as aliens for the duration of the First World War. At the end of the war the family sought to settle in Britain but were refused entry and moved instead to Hamburg. There Rowland was a member of the Hitler Youth, but his father's anti-Nazi sentiments caused him to lose his business, and the family moved to England. Young Roland was sent to Churchers College at Petersfield. His first job after school was with a firm of shipping agents, for which he travelled widely.

In Berlin in 1939 he was jailed for eight weeks for associating with anti-Nazis. In that year he changed his surname – forming Rowland by inserting his middle initial into the first syllable of his Christian name. The origin of the nickname 'Tiny' – with which he signed all official correspondence – is obscure; he was tall, well-built and strong-jawed.

His two elder brothers served in the German army, but Rowland was enlisted in the Royal Army Medical Corps and was in Norway in 1940. But his parents were again interned, this time on the Isle of Man. Rowland refused to continue serving while they were detained. He was discharged and detained for a time with them. His mother died in detention; her treatment by the authorities was often cited as an explanation of her son's hostility to British officialdom.

Thereafter Rowland took various jobs, including a spell as a porter at Paddington station and as a waiter at the Cumberland Hotel. After the war he made money selling refrigerators and car radios, but in 1947 he decided to emigrate, first to South Africa and then to Southern Rhodesia. There he bought two farms and had interests in gold mines. He acquired the Mercedes franchise for Rhodesia, and became an agent for Rio Tinto Zinc. When Ogilvy recruited him in 1961, Rowland's own group of businesses, Shepton Estates, was exchanged for 1.5 million shares in Lonrho. The holding was the foundation of a personal fortune estimated to have reached £200 million by the late 1980s.

Always impeccably dressed and tanned, Rowland lived in discreet opulence, with mansions in Buckinghamshire and Chester Square. He was fiercely protective of his family's privacy. He collected African and German expressionist art, and had a taste for Siamese cats, but otherwise had few interests outside his work.

Tiny Rowland did not marry until he was fifty, in 1967, when he took as his bride his goddaughter Josie Taylor, many years his junior. She was the daughter of his farm manager in Rhodesia. They had a son and three daughters.

24 July 1998

Lord Spens

1942–2001

Guinness trial defendant

The 3rd Lord Spens was acquitted of charges of dishonest dealing during the controversial Guinness takeover of Distillers, but spent the rest of his life seeking redress for the damage to his reputation.

Patrick Spens was a City maverick: an outspoken, ebullient, cigar-smoking merchant banker who relished the buccaneering tactics that often win takeover battles. He provoked loyalty and admiration on his own side, but often made enemies of his opponents.

He was managing director of the small banking house of Henry Ansbacher when Guinness chief executive Ernest Saunders launched a £2.2 billion bid for Distillers, makers of Johnnie Walker whisky and Gordon's Gin, in January 1986. Another merchant banker, Roger Seelig of Morgan Grenfell, asked Spens to help set up a scheme to support Guinness's share price, in order to make the offer to Distillers' shareholders look more attractive than a rival bid from the supermarket group Argyll. This involved rewarding a number of investors, including the property tycoons Gerald Ronson and Sir Jack Lyons, for buying and holding Guinness shares, while indemnifying them against any losses they might incur. Ansbacher ended up holding a block of shares, funded by money from Guinness – tantamount to Guinness buying its own shares, which would have been illegal.

By general consensus these manoeuvres crossed the line of City propriety, but the law was unclear about the totality of the scheme, which was by no means unusual in the City. A 1988 tribunal chaired by Lord Grantchester examined six similar schemes, all involving Spens; among the clients he had acted for were United Newspapers and Robert Maxwell. Argyll's directors considered themselves cheated of the bid, and a DTI investigation began with a raid on Guinness's offices in December 1986. A month later, the Bank of England forced Ansbacher's chairman to dismiss Spens.

The Bank had earlier warned Spens about his *modus operandi*, but had received a high-handed answer: 'I told them, "Fine – that's your opinion, but that is what Ansbacher and I do well, and I intend to carry on doing it."' Throughout all the proceedings that followed, he refused to acknowledge that there was anything inappropriate in what he had done – and indeed the City's Takeover Code did not specifically preclude indemnified share-support schemes until it was amended in 1987. The Government, however, was determined that examples should be made which would persuade the City to clean up its act. At 6.45 a.m. on 10 March 1988 Fraud Squad detectives arrived to arrest Spens at his Tudor mansion in Kent on charges under the Theft Act and the Companies Act.

Saunders, Ronson, Lyons and a fourth defendant, the stock-broker Anthony Parnes, were all convicted in the first Guinness trial in 1990. Seelig and Spens finally appeared in court in September 1991, by which time Spens had suffered a heart attack followed by bypass surgery, and Seelig was suffering severe depression. In February 1992 the trial was abandoned, but the judge, Mr Justice Henry, refused to give Spens a formal verdict of Not Guilty or to allow him the £400,000 of costs he had incurred before being granted Legal Aid, on the grounds that he had 'brought the prosecution on himself'. On appeal, however, he was formally acquitted, and Seelig was also cleared. Spens continued to speak out robustly in defence of his own name and in criticism of both the judicial processes and the DTI report on Guinness which finally appeared in 1997.

He also turned his attention to suing the Bank of England for 'abuse of power', claiming that the Bank had threatened to revoke Ansbacher's banking licence if he was not sacked. This was to have come to court in 1999, but at the last moment the Legal Aid Board refused Spens further funding, obliging him to abandon the case. It was still in the hands of the ombudsman when he died.

Patrick Michael Rex Spens was born on 22 July 1942, and was educated at Rugby and Corpus Christi College, Cambridge, where he read law. He went on to take articles in accountancy with the firm of Fuller Wise Fisher – the Fisher in question being his wife's grandfather – qualifying in 1967. Two years later he joined the corporate finance department of Morgan Grenfell, where he became a director in 1972 and a close colleague of Roger Seelig. He moved to Ansbacher as managing director in 1983. He was also a director of London & Midland Industries and Arlington Securities.

After his departure from Ansbacher he set up a corporate finance consultancy, Castlecrest, and in later years he re-established himself as a chartered accountant, with his own firm based in the West End of London. He reckoned to have had a hand in 350 takeovers and share issues during his career.

He had succeeded as the 3rd Baron Spens in 1984. The barony had been created for his grandfather, Sir Patrick Spens, who was chief justice of India from 1943 to 1947, and sat as a Conservative MP, first for Ashford in Kent and later for South Kensington. The second baron, Patrick's father, was the founder and director of the Federation of British Carpet Manufacturers – but was also a compulsive gambler and was jailed for two years in 1974 for stealing from the Federation. In one of several tribulations in his personal life, Patrick had to raise substantial sums of money to cover his father's debts.

By way of relaxation, Patrick Spens was an avid stamp collector. He was a fellow and medal-winner of the Royal Philatelic Society, to which he presented a paper on 'Queen Elizabeth II Waterlow High Values'. But in 1990 he was forced to sell his beloved collection to cover his legal costs.

He married, in 1966, Barbara Fisher, daughter of Rear Admiral Ralph Lindsay Fisher. She stood resolutely by him through all his difficulties; they had a daughter and a son, also Patrick, born in 1968, who succeeded to the barony.

5 January 2001

Edouard Stern

⟶ 1954–2005 ⟵

Banker murdered in a sado-masochistic ritual

Edouard Stern, who was found dead in his Geneva apartment having been shot while wearing a flesh-coloured latex suit, was one of France's best-known financiers, with a reputation as an abrasive and uncompromising deal-maker.

Stern was for some years the heir apparent to his father-in-law, Michel David-Weill, who was chairman and controlling shareholder of the investment bank Lazard Frères. David-Weill, a great-grandson of one of the firm's founders, had run the tripartite group, which had operations in Paris, London and New York, since 1977; in 1992 he brought in Stern to be a senior partner in Paris and New York.

Stern also became a significant shareholder in Lazard's holding companies, and a power struggle swiftly ensued between the two men. It was reported that Stern's aggressive manner caused him to be ejected from two of the bank's senior committees; and he departed angrily in 1997 to run his own investment fund – leaving a vacuum that was filled by the arrival of the Wall Street veteran Bruce Wasserstein as David-Weill's eventual successor.

Stern had close links with two of Lazard's biggest French customers, the Elf oil company and the cosmetics group L'Oréal. But according to David-Weill, smooth handling of clients was not his strong suit: 'He is much more talented as a businessman than in service activities.' The French press labelled him *'le gendre incontrôlable'* (the uncontrollable son-in-law).

Stern led a private and somewhat mysterious life in Geneva. Three weeks after his death, a former call girl, Cecile Brossard – Stern's girlfriend of four years' standing, whom he liked to address as Maîtresse Alice – confessed to having shot him four times in what she claimed was a moment of madness during a sadomasochistic sexual encounter.

Edouard Stern was born on 18 October 1954, the son of a Jewish father and a French mother. He graduated from the Ecole Supérieure des Sciences Economiques et Commerciales in Paris, and joined his family's private investment house, Banque Stern, in 1977. Two years later, he ousted his own father from control of the business, which he sold to a Swiss bank in the late 1980s, though he remained chairman until 1998. After his departure from Lazard, Stern deployed his Geneva-based €600 million investment fund, Investment Real Returns, to become one of the most controversial players in the European corporate scene.

Typical of his style as an active shareholder was his intervention at Rhodia, the troubled French chemicals company, where he was co-opted as a director and promptly called for the group to be broken up to maximise shareholder value. Rhodia's annual general meeting in 2003 rejected his proposal to oust the chairman, Jean-Pierre Tirouflet, and instead ejected Stern himself from the board.

He was also involved in ructions with Suez, the industrial conglomerate, and the Vivendi media group. In Britain, his name was connected in 1999 with an attempt to gain control of the troubled textile group Coats Viyella, in combination with Lord Rothschild and the company's former chairman Sir David (later Lord) Alliance. In 2003 Stern became chairman of Delta, the electronic components maker, of which he owned 26 per cent.

Edouard Stern's only known hobby was a passion for game-shooting and collecting guns. He married Beatrice David-Weill in 1983, but they separated; they had three children.

1 March 2005

·≈ PART THREE ≈·

ENTREPRENEURS

HAROLD CREIGHTON – Spectator *proprietor*
DAME HILARY CROPPER – *head of a software business for women*
JENNIFER D'ABO – *serial rescuer of businesses*
SIR JAMES GOLDSMITH – *billionaire investor and campaigner*
LORD HANSON – *classic 1980s entrepreneur*
LORD KING OF WARTNABY – *rescuer of British Airways*
SIR FREDDIE LAKER – *pioneer of cheap air travel*
RONALD LYON – *property dealer caught in the 1974 crash*
LORD MATTHEWS – *builder who bought the* Daily Express
ROLF SCHILD – *kidnap victim*
SIR ADAM THOMSON – *founder of British Caledonian Airways*
LORD WEINSTOCK – *creator of GEC*
LORD WHITE OF HULL – *Lord Hanson's swashbuckling partner*
SIR ISAAC WOLFSON – *stores magnate and philanthropist*

Harold Creighton

⊷≡⊚ 1927–2003 ⊚≡⊷

Spectator *proprietor*

Harold Creighton was a self-made entrepreneur in the machine-tool industry who became proprietor and editor of the *Spectator*. Creighton's ownership of the weekly magazine from 1967 to 1975 was a period of falling circulation and internal strife. He sacked two editors and parted company with a number of well-known contributors before taking on the editorship himself in 1973; by the end of his tenure the very survival of the magazine was in doubt. Nevertheless, he retained the *Spectator*'s reputation both for intelligent right-wing comment and for conviviality, and took a brave stance as the only national paper to call for a 'no' vote in the 1975 referendum on Britain's continued membership of the Common Market.

Harry Creighton was alerted to the fact that the *Spectator* was for sale in April 1967 by a diary paragraph in the *Evening Standard*, and was persuaded (by, among others, Lord Boothby over dinner at Wilton's) to buy it as a launching pad for his political and social ambitions. The magazine was then under the editorship of Nigel Lawson and the ownership of the Conservative MP Sir Ian Gilmour, who had tired of losses of £20,000 a year, and had asked the financier Jim Slater to find him a buyer. Creighton had done business with Slater before, and a deal was quickly put together at a price of £75,000.

Under arrangements dating from 1928, a new proprietor had to secure the approval of a committee of trustees (to include representatives of the Headmasters' Conference and the by then extinct London County Council) charged with ensuring that the magazine did not fall into the wrong hands. Harry Creighton duly went before the committee – whose chairman turned out to have shooting rights over Creighton's estate near Chichester. Several other potential bidders were in the wings (among them Woodrow Wyatt, George Weidenfeld and at least one wealthy American) but

Slater pressed Creighton's suit and Gilmour was anxious for a swift conclusion.

Creighton and Lawson (who had tried to put together a bid of his own) did not warm to one another, the latter insisting firmly on editorial independence. Creighton did however prevail in a wish to see more financial coverage in the magazine – to attract more financial advertising – and earned the gratitude of his staff by reinstating a dining room in the basement of the magazine's rambling offices at 99 Gower Street: the designer David Hicks was called in to advise on the colour of the walls. But proprietor and editor could not agree on the colour scheme for the magazine's cover, Lawson favouring mauve while Creighton pressed in vain for green.

In 1970, after Lawson was adopted as a parliamentary candidate, Creighton dismissed him, offered the job to Bernard Levin who turned it down, and finally appointed the political columnist George Gale to the chair. The circulation of the magazine had fallen from 36,000 in 1966 to around 25,000, and it galled Creighton that he was unable to make it run efficiently and profitably like his machine-tool businesses. He once told an interviewer that at least 'our stapling is a lot better' than that of the rival *New Statesman*. He cut the editorial staff from five to four – while increasing the size of the advertising sales team, to little effect except for a rush of small ads for saunas and massage parlours. Finally in September 1973 he sacked Gale (though they remained on friendly terms) and took over as editor himself.

The *Spectator*'s managing director of that era, George Hutchinson, described Creighton as 'not without aptitude, albeit of a somewhat slapdash, capricious sort'. He could be choleric or charming by turns, and he was immensely hospitable, hosting lunches in Gower Street almost daily. He loved gossip, especially about celebrities and his business acquaintances – about whom he contributed his own column, 'Skinflint's City Diary'.

At a low ebb in Conservative fortunes Creighton maintained the magazine's traditional allegiance, refusing to allow Patrick Cosgrave to write a leader in February 1974 urging readers to vote Labour. But after the election he dedicated the *Spectator* to the cause of evicting Edward Heath from the Tory leadership, becoming an ardent supporter of Margaret Thatcher. He was even more single-minded in his opposition to British membership of the Common Market, providing office space in Gower Street for the cross-party Get Britain Out campaign group assembled for the June 1975 referendum – which produced a 2:1 majority for staying in. By this stage, predictions of the magazine's imminent demise were commonplace. Circulation continued falling, to below the 17,000 figure claimed for 1974. Weekly losses and a run of libel suits against the magazine had depleted Creighton's resources. The Gower Street building was crumbling. The magazine's abusive tone during the referendum campaign was, according to the *Spectator*'s historian, 'coming to sound like a death rattle'.

But Creighton had by then let it be known that the *Spectator* was for sale again. It was fortunate both for him and for the magazine that another wealthy businessman with political aspirations – Henry Keswick, chairman of the Hong Kong trading house Jardine Matheson – was prepared to pay him £75,000 for it in August 1975. Creighton sold 99 Gower Street separately and the magazine moved to a new home in Doughty Street to be revivified by the editorial hand of Alexander Chancellor. Some months later, Creighton acknowledged that Chancellor's *Spectator* was 'very good indeed . . . although I don't go all the way with his liberalism'.

The son of a clergyman, Harold Digby Fitzgerald Creighton was born on 11 September 1927. He was educated at Haileybury. After a national-service commission in the Royal Armoured Corps in India and Egypt and a couple of years in the tin-smelting business in Penang, he returned to London and went into the machine-tool business as sales director of a company called MC Layton, dealing in second-hand machinery.

In 1956 he branched out on his own as Tate Machine Tools, and for a time he also owned a printing works in Fulham. In 1963 he sold Tate for £250,000. He invested in another business in the same trade and two years later, with Jim Slater's guidance, he carried out a reverse takeover to gain control of a Glasgow-based public company, Scottish Machine Tool Corp, of which he became chairman and principal shareholder.

Creighton was in fact Slater's first client for this sort of transaction, and Slater's firm, the investment group Slater Walker, proposed to charge only £1000 for the service. Creighton told Slater that he obviously knew little about City fee scales, and should charge at least £5000 – the figure on which they finally agreed.

Towards the end of his time at the *Spectator*, Creighton started to develop other publishing ideas in the field of 'girlie' magazines. He bought *Lilliput*, a title which had not been published since 1961, intending to relaunch it with a mixture of short stories and nude pictures to fill a market gap 'somewhere between *Reveille* and *Reader's Digest*'; the project never came to fruition. He also invested £10,000 in a new magazine, *Cockade*, which folded after one issue. In later years he maintained a portfolio of industrial and other business interests, but was little heard of in the public arena.

Harry Creighton married, in 1964, Harriet Wallace; they had four daughters.

3 July 2003

Dame Hilary Cropper

⋆═▷ 1941–2004 ◁═⋆

Head of a software business for women

Dame Hilary Cropper was one of Britain's most respected business-women as chairman and chief executive of the computer services group Xansa, formerly FI – a company which from its foundation set out to give women the opportunity to develop careers in the largely masculine world of computing.

Originally called Freelance Programmers, Xansa was founded in Hemel Hempstead in 1962 by a German Jewish refugee, Stephanie Shirley (later Dame Stephanie), to offer part-time and home-based work for women like herself with computer-programming skills and children to care for: she signed herself 'Steve' to gain acceptance with male clients, but for many years she employed no men.

By the time Hilary Cropper was recruited from ICL to join the company – by then called Freelancers International, or FI – in 1985, it was no longer all-female but still predominantly so, with a majority of women on its board, and still strongly influenced by the founder's collectivist ideals. Hilary Cropper disliked being stereotyped as a 'superwoman' of the boardroom; she advocated equal opportunities and a healthy mixture of the sexes in business. 'In a culture that is very male-dominated, there does tend to be more competition than co-operation,' she told an interviewer in 2002. 'If there are a good number of women in the business, then you do get a more open culture.'

Under her leadership, FI developed as a major provider of solutions to information-technology problems for consumer-based businesses such as supermarket chains, banks and utility companies. Turnover rose from £7 million a year in 1987 when she became chief executive, to £450 million in 2002, when she stepped down as executive chairman.

In 2000, FI acquired an IT management consultancy group, Druid, founded by a group of young male entrepreneurs. Concerned at the risk of a gender clash, one analyst described the takeover as 'like Bath rugby club merging with Cheltenham Ladies College lacrosse team'. Asked which was the rugby club in this analogy, Cropper retorted: 'If you're implying that we girls are a bit tough, you're probably pretty accurate.'

She was particularly admired for successfully repositioning the group in new business areas – notably low-cost 'outsourcing' of IT services from India – when conditions became more difficult after the demise of the late-1990s technology boom.

Hilary Cropper led a management buy-out of FI in 1991 in which many of its staff became shareholders. When the company was floated on the stock exchange in 1996, more than a third of it remained owned by its staff, many of whom became millionaires as the shares soared. Cropper described this wide participation in the company's success as 'the proudest achievement of my career'. She herself was one of Britain's highest-paid women.

Hilary Mary Trueman was born in Macclesfield on 9 January 1941, the daughter of an accountant, and was educated at a convent in Stockport. She combined a degree in mathematics at the University of Salford with an apprenticeship in computer programming in an engineering company which became part of GEC. She recalled that the factory in Trafford Park made 'thundering big gas turbines and industrial engines' and that there were 'hundreds of blokes and three women ... You had to prove yourself, over and over again. If you weren't better than the average guy you weren't going to get on. It kept you sharp'.

In 1963 she married Peter Cropper, who made his career in telecommunications, and in 1970 she moved to join ICL, the mainframe computer manufacturer, where she was able to work part-time while the couple's children were small. She described ICL as 'very male-dominated', but was nevertheless promoted (as the group's most senior woman) to run a division supplying software to customers, until she was headhunted to run FI's British operations in 1985.

Hilary Cropper sat on the boards of TSB, Barclays, the Post Office, and London First, the development agency for the capital, where she encouraged businesses to work with the young unemployed. She was a member of the government's New Deal Taskforce, and a governor of the University of Hertfordshire. She was appointed CBE in 1999 and raised to DBE in 2003.

In 2001 she was diagnosed with ovarian cancer, though she concealed the illness from her business colleagues – receiving chemotherapy at weekends and on short holiday breaks – until 18 months later, when she announced her final retirement as non-executive chairman of FI. 'People describe you as dying of cancer but I say I'm living with it,' she said in 2003, the year before her death.

She became an active fundraiser for CancerBACUP, a charity which provides help lines for cancer sufferers and their families.

Hilary and Peter Cropper had a son and two daughters.

26 December 2004

Jennifer d'Abo

⤛⟶ 1945–2003 ⟵⤜

Serial rescuer of businesses

Jennifer d'Abo was one of Britain's best-known women entrepreneurs and the first to lead a successful hostile takeover bid. Statuesque and strong-voiced, Jennifer d'Abo was a striking presence at any gathering, not least for her trademark heart-shaped spectacles. She made a dynamic impression on everyone she met, and had a knack of charming financiers into backing her projects. But she sometimes felt herself patronised and discriminated against in the male-dominated world of big business.

'The City is still terribly cautious about women,' she told one interviewer. 'If I put up a feasibility study for a business project, it's read by ten analysts as opposed to two because I'm a woman.'

Jennifer d'Abo's motivation was the thrill of the deal and the satisfaction of turning round moribund companies, rather than personal gain. She acted intuitively, brought a sense of fun into her business dealings, and was never afraid to break rules. Though she invested in many different ventures – by no means all successful – she was best known for her achievement in reviving Ryman, the stationery chain.

Shopping in a Ryman branch one day in 1981, she was horrified to find how shabby it had become. Ryman's owner, the Burton group, turned out to be willing to sell, and d'Abo and her management team moved in to revolutionise the Ryman image, giving it a complete facelift and a lively new product range. Filing cabinets, for example, now came in bright pinks and greens, rather than gunmetal grey. Perhaps d'Abo's cleverest innovation was the introduction of the self-adhesive Post-It note. She returned from a Frankfurt trade fair with a sample of the gummed notepads, then only available in white. But she sensed that they needed to be more eye-catching, and ordered them for Ryman in yellow, pink and blue. They became an essential item on every British office desk.

Ryman survived financial peril and struggles with its unions to become one of the sharpest retail brands of the 1980s. It was floated on the stock market in 1986 and taken over by Pentos – for £20 million, double the flotation price – a year later.

Meanwhile, another City play produced a less satisfactory outcome. Through a shell company called Stormgard, d'Abo launched a hostile bid in 1986 for Selincourt, a small, traditional textiles group. The battle was hard-fought and just as it was won some of her bankers withdrew support, leaving her to find £25 million of new financing in three days. Having leapt that hurdle, she found herself locked in a two-year management struggle at Selincourt in which eventually she had no choice but to resign. She described this episode as 'the nastiest time of my life', but it did not deter her from a succession of other entrepreneurial gambits over the following decade.

Jennifer Mary Victoria Hammond-Maude was born in London on 14 August 1945. Her diplomat father was often away and her mother's health was poor, so Jennifer spent much of her childhood with her grandmother. She attended nine schools; the last was Hatherop Castle in Gloucestershire where she passed five O-levels and showed artistic promise. She went on to a Paris finishing school, but hopes of going to art school were abandoned after her mother's death when Jennifer was 17. A year later she married David Morgan-Jones, a Life Guards officer, by whom she had a daughter, Sophie.

One of her first jobs as a teenager had been as an office junior at Keith Prowse, the theatrical ticket agency owned by Peter Cadbury, a scion of the chocolate dynasty whom she met when he bought her grandmother's house. In 1970, having divorced Morgan-Jones, she married Cadbury, who was her senior by 27 years, and had a son by him, Joel, who became a restaurateur in London. She was a strong support to Peter Cadbury in his sometimes colourful business dealings. In particular, Cadbury credited Jennifer with helping him to weather a crisis at Westward Television, where he was ousted as chairman in a blaze of media attention, only to be reinstated eight days later.

She also took over the running of his investment portfolio – a skill she had learned from her grandmother, a keen investor – and was irritated to find that women were still barred from taking the stock exchange exams. In 1973, to Peter's initial fury, she decided to sell all his shares; the market crashed a few weeks later, and her husband's rage turned to grateful admiration.

Life with Cadbury was a glamorous whirl of hunting, holidays in Nassau, Rolls-Royces and private planes – husband and wife both held pilot's licences. But the marriage lasted only six years; according to Cadbury at the time, it broke up because 'she's a better entrepreneur than I am'. They remained good friends – as indeed she did with both of her other ex-husbands, sometimes in later years entertaining all three to dinner at the same time.

Her third marriage, which lasted until 1987, was to the stock-broker Robin d'Abo. Initally they were relatively poor, and Jennifer set out to earn a living by taking on a Wavy Line grocery-shop franchise at Alton in Hampshire. The work was backbreaking, but gave her a taste for the retail trade. In 1977 she acquired Burlington Furnishing, a Basingstoke department store which she revamped in the style of Peter Jones and sold for a healthy profit. Her next investment, in 1980, was Jean Sorelle, a Peterborough-based maker of 'champagne bubble bath' and other toiletries and fragrances.

In 1988 d'Abo and her former Ryman team acquired Roffey Brothers, a compost-making company, to which in due course they added T Parker & Sons, a supplier of 'turf dressings' to golf courses. When the golf-course boom went into reverse in the recession, these businesses also suffered and were eventually sold. But Jennifer d'Abo had better luck with her last major investment, the florist Moyses Stevens, where she developed a successful import-export business in ceramic and dried flowers.

She was also at various times a director of Channel 4 Television and the London Docklands Development Corporation, a member of the Industrial Development Board for Northern Ireland, a trustee of the Natural History Museum and a council member of Cancer Research UK.

In 1998 Jennifer d'Abo was herself diagnosed with cancer and was advised to give up all her business interests. But she continued to live life to the full, and remained a generous hostess to a wide and eclectic circle of friends – who were, in turn, devoted to her. She was a brilliantly creative cook: no two meals at her table were ever the same.

She published in 1999 *Jennifer d'Abo at Home*, subtitled 'Recipes for stylish people in a hurry', offering tips from a range of celebrity contributors.

In the last year of her life Jennifer d'Abo moved to southwest France, where she renovated a beautiful home.

30 April 2003

Sir James Goldsmith

❖═◉ 1933–1997 ◉═❖

Billionaire investor and campaigner

Sir James Goldsmith was a mercurial stock-market predator, a quixotic political thinker and a man of volcanic passions whose private life defied all convention.

Having retired from active business after amassing a gigantic fortune in the 1980s, Goldsmith was known in later years principally as a European political pundit. Operating from a vast private estate – virtually a kingdom – in the Mexican jungle, he waged a campaign against the globalisation of free trade and the signing of the GATT agreement, which he believed would damage the interests of the developed world.

Encouraged by the success of *Le Piège* (*The Trap*), a book-length interview on these topics published in 1993, he went on to found a political movement, *L'Autre Europe*, which campaigned for a decentralised, trade-protected Europe of democratic nation states. On this platform he was elected a member of the European Parliament in 1994.

Next he launched the Referendum Party in Britain, to lobby for a referendum on the nature of Britain's relationship with Europe. Goldsmith committed £20 million to this campaign, whilst declaring that he sought 'no wider role on the political stage' for himself. Indeed, he promised to dissolve the party if it ever achieved its aim of forcing a referendum on Britain's place in Europe. In the 1997 General Election the Referendum Party fielded a candidate in every constituency – 546 in all – in which it considered the sitting member to be unsound on European issues. The candidates Goldsmith persuaded to stand included many friends and celebrities, among them the casino owner John Aspinall, and Margaret Thatcher's economic guru Sir Alan Walters.

The party polled a total of some 800,000 votes. More than a dozen Conservative members were unseated by a margin smaller than the Referendum's vote against them. Goldsmith himself stood in Putney against the Conservative ex-minister David Mellor – chosen as an opponent partly because his private life was colourful enough to distract attention from Goldsmith's own complex domestic arrangements. Although Mellor was unseated by Labour, Goldsmith (whose advancing pancreatic cancer had restricted his campaigning) polled only 1,518 votes and lost his deposit. Nevertheless, Goldsmith took delight in standing on the platform at the declaration and joining hecklers from the crowd in chanting 'Out! Out! Out!' whilst pointing and guffawing at the enraged Mellor. For his part, David Mellor advised Sir James: 'You can get off back to Mexico knowing that your attempt to buy the British political system has failed. Up your hacienda.'

Such confrontations were grist to Goldsmith's mill, as he showed in full force in 1976 in his legal battle with *Private Eye*. The satirical magazine had published an article which suggested that Goldsmith had helped his friend Lord Lucan to flee after the murder of the Lucan family nanny, Sandra Rivett, and that he and others had then driven to suicide another member of their circle, the painter Dominic Elwes, who had talked too freely to the press.

This was all based on the (incorrect) claim that Goldsmith had attended a lunch of Lucan sympathisers on the day after the peer's disappearance. A second article blackened Goldsmith's name on several other fronts, *inter alia* by linking him with business corruption. Three days after the second article appeared, the enraged Goldsmith issued 63 writs against the magazine and its distributors, followed by an application to bring a criminal libel charge (carrying a threat of imprisonment) against its editor,

Richard Ingrams. Goldsmith was convinced that the magazine was subversive. It was, he said, staffed by 'maggots and scavengers', who were motivated by a desire to undermine his attempt to rescue Slater Walker, a troubled City finance house of which – with the blessing of the Bank of England – he had recently taken over as chairman. *Private Eye* meanwhile dubbed its persecutor 'Goldenballs', encouraging the public to regard him as a sinister foreign megalomaniac.

The case lasted 18 months and involved ten hearings. Eventually Goldsmith (who by then had aspirations to acquire the *Daily Express*) was persuaded to drop the charges in exchange for a full apology from the magazine, a decision which he later said he regretted. The experience soured his view of Britain, which he saw as an anti-enterprise culture, riddled with 'snobbism and frustrated sex'.

After the *Private Eye* case, Goldsmith largely withdrew from British business, concentrating his interests in France and the United States. He took Cavenham Foods, his British holding company back into private ownership – a move which helped him to become, in later years, 'richer than I had ever dreamed of'. Disenchantment with Britain fuelled a residual ambition on this side of the Channel, however: Goldsmith's urge to find a platform for his opinions by becoming a press baron. He already owned a successful French news weekly, *L'Express*, and in 1979 he launched a similar product in London, *Now!* But the format did not excite British readers, and the magazine closed after less than two years, having cost Goldsmith £10 million.

James Michael Goldsmith was born on 26 February 1933 in France, where he was always known as Jimmy. He was the second son of Major Frank Goldsmith OBE, a grand hotelier, former MP and ubiquitous social figure of the interwar era. The Goldsmiths were descended from Moses von Schaffhausen, a goldsmith from Nuremberg who was driven out of that city by official persecution of Jews in 1499. The family settled in Frankfurt, took the name Goldschmidt, and prospered as bankers. By the beginning of the 19th century they were (like their more famous Rothschild cousins) providing finance for most of the governments of Europe.

The family patriarch during that era was Benedict Hayum Goldschmidt, a father of 14. He passed the Frankfurt banking house to two of his sons, Maximilian and Adolph, who disagreed on business strategy and eventually decided, in 1893, to close the business. Adolph and his English-born wife moved first to Paris and thence to London and Suffolk, where their son Frank adopted the style of the English gentry.

In 1910 Frank Goldsmith was elected to Parliament as Conservative MP for Stowmarket. Although he was a friend of Churchill and a captain in the Loyal Suffolk Hussars, he and his family became, in 1914, objects of anti-German sentiment which he found deeply hurtful. Having fought at Gallipoli and been promoted major, Frank decided at the end of the war to make his home in France. He put his fortune into the hotel business. Known as 'Monsieur le Majeur', he came to control 48 of France's finest hotels, including the Carlton in Cannes and the Hermitage in Monte Carlo. It was in this gilded world that Jimmy Goldsmith spent his childhood, before the Nazi threat forced the family to evacuate, via a refugee ship from Bayonne and a suite at Claridges, to the Bahamas for the duration of the war.

A precocious child, already fascinated with gambling, Jimmy was immune to educational discipline. A spell at a tough Canadian college, St Andrew's in Ontario, was not a success. Determined that his sons should acquire the manners of English gentlemen, Frank dispatched them next to Millfield, and Jimmy in due course to Eton.

There his chief preoccupation was betting on horses, and in 1949, aged 16, he invested £10 on a three-horse accumulator at Lewes, winning £8,000. He decided to leave Eton immediately, declaring to a celebratory house dinner that 'A man of my means should not remain a schoolboy'.

The next period of his life was spent playing poker and chasing girls at Oxford with his undergraduate brother Teddy and a louche circle led by John Aspinall. Despite his father's promptings, Jimmy showed no enthusiasm for training in the hotel trade. Surprisingly however, he adapted well to the rigours of national service with the Royal Artillery, emerging with a commission.

On leaving the army in 1953, Goldsmith set out to make his fortune, using as his vehicle a small pharmaceutical company set up by his brother. By ruthless salesmanship and the acquisition of licences to sell products such as Alka Selzer, he achieved dramatic growth. He set up his own manufacturing operation to undercut leading brands. But he lacked cash to fund this expansion, and in July 1957 the business was on the edge of bankruptcy. He was saved by a bank strike, which allowed time to negotiate the sale of the company. This was, he said later, 'the only really lucky thing that ever happened to me in business'.

Only slightly chastened, Goldsmith rebuilt a similar business, selling cortisone derivatives, and later slimming and tanning products, on both sides of the Channel. In partnership with Selim Zilkha, a wealthy Iraqi-born banker, he developed the concept of the Mothercare stores chain – although he lacked capital to keep pace with Zilkha, and eventually withdrew from the venture.

His French interests grew to equal those in Britain, and in the 1960s Goldsmith began to build one of the world's largest food conglomerates. He acquired, among other products, Slimcea and Procea bread, Carr's water biscuits, Hollands toffees and Elizabeth Shaw mints. He called his British group Cavenham Foods, after his father's Suffolk estate, whilst his French holdings came under the umbrella of Générale Occidentale.

By the early 1970s, he commanded a substantial multinational empire, which included banking, retailing and manufacturing. Audacious takeovers of Bovril and Allied Suppliers confirmed his reputation as a stock-market predator. In the United States he bought the Grand Union supermarket chain. On one occasion, unable to agree terms for a business he wanted to buy from the financier Jim Slater, Goldsmith calmly played backgammon for the last million of the acquisition price, and won.

During this period he became influential with both Edward Heath and, after the 1974 election, with Harold Wilson – on one occasion bringing the two leaders together as his dinner guests. He received a knighthood in Wilson's controversial 1976 farewell honours list, 'for services to exports and ecology': it was true that he had funded his brother Teddy's ecological research, but the citation was interpreted in some quarters as a reference to Goldsmith's efforts to clean up the press by persecuting *Private Eye*.

In the 1980s (having declared that he now only came to Britain 'for my hobbies') Goldsmith evolved into a Wall Street raider, gradually shifting his focus from food businesses to natural resources. He acquired oil interests in Central America and took over Diamond International, a giant timber concern which he broke up at a profit of some $500 million. He went on in 1985 to acquire another forest products company, Crown Zellerbach, which netted him a further $400 million. He now controlled 3.5 million acres of American forest, as well as the Grand Union supermarket chain, a French publishing empire, a Guatemalan oilfield and many other assets.

But perhaps the smartest coup of Goldsmith's later business career was his decision to sell the bulk of his stock-market holdings on the eve of the 1987 stock-market crash, consolidating much of his vast fortune in cash. Thereafter, though he occasionally gave his backing to takeover consortia or took huge speculative positions in the commodity markets, he described himself as having retired from business. His energies were undiminished, but were increasingly absorbed by political and ecological causes.

Goldsmith's private life was extraordinary, and a major factor in his confrontational relationship with the media. In 1954, he eloped from Paris with the beautiful, pregnant 18-year-old Isabel Patino, heiress to a Bolivian tin-mining fortune. They were married in Scotland, in what one columnist called 'the motorised version of Lorna Doone', but were separated by tragedy soon afterwards. Isabel suffered a cerebral haemorrhage and died shortly after her child – also named Isabel – was delivered.

His second wife was Ginette Lery, daughter of a Paris Metro worker, who had joined him as a secretary in 1956. She gave birth to his son in 1959 and (although Goldsmith was preoccupied at the time with an English mistress, Sally Crichton-Stuart, later the Begum Aga Khan) the couple married in 1963, and had another child, a daughter. In 1964, Goldsmith took up with another English beauty, Lady Annabel Birley (daughter of the Marquess of Londonderry and wife of the nightclub owner Mark Birley) whom he eventually married in 1978, having divorced Ginette. Lady Annabel bore Goldsmith two sons and a daughter (Jemima, former wife of the Pakistani cricketer Imran Khan).

Divorce and remarriage legitimised Goldsmith's English children, but did not alter his preferred pattern of life, which was to divide his time, as he had already done for many years, between the two families, one in Paris and one at his mansion on the edge of Richmond Park. 'Not one iota' of his relationship with Ginette was changed by divorce, he said. He also declared, 'If you marry your mistress, you create a job vacancy.' Accordingly, he took up with a third companion, Laure Boulay de la Meurthe, a New York-based *Paris Match* journalist and niece of the Comte de Paris, pretender to the French throne. She and Sir James had a son and a daughter. 'Jimmy has always lived his life in compartments,' one friend observed.

'I could not live it any other way,' was Goldsmith's response.

19 July 1997

Lord Hanson

✦⇢ 1922–2004 ⇠✦

Classic 1980s entrepreneur

Lord Hanson was often named by his contemporaries as the most admired British industrialist of the Thatcher era. A master of the arts of corporate takeover and surgery, he assembled a robust and highly profitable portfolio of businesses on both sides of the Atlantic together with Lord White, his business partner for more than thirty years until White's death in 1995.

Hanson perfected a strategy which seemed, at the peak of their powers in the late 1980s, to be virtually invincible. Having identified an undervalued company, Hanson would name his bid price and stick to it; if the bid succeeded, a team of 'ferrets' – sharp-pencilled Hanson accountants – would descend on the purchase, strip it of unnecessary costs and sell off superfluous assets. Pared to the core, the acquired business would be left to thrive under its own management, subject only to profit targets and cash controls from Hanson's head office. Capital expenditure of more than £500 had to be approved by Hanson himself.

In their early years together, Hanson and Gordon White were branded as asset-strippers, and their names were linked with the controversial financier Jim Slater. But their judgment stood the test of time when less shrewd takeover practitioners came to grief in the 1970s. Although Hanson Trust (as the company was then called) took quick profits on some of its deals, it also nurtured for the long term a collection of solid, unglamorous businesses – in bricks, sacks and American coal mines, for instance – which could be relied upon to generate cash year after year.

White moved permanently to the United States in 1973 to build the American half of the empire. But the two men remained in constant, almost telepathic communication, with White's genius for takeover ideas complementing Hanson's managerial skills.

Both men were unusually tall, fit and well preserved, declaring their intention to continue working until their mid-seventies. Hanson however was much less flamboyant than his partner in his private life and utterances. Courteous but demanding, sensitive to criticism and intrusion, prone to short temper, he was respected and feared by staff and outsiders.

The bruising takeover of Ever Ready batteries in 1981 was a classic example of Hanson's ability to improve the performance of companies he bought. The company's head-office staff was promptly cut from 550 to 75, removing six of its nine layers of management. But the profitability of the battery brand name, which had been in sharp decline, was revived substantially. Other British acquisitions included United Drapery Stores and the London Brick Company, whilst Hanson Industries grew to rank among the largest 150 companies in the United States. Long-term shareholders in Hanson were rewarded with many years of rich returns.

The group's zenith was perhaps reached in 1985–86, when SCM (a conglomerate which included Smith Corona typewriters) was added to the American portfolio, and Imperial, the brewing and tobacco group, on the British side. The cost of both purchases,

$930 million and £2.5 billion respectively, was recouped within a few months by the sale of subsidiary businesses which did not fit the Hanson mould.

Hanson was undoubtedly tough on his managers and auto-cratic in the boardroom. A MORI opinion poll conducted among company directors nominated Hanson as the most impressive industrialist in Britain each year from 1988 to 1992. The biggest deal yet came in 1989: the addition of Consolidated Goldfields to the Hanson stable. At the end of a hugely successful decade, Hanson would have been more than entitled to rest on his laurels. With £7 billion of cash resources still at his disposal he showed no inclination to slow down, but the changing national mood at the end of the Thatcher era brought with it a decline in admiration for the model of the ruthless entrepreneur which he represented.

A proposal by Hanson in 1990 to buy Powergen, the electricity generating body then about to be privatised, evoked a sullen response. In the following year, he met outright hostility when he played the opening gambit in a campaign to take over ICI. Hanson declared that his 3 per cent stake in the chemical giant was 'for investment purposes' and that he was open to discussion of business co-operation between the two groups. But it was universally assumed that a full bid was likely to follow; it was within Hanson's price range, and would have created the largest company in Britain. The ferocity of the response from ICI and its advisers took Hanson by surprise. There was particular concern, supported by voices from the academic world, that ICI's dedication to research and development would not be sustained under a cost-slashing Hanson management. There was also emotional reluctance to see one of the few remaining great names of British manufacturing industry subsumed into the Hanson portfolio. A lurid case was painted against Hanson in the press. Openly criticising his own advisers for losing this public-relations battle, Hanson eventually withdrew and sold his ICI stake – collecting £40 million profit as he did so.

During the 1990s Hanson's business was increasingly unfashionable – both in its management style and in its low-technology content. There were concerns that Hanson was unwilling to cede power to a successor, and his shareholders were a good deal less contented than they had been in the group's expansive heyday. But a series of reincarnations followed: buying Eastern Electricity in 1995; floating off Imperial Tobacco in 1996; and finally, in 1997, splitting off the energy interests to refocus the rump of Hanson plc as a group of building-materials businesses whose investment merits became more evident when technology stocks collapsed at the end of the decade.

Hanson stepped down as chairman to become chairman emeritus – and sometimes expressed surprise that the new generation of managers only rarely consulted him. As the Thatcher era faded into memory his influence in Conservative Party circles, once considerable, also waned; but he found a new outlet for his robust opinions as an occasional columnist in the *Daily Telegraph* and elsewhere.

James Edward Hanson was born on 20 January 1922 in Huddersfield, where his father Robert ran a haulage firm. The business dated back to the 1840s, when Robert's great-great-grandmother had begun carting wool to and from local mills by packhorse. At the time of James's birth, Robert had fallen temporarily on hard times after a disastrous warehouse fire, but by the early 1930s his fortunes were restored and the family lived in comfortable style. James was educated at local schools.

In 1939 James was enlisted in the army, having first served as a Territorial with the Duke of Wellington's Regiment in Halifax. He was commissioned in the Royal Army Service Corps, and was for a time an announcer on Forces radio. Demobbed in 1946, he joined his father's company.

Robert Hanson, by then a prominent citizen of Huddersfield, passed on to his elder son a no-nonsense approach to business: tight financial control, a habit of repaying his bankers earlier than expected in order the better to persuade them to lend a little more next time, and minimal bureaucracy. After the family company was nationalised in 1948 (the family later bought it back) James and his younger brother Bill applied those principles to a new haulage venture in Hamilton, Ontario.

Bill was the more dashing and imaginative of the two brothers, while James had a talent for organisation. At 19, Bill had been the youngest major in the British Army; after the war he was a member of the national showjumping team, but he died suddenly, in 1954, of stomach cancer.

James inherited from his brother a friendship with Gordon White, whom Bill had met in the Army. White was then working in his father's publishing business in Hull. As bachelors, James Hanson and Gordon White shared playboy tastes for fast cars, gambling and the pursuit of starlets in London and Hollywood – Hanson escorted Jean Simmons, and was briefly engaged to Audrey Hepburn.

Hanson and White were involved in transport businesses together in the late 1950s, but their first major new venture was in importing humorous greetings cards from the United States. It was not a notable success. In due course it was sold, taking with it the trade name 'Hanson-White'. Unable to reuse that conjunction, the two partners tossed a coin as to whose surname should prevail. Thus it was that the conglomerate they began to build in 1964, with the acquisition of a fertiliser company called Wiles, carried Hanson's name alone.

James Hanson was knighted in 1976, in the notorious farewell honours list said to have been compiled for Harold Wilson by his secretary Marcia Williams (Lady Falkender) on lavender notepaper. But Hanson detested socialism and became a fervent supporter of Mrs Thatcher and a generous contributor to Conservative funds; his support for her preferred rescue plan for Westland Helicopters cost his company some £6 million. Thatcher returned the admiration, citing Hanson's US interests as a model of what British companies could achieve abroad. Hanson was created a life peer in 1983.

When in London, Lord Hanson worked long hours in his relatively austere headquarters overlooking the gardens of Buckingham Palace. But in later years he spent several months of each year at a second home in Palm Springs, California, whence he continued to run his empire from a poolside telephone.

He enjoyed the trappings of great wealth – his Bentley carried the number plate JH1 – and occasionally moved in celebrity social circles, hosting parties for Frank Sinatra and giving the Duchess of

York helicopter-flying lessons as a wedding present. But he also placed a high value on family life and privacy.

James Hanson married, in 1959, Mrs Geraldline Kaelin, a New Yorker. He was survived by two sons and a stepdaughter.

1 November 2004

Lord King of Wartnaby

⋆⇒ 1917–2005 ⇐⋆

Rescuer of British Airways

Lord King of Wartnaby was formerly chairman of British Airways and one of Britain's most colourful industrialists. King's achievement at BA is part of the folklore of the Thatcher era. When he took on the chairmanship of the state-owned airline in February 1981 (against the advice of some of his friends), it was badly run, demoralised and overmanned. Its aircraft fleet and route network revealed chronic failures of business planning. It had been making heavy losses.

King set about his task in the rumbustious, sometimes bruising style which was his hallmark. The old guard of senior managers was abruptly replaced by newcomers such as Colin (now Lord) Marshall, a brilliant marketing specialist who joined King as chief executive. Staff numbers were cut from 52,000 to 37,500 within two years. Surplus aircraft and other assets were sold off.

By 1983 BA had returned to profit and its reputation with travellers had improved beyond measure. Its stock-market flotation in 1987 was highly successful. Advertising prompted by greatly increased passenger numbers claimed BA to be 'the world's favourite airline'. It was certainly among the most profitable of the decade. And King himself was often described as Mrs Thatcher's favourite businessman.

But the sum of his business achievements was much greater than simply the turnaround of BA. From the humblest of origins, he was a substantial industrialist in his own right long before he came to national prominence. And, in parallel with his more newsworthy reign at BA, he was chairman for more than twenty years of FKI Babcock, a world leader in power-station engineering.

He found time also to be a famously bold Master of Foxhounds, a landowner who gave his occupation as 'farmer' in his passport, a ubiquitous social figure and a devoted *pater familias*.

John Leonard King was born at Brentwood, on 26 August 1917, although he disliked enquiries into his early life and preferred not to reveal the precise date. He was the son of an Army sergeant who became a Surrey postmaster and an Irish Catholic mother who took in washing. It was his mother who was the strongest influence on his childhood, but he left school with no qualifications and was remembered as an unpromising pupil. He went to work first as a petrol-pump attendant and a factory hand, then more successfully as a car salesman in Guildford.

At the outbreak of the Second World War, King saw his first opportunity to go into the engineering business. Aged 21, he set up Whitehouse Industries to manufacture aero-engine components, using American machine tools provided under the lend-lease arrangements. His flair for salesmanship and entrepreneurial risk was already evident. At the end of the war he moved his engineering equipment from Whitehouse Industries into a Midlands company called Pollard, which manufactured ball bearings. The product appealed to him as 'one of the most basic things you can make', with a multiplicity of applications. He became managing director of Pollard and transferred the company lock, stock and barrel to a vacant site at Ferrybridge in Yorkshire, where he restored employment and community life to a virtually derelict mining village – an experiment which, he later admitted, showed some influence of postwar socialist thinking. He counted it among his proudest achievements.

Pollard grew from 50 employees to 2000 by the 1960s. It became one of the top three British companies in its field, and made King a millionaire. In 1969 the then Labour government forced the merger of Pollard with another bearing maker, Ransomes & Marles, in the hope of resisting foreign competition. Pollard was sold for £9.8 million, of which King's portion was said to have been £3 million.

His next major investment, in 1970, was in Dennis Motor Holdings, which built fire engines and dust carts. Again he was able to sell out profitably, and in 1972 he took the chairmanship of Babcock & Wilcox (later FKI Babcock), a maker of power-station turbines and heavy equipment. At Babcock his role was to reorganise the senior management structure and to lead the overseas sales effort. He was known as a pragmatic decision-maker and an effective delegator, insistent on good internal communications. He kept his headquarters at Babcock's St James's Square head office, rather than at BA, for the remainder of his career.

King was on good terms with the Labour government and undertook a number of public committee roles, including the chairmanship of the British Olympic Appeal in 1975. He was knighted in James Callaghan's 1979 farewell honours list. But it was on the arrival of Margaret Thatcher in Downing Street that his star really began to rise.

When the board of the National Enterprise Board resigned *en masse* after the election, King stepped in, first as deputy chairman and then in 1980 as chairman to oversee the disposal of many of its holdings. He became an ardent public supporter of Mrs Thatcher, going so far as to withdraw Babcock from CBI membership when the then CBI president, Terence Beckett, publicly criticised her policies towards industry.

King was said to have declined the offer of the chairmanship of British Steel before accepting BA. He received a life peerage in 1983, as the success of his surgery on the airline became evident. Perhaps the most remarkable feature of his long tenure at BA was the relentless and single-minded energy with which he led the airline's battles with its competitors and when necessary with government. He was a magnet for publicity, with a capacity for mercurial gestures and blunt statements that kept him and the airline constantly in the eye of the press. When he felt that the Conservative government had ceased to take proper care of BA's interests, he stopped the company's contribution to Conservative Party funds. And when business was bad in the depths of the recession he simply gave away 50,000 tickets to get people back into the air.

He was particularly enraged by the transfer of some BA's

London–Tokyo routes to Richard Branson's Virgin Airlines and by a decision to allow Virgin to operate from Heathrow in 1991. A highly publicised mercy mission by Branson to fly home hostages who had been held by Saddam Hussein in Baghdad added to the irritation, and King was reported to have told his subordinates to 'do something about Branson'. This led to the notorious 'dirty tricks' campaign, in which BA went to extraordinary lengths to undermine Virgin's business.

Branson sued King and BA for libel; King countersued, and the case went to trial in 1993. The court found in favour of Branson and Virgin, and BA paid damages to Branson of £500,000 and a legal bill of some £3 million. King remained defiant, but soon afterwards stepped down as chairman of BA to become president emeritus.

King's public aggression masked the private insecurity which made him hide the details of his early years. But he amply fulfilled a role which, he said, he had always imagined for himself: he relished the limelight, the trappings of an international tycoon and a country gentleman, the social prominence that brought him into contact with celebrities, royalty and Presidents of the United States.

Those close to him described a warmer man under the gruff exterior. He liked to describe himself to interviewers, of whom there were many, as a dreamer and a romantic. He would take border terriers into his office, and once had a special trolley constructed for a Labrador whose hindquarters had been crushed.

Hunting was an essential part of the King legend. Lord White, who with his business partner Lord Hanson had been friends of King since their days in Yorkshire together in the 1950s, described him as 'the bravest fellow I've ever seen in the hunting field'.

King was Master of the Badsworth in Derbyshire from 1949 to 1958 and of the more prestigious Belvoir, the Duke of Rutland's pack, from 1958 until 1972. His 2000-acre estate at Wartnaby, near Melton Mowbray in Leicestershire, was in the heart of Belvoir country, and he became the hunt's chairman when he retired from the Mastership. He was also a racing enthusiast, and held a private pilot's license.

King was a director of the *Daily Telegraph* and the *Spectator*.

Amongst many charitable activities he was a successful fundraiser and chairman for various cancer relief groups.

He married first, in 1941, Lorna Sykes, daughter of the garage owner with whom he had been in business in Guildford. A devoted marriage produced three sons and a daughter. He was deeply distressed by Lorna's early death in 1969, and was said to have bought a £20,000 pearl necklace to place with her in the coffin. Her sister had married the architect John Poulson and, at Lorna's wish, (although never previously involved in business with him) King made strenuous but unsuccessful efforts to rescue Poulson's companies as they went down.

He married secondly, in 1970, Isabel Monckton, daughter of the 8th Viscount Galway; they met on the hunting field.

12 July 2005

Sir Freddie Laker

⟡ 1922–2006 ⟡

Pioneer of cheap air travel

Sir Freddie Laker pioneered the idea of cheap air travel with his Skytrain to America in 1977; his entrepreneurial spirit brought him immense public affection and the wrath of rivals who conspired successfully to break his business.

Before Skytrain, international flights were largely the preserve of the rich. After the Second World War it was thought that competition between airlines might prejudice passenger safety, and hence the market was strictly regulated by the International Air Transport Association. This allowed state airlines to maintain an inefficient monopoly offering identical services at high prices. By 1971 the only exception was charter airlines catering for the growing package holiday trade. Under a bizarre IATA rule intended to preserve the monopoly, charter passengers needed six months' membership of an 'affinity group' whose main purpose was not travel, groups such as the Dahlia Society or the Left Hand

Club. Backdated membership soon became openly obtainable at airports.

Laker, whose airline was being regularly fined for carrying large numbers of bogus members of rose growers' societies to America, proposed an easier system. Passengers who wanted a cheap flight could queue for a ticket at the airport, just as they would at a railway station before taking a train. It took six years of strenuous argument to persuade the British and American governments to see the idea's merits.

The first Skytrain took off for New York in September 1977. Although Laker offered no frills (such as meals), at £59 it cost a third of any other ticket. He made £1 million profit in the first year, and by 1980 was carrying one in seven transatlantic passengers. Laker took a boyish delight in his success; he was memorably photo-graphed zooming around the Gatwick runway pretending to be a Spitfire. Yet his concern for the consumer's interest endeared him to the public. He was voted 'Man of the Year' and in 1978 knighted by the Callaghan government.

Then, in February 1982, Laker Airways abruptly went into receivership with debts of £264 million. The collapse was so sudden that its flights were turned round in mid-air. At first it appeared that Laker had overreached himself, borrowing heavily to finance 15 new planes just as the pound plunged against the dollar. The major airlines had also taken concerted action, offering cheap fares for the first time; and when Pan Am cut the price of its regular service by two-thirds in October 1981, Laker's passengers deserted him. In 1983 the liquidators Touche Ross began an antitrust action in America, claiming a billion dollars from ten major airlines. The allegations went beyond predatory pricing; British Airways, Pan Am, TWA and Lufthansa were said to have met to plot Laker's downfall. In particular, several airlines had threatened the manufacturer McDonnell Douglas that they would buy elsewhere if it rescheduled Laker's debt. The Justice Department found the evidence in a school project by the daughter of a McDonnell Douglas director.

The action threatened BA's privatisation, and in 1985 the defendants settled out of court the £35 million owed to Laker's creditors, staff and passengers. Laker himself reluctantly accepted £6 million in compensation and retreated to the Bahamas.

Frederick Alfred Laker was born at Canterbury on 6 August 1922. His father, a merchant seaman, deserted the family when Freddie was five, and his mother then worked as a cleaner. At the local Simon Langton School Freddie did not shine academically, amusing friends by saying he was going to be a millionaire. His first job was delivering coal for an uncle.

At 16 he joined the flying-boat builders Short Brothers of Rochester as a tea boy and apprentice engineer, and studied maths and economics at night school. In the Second World War he worked for the Air Transport Auxiliary where he excelled at improvising repairs. He became flight engineer to Jim Mollison, Amy Johnson's husband, before qualifying as a ferry pilot himself.

By 1946 Laker knew every airfield in Europe, together with every type of aircraft and its payload. With a loan from a friend he set up Aviation Traders, dealing in war-surplus and then carrying passengers and freight in converted Halifax bombers. Laker made his first fortune from the Berlin airlift of 1948. The government chartered every available aeroplane from the many small independent airlines at generous rates. The subsequent round-the-clock operation instilled in Laker a mania for punctuality. His profit, however, came from selling spare parts to the other airlines.

When the airlift ended, Laker shrewdly judged the market to be overcrowded, and, as others went under, had his team at work smelting 6000 engines for a saucepan manufacturer. In 1951 he returned to charter, carrying troops for the Army in aircraft rebuilt from crashed ones. Laker himself survived a crash while landing at Hamburg in 1952, just evading the neighbouring crematorium when two engines failed.

In 1953 his Channel Air Bridge began flying passengers, and then cars, from Southend to Calais. Laker also found time to introduce the 'stop me and buy one' ice-cream man to Nigeria. In 1958 he sold his business, which was merged with others to form British United Airways (BUA). He became managing director of BUA, but though it grew into the largest independent, Laker hankered after his own airline. He liked to know all his employees and he liked to call the shots, increasingly difficult in the sprawling BUA. In 1965 he resigned, forming Laker Airways to capitalise on the booming package holiday trade. The launch was overshadowed by the death of his son by his first marriage, Kevin, in the sports car Laker had given him for his 17th birthday.

Three innovations made the airline successful. Laker chartered his aircraft to tour companies at a rate that cost them less the more they flew. He saved money on fuel by telling his crews to fly at higher altitudes than usual and by pioneering the reduced thrust technique on takeoff. He also kept his fleet busy off-season, flying winter tours to the Mediterranean and Muslims to Mecca for the Haj. Despite occasional scares, including involvement on the Mersey in the world's first – and short-lived – commercial hovercraft service, he was carrying half a million passengers by 1971 and ready to expand.

After Skytrain, Laker was disillusioned with Britain, and from his yacht concentrated on organising tours to Lonrho's Bahamian hotels for his friend Tiny Rowland. Then, in 1991, he returned to airlines, carrying passengers between Florida and the Bahamas, basing his operation at Freeport. The success of this venture persuaded him and his partner, the Texan oil tycoon Oscar Wyatt, to run flights from London to Florida in 1996. Despite technical problems that saw their first holidaymakers take off after two days at the airport, the service, rather more up-market than Skytrain, made a modest profit, but Laker abandoned the British package holiday market in 1998. The airline later closed down.

Laker revelled in the good life. At his peak he bought a Rolls-Royce each year and racehorses for his Epsom stud. Yet he never lost his Kentish accent and had a reputation for frugality. Once, noticing the loose sole of an employee's shoe, he extracted a vast bankroll from his pocket and handed the man the elastic band. He later lost large sums in the Lloyd's insurance market.

Tall and occasionally plump, Laker's management style was to dominate. He knew each aspect of his business as well as any employee, and, while inspiring great loyalty, knew his own mind and got his own way. He was a sharp, difficult negotiator whose ability to infuriate rivals was commemorated by his friend Prince

Philip in a clerihew: 'Sir Freddie Laker/may be at peace with his maker/but he is persona non grata/with IATA.'

Freddie Laker was married four times. He married his first wife, Joan, in 1942 (dissolved 1968); they had a daughter and his son who predeceased him. His second marriage, to Rosemary Black, lasted from 1968 to 1975; his third, to Patricia Gates (with whom he had a son and another son who died in infancy), from 1975 to 1982. He married, fourthly, Jacqueline Harvey, a former air hostess, in 1985.

9 February 2006

Ronald Lyon

⊰═⊙ 1928–2004 ⊙═⊰

Property dealer caught in the 1974 crash

Ronald Lyon was one of the most flamboyant casualties of the collapse of the commercial property market in 1974, going under with £52 million of debts; but he was also one of the most resilient, recovering from this and other financial catastrophes to create new property empires at home and abroad.

Ronald Lyon was born on 7 April 1928 at Halstead in Essex. His father, a builder, brought him up to believe that 'every salaried man is a slave'; young Ronnie started his first entrepreneurial venture at 15, supplying loudspeaker systems for local dances and fêtes. Having left school the following year, he started making and selling garden sheds, hiring a local youth to chauffeur him until he was old enough to drive himself.

By the early 1950s he had moved into developing simple, steel-framed industrial buildings. Despite setbacks – he was acquitted of fraud charges after the collapse of a scrap-metal business – his property interests continued to grow, and he made his first million before he was thirty.

'Business is just like driving a car – of which I have four, by the way,' he once observed. 'I moved up in stages, like changing gears.' A burly cigar-smoker, Lyon saw an opportunity at every turn and drove a very hard bargain. He put in long hours at his office and on site, but he and his wife Hazel – an interior decorator – also found time to enjoy the millionaire lifestyle with some gusto. Hazel once arrived at a charity lunch at the London Hilton with a pet cheetah (called Princess Roza) on a lead, and in 1967, shortly after the introduction of the breathalyser test, Lyon hired a fleet of fifty Daimlers to take guests home safely from his annual Christmas cocktail party. When the couple parted, they lived in separate mansions in Sunningdale – Ronald's being equipped, according to one report, with 'swimming pool, private projection room, the finest badger colony in southeast England and to cap it all, the perfect Jeeves-type butler'.

At his zenith he also owned a shooting estate in Hampshire, 10,000 acres of farmland in Wiltshire, a yacht in the south of France, a holiday house in Majorca, a Sloane Street flat and a collection of 21 paintings by L.S. Lowry (bought at very shrewd prices) as well as works by Monet, Cezanne and Renoir.

Meanwhile, Ronald Lyon Holdings, headquartered at Lyon Tower in Colliers Wood, south London, grew into an international property group worth £183 million – though valuations during the boom which preceded the crash were very much a moving target: the value attached to one of Lyon's house-building sites in Gloucestershire multiplied seven times between mid-1971 and late 1972. Among the group's prize assets were two residential blocks on Park Lane, Fountain House and Alford House, which Lyon intended to redevelop. As market conditions deteriorated in early 1974, however, he tried to sell the two buildings to Kuwaiti interests to ease his cash flow. The collapse of the deal left Lyon Group in breach of its loan arrangements; when negotiations with the lenders broke down on 16 May, coinciding with similar problems in another major property company, Stern Holdings, the *Daily Telegraph* announced that 'the great property bubble finally burst yesterday'.

In due course the celebrated City accountant Kenneth Cork – 'the Great Liquidator' – was called in to unwind Lyon Group's affairs. Lyon himself had given personal guarantees for the company's loans, and was obliged to sell almost everything he owned. At a press conference in his boardroom shortly after the news broke, journalists noted that the picture hooks were still in the panelling, but the paintings had already gone. The new 187-foot yacht which he had ordered from a Dutch shipyard was completed but eventually sold off for several million pounds by Lyon's bankers – Fidel Castro was briefly rumoured to be a potential buyer.

Undaunted, Lyon declared in 1975 that he hoped 'it will not be very long before I can think of buying myself another yacht'. He was quickly back on his feet, developing residential property in Dubai, and in 1979 he re-emerged on the British property scene – in the chauffeured Rolls-Royce which had somehow survived from Lyon Group days – with a new company called Arunbridge. Backed by Middle Eastern interests, Arunbridge built industrial estates on the former Wembley Exhibition site and elsewhere, and became involved in trying to develop a controversial 12-acre site at Vauxhall (where the MI6 building now stands) which ran into intractable planning difficulties.

But having failed to find sufficient tenants for the Wembley scheme, Arunbridge went into liquidation with debts of some £8 million in 1983. For a time Lyon ran a chicken hatchery business in Egypt, and in 1990 his name was connected with another collapsed British property venture, Kingswood Estates. Yet again he rebounded, this time having spotted the real-estate potential of the former East Germany after reunification; by 1994 he had assembled a huge development site in Berlin. Finally he returned to London to launch a venture with interests in the redevelopment of the Thames Gateway.

Ronnie Lyon was a larger-than-life figure whose generosity and dry sense of humour won him a huge circle of friends. He had a great love of big-band music and contemporary jazz. He and Hazel were married in 1959, and had a son, Marcus. The marriage was later dissolved. He also had a daughter Camilla. Hazel died in 1982. He married secondly, in 1980, Rosemary Henri, who had three children by a previous marriage.

26 November 2004

Lord Matthews

⊸⊜ 1919–1995 ⊜⊷

Builder who bought the Daily Express

Lord Matthews was a London builder who became, as proprietor of the *Daily Express*, a powerful press baron in the last years of the Fleet Street era.

In a highly successful partnership with Sir Nigel Broackes, Matthews had built up the Trafalgar House group, a conglomerate whose interests included commercial-property development, the Cunard shipping line, the Cementation civil engineering group and the Ritz Hotel. In June 1977, Trafalgar emerged as a last-minute bidder for the Beaverbrook empire, which owned the *Daily Express*, the *Sunday Express* and the *Evening Standard*. 'I was not after a newspaper,' Matthews later insisted. 'It just happened to be an opportunity. As far as I was concerned the *Express* was a casualty. My task was to mend it.'

Matthews' humble background and unvarnished style were sometimes caricatured – *Private Eye* dubbed him Lord Whelks – but there was no doubting his shrewdness. An early admirer of Margaret Thatcher, he wanted the *Express* to be 'a family newspaper crusading for what is good in Britain'. He personally approved the paper's leading articles, and would have no truck with investigative journalism (such as the British Leyland 'slush fund' story in 1978) which he felt might damage the national reputation. Six *Express* editors came and went under his chairmanship.

Matthews made no secret of his aim to be the first Fleet Street publisher to break the grip of the trade unions. He later declared that he would have cut the *Express* workforce by two-thirds if the unions had let him. Immediately after the takeover he found himself in a nasty confrontation involving sabotage of the printing presses with the engineers' union, over a 70 per cent pay claim and the shedding of 46 jobs. Matthews demanded 'the right to manage'; he rapidly revised his declared intention of investing a further £10 million in his newspapers. Of the unions, he said, 'Some of them are hell-bent on self destruction. Well, let it be, but not with our money.'

He also spoke of the possibility of closure – no idle threat, since the development value of the *Express*'s famous Fleet Street headquarters exceeded the £13.7 million Matthews had paid for the Beaverbrook group.

Despite protestations that 'I don't have ink in my veins', Matthews quickly adapted to the newspaper business, and took satisfaction from the fact that production continued from the *Express*'s Manchester plant; an edition appeared with the headline: 'We shall not be moved'. If the Fleet Street workforce was too entrenched to be easily reduced, Matthews determined to make it produce more newspapers instead. There were plans for new Sunday and daily titles and a third London evening paper, intended to be down-market from the *Standard* and in competition with Associated Newspapers' *Evening News*. Of these projects, only the *Daily Star*, Britain's first new national daily for 75 years, came to fruition – again making use of Manchester presses. The *Standard* meanwhile merged with the *Evening News*, in a joint-venture arrangement with Associated Newspapers.

The *Express* lost £5 million in the first year of Trafalgar's owner-ship, and the newly launched *Star* was losing £1 million per month. The unions remained uncooperative.

Matthews let it be known in 1981 that all the titles were for sale: among the interested parties were Tiny Rowland, Robert Maxwell (who acquired a 20 per cent stake) and Sir James Goldsmith. But Matthews chose to hold out, and by 1984 the group's publishing and media interests, de-merged from Trafalgar House as Fleet Holdings, were achieving satisfactory profits.

He was created a life peer as Baron Matthews in 1980, but rarely took part in debates in the Lords. 'Goodness knows when I will go next,' was his only comment after his maiden speech. 'I shouldn't think I'll be going there as regularly as most people because I have such a large organisation to run.'

After stepping down from Fleet Holdings he retired to tax exile in Jersey. 'I have made a lot of money for a lot of people,' he said. 'I have done my bit.'

Victor Collin Matthews was born in Islington on 5 December 1919, and was brought up by his widowed mother. He was educated at Highbury School, and gained an early introduction to the newspaper business as a paper boy for a shop in St Paul's Road, Islington, earning half a crown per round. His first job after school was as an office boy in a tobacco company. He was also a talented footballer, and might have played for Arsenal but for the outbreak of war.

As an ordinary seaman in the RNVR, he was in a small boat at Dunkirk and later took part in the commando raid on Dieppe. But in six years of service he advanced only to able seaman: 'I hated the sea,' he said later, 'and I didn't have much ambition.'

After the war he joined the City building firm of Trollope & Colls, at first as a clerk and later as a surveyor. Among the jobs which he supervised in the 1950s was the restoration and re-roofing of the Guildhall.

In due course he changed to another firm, Clark & Fenn, which undertook contracts in the BBC television studios and the American embassy. Gradually he became more ambitious, and his entrepreneurial talent emerged: recognising Matthews' potential, his boss at Clark & Fenn helped him in 1960 to buy a small building firm of his own, Bridge Walker, based in Brixton. It had capital of £5000 and turnover of £250,000; over the next four years he multiplied the latter figure by ten.

One of the up-and-coming property men with whom he did good business was Nigel Broackes of Trafalgar House; by 1967 he had sold his company to Trafalgar and joined the board there. When Trafalgar also acquired Trollope & Colls, Matthews became chairman of his old firm. He was managing director of the Trafalgar House group from 1968, and chief executive from 1977.

He and Broackes developed a predatory reputation in the takeover market. Among the early targets which evaded their grasp were the Metropolitan Estates Property Co, Bowater and the Savoy Group. Trafalgar's first major diversification, in 1971, was the ailing Cunard shipping line, owner of the *QEII*. Matthews described it as 'a terrific purchase' at £28 million, and took patriotic pride in ownership of the *QEII*, whose viability had previously been in doubt.

By a process which he described as 'simple horticulture', he achieved a radical improvement in Cunard's profitability, dispensing with all but two of Cunard's directors, 15 cargo ships and a variety of loss-making subsidiaries. The London Ritz, struggling in the aftermath of the oil shock, was acquired as a second flagship for the group in 1976.

The two partners were in some respects an unlikely combination: the suave, Stowe-educated Broackes, precociously successful, was the younger of the two by 14 years. Relations between them were strained in 1979 by the publication of Broakes's autobiography, *A Growing Concern*, which, whilst acknowledging that the *Express* takeover was really Matthews' story, seemed otherwise to play down the older man's role in building up Trafalgar House, and offered an ambiguous portrait of him: 'He has a keen sense of humour, he responds well to flattery, and to others must seem a cheerful, contented man; but in private he is often morose and pessimistic, doubtful and suspicious of the future. This is nothing new: he was just the same fifteen years ago . . .'

Broackes implied that he had agreed to the Beaverbrook takeover principally in order to provide Matthews with an invigorating new challenge. Matthews, who had not known that the book was in preparation, responded in a barbed review in the *Evening Standard* that he thought enviously of his partner 'idling his time away in the South of France'.

The tension between them did not amount to a serious falling-out, but in due course it made commercial sense to separate the newspaper interests from the rest of Trafalgar House. The *Express* titles were grouped together, along with the successful magazine publisher Morgan Grampian and stakes in Reuters and TV-AM, under a new umbrella, Fleet Holdings, which was partially de-merged in March 1982 and finally divorced in the following year.

Matthews resigned as chief executive of Trafalgar and sold a large part of his personal shareholding. He remained chairman of Fleet and non-executive deputy chairman of Trafalgar until 1985, when Fleet succumbed to a £286 million takeover bid from United Newspapers.

From 1977 to 1982 he had also been a director of Lew Grade's company, ACC. During the boardroom dramas which culminated in Grade's abrupt ousting by the Australian entrepreneur Robert Holmes à Court, it was thought that Matthews himself might have led a bid for ACC which would have been more palatable to Grade; but the pressure of Trafalgar group commitments prevented him doing so.

Retirement allowed him to concentrate on horses and golf. He was a keen owner and breeder but disliked betting. 'I do not believe in luck,' he said.

Victor Matthews married, in 1942, Joyce Pilbeam. They had a son.

5 December 1995

Rolf Schild

1924–2003

Kidnap victim

Rolf Schild was an entrepreneur and inventor in the field of medical equipment but was perhaps better known for surviving, with his wife and daughter, a traumatic kidnapping by Sardinian bandits.

An emigré from Nazi Germany, Rolf Schild was acknowledged in his professional field for his work on the development of the first 'iron lung' and other pioneering medical devices. The company he built up, Huntleigh Technology, sold its products all over the world and received Queen's Awards for exports and innovation. But his name was also known to the wider world for the series of events which began in the summer of 1979, when he and his family were subjected to a seven-month kidnap ordeal which arose out of a fatal misunderstanding. The ill-educated villains concerned had mistaken him for a Rothschild. In the early hours of 22 August 1979, Schild, his wife Daphne and their 15-year-old daughter Annabel returned to their holiday villa at Palau on the north coast of Sardinia after a dinner with neighbours, to find a gang lying in wait. Blindfolded, they were driven for four hours to a cave in the central mountains then manhandled roughly from one hide-out to another over the following days. The Schilds' car was found burned out and abandoned on a remote track.

Elements of the British press – never to be forgiven by Schild for what he regarded as irresponsible coverage of the story – speculated that the family's disappearance might be connected with complications in Schild's business affairs. But the truth was that kidnapping was rife on the island, and that the Schilds were among more than a dozen victims, mostly rich Italian holidaymakers, to fall into bandit hands that season.

Rolf Schild himself was found in a dishevelled state on a mountain road on 5 September, having apparently been driven in circles for some hours before being released so that he could set about meeting the kidnappers' huge ransom demand. There was speculation that this was more than £1 million. Over the months that followed – as Daphne and Annabel spent a fearful, cold and uncomfortable winter in the custody of guards they nicknamed 'Funnyman' and (for his odour) 'Monkey' – Schild became increasingly sceptical of the efforts of the Sardinian police to find them. He sought a negotiating channel with the kidnappers through local intermediaries, and some money was reported eventually to have changed hands. Daphne was freed in mid-January. A month later eight peasants from the village of Orani were arrested in connection with the kidnap, but bandit leaders continued to ask for more cash. Finally, Annabel was handed over on 21 March; the ransom paid was never revealed.

The son of a Jewish textile entrepreneur, Rolf Schild was born at Lindental in Germany on 18 May 1924. He went to school at Cologne, where in 1939 his headmaster arranged for about a hundred pupils, including Rolf, to be evacuated to England by the so-called *kindertransport* route. Rolf's elder brother was already in England, but his parents were not permitted to follow, and both died in Nazi camps.

Rolf spent three years in hostels in Liverpool, Wales and Manchester, where he took his first job in 1943 as a machine operator while studying at night school to qualify as an electrical engineer. After the war he moved to London and found work with a small medical instruments company, New Electronic Products. There he developed a phono-cardiograph to measure and record the sound of the heart, and a transducer device to measure pressure within the heart.

His next career move came when he was approached by an aero-engine manufacturer who needed a device to measure engine pressures. Schild's view was that 'an engine is just a pump, similar to the heart' and that it was only a matter of adopting the medical technology. His boss thought the potential in the aviation industry too limited, and was not interested in diversifying, but Schild had what he called '*fingerspitzengefuhl*' – a feeling in his fingertips – about the new product.

Schild was blunt and determined in manner, and remained Germanic in expression even after many years in Britain. Initially he was allowed to continue his day job at New Electronic Products while developing the aero-engine transducer in a basement in his spare time, but in 1956 he was asked to leave.

He set up his own company, SE Laboratories, with a partner, Peter Epstein. They began assembling components in Schild's Hampstead kitchen for manufacturers such as De Havilland and English Electric. After winning a government contract to provide transducers for ballistic missiles, they took over a rented factory and the business took off. SE Laboratories went on to contribute to the development of the first heart and lung machine – the iron lung – at Hammersmith Hospital and was floated on the stock exchange in 1963 with a value of £2.4 million. The share issue was a record 176 times oversubscribed. The company was taken over by EMI in 1966, but Schild fell out with his colleagues over the development of body scanners, and left the group in 1973.

He went on to invest in Hymatic Engineering, a military equipment manufacturer, which became Huntleigh in 1975. He developed a new range of medical products, and in 1983 he led a management buy-out of the medical side of the business, Huntleigh Technology, which again he took to the stock market. The company, based at Luton, focused on products such as pneumatic garments to assist blood flow, special mattresses and hospital beds, and hand-held diagnostic instruments. The Schild family's stake in the company was estimated to be worth almost £100 million.

Rolf Schild was appointed OBE in 1997, and was also honoured in Germany for his contribution to Anglo-German relations. He remained chairman of Huntleigh until his death, declaring it to be 'an easy job. You just think about new products and what the salary is for the new office girl'. He also remained a practising engineer, both in the research department of Huntleigh and as a hobby, and travelled widely in search of new ideas. Shortly before his death he designed the 'air walker', an exercise device to help airline passengers avoid deep-vein thrombosis. He was a fellow of the Institution of Electrical Engineers.

Rolf Schild was a generous supporter of a wide range of charities. In later years he spoke little about the kidnapping episode, except to observe that it had made the Schilds a very close family.

He was survived by his wife Daphne, their daughter Annabel and their sons Julian and David, who were both directors of Huntleigh.

14 April 2003

Sir Adam Thomson

◆═◇ 1926–2000 ◇═◆

Founder of British Caledonian Airways

Sir Adam Thomson was the founder and chairman of British Caledonian, one of Britain's most successful independent airlines. From humble Glaswegian origins and service in the Fleet Air Arm, Thomson emerged as the most enduring of a generation of postwar aviation entrepreneurs. With small capital and little help from government, he battled for 27 years to build a niche for British Caledonian (BCal) in an industry dominated by state-backed national carriers and US giants.

From a single Douglas DC7 flying charter flights in 1961, BCal grew to be the ninth largest European airline, with a fleet of 27 jets serving almost 50 international destinations. Passengers warmed to

BCal's proudly Scottish image, with tartan-clad cabin crew ('Wish they all could be Caledonian girls,' went the jingle, borrowed from the Beach Boys) and the lion rampant on its tailplanes. At the peak of its success in the early 1980s, it was voted by travel writers to be the best airline in the world.

But in the fiercely competitive market of the 1980s – particularly on North Atlantic routes – BCal lacked critical mass to hold its own, especially as the Thatcher government leaned strongly in favour of British Airways in the run-up to privatisation. After losing a crucial row with BA over route allocations in 1984 and suffering a series of other commercial misfortunes, BCal fell – to Thomson's deep and evident regret – to a takeover bid from BA in 1988.

Small, quiet and deliberate in manner, Thomson was tough as nails at the boardroom table and in the defence of BCal's interests. But he was well liked by his 7000 staff; BCal had an excellent industrial relations record, and paid 5 per cent of its profits into a staff share fund. And though he became a powerful and respected businessman, he remained an aviator at heart.

In New York on one occasion in the 1960s to negotiate a loan for new aircraft, he received an urgent call to say that the pilot of a BCal New York–Bermuda flight had been taken ill.

'You're the nearest pilot, chairman,' said the caller. 'There's a uniform waiting in the cockpit.'

'So I flew the darned thing,' Thomson recalled. 'And I loved it.'

Adam Thomson was born on 7 July 1926, the son of a shunter on the London Midland and Scottish Railway. Brought up in a Glasgow tenement, he was educated at Rutherglen Academy, Coatbridge College and the Royal Technical College (now Strathclyde University). At 17, in 1944, he volunteered for the Fleet Air Arm and was sent to Canada for pilot training, earning his wings in a Fairchild Cornell trainer.

After demobilisation Thomson was keen to venture out on his own. He tried starting a business flying 'joyrides' for holidaymakers at Largs on the Clyde, but financial backing was impossible to find. Instead, after a stint with the Ministry of Civil Aviation as a pilot instructor, he joined Newman Airways to fly biplanes from the Isle of Wight to the Channel Islands. In 1951 he joined British European

Airways (BEA) and two years later he became a captain with West African Airways, based in Lagos. From there he transferred to Britavia, flying Handley Page Hermes aircraft transporting troops in Africa and to Singapore. He once recalled the experience of low bush-flying through a 'line-squall' during the African rainy season, as being 'like a wet cliff coming at you'.

Thomson had ideas for Britavia route developments, but eventually decided it might be more fruitful to 'have a go at them myself'. In partnership with a former BEA steward, John de la Haye, he raised £54,000 from investors – including some Scottish Americans – to charter a DC7 on a 'pay-as-you-fly' basis from the Belgian airline Sabena. The first Caledonian Airways flight, a charter carrying immigrants from Barbados, took off appropriately on St Andrew's Day, 1961.

The airline survived a tragic early setback when one of its first planes crashed in Africa with the loss of 100 lives. The finances were precarious, and at every turn Caledonian was up against what Thomson called 'International Goliath Airways', the cartel of national carriers, backed by their governments, which controlled scheduled routes and fares. Caledonian could grow only by offering low-fare charters and package-holiday flights from Gatwick and Prestwick; it specialised in transatlantic deals for 'affinity groups' with names such as Ma Brown's Paisley Buddies. It also flew pilgrims to Mecca and migrants to Australia. Many of Thomson's charter competitors failed, but by 1968 Caledonian was running Boeing 707s on regular services from Gatwick to New York, Los Angeles and Singapore.

Meanwhile, the Labour government had responded to increasing consumer pressure for cheaper flights by appointing the Edwards Committee, which recommended that the national carriers BEA and BOAC (to be merged, in 1971, as British Airways) should be gingered up by competition from a 'second-force' airline such as Caledonian. On the strength of this, Thomson raised more capital – from, among others, the Royal Bank of Scotland and the Glaswegian Sir Isaac Wolfson's Great Universal Stores – and acquired the ailing British United Airways, where Freddie Laker had once been managing director.

Relaunched on St Andrew's Day 1970 as British Caledonian, the airline acquired scheduled routes to South America, West Africa, Europe and within the UK, and in due course to several US cities. But conditions remained challenging for a small operator – despite the Edwards Committee findings, BCal was never able to increase its routes to much more than a tenth of British Airways' network. And the collapse of the package-holiday trade (particularly Horizon Holidays, for which it was the main carrier) after the 1973–74 oil crisis brought BCal temporarily to its knees. Planes were grounded and staff laid off, but Thomson fought back, and by the end of the decade BCal was carrying two million passengers a year. It provided more than half of the traffic at Gatwick, and acquired new scheduled routes to Hong Kong as well as (after Laker Airways' collapse in 1982) New York and Los Angeles.

Such a paragon of gritty entrepreneurship might have been expected to thrive in the Thatcher years. But the Conservative government was anxious to ensure the successful privatisation of British Airways, under the leadership of the pugnacious Lord King of Wartnaby. A 1983 proposal by Thomson for the transfer of a significant portion of BA routes to BCal – dismissed by King as a 'smash and grab raid' – was partially endorsed in the following year by the Civil Aviation Authority, only to be rejected by ministers for fear of damaging BA's flotation prospects.

In the same period, BCal suffered a series of other blows beyond its control. It lost its Buenos Aires route because of the Falklands war, and Tripoli because of tensions with Libya. Fear of terrorism reduced passenger demand on North Atlantic routes, and economic chaos in Nigeria hit the profitability of its Lagos service. Finally, in 1987, BCal's lucrative helicopter service between Heathrow and Gatwick was halted on environmental grounds.

As BCal's finances weakened, BA was going from strength to strength: having floated on the stock exchange, it decided to put an end to competition from BCal by means of a £235 million take-over bid. The proposed merger was approved by the Monopolies and Mergers Commission on condition that some of BCal's domestic and European routes would be surrendered to smaller carriers. Thomson responded by inviting Scandinavian Airlines

System to become a major shareholder in BCal, but an increased bid from BA won the day. For a while the British Caledonian name survived, with the fleet repainted in BA colours; but in due course it was subsumed altogether. Though only 61 and in full vigour, Thomson chose to retire rather than sit on the board of the merged airline.

Thomson was chairman of the Association of European Airlines in 1977–78 and of the Institute of Directors from 1988 to 1991. He was also deputy chairman of Martin Currie Pacific Trust and a director of Williams & Glyn's Bank, Royal Bank of Scotland, Otis Elevators and the property group MEPC.

He was appointed CBE in 1976 and was knighted in 1983. He published, in 1990, *High Risk: The Politics of the Air*.

Adam Thomson lived modestly in the same house near Gatwick throughout most of his working life; he enjoyed golf, and kept a small sailing boat in Majorca. His only luxury was a constant supply of Havana cigars.

He married, in 1948, Dawn Burt; they had two sons.

23 May 2001

Lord Weinstock

⊶═══ 1924–2002 ═══⊷

Creator of GEC

Lord Weinstock built the General Electric Company into one of Britain's leading industrial conglomerates, but lived to see it virtually ruined by his successors. Arnold Weinstock was admired and feared as one of the most dynamic figures in British industry over more than three decades. His heyday was the era of Harold Wilson and Edward Heath; in the Thatcher years he was out of step with fashionable thinking, and the fortunes of GEC were relatively subdued. Though the merits of his unbending management style were evident again in the recession of the early 1990s, in which the group turned in profits of £1 billion a year and hoarded cash reserves of more than £3 billion, City investors felt that change at the top of GEC was long overdue.

Weinstock finally stepped down in 1996 after 33 years as managing director to become honorary 'chairman emeritus' and to make way for Lord Simpson of Dunkeld as his chosen successor. Simpson renamed the company Marconi to underline the end of the Weinstock era, and pursued bold new strategies which brought it to disaster.

Weinstock's faded reputation in the 1990s was in sharp contrast to his heroic status in the late 1960s, when he became the embodiment of the kind of meritocratic management revolution about which Harold Wilson liked to preach; Weinstock himself spoke of 'a crusade'. By means of two major acquisitions – of Associated Electrical Industries and English Electric – Weinstock turned GEC into one of Britain's largest businesses, rationalising a significant part of the nation's manufacturing capacity as he did so.

In this he had the full support of the Labour government, despite savage job cuts – 12,000, including the giant English Electric factory at Woolwich, in 1969 alone – and fierce criticism from union leaders. The AUEW leader Hugh Scanlon dubbed Weinstock 'Britain's largest unemployer'. Praise was more common, however. In 1978 Professor William Gosling said that 'without Sir Arnold and his company, Britain's balance of payments would be unmanageable'.

For some years, Weinstock virtually controlled Britain's nuclear power-station programme – until he fell out with the energy minister, Tony Benn. Close relations with successive governments helped GEC to profit steadily from cost-plus equipment contracts for the Ministry of Defence and (before the advent of British Telecom) the GPO.

When the Conservatives came to power in 1979, they looked to Weinstock as a natural ally. Sir Keith Joseph, the new industry minister, immediately considered asking GEC to take Rolls-Royce off the government's hands. But Weinstock was sparing in his offers of help, and was rapidly eclipsed in the public eye by a new generation of Thatcherite industrialists. In the years which followed, GEC suffered a series of dents to its reputation. The House of Commons criticised the long-running and expensive GEC torpedo programme. British Rail sued the company for faults in the design of the aborted High Speed Train. And in 1985, the Nimrod Airborne Early Warning contract – on which GEC's Marconi subsidiary had been working for nine years at a cost to the taxpayer of £1 billion but had failed effectively to deliver – was cancelled in favour of an American alternative.

Nevertheless, GEC's finances remained strong, as Weinstock accumulated what was frequently described as his 'cash mountain'. Having once been thought of as a bold adventurer, he was now seen by the stock market as excessively cautious. He was accused of spending too little on research, of failing to compete in the glamorous market for consumer electronic products, of being over-reliant on government contracts; in effect, of resting on his laurels.

Weinstock in turn expressed his contempt for the sort of entrepreneurs, then – and a decade later – very much in fashion with the City, who created spectacular results through highly geared takeovers. 'We don't deal in companies,' he said. 'I don't approve of raising money to plunder other companies.'

He did however bid £1.7 billion for Plessey, a rival electronics firm, in 1986. GEC was eventually warned off by the Monopolies and Mergers Commission, whilst a consortium led by Plessey sought unsuccessfully to bid for GEC in return. Much was made of the clash between Weinstock, a Jewish tailor's son, and the sporting Harrovian Sir John Clark, chairman of Plessey. But the game went to Weinstock in the end: GEC joined forces with the German group Siemens to acquire Plessey in 1989.

The possibility of a takeover and break-up of GEC was raised on other occasions: Sir John Cuckney, former chairman of Westland, led one hostile consortium, and a potential challenge from another fronted by Lord King was thought to have the blessing of Margaret Thatcher, who had declared herself 'disapppointed' with Weinstock. But nothing transpired. GEC remained intact, consolidating its market position in the early 1990s by a series of European joint ventures. It was inevitably first to be mentioned as a potential saviour of its less robust competitors, notably British Aerospace and what remained of Ferranti after GEC acquired its defence business. Weinstock – enigmatic, sceptical, uncompromising and hostile to criticism – remained firmly in control.

But he suffered a terrible blow in May 1996 when his only son Simon, whom he had once hoped to see succeed him at GEC, died of cancer aged 44. In September of that year he made way for Simpson, whom he had courted as a potential recruit since meeting him as a British Aerospace executive some years earlier. Weinstock handed over a profitable company worth £10 billion on the stock market and with £3 billion in the bank.

Simpson proceeded to sell off the defence manufacturing businesses which had been the jewel in Weinstock's crown and to turn GEC into Marconi, a specialised telecommunications group which spent all its cash and more on high-priced acquisitions in the United States and elsewhere. The stock market applauded, and the shares soared. But when the technology bubble burst, Marconi was left with heavy losses and crippling debts. In July 2001 its shares collapsed and Simpson was forced out. Weinstock – still the largest private shareholder – involved himself in the search for a new boardroom team to lead a rescue, but little could be done to save the once-great company's reputation or its investors' cash: shares which had been worth £12.50 each at the height of the stock market boom had fallen to four pence. Weinstock's own stake, once worth £480 million, was reduced to £2 million.

Arnold Weinstock was born in north London on 29 July 1924, the son of a Polish tailor who had arrived in England in 1906. Both parents died while Arnold was a child, leaving him to be brought up in Stoke Newington by a brother 17 years his senior, who was a hairdresser. Young Arnold was educated at Albion Road Central School until evacuated to Warwickshire at the outbreak of war. He went on to the London School of Economics (then temporarily relocated to Cambridge) where he studied statistics, before being drafted into the Admiralty at Bath as an administrative officer.

In 1947, Weinstock's elder brother found Arnold a job with one of the clients of his hairdressing salon, Louis Scott, a West End property developer – who in due course introduced Weinstock to the Sobells, a family of Polish Jews who had migrated to England via Austria at the turn of the century. Arnold married Netta Sobell in 1949.

After a seven-year apprenticeship with Scott, Weinstock moved to join his father-in-law, Michael Sobell. The latter had sold his first electrical business to EMI and was embarking on a new one, Radio & Allied Industries, based at Slough. Weinstock took charge of television manufacture, showing himself to be ruthlessly effective both in salesmanship and in labour relations. Sales boomed with the introduction of commercial television channels in 1955. By rigorous control of factory costs, Radio & Allied produced cheaper sets than their competitors, including the first 14-inch model. The company prospered, and went public in 1958. Three years later, Weinstock engineered a reverse takeover of the much larger General Electric Company – a sprawling conglomerate which was, in his words, 'on the brink of ruin'. Shortly afterwards, at the age of 38, he became GEC's managing director.

Weinstock's *modus operandi* was often compared to that of a spider. The centre of the web was his dimly lit office in Stanhope Gate, adorned only by pictures of his winning racehorses. From there he controlled more than 160 companies in his group, employing more people than the British Army. Management decisions were devolved, strategic planning minimal; Weinstock rarely visited factories or customers, but tirelessly monitored the performance of each unit, with a sharp eye on costs and salary levels. He had a lively sense of humour, but a brisk and unforgiving temper. Among his managers he provoked loyalty, pride and exasperation in equal measure.

He was, he said, 'a creature of reason', motivated neither by money nor technology, but by logic. 'The secret is to see what the market will pay for a product. You then see if you can manufacture at that price. You then work out what you can get off the costs by squeezing a discount out of the suppliers, producing in bulk, reducing your manpower – and that is your profit.'

An introvert, he shunned personal publicity. A succession of ex-ministers – Lords Aldington, Carrington and Prior – were recruited as chairman of GEC, to act as ambassadorial front-men on

Weinstock's behalf. All three came from the Heathite wing of the Conservative party.

In the House of Lords, Weinstock sat on the cross-benches. From there he voiced opposition to the privatisation of British Telecom – partly on the grounds of its monopoly power and partly because of the implied threat to equipment suppliers like GEC. In 1985 he joined with other industrialists in criticism of the Thatcher government's industrial policy: his chief concern was that an indigenous manufacturing base should be safeguarded, rather than allowing the economy to become reliant upon service industries and foreign-owned assembly plants.

To the extent that Weinstock ever relaxed, he did so on the Turf, but he approached bloodstock breeding with the same obsessive attention which characterised his business life. It was in 1957, in partnership with his father-in-law, that he bought his first horse, a doubtful prospect called London Cry, for £3,500. They were advised by the great jockey and trainer Sir Gordon Richards, later their racing manager. Richards had guessed that London Cry might improve with a change of stable; the three-year-old stallion went on to win six of his first nine races, among them the 1958 Cambridgeshire at 20–1, carrying a record weight.

Encouraged by early successes, Sobell and Weinstock bought up the racing interests of the late Dorothy Paget, which included a string of horses in training with Richards and the Ballymacoll Stud in Ireland. Later, Dick Hern's stables at West Isley became part of their racing empire, until sold on to the Queen. Among the many great horses to carry the Weinstock-Sobell colours were Reform, Sun Prince and the ill-fated stallion Troy, winner of the 1979 Derby. Other Classic victories included Sun Princess in the 1983 Oaks and St Leger.

Weinstock was a cultured man, with elegant homes in Grosvenor Square and Wiltshire. He was a trustee of the British Museum and the Royal Philharmonic. He confessed that music, especially opera, sometimes moved him to tears in the privacy of his dressing room; on *Desert Island Discs*, all his musical requests were recordings of performances under the baton of his friend Riccardo Muti, at which Weinstock himself had been present.

Arnold Weinstock was knighted in 1970 and became a life peer in 1980. He was survived by his widow and a daughter.

23 July 2002

Lord White of Hull

⤙⟺ 1923–1995 ⟺⤚

Lord Hanson's swashbuckling partner

Lord White of Hull possessed an extraordinary instinct for corporate takeovers and, in a partnership with Lord Hanson which lasted more than thirty years, helped to build one of Britain's most successful industrial conglomerates.

Rarely out of the gossip columns, White described Hanson and himself as 'the last of the swashbuckling whizz kids'. He relished the image of a stylish corporate shark, for which *Fortune* magazine once awarded him 'four fins', and which inspired a thinly disguised portrayal by the actor Terence Stamp in the film *Wall Street* (1987), a lurid fable of stock market pirates. But he fiercely resented accusations that his method relied on asset-stripping.

Although he was the creative force behind all Hanson's major bids, White's particular achievement was in building up the American side of the group. Disillusioned with the atmosphere of 1970s Britain – where success, he felt, had become a dirty word – he crossed the Atlantic in 1973 with only $3,000 of capital, the maximum then permitted by exchange control. A series of bold deals rapidly followed. By 1984, Hanson Industries had become one of the 150 largest companies in the United States, all achieved through White's nose for identifying under-performing companies and his ability to squeeze value out of them. He was unashamedly ruthless, both in ridding his acquisitions of layers of cost (usually their senior management) and in reselling their peripheral assets. Some critics felt he treated business as a game, and he taunted them by claiming never to visit the factories he bought, nor even the Hanson administrative offices in New Jersey; in his view, the superfluous 'bossmanship' of such visits merely got in the way of corporate performance.

He was robust in defending the principle of takeovers as a means of galvanising slack management and as a catalyst for positive change. When an American court that was investigating one of his bids asked the significance of the knighthood awarded to him in 1979, he said that it made him a 'white knight'.

Typical of his approach was the purchase of SCM Corporation (a conglomerate which included Smith Corona typewriters) in 1986: within a few months, Hanson's entire purchase costs had been recouped by selling off a third of the acquired group. Most of the £2.5 billion paid for Imperial, the British brewing and tobacco combine, was recovered in the same way. Of Kidde Inc, another American purchase, White remarked with typical bluntness, 'We have got the company cheap and we can turn it into a jewel.'

Vincent Gordon Lindsay White was born at Hedon, near Hull, on 11 May 1923, the son of a successful local printer and publisher. He was educated at De Aston School in Lincolnshire where, by his own account, he was 'an idle and indifferent scholar'. He left at 16, against his father's wishes, and worked briefly for a timber firm before joining the Army.

Commissioned into the Special Operations Executive and subsequently Force 136, he spent four years in clandestine missions in India and Burma. The independence allowed to such operations was very much to his liking.

Afterwards he joined his father's business, and found time to indulge in the enjoyment of fast cars, horses, gambling and the company of pretty girls. His fellow Yorkshireman James Hanson (met through friendship with an elder Hanson brother, Bill, who died in 1954) had similar tastes, and together they explored the high life, not just in London but as far afield as Hollywood, where they were regular visitors. In due course the two became business partners.

Their first venture was in humorous greetings cards, and was sold on for a modest profit – taking with it the trade name 'Hanson-White'. Unable to reuse that conjunction, the two partners eventually tossed a coin as to which of their surnames should prevail. Thus it was that 'Hanson Trust' was the name adopted for the conglomerate they began to build in 1964 with the acquisition of Wiles, a maker of fertilisers.

They went on to accumulate a portfolio of mature, low-technology, cash-generative businesses – in sacks, bricks and paint, for example – which stood the test of time when other takeover specialists struggled for survival in the early 1970s. The real success of the group lay in the assets which it nurtured for the long term, as well as the profits from those of which it was quick to dispose.

As the run of unbroken growth continued through the 1980s, both in Britain and in the United States, the Hanson group became one of the most admired British companies of the Thatcherite era. White, in turn, was an ardent supporter of Mrs Thatcher, both for her encouragement of enterprise and for her firmness in other areas. He was made a peer as Baron White of Hull in her farewell honours list.

But it was symptomatic of a new mood which coincided with the change of premier that the purchase by Hanson of a stake in ICI in 1991 – interpreted as the first move in a takeover campaign – was greeted with hostility. The substantive point at issue was whether, if the Hanson group was to become the owner of ICI, it could be trusted to maintain the chemical giant's investment in costly research and development, an area not traditionally given priority in pared-down Hanson companies. A ferocious campaign by ICI's defenders chose to highlight anomalies in Lord White's position: that he was not a main board director of Hanson (he had stepped down as deputy chairman in 1974), and his remuneration was thereby concealed from shareholders; and that he enjoyed great luxury at the company's expense. Lord Hanson's riposte was to point out that White's remarkable talent had contributed many millions to the combined wealth of the group's investors over the years; that, in effect, they were lucky to have him at any price.

'Gordy' White's lavish private life made him a soft target for tabloid attention as well as corporate snipers, and he was never shy of rakish publicity. His pattern of work allowed for an energetic social life on both sides of the Atlantic and both coasts of the United States. His homes included the former studio of the painter John

Singer Sargent in Chelsea, a mansion in Beverly Park, Los Angeles, and a spectacular yacht in the Mediterranean.

In the racing world, White was an enthusiastic owner and patron. He kept a string of 30 thoroughbreds in training at Newmarket, and was part-owner of one Derby winner, Reference Point. It was at his instigation that the Epsom classic became the Ever Ready Derby, under the sponsorship of Hanson's battery-making subsidiary.

He also involved himself in a variety of fundraising efforts, including a London Zoo appeal and the promotion of City Technology Colleges.

Tall, lean, and photogenic, White was proud of his physical fitness long past the age at which other men might have retired both from wheeling and dealing and from gallivanting. He held a pilot's licence and was a keen rider and speed walker. Although he did not take to the pistes until his fifties, he became a notably bold skier. A bizarre incident in the winter resort of Aspen in 1991 brought a flurry of headlines: White was arrested for an alleged assault on his girlfriend, Victoria Tucker, a former model forty years his junior. The charge was dropped when Miss Tucker attributed her injuries to a skiing fall; she later became his third wife.

White's name was linked with a long list of beautiful women, who included, in the 1950s, Kay Kendall, Ava Gardner, Rita Hayworth and, most memorably, Grace Kelly, with whom he was pictured at New York's El Morocco club and at the Cannes film festival.

He married first, in 1958, Elizabeth Kalen, daughter of a Swedish diplomat. They had two daughters. The marriage was dissolved and he married secondly, in 1974, an American actress, Virginia North, who gave him a son.

Divorced again in 1979, White made much-quoted remarks about the perils of marrying younger women; he returned for some years to glamorous bachelorhood, supported by a galaxy of dazzling escorts. But Miss Tucker became the third Lady White, concluding a turbulent seven-year courtship, in 1992.

23 August 1995

Sir Isaac Wolfson

⊸⟹ 1897–1991 ⟸⊷

Stores magnate and philanthropist

Sir Isaac Wolfson, Bt, the president of Great Universal Stores, was one of the great retailers of the 20th century and a philanthropist on such an outstanding scale that he became the first man since Jesus to have colleges named after him at both Oxford and Cambridge. At one point, Wolfson had more customers than any other tradesman in Britain. His business acumen and toughness were legendary.

'I always praise the management,' he said of his procedure in taking over other companies. 'It makes them feel better and some-times it even gets the shares a little cheaper. Then I wait six months to see if there is anyone who is actually any good at all. At the end of that time I send round a highly trained executive with a bag of gold.'

But although Wolfson's business achievements were remark-able, it was as a philanthropist that he was principally to be remembered. In 1955 he formed the Wolfson Foundation, mainly for the advancement of health, education and youth activities in Britain and the Commonwealth. The Foundation distributed millions of pounds, including £1.5 million to Wolfson College, Oxford, and £2 million to University College, Cambridge, which subsequently renamed itself after its benefactor – the first college to change its name in six centuries.

Wolfson left school at 14 and had been too busy with business to acquire an education, but he gloried in the many honorary degrees with which he was showered. They included a PhD from the Hebrew University, Jerusalem, a DCL from Oxford, and LLDs from London, Glasgow, Cambridge, Manchester, Strathclyde and Nottingham. When asked where he got all his degrees from he would say 'from writing'.

'And what do you write?'

'Cheques.'

Isaac Wolfson was born in Glasgow – he retained a Scottish accent – on 17 September 1897. He left school to earn 5 shillings a week in his father's furniture workshop and then 'went on the road' canvassing for orders, but it was not until 1932 that he found real scope for his acumen.

Great Universal Stores, an old-fashioned mail-order business, offered shares to the public and appointed a new managing director. His name was Isaac Wolfson. Within five years 'Gussies' was the largest mail-order business outside America, and Wolfson was well on the way to becoming the takeover 'king' of Britain. He was appointed chairman of the company in 1946, and was made life president in 1987.

He bought up competitors, drapery stores, furniture shops, factories. A guiding principle was to concentrate on areas in which Great Universal Stores already had expertise. In his invasion of the high streets he spent millions in cash and shares on buying up shops selling furniture, shoes and men's and women's clothing. He bought factories to supply the shops, and warehouses to store the goods. The success of this policy was reflected in the unrelentingly forward progress of 'Gussies', which turned in rising profits with astonishing consistency: 26 consecutive years of record profits reached a landmark in 1977, when the company was able simultaneously to report total sales of more than £1000 million and profits of more than £100 million. He denied that he was a financier, though. 'I am a *merchant*,' he said. 'Selling is my job, not finance.'

Wolfson, who was short and sturdy, with a face as impassive as a mask, spoke with great rapidity. When he met Khrushchev in Moscow in 1961 it was said that the Russian leader failed to get a word in during a ten-minute 'conversation'. This caused pleasure but no surprise to Wolfson's business associates.

It was once said that Sir Isaac's employees could set their watches by the time he reached his office, which was invariably 8 a.m. He neither drank alcohol or smoked, and took his only relaxation in the cinema – to him business was 'fun'. He once summed up his philosophy on money to a friend. 'No man should keep more than £100,000,' he said some years before he died. 'That's enough for any man. The rest should go to charity.'

By 1980, when the Wolfson Foundation had been in operation for 25 years, it had given away £42,862,741 – £15 million of this towards university buildings. The generosity was accompanied by an acuity similar to that which Sir Isaac displayed in his business transactions. In 1968, for instance, the Foundation gave grants totalling £1,505,200, more than £1 million of which went to a new venture to support technological projects that would help the modernisation of industry and improve Britain's commercial and economic position.

In the same year Sir Isaac commissioned Sir Solly Zuckerman, the scientific adviser and polymath, to carry out an appraisal of sixty projects, to which a total of £4 million had been given. The resulting report declared the Foundation to be a startling success. Wolfson was elected a Fellow of the Royal Society in 1963; he was also a member of the Court of Patrons of the Royal College of Surgeons and an honorary Fellow of the Weizmann Institute of Science in Israel. In 1967 Wolfson won the Einstein award for philanthropy; and he was made a freeman of the City of Glasgow in 1971.

In 1962 he became president of the United Synagogue, the leading synagogal organisation of Anglo-Jewry, which he would sometimes rule as if it were a subsidiary of Great Universal Stores. It was a critical time in the life of the community, which was nearly torn asunder by what came to be known as the Jacobs Affair.

Rabbi Jacobs had expressed views which seemed heretical to Dr Israel Brodie, the then Chief Rabbi, and he was prevented first from becoming principal of Jews' College and then from returning to the pulpit he had previously occupied in the new West End synagogue. Sir Isaac was no theologian, but he believed in the authority of the Chief Rabbi and supported him to the hilt. Later when Dr Brodie retired, he busied himself to find a successor of sufficient orthodoxy and alighted on Emmanuel Jakobovits, who was in many ways his personal choice. 'I've always been good at picking winners,' he would say.

In his philanthropy he was ably supported by his wife, the former Edith Specterman, in whose honour a forest of 50,000 trees was planted in Israel, to acknowledge her social work in that country.

He was created a baronet in 1962. His wife died in 1981. The heir to the baronetcy was his son, Leonard, born in 1927, who was knighted in 1977 and created a life peer as Baron Wolfson of Marylebone in 1985.

20 June 1991

~=∞ PART FOUR ∞=~

INFLUENCERS OF TASTE

ALDO BERNI – *creator of the steakhouse dining experience*
JOHNNY HOLBECH – *Gordon's Gin salesman*
SIR BERNARD MILLER – *chairman of the John Lewis Partnership*
AKIO MORITA – *father of the Sony Walkman*
LAXMISHANKER PATHAK – *Indian pickle maker*
GAD RAUSING – *Tetra Pak billionaire*
WILLIAM RUSSELL – *designer of the Russell Hobbs kettle*
LORD SAINSBURY – *the first British supermarket tycoon*
LORD SIEFF OF BRIMPTON – *dynamic head of Marks & Spencer*
LESLIE SMITH – *creator of Matchbox toys*
SIR NOEL STOCKDALE – *founder of ASDA supermarkets*
SIR GERALD WHENT – *mobile-phone pioneer*

Aldo Berni

⇢ 1909–1997 ⇠

Creator of the steakhouse dining experience

Aldo Berni was one of two brothers who founded Berni Inns, the chain of steakhouses that became a byword for plush down-market eating-out in the 1950s and '60s. The success of Berni Inns was based, in Aldo's words, on 'giving patrons what they like to eat at prices they like to pay'. An icon of postwar British culinary taste, the Berni dining experience was once a natural choice for a provincial night out. The menu offered a half-pound Argentinian rump steak with chips and peas, roll and butter and pudding or cheese for seven shillings and sixpence. At the top of the range, a prawn cocktail and fillet steak or scampi combination cost less than a pound. Diners were made comfortable with a schooner of medium sherry in a décor dominated by red, with paper napkins and velvet banquettes.

Inspired by limited-menu steakhouses the brothers had seen in America – where Aldo once dined with Frank Sinatra – the Berni formula was first developed at Horts restaurant in Bristol, where they established themselves after the war. At the end of the rationing era, when good meat was still a considerable luxury, the venture proved hugely successful, with customers queuing for tables.

The format was replicated all over the country, often in ancient hostelries like the Rummer in Bristol market – which Aldo described as 'a goldmine' – the New Inn at Gloucester, and – much loved and abused by bread-roll-throwing undergraduates – the Mitre at Oxford. At the height of the chain's success a new Berni Inn opened every month, until there were 147 around Britain and several in Japan.

Frank Berni, the elder of the brothers, was the financial brains of the business, while Aldo was a genial front man, popular with diners and suppliers alike and immensely hard-working. After Frank retired to the Channel Islands, Aldo became chairman, but in 1970 he sold the business for £14.5 million to Grand Metropolitan, which absorbed its own Schooner Inns under the Berni brand name. In 1990, the Berni chain was sold to Whitbread, which rebranded it as 'Beefeater Pubs'.

Aldo Berni was born on 14 March 1909 at Bardi in the Appennine Mountains of northern Italy, where he would ski to school in winter. At 15 he set off to join his father who had migrated to Ebbw Vale to seek his fortune in the café trade amid the prosperity of the Welsh coalfields. Though his two elder brothers retained strong traces of their Italian origins, Aldo acquired a distinctive Welsh lilt as a young man and was later proud to call himself a Bristolian.

He was a contemporary and friend of Charles Forte, whose family had followed a similar path from Italy: 'They were talented, we were lucky,' Aldo once remarked.

When Aldo's mother died, he and Frank invested their modest inheritance in a café in Exeter, and by the early years of the Second World War they had branched out to Plymouth and Clifton. Both his brothers were interned, but Aldo was allowed to work in a garden nursery, continuing to run his business by bicycle in the evening. The cafés suffered war damage, but trade recovered and after floating their company on the Bristol stock exchange in 1948, the brothers were able to acquire Horts, one of the city's most fashionable watering holes, and to go on to build a substantial catering empire. After the sale to Grand Metropolitan, Aldo was on close terms with Sir Maxwell Joseph, Grand Met's founder, and retained a non-executive role in the business until the late 1970s.

Aldo Berni was good company – well read, generous-spirited and full of good humour. In retirement he devoted himself to golf and dining out – which he did as often as he could, relishing every kind of cuisine except Indian. But he did not flaunt his wealth, and he quietly helped many people less fortunate than himself.

He married, in 1947, Esmé Clifton; they had a daughter.

12 October 1997

Johnny Holbech

◦⊷⊜ 1921–2004 ⊜⊶◦

Gordon's Gin salesman

Johnny Holbech was the managing director of Gordon's Gin and was responsible for making it one of Britain's best-recognised brands.

Holbech took a job as a sales rep for Gordon's in the West End of London in 1950, and became a tireless advocate and consumer of his product, declaring, 'There are only three elements in life: oxygen, nitrogen and Gordon's.'

His day began at 10 a.m. with calls on wholesalers and off-licences, and continued with bars and drinking clubs; an afternoon nap at his flat off Park Lane prepared him for an evening round of restaurants and hotels, and nightclubs kept him busy into the early hours. Within a few years he made Gordon's the most fashionable gin in the West End – which had not been the case before the war – and in due course it became the best-selling gin in the country.

He was promoted to home sales director in 1957 and made managing director of Gordon's in 1971 – also taking responsibility for promoting Tanqueray Gin in the United States, where Gordon's itself was licensed to another distiller. Tanqueray subsequently became America's top imported gin, with sales of more than a million cases a year.

Holbech became the first honorary member of the International Bartenders Association, and was celebrated in the trade for the hospitality of his boardroom at Gordon's Clerkenwell distillery, where his birthday lunches traditionally ended with Silver Streaks – equal measures of gin and kümmel.

John Ronald Christopher Holbech was born on 12 December 1921, the third son of Ronnie Holbech who – though wheelchair-bound by polio – was a prominent figure in Warwickshire and Oxfordshire life. The family seat, Farnborough Hall near Banbury (now a National Trust property) had been acquired in 1683 by Ambrose Holbech, the son of a prosperous lawyer, and was inherited by Ronnie on the death of his elder brother at Ypres in 1914.

Johnny was educated at Windlesham House prep school (which he described as 'miserable rotten' in his first letter home) and Stowe, where his greatest achievements were on the tennis court, though he also played trumpet and accordion in the school band and won the poetry prize – later hinting that the winning poem might not have been entirely his own work. The possibility of going to Oxford was discussed with his father – a Magdalen man – but since Johnny's ambition at the time was to become a journalist, they agreed instead that he should enrol at the Marlborough Secretarial College, where he learned shorthand and typing in a class consisting of him and 22 girls. Having failed his Army medical due to a burst appendix, Holbech enlisted in the Home Guard and became a bombardier in an artillery unit in Hyde Park that was credited with shooting down a German bomber.

The war ended with a family tragedy: Johnny and his eldest brother Edward, a decorated RAF officer to whom he was very close, were involved in a car crash after a party in Warwickshire on VJ Day; Edward was killed but Johnny survived with broken bones.

Holbech often joked that as the youngest son of a country squire he should have gone into the Church, as many of his forebears had done. Instead he found work during and after the war in publishing, but without much enthusiasm: he was sacked from one job for taking afternoons off to go racing, and was reduced for a time to selling advertising space on railway maps. It was his surviving brother Geoffrey – then the Midlands representative for Gordon's – who suggested he apply for the sales job in the West End, and from there his career blossomed.

Later, Holbech was a director of the Distillers Company, Gordon's parent company, and chairman of its white spirits division, which also made Booth's and High & Dry gin, Cossack Vodka and Pimm's. He retired in 1986, shortly after the takeover of Distillers by Guinness, which brought an end to the convivial corporate life of earlier days.

Away from work, Holbech loved racing and gambling to which he had been introduced by his father – at whose burial in 1956 he threw a bookmaker's ticket into the grave. In the bachelor days between his two marriages, Johnny's summer holiday consisted of a week at Goodwood and a fortnight in Monte Carlo; he once lost almost a year's salary attempting to bail himself out on the last race at Ascot, and was only persuaded to give up high-stakes poker by his second wife Liz, who was a steadying influence throughout his later years.

He was also a keen golfer at St Andrews, in White's club tournaments and latterly at the New Zealand club in Surrey. His greatest success was victory with the American player Fuzzy Zoeller in a pro-am tournament before the World Matchplay event at Wentworth in 1979: Zoeller autographed his match card with the observation that Holbech was 'a useless golfer, but a one-handicap at the bar'.

Johnny Holbech married first, in 1946, Jean Palethorpe, the daughter of a sausage manufacturer. The marriage was dissolved in 1950 and he married secondly, in 1962, Elizabeth Matthews; they had twin sons.

30 August 2004

Sir Bernard Miller

⤛⥱ 1904–2003 ⥱⤜

Chairman of John Lewis Partnership

Sir Bernard Miller was chairman of John Lewis Partnership, the department store group, in succession to the founder Spedan Lewis – whose radical principles of employee ownership he nurtured and developed.

Spedan Lewis inherited the drapery stores of John Lewis in Oxford Street and Peter Jones in Sloane Square and formed them into a partnership for the benefit of their employees in 1929, declaring: 'I want no more money for myself. The fortune I have inherited from my father is a sufficient prepayment for my life's work.' Bernard Miller, who had joined him from Oxford two years earlier, was one of his closest associates in the development of a radical, and in some respects unique, corporate model: all permanent staff of the group could become profit-sharing partners, and senior management was accountable to an elected council.

Spedan Lewis was an inspirational figure who treated Miller almost as a son, but was also, at times, extraordinarily difficult. He originally intended to remain in office until he was 75 in 1960, and then to hand over to his son Edward. But in 1951, while an undergraduate at Oxford, Edward himself declined the succession on the grounds that he would be too young to take charge, and Spedan Lewis turned instead to Miller, who held the title of 'general inspector' of the group.

Miller became deputy chairman, and succeeded as chairman in 1955. But Spedan Lewis made it clear that he had no intention of retiring quietly from the partnership's affairs. Five years later, he became convinced that his protégé was straying from the path of wisdom and complained in the *Gazette*, the partnership's weekly newspaper, that Miller was guilty of 'grave errors of judgement' on the matter of fair pay. Lewis claimed to have been 'gagged and sent to Coventry'. The Partnership's council voted heavily against proposals from Lewis that Miller should be compelled to follow Lewis's guidance, and that former chairmen 'not certified to be incapacitated by mental illness' – meaning, of course, Lewis himself – should be able to commandeer space in the *Gazette*.

Lewis went on to describe Miller as 'a very sincere, well-meaning person, but not very clever and exceedingly obstinate. If I had known that the effect of giving him the chairmanship would be what it is I would have left him in the general inspectorate.' A man of quiet authority, Miller handled this onslaught with patience and loyalty, and remained privately on good terms with Spedan Lewis until his death in 1963.

Oswald Bernard Miller was born in Chelsea on 25 March 1904. He was educated at Sloane School and Jesus College, Oxford, where he took a First in history and won the Stanhope Prize for an essay on Robert Harley, Earl of Oxford which was published as a biography. His ambition was to be a civil servant or a schoolmaster until a careers officer arranged an interview with the captivating

Spedan Lewis, who he found to be 'almost on the point of explosion all the time'.

He joined the firm and (though colour blind) became a salesman in John Lewis's Oxford Street silk room. When Spedan Lewis's father John, a Victorian tyrant then 92, came in his Rolls-Royce to inspect, Miller had to don a Homburg hat and pretend to be a customer, since Lewis père strongly disapproved of his son's habit of recruiting intellectuals rather than traditional drapers. Old John Lewis died in 1928, and Spedan set to work devising the partnership constitution. Miller was his first personal assistant, and over the following years he was one of an inner group which carried the task of turning Spedan Lewis's ideas into practice. He became a director in 1935 and was the firm's financial controller, introducing pioneering systems of budgetary control.

During Miller's chairmanship from 1955 to 1972, the number of partners expanded from 12,000 to 20,000, and distribution of profit rose steadily from 8 per cent of annual pay to more than 13 per cent. The group's sales rose from £25 million a year to more than £100 million, the Oxford Street store was redeveloped, and the Waitrose supermarket subsidiary grew. Miller maintained the group's value-for-money reputation and put his stamp on the partnership in an unobtrusive way, increasing the powers of its central council and maintaining lively communication with partners at every level. The precepts of partnership were central to his credo, and he had no interest at all in personal wealth.

When he retired from the chair in 1972 he nominated his own successor under a procedure laid down by Spedan which involved lodging in a bank vault a secret list of possible successors in preferred order. Miller's choice fell on Peter Lewis, a grandson of Spedan.

Bernard Miller was chairman of the Retail Distributors Association, and a member of the Monopolies Commission, the Economic Development Council for the Distributive Trades, and the Council of Industrial Design. He was also pro-chancellor of the University of Southampton, chairman of the Glyndebourne Festival Society, a council member of the Royal Society of Arts and a governor of Milton Abbey School. He was knighted in 1967.

Bernard Miller was a voracious reader of newspapers, a music lover and a fisherman. Long into old age, he remained active in the social life of the partnership and its pensioners.

He married in 1931 Jessica ffoulkes, who was a John Lewis buyer; they lived for many years on the partnership's estate at Cookham in Berkshire, and had three sons, two of whom also rose to senior positions in the partnership. Lady Miller died in 1985.

23 February 2003

Akio Morita

⊷⟟⟾⟾⟾ 1921–1999 ⟾⟾⟾⟟⊷

Father of the Sony Walkman

Akio Morita was one of the most influential industrialists of the 20th century; he was chairman and co-founder of Sony Corporation, the Japanese electronics giant. Morita was virtually unique among Japanese corporate chiefs in becoming an international household name in his own right. With his business partner Masaru Ibuka, he pioneered electronic products which entered the lives of hundreds of millions of people: the transistor radio, the Walkman personal stereo and the hand-held video camera.

A man of tireless energy, Morita was a marketing genius and an outspoken pundit on international trade issues. He possessed the chameleon qualities and boundless confidence of a super-salesman, coupled with a gift for lateral thinking and fearless speech – all un-Japanese attributes which caused him often to be described as a Westernised maverick. But he remained at heart deeply Japanese.

Akio Morita was born in Nagoya on 26 January 1921, the eldest son of Kyuzaemon Morita, a 14th-generation head of a sake brewery founded in the 17th century. The family was wealthy, and socially prominent: a bronze statue of a 19th-century Morita patriarch stood in Kosugaya, the family's native village. Young Akio was expected to succeed his father in the family business, but from an early age he showed a preference for science.

Graduating in physics from Osaka Imperial University in 1944, Morita joined the navy as a cadet technical officer. It was at meetings of a secret research committee that he first met Ibuka, then a small-time supplier of electronic equipment to the military. After the war they made contact again. Morita had obtained a teaching post at the Tokyo Institute of Technology, but General MacArthur issued an order banning former military officers from such appointments. By 1946 Ibuka was making voltmeters and crude electric rice-cookers from a workshop in a bombed-out Tokyo department store. Morita persuaded his father to let him join the nascent electronics enterprise rather than returning to the sake trade. In May 1946, Morita and Ibuka incorporated Tokyo Telecommunications Engineering Co, with $500 of capital.

From its earliest days – although operating from little more than a shack in suburban Shinagawa – the company declared high ideals in terms of use of technology and of enlightened management of its workforce. Its initial achievement was to develop Japan's first tape recorder. The two partners had complementary skills. Both were skilled engineers, but while Ibuka was a perfectionist in product development, Morita had a genius for marketing and a shrewd understanding of finance. 'My mission became to realise Ibuka's dream,' he said.

Since vinyl was unavailable, the tape was made of paper, requiring a mechanism of great precision in order to minimise tape breakages. The first machine was sold to a noodle shop for use in a form of karaoke, but real progress came when the ministries of justice and education began to buy the machines for courtrooms and schools.

Morita went to the United States for the first time in 1953, to negotiate for $25,000, then a huge sum for his company, a licence to make transistors, a seminal advance in the miniaturisation of electrical circuitry. The holders of the patent, Western Electric Co, told him that the device was so limited in its power that it could be used only in hearing aids. The Ministry of Trade and Industry, engine room of the Japanese economic miracle, was reluctant to lend its support.

But Ibuka and Morita were determined to use transistors to

make radios. They set out to design radio sets which were truly portable. The first model, the TR-55, appeared in 1955. The TR-55 also used the brand name 'Sony' for the first time. It was intended to combine echoes of 'sonic' and 'sonny': 'We are a couple of sonny boys,' Morita liked to say. Sony became the company name in 1957.

At the end of his 1953 trip, Morita had also visited Britain and continental Europe for the first time, travelling to Eindhoven in rural Holland to see the mighty Philips electronics company. He was deeply impressed that a high-tech company of world standing could be built by one man (Dr Gerard Philips) in such an out-of-the-way place. 'Maybe,' he wrote later, 'we could do the same thing in Japan.'

Although by no means the biggest Japanese electronics company, Sony was a leader in raising the reputation of Japanese goods abroad, and in developing new products. Morita believed in challenging conventional wisdom, and in leading consumer tastes rather than reacting to them. The Walkman was his own inspiration: he believed that it would never have come to the market if the firm had commissioned research beforehand to ask whether people would buy it. He even named the product himself.

Perhaps Sony's only real failure in this respect was the development of the Betamax video-recording system. The decision that their tape cassette should be no larger than an airport paperback meant, crucially, that in the early competition against the rival VHS system, a Betamax tape was too short to record an entire American baseball game. VHS consequently became the standard format.

Other Sony successes, however, included the Trinitron portable colour television, the pocket-sized television ('Watch-Man') and the video camcorder. Under Morita's influence, Sony became truly international, one of the first to appoint non-Japanese executives to senior positions. Morita himself travelled relentlessly, and was president of the American subsidiary from 1960 to 1966. Plants were established in America and Europe, including the one at Bridgend, South Wales. Morita frequently lectured his fellow Japanese on the need to open up to Western business influences and products. But he was also highly critical of the rest of the world, particularly the United States. American decision-makers were too short-term in their thinking, he said, looking ahead ten minutes rather than ten years.

In 1989, he contributed to *The Japan That Can Say No*, a controversial book attacking US trade and foreign policy which included (largely on the part of his co-author, right-wing politician Shintaro Ishihara) accusations of racial prejudice, intimidation and hypocrisy. When a pirate translation began to circulate in Washington, Morita disassociated himself from it, saying that in highlighting 'defects' in America, he had spoken out merely as 'a friend who is worried'.

Morita seemed more genuinely Anglophile. He took pride in the achievements and atmosphere of Sony's Bridgend plant, though in the 1970s he despaired of the power of British trade unions and lamented Britain's lack of respect for engineering and manufacturing. 'Someone once mentioned to me that many UK corporations are headed by chartered accountants,' he told an audience at the Royal Society in London in 1992. 'This strikes me as very curious.' Over breakfast in Tokyo, he advised Margaret Thatcher to 'change your society's concept to make people respect engineers'.

Morita stepped down as president of Sony in 1989, but remained active as an ambassadorial chairman. Export profitability declined with the recession, and product innovations failed to sustain the clear market leadership achieved by earlier successes. But Sony remained in the forefront of new ideas. Among these was the breaking down of barriers between the electronic and media industries. Sony acquired Columbia Pictures and CBS records at a total cost of $8.5 billion, combining the 'software' of film and music production with the 'hardware' of its consumer products, and established a link with Apple computers.

Morita was a vice-chairman of Keidanren, the Japanese CBI, and had been expected to succeed as chairman. He was said to have declined the post of Foreign Minister, and was touted as a possible Finance Minister in the cabinet of reformist premier Morihiro Hosokawa after the 1993 general election.

Morita had a deep love of music, and counted Leonard Bernstein and Herbert von Karajan among his personal friends. His proudest possessions included a 1910 baby grand player-piano with a vast collection of piano rolls, including recordings of Gershwin and Rachmaninov playing their own works.

His autobiography, *Made in Japan: Akio Morita and Sony,* was published in English in 1987. He was appointed honorary KBE in 1992.

Morita married, in 1950, Yoshiko Kamei. They had two sons (educated at English boarding schools and American colleges) and a daughter. The family home, a hill-top mansion in suburban Tokyo, was an eclectic mixture of Japanese and Western styles, equipped with 200 hi-fi speakers.

3 October 1999

Laxmishanker Pathak

1924–1997

Indian pickle maker

Laxmishanker Pathak was the founder of one of Britain's most successful Asian food businesses. Pathak began his enterprise with £5 in 1956 and laid the foundation of a multimillion-pound empire, based on authentic Indian recipes and ingredients. Patak's (the 'h' was dropped from the brand name to make it easier to pronounce) supplied pastes, sauces, pickles, chutneys and pappadums to the vast majority of Britain's 10,000-plus Indian restaurants, and to more than forty other countries. With the growth in enthusiasm for ethnic cooking at home, the Patak range also became familiar to millions of supermarket customers. Patak products were even smuggled back into India by black-marketeers.

In India itself, Pathak was best known for his accusations of fraud against former prime minister N.V. Narasimha Rao. Pathak alleged that, after a meeting with Rao in New York in 1983, he had paid $100,000 to Rao's personal guru, known as Chrandraswami, on the understanding that Rao (who was then foreign minister) would secure for Pathak a government contract to supply newsprint and paper pulp. The contract never materialised. Confined to a wheelchair by illness, Pathak gave evidence to the high court in New Delhi a few months before he died.

Laxmishanker G. Pathak, usually known as Lakhubhai Pathak, was born in India in 1924. His family emigrated in the 1930s to Kenya, where they ran a successful shop selling Indian sweets and savouries. But the Mau Mau terror in 1956 forced them to move again, and Pathak arrived in London with his young family and £5 in his pocket. The only work offered to him was drain-cleaning for Camden Council, which he declined. Instead he began making sweets and samosas in the basement of a rented house in Kentish Town. Having borrowed money from a relative he sent his sons to an Irish boarding school run by nuns, from which one of them returned to surprise the Hindu Pathaks by announcing in an Irish accent his ambition to become Pope.

Meanwhile, Pathak and his wife worked 18 hours per day, hawking their products around London's growing Indian community. By the late 1950s they had saved enough money to buy a shop. Ten years later, the company was supplying spices, pastes and sweetmeats to most of Britain's Indian restaurants, but Pathak burned his fingers in a dubious distribution contract and bankruptcy threatened. The operation had to be rebuilt, with Pathak's eldest son Kirit recalled from college to run an outlet in Golders Green which took little more than £2 a day.

But the family prospered again in 1972 with the arrival in British transit camps of many thousands of Asians expelled from Idi Amin's Uganda. Pathak won the contract to supply food to the camps and also provided new arrivals with valuable information about life in Britain, including printed instructions on how to use a Western lavatory. When many refugees went on to open their own shops and restaurants, they asked Pathak to supply them.

In 1976, Pathak handed over the day-to-day running of the business to Kirit and Kirit's wife Meena, a graduate in food technology. Two years later the operation moved to Wigan, taking advantage of the damp air for the storage of spices. Pathak himself made his home in Bolton and was involved in a range of other trading activities. Kirit described his father as 'a hard taskmaster', often critical of the younger generation. But Patak's came to be quoted as a model of brand-name development in business school textbooks, and the family's wealth was estimated at £60 million.

In 1988 Lakhubhai Pathak established a charitable foundation to promote health and education for the poor in India and elsewhere.

He was survived by his wife Shanta, their four sons and two daughters.

31 March 1997

Gad Rausing

◆►══◑ 1922–2000 ◑══◄◆

Swedish Tetra Pak billionaire

Gad Rausing, the Swedish industrialist, was one of the world's richest men – thanks to his father's development of the Tetra Pak milk carton. Rausing and his younger brother Hans controlled what was virtually a worldwide monopoly in milk and fruit juice cartons, with sales in 170 countries amounting to more than 68 billion cartons per year. Their fortune was estimated at up to £5 billion, but both their business affairs and their personal lives were conducted in total privacy. Though Gad Rausing was for much of the 1980s and '90s one of London's richest residents, he was almost completely unknown, even to the most avid readers of gossip columns.

Gad Rausing was born in Bromma, near Stockholm, in May 1922. The family's original name was Andersson – which is very common in Sweden – but Gad's father Ruben changed it to the more distinctive Rausing, derived from his native village of Raus.

Ruben trained as an economist and studied in the United States; having observed American advances in retail distribution, he returned to Sweden in the early 1920s and founded a rudimentary packaging business, breaking down sacks of flour and sugar into smaller, more saleable packets. In 1944, Ruben was watching his wife make sausages in the family kitchen at Lund in southern

Sweden when the idea of the Tetra Pak carton came to him. Observing how the sausage skins were pinched at each end to close them, he decided to test the principle on milk cartons.

He employed a research scientist to perfect the design, based on a tetrahedron, in which the hygienic seal removed the need for refrigeration. Ruben acquired the patent, and by 1952 the Tetra Pak was in commercial production.

Gad was the eldest of Ruben's three sons. He studied chemistry, economics and statistics at Lund University before joining the family business, by now a diversified industrial group. It was his younger brother Hans, however, who was the most business-minded, and emerged as Ruben's heir apparent.

By the mid-1960s, the business was struggling for lack of profits, and the family sold out – but wisely bought back all the rights to the Tetra Pak. From then on their business – ultimately controlled in Liechtenstein – was conducted in some secrecy, with no outside shareholders. They developed numerous variations of the product (the Tetra Brik, for example, and aluminium foil linings) while maintaining vigorous control of their patents; profits multiplied many times over.

In due course the original cardboard Tetra Pak – which could often be difficult to open – was improved by the introduction of resealable plastic tabs, for which ironically, the company had to pay royalties to a rival Norwegian packaging group.

Ruben Rausing died in 1983 and at around the same time Gad and Hans moved to England to escape punitive Swedish tax rates. They gradually handed over management control to younger executives, but the company continued to expand its geographical reach, exporting to Eastern Europe, China and Russia, and was enlarged in 1991 by the acquisition of another Swedish industrial group, Alfa Laval.

Gad lived in discreet opulence in Holland Park, while Hans acquired an estate in Sussex. For a family of such wealth they maintained a remarkably low profile, their appearances in the press being largely confined to annual listings of Britain's richest residents.

In the mid-1990s, Gad bought out his brother's 50 per cent

shareholding in Tetra Laval for an estimated £4 billion and quietly moved to Lausanne in Switzerland. He retained what was described as a 'summer cabin' in Sweden, but in 1995 it was reported that he had objected – on the grounds that he was rarely there – to a £2.50 surcharge on the annual rate for refuse collection.

Gad Rausing was more easy-going than his brother Hans, and enjoyed telling funny stories. His real passion was archeology: he wrote a doctoral thesis on Viking weapons, funded archeological projects in Sweden and was a member of the Royal Swedish Academy of Letters, History and Antiquities.

He married, in 1949, Birgit ('Bib') Mayne, daughter of the Swedish artist Henry Mayne. They had met on an archeological dig in Sweden during their university days. Their sons Finn and Joern continued to run the business empire; a daughter, Kirsten, became a racehorse breeder at Newmarket.

28 January 2000

William Russell

⊶⊫⊳ 1920–2005 ⊰⊨⊶

Designer of the Russell Hobbs electric kettle

William Russell was the designer of the Russell Hobbs electric kettle, one of the most iconic domestic appliances of the postwar era. Russell went into business with Peter Hobbs in 1952 to design and manufacture a coffee percolator capable of keeping coffee hot – but not boiling – after it had been made. They also produced an automatic tea-maker, though it struggled to compete against the ubiquitous Goblin Teasmade. But it was the K1 kettle, launched in 1956, that established the reputation of Russell Hobbs for elegant modernity and innovation.

Earlier electric kettles were essentially Victorian in appearance, and hazardous in operation because they lacked reliable automatic mechanisms to switch them off when they boiled. Bill Russell's design combined the handle and switch housing into one sleek shape and incorporated a bimetal strip, activated by steam, that triggered the disconnection of the heating element.

A modest, self-effacing man who believed that a well-designed product would sell itself without extravagant marketing, Russell was an engineer with an unusually romantic streak, enthralled by the processes of design and manufacture. His 1960 K2 kettle – an improved version of the K1 – remained in production until the late 1970s and was in use in many British kitchens long after that; an example of it was acquired by the Design Museum in London.

William Morris Russell was born on 22 July 1920. It was his father, a printer, who pointed him towards electrical engineering as a career, but his aptitude for design may have come from his mother's family, in which there were a number of artists: it was she who chose to name him after the founder of the Arts and Crafts movement. At 13, he won a scholarship to High Wycombe Technical Institute; he went on to become an apprentice with the Rheostatic Company in Slough, a maker of automated controls and switchgear, where he completed a diploma in engineering.

Although he was in a 'protected profession', Russell volunteered for REME in 1943 and was commissioned, serving in anti-aircraft batteries until the end of the war. He was then posted to train troops in India and Ethiopia, and was demobilised as a major in 1947, when he joined Morphy Richards, a maker of domestic appliances. There he contributed to the design of three essentials of the middle-class postwar household: the pop-up toaster, the electric iron and the hairdryer. Peter Hobbs, meanwhile, had been running Morphy Richards' South African arm, but after returning to England he worked for another company which was trying to use a German patent to perfect a coffee percolator – the problem being the introduction of an electric element into a ceramic pot. Hobbs consulted Russell and a solution was found – but the two swiftly agreed that it would be better to apply it in a venture of their own.

Russell Hobbs came into being in a run-down factory in Croydon, with Russell in charge of product development and Hobbs as sales director. Packaging prototypes were handmade on the Russell living-room floor and manufacturing tools devised with the help of Meccano. Russell liked to claim that his final safety test for any new product was to 'pour half a pint of boiling gravy on it'.

The business was in profit from its first year, and Russell Hobbs percolators and kettles became fixtures of every wedding list of the era. By 1963, pressure to expand production forced the partners to look for new capital, and they decided to sell to the conglomerate Tube Investments (TI), which owned several other consumer electrical brands. Production was relocated to a factory in Staffordshire which was shared with Creda, a TI subsidiary that made cookers. Russell in due course became technical director of Creda before moving to run Turnright, a Portsmouth-based TI company that made control and regulation devices. Russell Hobbs itself was eventually sold by TI to Polly Peck, the group run by the entrepreneur Asil Nadir. After Polly Peck collapsed, it was sold twice more, but retained its distinctive brand identity; it is now under American ownership.

William Russell was a dedicated gardener at his home near Chichester, and a keen sailor in earlier years. He had a great love of music, especially Wagnerian opera. He married Anne Swabey in 1944; they had two sons.

16 February 2005

Lord Sainsbury

◦═══◦ 1902–1998 ◦═══◦

The first British supermarket tycoon

Lord Sainsbury was joint president of J Sainsbury, the grocery chain, and the senior member of Britain's richest business dynasty. 'Mr Alan', as he was known within the company, was a spirited and forward-looking entrepreneur, who pioneered the concept of self-service supermarkets in Britain. His fiery personality found expression both in the promotion of the Sainsbury brand name and in the field of politics, where he was a champion of consumer rights.

For thirty years he worked in harmonious partnership with his less flamboyant younger brother, Robert. While Robert took care of the administrative functions, Alan drove the firm's trading activities and was its public spokesman. Between them they modernised and expanded Sainsbury's, making it one of Britain's most successful businesses, and a hallmark of quality in the grocery trade. They also consolidated a family fortune estimated at some £2.5 billion.

After the end of the Second World War, the Ministry of Food was keen to promote improvements in British food retailing, and in 1949 Alan Sainsbury was provided with a diplomatic passport to visit the United States and study innovations there. He returned 'thrilled and stimulated at the potential of self-service trading', and ordered the conversion of Sainsbury's Croydon branch to that purpose. When the store re-opened as Britain's first real supermarket in June 1950, reaction was mixed. One customer, offered a wire basket by Alan at the entrance, threw it back at him in contempt. At the Purley branch, a judge's wife hurled abuse at him when she discovered that she was expected to carry her own purchases. Competitors declared that the idea would never catch on. 'How wrong they were', Alan said later, 'and how lucky we were that they were wrong.'

Alan John Sainsbury was born on 13 August 1902. He was the elder son of John Benjamin Sainsbury by his wife Mabel, née Van den Bergh, whose family, of Dutch Jewish origins, made a fortune from the manufacture of margarine. John Benjamin (known as 'Mr John') was in turn the eldest son of John James and Mary Ann Sainsbury, whose wedding day, 20 April 1869, is regarded by the firm as its official foundation date – though their first shop, selling butter, eggs and milk at 173 Drury Lane, opened for business some months earlier. Under Mr John's leadership the firm grew to become a chain of 250 grocery shops throughout the south of England, East Anglia and the Midlands. Mr John was chairman of J Sainsbury from his father's death in 1928 until his own in 1956.

Young Alan was educated at Haileybury before joining the family business in 1921. He learned all aspects of trading, beginning with the buying of eggs and dairy produce under the supervision of two of his uncles, Arthur and Alfred Sainsbury. He also spent a period incognito on the sales counter of the Boscombe branch. Alan became a director of the company in 1933, and joint general manager, with Robert, in 1938, when their father yielded executive power after a minor heart attack. The brothers steered the business through the many difficulties of the war years – which included food shortages, drastically reduced sales and bombed-out stores. Alan served on a number of wartime consultative committees at the Ministry of Food.

In the 1950s and early '60s the group continued to expand by opening larger, purpose-built self-service stores. Alan also pioneered other developments. Clean, modern designs were adopted for own-label packaging, and the slogan 'Good Food Costs Less at Sainsbury's' was introduced. Frozen 'oven-ready' chicken and many other frozen food lines changed everyday British eating habits. Fresh fruit and vegetables were added to the product range. Old-fashioned outlets, including his grandparents' shop in Drury Lane, were closed down. Alan was chairman of the company from 1956 to 1967, but he and Robert continued to use the title of joint general manager until 1962, when they began to hand over day-to-day responsibility to the next generation.

Alan's three sons had all entered the business: the eldest, John ('Mr JD' within the firm, and later Lord Sainsbury of Preston Candover), was to become chairman in 1969; the younger sons, Tim (Sir Tim and the former MP for Hove) and Simon, were also directors. In retirement, Alan and Robert became joint life presidents.

Alan Sainsbury was, at various times, a member of several political parties. He stood as Liberal candidate for Sudbury in the general elections of 1929, 1931 and 1935. Having publicly welcomed the Beveridge Report outlining the postwar welfare state – which was attuned with Sainsbury's progressive company policies on staff welfare – he joined the Labour Party in 1945, and became a generous financial supporter. When he was created a life peer on the recommendation of Hugh Gaitskell in 1962, he took the Labour whip. But in February 1981, he was one of a list of 100 prominent supporters published by Labour's 'Gang of Four' as they broke away to form the SDP.

As Lord Sainsbury, he played an active part in the House of Lords, particularly on consumer issues. In the mid-1960s he had campaigned vigorously against trading stamps, which some of Sainsbury's competitors were giving away to attract customer loyalty; he believed the stamps to be an unfair trading device that could only lead to higher prices. He also opposed retail-price maintenance, which again he felt was against the customers' interests. At the time of his retirement from business in 1967 there were rumours that he might be offered a post in the Wilson government.

Sainsbury sat on innumerable public committees relating to food and commerce, including the 'Little Neddy' for the distributive trades in the late 1960s. He was chairman of the Food Research Advisory Committee, and of an inquiry into the relationship between the pharmaceutical industry and the National Health Service. He was also president of the Multiple Stores Federation, the Grocers' Institute, the International Association of Chain Stores and the Royal Institute of Public Health and Hygiene. He was a generous benefactor of many Third World charities, and was president of the Pestalozzi Children's Village Trust.

Alan Sainsbury married first, in 1925, Doreen Davan Adams, who was a dancer in the early days of the Royal Ballet company; they had three sons. The marriage was dissolved in 1939 and he married secondly, in 1944, Anne Lewy, by whom he had a daughter. Both wives predeceased him.

21 October 1998

Lord Sieff of Brimpton

⋈ 1913–2001 ⋈

Dynamic head of Marks & Spencer

Lord Sieff was chairman of Marks & Spencer from 1972 to 1984 and a tireless evangelist for the philosophy on which it had been built. He was also a leading figure in British Zionism.

The third generation to run the family business, Marcus Sieff was descended from two penniless immigrants from Poland. One of them, Ephraim Sieff, had established a business in Manchester sorting and reselling cotton waste; whilst the other, Michael Marks, had borrowed £5 to buy goods to peddle in the villages around

Leeds, and went on to establish a stall in Leeds market under the slogan 'Don't ask the price, it's a penny'.

Michael (to whom the trademark 'St Michael' was a tribute) established Marks & Spencer as a chain of 'penny bazaars' in 1894. The Sieff and Marks families were neighbours in suburban Manchester. The second generation, Israel Sieff and Simon Marks (both later to become peers), were schoolfriends who married each other's sisters. Their business partnership was cemented in 1917, when control of Marks & Spencer was bought back, after a falling-out, from the successor of the original Spencer partner.

The management precepts of which Marcus Sieff was to become an eloquent exponent were largely developed by his uncle, Simon, and put into practice by his father, Israel, as the shop chain expanded in the 1930s. The first principle was one of quality control and value for money, which involved long-term co-operation with suppliers of merchandise and meticulous scrutiny of their manufacturing processes. Equally important was staff welfare – including a range of benefits from restaurants to hairdressing and chiropody. Executives were encouraged to minimise bureaucracy and to keep in touch with day-to-day business.

Marcus Sieff reached the top of the firm in the late 1960s. His tenure at the top of the firm coincided with the darkest period of British labour relations and industrial decline. He repeatedly preached the merits of Marks & Spencer's version of free enterprise 'with a human face'; as well as the harmful effect of high taxation and government interference. He also emphasised the firm's then policy of buying more than 90 per cent of its merchandise from British manufacturers, urging other retailers to do likewise.

An ebullient, strong-jawed extrovert, Sieff admitted in his autobiography that he was 'never modest' and that he enjoyed the sound of his own voice. But the business he ran spoke for itself, both in its sustained profitability and in the extent to which it entered the national consciousness as a hallmark of good value.

Devotion to the Zionist cause was the second great theme of Sieff's life, and also very much a family tradition. His earliest recollection was of being taken at the age of four, in November 1917, to a meeting in the Manchester Free Trade Hall to celebrate the announcement of the Balfour Declaration. The principal speaker was Dr Chaim Weizmann, a friend of Sieff's parents and later first president of Israel. Marcus himself first visited Palestine as a schoolboy in 1929, when it was still largely desert and swamp. His mother, Becky, a formidable activist for the Women's Zionist Movement, bought farmland near Tel Aviv in 1935.

When the state of Israel was declared in 1948, Sieff received a message from the Prime Minister David Ben Gurion, requesting his help in the impending conflict with Israel's Arab neighbours. Although still a colonel in the British Army Reserve, Sieff became transport adviser to the Israeli ministry of defence. Throughout Israel's War of Independence, Sieff participated in Ben Gurion's innermost councils, bringing his wartime experience (as a movements control officer in the North African desert) to bear on the Israeli forces. He was close to President Weizmann, whom he described as his mentor, and was later chairman of the Weizmann Institute Foundation. He also befriended many of the future leaders of Israel, from Golda Meir to the young Shimon Peres.

Sieff remained a constant supporter and fund-raiser for the Israeli cause, although always in favour of peace. His memoirs revealed that in 1974, James Callaghan, as Foreign Secretary, had offered him the post of British ambassador to Israel. He declined, saying, 'No one would believe that I would put the United Kingdom's interests first, even if I was doing so.' After the Camp David agreement in 1979, Sieff sought to help the peace process by offering commercial advice to Egypt. He had a series of meetings with President Sadat, for whom he developed a warm regard.

During the premierships of Begin and Shamir, Sieff was sometimes critical both of Israel's lack of firm economic management and of its intransigent foreign policy, which he feared would not allow peace in the region in his lifetime. But he remained a supporter of Shimon Peres as prime minister and later as foreign minister, and lived to welcome the 1993 accord with the Palestine Liberation Organisation.

Marcus Joseph Sieff was born in Didsbury, Manchester, on 2 July 1913. The Sieff household was traditionally Jewish, although not orthodox. Young Marcus was educated first at Manchester

Grammar School, then – the family having moved to London in 1926 – at St Paul's. He went on to read economics at Corpus Christi College, Cambridge, and entered the family business, working in its Hammersmith Broadway store at £2 10 shillings per week, in 1935. At the outbreak of the Second World War, Sieff was a subaltern in a Territorial unit of the Royal Engineers. Posted first to North Africa and later to Italy, he became an expert in movement control and achieved rapid promotion despite a headstrong and sometimes arrogant style.

Told that he would be responsible for forthcoming deployments in Istanbul, he embarked on a reconnoitre disguised – ineffectively – as a tourist and was ordered out of the country by Turkish police. On the eve of El Alamein, he adopted an order of battle intended to bring men and munitions more quickly to the front line, overriding instructions to abide by conventional transport plans. The threat of a court of inquiry was deflected by a telegram of thanks to his unit from General Montgomery after the battle was won.

After the war Sieff returned to Marks & Spencer, but took leave of absence in May 1948 to go to Israel. He returned three years later, and joined the board of Marks & Spencer in 1954. He was responsible for the food department, the growth of which was perhaps his chief legacy to the business, and later took charge of store operations and personnel.

Although his relations with the stubborn Simon Marks – who held the chair until his death, in his office, in 1964 – were often turbulent, Sieff was clearly destined to lead the company. He became a joint managing director in 1967 and succeeded his uncle Edward Sieff as chairman from 1972 to 1984.

During the 1970s and 1980s high-street trade was consistently strong, and resistant to recession, but other aspects of the business were more troublesome. Overseas developments, in France and Canada, encountered difficulties. In 1982, a scheme by which Sieff and other directors had sold their houses to the company and leased them back on favourable terms received much adverse publicity; Sieff later acknowledged it as an error of judgment.

In retirement, Sieff was honorary president of Marks & Spencer, non-executive chairman of the *Independent* newspaper and a trustee of the National Portrait Gallery. He published an auto-biography, *Don't Ask The Price* (1987), and also found more time for his preferred form of relaxation, trout-fishing on the Kennet.

Although his personal tastes ran to fine claret and good cigars, Sieff made a point of dressing from head to toe in Marks & Spencer merchandise. And he continued to take pride in the quality of the stores' food products, which in the 1980s brought new sophistication and convenience to middle-class dinner tables.

Sieff was appointed OBE in 1944, knighted in 1971 and received a life peerage in 1980 – the first son of a life peer to be ennobled. He had the reputation of being something of a man about town in his youth, and married four times: first, in 1937, to Rosalie Fromson, a dancer in the Dorchester Follies. The couple were separated for five years by Marcus's war service, and divorced in 1947. They had a son, David, who became a director of Marks & Spencer.

Sieff's second wife was Elsa Gosen, an executive of a New York hairdressing chain to whom he was introduced by the hall porter of the Carlton Hotel in Cannes. They married in 1951 but were divorced in 1953. Next, in 1956, he married Brenda Beith, an actress and BBC announcer. Their daughter, Amanda, also joined Marks & Spencer.

Divorced for the third time in 1962, Sieff remarried in the following year, to the Polish-born Mrs Pauline Lily Moretzki née Spatz, by whom he had another daughter, Daniella. Lady Sieff nursed him through the initial years of his debilitating illness, but she died in 1997.

23 February 2001

Leslie Smith

╌═◉ 1918–2005 ◉═╌

Creator of Matchbox toys

Leslie Smith played an important part in the lives of postwar children as the maker of Matchbox cars, a range of authentically detailed miniature vehicles which fitted snugly into small hands.

While he was the managing director responsible for Lesney Products' sales and marketing, his partner Jack Odell was the engineer in charge of manufacturing. Within little more than 15 years they were selling more than a million cars a day to more than 100 countries, and had 14 factories around the world. The company did not have the market to themselves, but for a long time it maintained a lead, thanks to Odell's flair for constantly improving the detail on their models, which included dashboards with the dials in the right place and doors and bonnets which opened. When the company wanted to produce a model of the Maxwell Roadster of 1911 for its American market, a team was dispatched to Texas to photograph and measure an original.

Smith was also responsible for the welfare of the workforce at their main factory at Hackney Marshes, ensuring that women workers were able to pick up their children from school by conveying them in a fleet of buses.

He avoided the problem caused by having too many models for merchants to stock by limiting their number to 75 at one time, regularly withdrawing some to make way for others. When Smith found that Queensland would not permit any lead in toys, he took the expensive decision to use a lead-free paint, which proved a problem because the colours were not strong enough at first; but he was later proved a pioneer in the field.

The son of a carpenter and jobbing builder, Leslie Charles Smith was born on 6 March 1918 in Enfield, Middlesex, where he was to live throughout his life. He worked as an exporter of carpets to Australia before joining the Royal Navy to become a signals rating in 1940. Young Les and his three brothers were advised to join the Navy by their father, who, having served in the trenches during the First World War, said they could at least expect a bed for the night aboard ship. His first vessel was the converted trawler *Phineas Beard*, which he left a week before it was bombed and sunk. After being commissioned at HMS *King Alfred*, Brighton, he commanded a motor torpedo boat on the Dieppe Raid, then served in landing craft at Sicily and Salerno before commanding a minesweeper off Gold Beach at D-Day.

With the return of peace, Leslie and Rodney Smith, who was no relation, decided to invest their combined service gratuities of £600 in a die-casting company which they set up in a bombed-out pub at Tottenham. Called Lesney after the beginning and ending of their Christian names, it used zinc to make car-engine parts until the government commandeered all zinc supplies for the Korean War. Rodney Smith left to emigrate to Australia, but they had been joined by another partner, Jack Odell, an engineer with a love for model-making who had made his first miniature vehicle for his daughter when she was told she could bring no toy to school that could not fit into a matchbox.

Soon they started to produce models of a steamroller, tractor, dumper and cement mixer before embarking on a more ambitious project, the State Coach with the figures of King George VI and Queen Elizabeth inside, for the approaching royal silver jubilee. The prototype was already complete when the lack of zinc halted the project. By the time the zinc restrictions were lifted, the King had died. However, Lesney resolved the problem for the Coronation the following year. The figure of the former Queen was now deemed to be her daughter Elizabeth II, though sharp-eyed children might spot that the new Queen had a spare pair of trousered legs beside her, where the late King's upper body had been removed. Produced in two sizes, the larger one selling for £2 11s and the much smaller one for 1s 11d, a million copies were sold.

The Matchbox series, beginning with smaller versions of the first models they had produced, was then launched. An ever-increasing number of would-be young motorists, keen to spend their pocket money on its products, sent Lesney's fortunes rocketing. The company, which was launched on the stock exchange in 1960, continued to expand until 1968, when Smith and Odell were both appointed OBE and the company shares reached £6 16s; it had a market capitalisation of £120 million, about one third of British Leyland's.

But their operations gradually became affected by economic turbulence and the emergence of rivals in Hong Kong, where Smith had declined to open a factory because he did not want to sack the Hackney workforce and thought that Chinese craftsmanship would not prove sufficiently skilled. He and Odell responded by cutting their own salaries by 75 per cent to £25,000; 'No man is worth £100,000,' Smith explained.

The company continued to widen its appeal, bringing out Superfast cars, Tomcat fighter aircraft and dolls, but it was hit by the oil crisis, raging inflation and shop-floor problems as one of the largest firms in London, along with Kodak, which had no in-house unions. It finally went into receivership in 1982, though Matchbox toys continue to be made by its American rival Mattel Toys.

Although saddened, Smith found plenty to occupy him in retirement. Always a keen yachtsman, he once dived into the sea to rescue a crew member who had fallen off his yacht *Breakaway* in a collision with a cargo ship; he also developed a successful marina at Poole, Dorset. In addition, he took great delight in planning his two-acre garden and also in his role as chairman of the governors for two schools at Winchmore Hill and at Enfield, where he lived throughout his life.

Leslie Smith was survived by two sons and a daughter; in later life he had to buy them a set each of Lesney Matchbox models from a dealer because he had never bothered to collect them himself.

26 May 2005

Sir Noel Stockdale

◈══ 1920–2004 ══◈

Founder of ASDA supermarkets

Sir Noel Stockdale was a founder of ASDA and a pioneer of grocery superstores in Britain, after courageous wartime service in the RAF.

Stockdale was vice-chairman of Associated Dairies – a Leeds-based foods group founded by his father – when he was approached in 1964 by Peter Asquith, a Yorkshire butcher with bold retailing ideas but insufficient capital to develop them. Asquith and his brother Fred – a teacher by profession – had built up a butchery business in Pontefract, and then converted a cinema in Castleford into a supermarket. They had experimented with discounting, and saw the Heath government's proposed abolition of resale price maintenance (which allowed manufacturers to control retail prices) as an opportunity to create an aggressive, cut-price supermarket format.

ASDA Stores was duly launched with Stockdale's backing – the name combining Asquith and dairies – and began as a small chain of conventionally sized supermarkets, usually no more than 10,000 square feet. Within a few months, however, the opportunity arose to buy the premises in Nottingham and Leeds of an American company, Gem International, which built superstores and leased space in them to a variety of retailers.

The Nottingham store covered 70,000 square feet – huge by 1960s standards – but was making hefty losses. When Stockdale and Peter Asquith visited, they found more staff than customers and observed that grocery turnover was only £6000 a week: Asquith reckoned he could achieve £25,000. The buildings were acquired for virtually nothing, and the ASDA discount superstore concept was born. The company's aim was 'to sell as much as possible at a smaller profit margin, rather than a little bit at a large profit', offering clothing and furnishings as well as food, and petrol in the car park: one of Stockdale's observations was that, in an era of rapidly growing car ownership, consumers attracted by low prices were happy to drive a few miles to find them.

While its supermarket rivals were still largely confined to high-street sites, ASDA rapidly acquired and converted old mills, cinemas and industrial workshops throughout the north of England: Stockdale reckoned he had 'seven years' start' in the superstore race.

Noel Stockdale was chairman of ASDA from 1969 to 1986. During his tenure the group opened a new superstore on average every three months: by the mid-1980s there were more than 100 of them, turning over almost £2 billion and making more than £100 million of profits.

A modest, friendly man, never happier than when walking the aisles talking to shelf-stackers and checkout operators, he saw himself as the leader of a team in which Asquith and successive managing directors provided the entrepreneurial fireworks. As consumer tastes shifted upmarket so did ASDA, with in-store delicatessens and bakeries, and greater emphasis on fresh rather than canned and frozen food. But the competition was also increasingly sophisticated, as Tesco and Sainsbury emerged to lead the superstore market.

As a defensive measure, urged on by the City, ASDA merged in 1985 with the discount furniture chain MFI, a move which proved a disastrous drain on resources and heralded an era of mixed fortunes and management change. Stockdale – who became life president – nevertheless remained a much-loved figure within the company, which was turned around in the 1990s by a new team led by Archie Norman and Allan Leighton and was later acquired by the American retailing giant Wal-Mart.

Arthur Noel Stockdale was born at Pately Bridge on 25 December 1920 and educated at Woodhouse Grove School near Bradford. His father Arthur started in the pork butchery trade before establishing Hindells Dairy Farmers, a West Riding co-operative which absorbed a number of similar ventures in Yorkshire and Lancashire to become Associated Dairies & Farm Stores (Leeds) Ltd in 1949. Noel's father Arthur was its managing director until his death in 1961.

Noel worked briefly for Hindells after leaving school, and embarked on a dairying diploma at Reading University until his studies were interrupted by war. He volunteered for the RAF in 1940 and trained as a pilot in England and Canada, first in Tiger Moths and Oxfords, then in Wellington bombers. He joined No 70 Squadron, and flew in his first 1000-aircraft raid on Cologne in August 1942. By October of that year the squadron had moved to North Africa, and went on to support the invasion of Sicily in 1943. In late 1942 Stockdale was awarded the Distinguished Flying Medal for a mission in which, having seen planes ahead of him shot down by an unexpectedly fierce barrage, he dived low to enable his own gunner to take out the anti-aircraft emplacements. Having flown a large number of dangerous missions, he ended the war a squadron leader and flying instructor. On demobilisation he returned to business, joining the board of Associated Dairies in 1950.

Noel Stockdale was knighted in 1986. He was a former chairman of Leeds Rugby League Club and a passionate supporter of Yorkshire county cricket. He loved salmon-fishing on the Dee and the Tweed, and was a keen gardener.

He married Betty Shaw in 1944; they had two sons.

2 February 2004

Sir Gerald Whent

⤙▭ 1927–2002 ▭⤚

Mobile-phone pioneer

Sir Gerald Whent was the founder of Vodafone and one of the fathers of the British mobile-phone industry. Gerry Whent was a senior executive of the Racal Electronics group, in charge of its military radio division, when he spotted the moneymaking possibilities of mobile telephony for the consumer and business market in August 1982. The DTI was about to offer the first British franchise to compete against British Telecom in the mobile sector, but none of the leading British electronics firms, Racal among them, was initially keen to venture into an unknown field which would demand massive investment.

Whent was approached by a Swedish telecoms entrepreneur, Jan Stanbeck, who was more interested in Racal as an equipment manufacturer than as a partner in mobile networks. But Whent swiftly realised that the real opportunity was in owning the network. Racal duly entered a bid, with Stanbeck as a minority partner. The licence was won, and Racal Telecom started business in April 1985 with Whent as its chief executive.

As a manager, Whent was ebullient, decisive and swift to act. He worked with a small, loyal team, and had a sharp eye for detail but little time for paperwork. He described himself as a benign dictator: 'I listen and I take on board, but in the end someone has to say this is what we do and this is the way we do it. Leadership is something you just have. It's like spots.'

In the early years, Racal took more than half of the British mobile market; BT's Cellnet venture was its only competitor. The mobile-phone business became a cuckoo in the Racal corporate nest, worth more than the market capitalisation of its parent. As a defensive measure against the possibility of a takeover, Racal Telecom was partially floated on the stock exchange in 1989, though Racal retained a majority interest. Two years later, renamed Vodafone, it became an independent public company with a value of some £3.5 billion. It had already garnered 700,000 subscribers, and the market as a whole clearly had vast potential.

Whent, however, was concerned that Vodafone's prospects would be damaged by a further deregulation which doubled the number of network operators and encouraged a price-cutting war. Though he initiated Vodafone ventures in a dozen other countries, he readily admitted that he did not foresee the explosive growth of the business – and its share value – which was to happen under his successor Sir Chris Gent, who took over as chief executive on Whent's retirement, aged 69, in 1996. Whent sold the bulk of his own Vodafone shareholding long before the company's stock market peak.

Gerald Arthur Whent was born in Ferozepore, India, on 1 March 1927, the youngest of four children of Major Albert Whent, a Royal Artillery officer whose ancestors were migrant cloth merchants from the Low Countries and who was a devoted gambler on cards, chess and horses. When he was posted to Palestine in 1938, the family remained in Southampton, where Gerry was educated at St Mary's College.

More interested in sport than study, he left school at 16 to become an apprentice in an aircraft factory, then joined the Army as a regular soldier in 1945. He was sent to Palestine as a sergeant in the Royal Horse Artillery and went on to serve in Egypt and Italy, but did not want to follow his father and two elder brothers in a military career. In due course he saw a careers officer and said: 'You know in films there's often a fellow with a big desk who keeps picking up phones and saying "sell" and "buy". That's what I'd like to do.'

'You'd better be a management trainee,' he was told, so in 1952 he joined Dent Allcroft, a manufacturer of gloves and leather goods, where he gained what he called a 'damn good training'. After ten years, he moved to the electronics group Plessey to become a divisional manager in charge of cost control. In 1966 he was recruited by another electronics firm, Control & Communications, which was taken over three years later by Racal, the defence electronics group built up by Ernie (now Sir Ernest) Harrison. Whent ran several of Racal's businesses before becoming managing director of its radio group in 1980 and a main board director in 1982.

He and Harrison (who was chairman of Vodafone throughout Whent's tenure as chief executive) were closely attuned, bouncing entrepreneurial ideas off each other in daily telephone conversations. Harrison described Whent as 'determined, full of common sense . . . a natural businessman'. Whent in return said, 'If Ernie taught me one thing, it was to do things with style.'

Whent certainly enjoyed life to the full, though his own style remained down-to-earth: he observed that his father had acquired 'champagne taste with beer money', but for him it was the reverse. The accents and friendships of his youth stayed with him throughout his high-flying career. In later life he treated himself to a chauffeured Rolls-Royce, but only on the basis that 'everyone over sixty is entitled to a Rolls; under sixty you look a jerk'.

Intensely competitive, he was passionate about sports: he loved watching rugby and cricket, and playing golf, snooker, chess and bridge. He also enjoyed fishing, and took a keen interest in the racehorses bred by his wife from the prize-winning stallion Bold Edge at their small stud farm near Newbury.

He was appointed CBE in 1989 and was knighted in 1995.

Gerry Whent married first, in 1956, Coris Bellman-Thomas; they had a son and a daughter. The marriage was dissolved and he married secondly in 1985 his former secretary Sarah Donaldson, who had two sons and a daughter by a previous marriage.

16 May 2002

⟶━ PART FIVE ━⟵

CAPTAINS OF INDUSTRY

LORD BROOKES – *engineering leader*
SIR MICHAEL CLAPHAM – *CBI chief*
SIR JOHN CLARK – *Plessey chief who battled GEC*
SIR REAY GEDDES – *Dunlop tyre chief*
SIR PETER HOLMES – *unconventional Shell boss*
JOE HYMAN – *textile tycoon*
LORD KEARTON – *cantankerous Courtaulds chairman*
SIR IAN MACGREGOR – *controversial head of the Coal Board*
SIR NIGEL MOBBS – *steward of Slough Estates*
SIR ALASTAIR MORTON – *combative Eurotunnel boss*
SIR ANTONY PILKINGTON – *innovative glass-maker*
LORD RIVERDALE – *Sheffield steel man*
LORD TROTMAN – *British head of Ford in the US*
SIR GEORGE TURNBULL – *motor industry leader*

Lord Brookes

⊸⟐⟐ 1909–2002 ⟐⟐⊷

Engineering leader

Lord Brookes, the life president of Guest, Keen & Nettlefolds (GKN) was a versatile, far-sighted and highly articulate industrialist.

GKN traced its origins to one of the world's oldest metal-working businesses, the iron foundry established by John Guest in Glamorgan in the late 18th century. As managing director from 1964 and chairman from 1965 to 1974, Brookes completed the firm's transition from a steelmaker and manufacturer of nuts and bolts to Britain's leading producer of metal components for the motor industry – a strategy which he had developed since the end of the Second World War. During his decade at the top of the firm, the profits and turnover of the group tripled, faltering only with the onset of the oil crisis in 1974.

Brookes once remarked that 'the best office you have is the boots you stand up in'. He put faith in intuitive business hunches based on long experience, and was never happier than when patrolling the shop floors of his factories. His strong sense of kinship with his workforce – reflecting a belief that 'people are more important than capital' – won him the trust of trade union leaders, whom he handled with exceptional skill.

But despite a streak of old-fashioned paternalism, and a ruminative, pipe-smoking style, Brookes was no soft touch. He was a forceful advocate of free enterprise and self-reliance long before Thatcherism made such concepts fashionable. Accusing the first Wilson administration of having 'fallen short of the nation's necessities', he pointedly announced a large corporate donation to the Conservatives a year before such declarations were required by law.

He was particularly exercised by extremist infiltration of the industrial unions. In a speech to the Society of Motor Traders and Manufacturers in October 1974, he called for a complete revision of Bennite industrial policy and declaimed that he, for one, 'would rather reach for the moon, aye for the sun, to shine on a proud Britannia, than spinelessly allow the moles of Marxism to succeed where Goering's Eagles failed'.

The son of a wholesale grocer's representative, Raymond Percival Brookes was born in West Bromwich on 10 April 1909. He was educated at West Bromwich Lodge Estate School, leaving at 14 to become an apprentice with Charles Bunn Ltd, a local firm of drop forgers and founders. Heeding the advice of his first boss not to become too specialised in one skill, he pursued evening courses in mechanical engineering, accountancy and law – a grounding which was to serve him well in his boardroom years. By the time he was 23, Brookes was already works manager of Bunns, and in 1939 he became managing director.

At the outbreak of war he became involved in the planning and commissioning of 'shadow' munitions factories. In 1941 this led – at the instigation of the Ministry of Supply and the Admiralty – to an approach to Brookes to join a GKN subsidiary, John Garrington & Sons at Darlaston, as manager of a new munitions factory. Having achieved the smooth functioning of the plant's innovative process for forging naval shells, and impressive output figures, he became a director of Garrington & Sons in 1944.

After the war, Brookes foresaw the potential for mass production of motor components. He persuaded GKN to commission a new plant at Bromsgrove, the 'B5 Forge', incorporating the most advanced technology of the day: high-speed forging processes, and coil induction heaters in place of flame furnaces. This fulfilled a promise made to the night shift at Darlaston during the war that in the forges of the future there would be 'no bangs, no flames, no sweat and no broken men'.

Component contracts were secured from the Ferguson tractor company and, after teething problems had been solved, from Rootes, Ford and other major car-makers. Garringtons' commanding position in this market was reinforced by GKN's acquisition of numerous competitors.

Another of Brookes's notable achievements was the establishment in 1951 of Blade Research & Development (BRD) at Aldridge, Staffordshire, to produce aero-engine gas turbine blades for the

Korean War. Brookes's innovations in the production process enabled blades to be turned out faster than ever before. When military demand declined in the later 1950s, he found a new market for BRD in the manufacture of universal joints and drive-shafts for four-wheel and front-wheel drive vehicles. Brookes advanced to managing director and later chairman of Garringtons, and joined the main GKN board in 1953. There he took charge of several more subsidiaries, including Joseph Sankey, which made everything, in his words, 'from soup to nuts' – in fact, from wheels to armoured fighting vehicles. During Brookes's chairmanship, several more acquisitions were made in the component sector, at a total cost of some £162 million. These were partly financed by compensation payments from the government following the renationalisation of the steel industry in 1967, but in 1974 Brookes bought back the Brymbo Steel Works in Wales. He also expanded downstream activities in steel stockholding, and developed a steel joint venture in Australia.

When Brookes retired from the chair of GKN, the title of life president was created for him to mark his unique contribution to the company. He was knighted in 1971 for services to export, and was created a life peer in 1975.

Brookes was a non-executive director of Plessey and ATV, and a part-time member of the British Steel Corporation. Among many public appointments, he was the first president of the British Mechanical Engineering Federation, and a past president of both the Society of Motor Manufacturers and Traders and the Motor Industry Research Association. He was vice-president of the Engineering Employers Federation, and served on the court of governors of Birmingham University. Failing eyesight limited his contributions to House of Lords debate in later years. In 1990 he resigned the Conservative whip in protest at the ousting of Margaret Thatcher, sitting thereafter as a cross-bencher.

Although often professing to dislike the game, Brookes was a keen golfer for more than forty years. He also derived pleasure from fly-fishing on the Upper Wye.

Raymond Brookes married, in 1937, Florence Edna Sharman. They had a son.

6 August 2002

Sir Michael Clapham

⤚⇒ 1912–2002 ⇐⤙

CBI chief

Sir Michael Clapham was a senior executive of ICI who became president of the Confederation of British Industry at a time of soaring inflation and constant industrial strife.

Michael Clapham was an unusual figure in the upper echelons of Imperial Chemical Industries, being neither a chemist nor an engineer. 'I don't really belong in chemicals at all,' he once remarked. 'I'm just a classics-educated printer gone wrong.' He was indeed a master printer by training and – as the son of a distinguished Cambridge economic historian – an intellectual both by upbringing and inclination. But having risen to be chairman of ICI's metals division in 1959, he joined the main board in 1961 as overseas director: he was the author of the group's first overseas investment policy, and travelled 100,000 miles a year, chiefly to the Far East and Australia.

In 1968 he became one of three deputy chairmen, with a reputation as a liberal-minded reformer and problem solver. He was in the running for the chairmanship in 1971, but the board chose a more conventional candidate in Sir Jack Callard, an engineer who had made his name as the father of ICI's Dulux paint brand. The Confederation of British Industry was, in effect, Clapham's consolation prize. He became deputy president in 1971, succeeding as president in 1972. Almost immediately he was involved, with his director-general Campbell Adamson, in a series of talks on voluntary pay restraint and price controls with the Prime Minister Edward Heath and trade union leaders, both at Downing Street and Chequers. The CBI team's impression was that Heath showed a good deal more consideration and deference to the unions than to the employers who were his natural allies; he had a rapport with the TUC leader Vic Feather, but neither could exercise much influence over the left-wing union men at the table, Jack Jones and Hugh Scanlon, and little progress was achieved.

Clapham was courteous and witty in face-to-face dealings, but a pungent phrasemaker on public platforms. He spoke of the CBI 'straining every sinew' to find a middle way in the tripartite anti-inflation talks, and called for public opinion to wage war on 'smash and grabbers' both among the unions and among the 'speculators' whom he accused of fuelling an incipient property boom.

As the situation deteriorated in 1973 and the Government struggled to win union support for its Price and Pay Code, Clapham dismissed profit restraints on industry as 'strangling the goose that used to lay the golden eggs', pointing out that profits were already substantially lower than they had been a decade earlier. As the pound fell and both inflation and unemployment soared, he warned that Britain stood at the edge of an economic precipice: without industrial progress its workforce would become 'the peasants of Western Europe'. At the same time, he strove to keep angry CBI members in line, urging them to engage in constructive dialogue with ministers, rather than 'having a go at the popular sport of Establishment-bashing . . . as a relief to the emotions'.

Michael John Sinclair Clapham was born on 17 January 1912 and was educated at Marlborough and King's College, Cambridge, where he had been a chorister as a boy and where his father Sir John Clapham was vice provost and professor of economic history. Michael read classics, but became a 'bastard economist', he said, by drinking tea with Marshall, beer with Pigou, and brandy with Keynes. He began his working life in 1933 as a printer's apprentice with the Cambridge University Press, at ten shillings a week. He went on to work for a Bradford printing firm before becoming manager of the Kynoch Press, part of ICI's metals division in Birmingham, in 1938. The director who recruited him warned that the job was a dead end because there could be no prospect of advancement within ICI for a man with Clapham's lack of technical qualifications.

But, as Clapham himself put it, 'Providence is an inveterate joker': early in the Second World War, while working on silk-screen printing techniques, he invented – accidentally, he claimed – an isotope diffusion barrier, and in consequence found himself seconded for four years to the Tube Alloys Project, Britain's first attempt to build an atomic bomb, and marked out for higher things.

In 1946 he returned to ICI's mainstream as personnel director of the metals division, going on to become a managing director of the division in 1952. He became a prominent figure in Birmingham, serving on the city's education committee and on the university council. A decade later, the metals division, which employed 28,000 people, was spun off by ICI as a separate public company, Imperial Metal Industries, with Clapham as one of its first directors; he was to be its chairman from 1974 to 1981.

Clapham's ICI career had been briefly disrupted in 1966 by the offer of the managing directorship of the newly formed – and controversial – Industrial Reorganisation Corporation (IRC), the Wilson government's vehicle for its interventionist industrial policies. Clapham was headhunted by IRC chairman Sir Frank Kearton – whom he had first met on the Tube Alloys project – and would readily have accepted. But the proposed appointment met the wrath of ICI's chairman, Sir Paul Chambers, who disapproved strongly of IRC, of Kearton – ICI's most aggressive competitor when chairman of the Courtaulds textile group – and of the fact that Clapham had been approached without the courtesy of asking Chambers' permission first. Other ICI directors tried to persuade Chambers to let Clapham go, but the chairman held his ground and the board vetoed the proposal.

Instead, Clapham became a non-executive director of IRC in 1969. He was a member of the National Economic Development Council, and served on committees on civil servants', doctors' and dentists' pay and numerous other public bodies. After retiring from the ICI board in 1974 he was chairman of BPM Holdings, deputy chairman of Lloyds Bank, a director of Grindlay's Bank and Associated Communications Corp, the Australian media group, and a member of General Motors' European advisory council. He was also president of the Institute of Printing and wrote scholarly articles on the history of the trade.

He was knighted in 1973.

Away from work, Clapham enjoyed boating: he kept a narrow boat on the Grand Union Canal, and a ketch in the Mediterranean, where he liked to explore out-of-the-way anchorages on the Greek and Turkish coasts. He was also an enthusiastic cook, made his own Christmas cards, designed some of his wife's clothes, and sometimes wore an opera cloak to the office. Long into his retirement he re-emerged in public as chairman of the residents' association of Mayfair, campaigning against the disruption that would have been caused by routeing the Crossrail link from Paddington to Liverpool Street under the area.

He married, in 1935, Elisabeth Rea, daughter of the 1st Lord Rea of Eskdale. She died in 1994; they had three sons and a daughter.

11 November 2002

Sir John Clark

⊷═⊙ 1926–2001 ⊙═⊷

Plessey chief who battled GEC

Sir John Clark was chief executive of Plessey, the electronics and telecommunications group built up by his father. For more than two decades he pursued a vigorous rivalry with Lord Weinstock of GEC, culminating in a series of corporate manoeuvres during the late 1980s in which Plessey was finally taken over and split up.

The Plessey company had originally been a manufacturer of piano actions and other mechanical devices in Holloway, north London. It was acquired shortly after the end of the First World War by Byron George Clark, an American who had done business with it in his capacity as the European representative of the United Shoe Machinery Co. Byron's son Allen went into the Plessey business after demobilisation from war service and in due course turned it into a manufacturer of radio sets under contract for Marconi, the pioneer of the broadcasting industry. Under Allen's leadership, Plessey expanded rapidly by concentrating on making radio (and later television) components for other manufacturers.

Sir Allen, as he became, was an outstanding salesman and an autocratic boss, who had been a boxing champion in his youth and shot for England in clay-pigeon championships in the 1930s. In the last year of Sir Allen's life, 1962, he and his sons John and Michael doubled Plessey's size by the takeover of Ericsson Telephones and Automatic Telephone & Electric Co. The latter brought with it some 40 per cent of the Post Office's orders for telephone-exchange equipment, under a 'preferred supplier' system which guaranteed strong growth for Plessey throughout the 1960s.

As a young chief executive, John Clark – already inviting comparisons with Weinstock, who had taken the reins of GEC through an audacious takeover in 1962 – was ambitious for further expansion. In August 1968 he sought an appointment with Lord Nelson of Stafford, chairman of English Electric Co (then one of the great names of British industry, and more than twice as big as Plessey) and surprised him with a merger proposal.

Nelson, however, was wary of the Clark family's aggressive business reputation, and encouraged instead the possibility of a tie-up with GEC, which had recently completed the takeover of another major player in the industry, Associated Electrical Industries. The Labour government's Industrial Reorganisation Corporation came down in favour of a GEC-English Electric deal – creating one of the world's biggest companies – and Plessey was effectively forced to withdraw. Plessey made a number of other acquisitions over the next 15 years, though the core of its business continued to be Post Office telephone exchanges.

Clark – wearing his father's gold watch and chain – continued to run the company very much in his father's style, though the family shareholding had long been diluted. Much was made over the years of the contrast in style between Clark as a sporting Harrovian man-of-action, and Weinstock the soft-spoken, cost-conscious son of a Jewish tailor. Clark himself liked to say, 'I am a manager, Arnold [Weinstock] is a banker.'

But the *Daily Telegraph* also observed that 'in outlook, temper and determination to get things done even at the expense of cutting cosy corners' the two had much in common. Their interests converged in the early 1980s in the 'System X' project, an electronic exchange, developed by Plessey, which both Plessey and GEC were contracted to supply to the newly created British Telecom.

The project was fraught with problems; the logic of bringing their telecom manufacturing activities together to achieve it was plain. But Clark was determined not to be subsumed within GEC. When Weinstock launched a £1.2 billion takeover bid in 1985, Clark's defence included an attack on GEC's technological record so colourful that Weinstock sued for libel, declaring that it 'would have done credit to Dr Goebbels'. Plessey lost the libel action, but the Monopolies Commission, with the support of the Ministry of Defence, ruled against the merger.

In the following year, Clark made a counter-proposal which resulted in the creation of a 50-50 joint venture, GEC Plessey Telecommunications (GPT), of which he became chairman. Far from creating harmony between the two groups, however, GPT was a focus for continued friction – and both Plessey and GEC were now subject to criticism in the City for their failure either to keep pace with technology or to provide sufficient rewards for their shareholders.

In 1988 GEC announced a new partnership with the German group Siemens to bid for Plessey a second time, at a price of £1.7 billion, with the intention of dividing its operations between them. Clark's response was pugnacious to the end. Lazards, his merchant bankers, announced that it was assembling a £7 billion consortium to bid for GEC – which would have been the largest takeover bid in British history, and an example of the so-called 'Pacman defence', in which the victim turns on its attacker. But the consortium was swiftly outmanoeuvred by Weinstock, and in September 1989, Clark yielded to a £2 billion final bid from GEC and Siemens. By then he had already announced his own intention to step down as chief executive.

John Allen Clark was born on 14 February 1926, and was educated at Harrow. He was commissioned in the RNVR during the Second World War, and spent a short spell at Cambridge before embarking on a business apprenticeship with Metropolitan-Vickers and Ford Motor Co, and a year with an American electrical manufacturer, P.R. Mallory. He joined the Plessey board in 1953. He was also a director of International Computers, in which Plessey was a founder shareholder, and president of the Institute of Works Managers and the Engineering Employers' Federation.

Sir John Clark was well over six feet tall and strongly built. He piloted Plessey's company helicopter himself and drove to work in an Aston Martin sports car. For relaxation he rode and shot at Redenham Park, his Hampshire estate, and played what one observer described as 'bashing' tennis.

He was knighted in 1971. He married first, in 1952, Deirdre Waterhouse; they had a son and a daughter. The marriage was dissolved in 1962 and he married secondly Olivia Pratt, by whom he had twin sons and another daughter.

3 December 2001

Sir Reay Geddes

⊷⟫ 1912–1998 ⟪⊷

Dunlop tyre chief

Sir Reay Geddes was a former chairman of Dunlop Rubber Company and a leading industrialist of the 1960s and '70s.

In the postwar era, Dunlop was a manufacturer of world renown. Founded in 1888 by John Boyd Dunlop, a Belfast vet who fitted the first pneumatic tyre to his son's tricycle, it was dominated for 56 years – from the appointment of Sir Eric Geddes, Reay's father, as chairman in 1922 to the retirement of Sir Reay in 1978 – by two closely allied families, the Geddes and the Beharrells.

When Sir Reay became chairman in 1968, Dunlop was the ninth largest company in Britain and one of its most successful – having doubled in size in the previous decade, when Geddes was managing director. Geddes himself was already a statesmanlike figure, having served as president of the Society of Motor Manufacturers & Traders and as a founder member of the National Economic Development Council ('Neddy'), and having chaired a groundbreaking inquiry into the problems of the shipbuilding industry.

On public platforms and at his own influential private dinner parties, Geddes did much to promote harmony between employers, unions and government – whilst also arguing for less state intervention in industry and lower taxes to promote private-sector investment. Tall, imposing and serious, he was complimented by one correspondent who encountered him at the Motor Show on his 'ministerial presence and proconsular profile'.

Geddes was determined that Dunlop should stay in the big league despite growing international competition in the tyre industry, and set out to look for a merger partner. Various possibilities were considered, until Geddes settled on the idea of 'a marriage of equals' with the Italian tyre-maker Pirelli. Sadly this proved, as a *Daily Telegraph* columnist later observed, 'one of the worst corporate decisions of Britain's postwar history', and a contributory factor in Dunlop's ultimate demise. Some of Geddes's colleagues expressed doubts at the time, but he pushed ahead, declaring Pirelli's management to be 'our class of people'. Pirelli had forecast its profit at £3 million for the first year of the union, 1971, but six weeks after Dunlop shareholders approved the deal, the forecast changed to a £7 million loss, and the actual deficit for the year turned out to be £18 million. While Dunlop's original businesses prospered during Geddes's chairmanship, Pirelli's losses continued unabated, steadily draining the group's resources. The union endured until 1982, by which time Dunlop itself was in difficulty: its European tyre business was sold to a Japanese company in 1983, and the remains of the group, which was collapsing under a mountain of debt, was taken over by BTR in 1985.

Anthony Reay Mackay Geddes was born on 7 May 1912 into a distinguished Edinburgh family. His father, Sir Eric, was director-general of military railways during the First World War and subsequently MP for Cambridge, First Lord of the Admiralty and Minister of Transport. In 1922, as chairman of a committee appointed by the Chancellor of the Exchequer, he wielded the 'Geddes Axe' over public spending. On leaving politics, he became chairman of Imperial Airways and Dunlop – rescuing the rubber company from a bout of near-disastrous over-expansion in the early 1920s.

Young Reay was educated at Rugby and Cambridge, where he went up to read economics but stayed only one year. Eager to enter the practical world of business, he joined the Bank of England as a trainee in 1932, and three years later moved to Dunlop.

Before the Second World War he worked for the company in France, Germany and India. Having trained as a reserve pilot, he was called up by the RAF in 1939 and saw service in South East Asia before becoming, at the age of 32, deputy director of air transport at the Air Ministry with the rank of group captain.

Returning to Dunlop as overseas sales manager, he joined the board in 1947, became domestic sales director in 1953 and managing director in 1957. In the following year, assuming the presidency of SMMT, he emerged onto the public stage as the chief spokesman of the motor industry, to which Dunlop was a major supplier. Though his style was thoughtful and reserved, Geddes had an aptitude for what would now be called the 'sound bite'. He spoke out in favour of steady expansion in car production, 'not a surge followed by restraint', and declared as his goal that there should be one car for every two families by 1968. He also accused the British of a Victorian attitude to cars, regarding them as 'a canary in a gilded cage', meaning a luxury for the few. Addressing the American Chamber of Commerce on the subject of Britain's future, he said that instead of trying to keep up with the Joneses, 'we should just set out to be the Joneses'.

His next major public appointment was in 1965, when he chaired an inquiry into the shipbuilding industry, which faced a combination of falling demand, rising competition from Sweden and Japan, and union strife. Geddes was widely praised for his committee's recommendations, which included a programme of rapid capacity reduction and strategic mergers, supported by cheap government loans. In practice, however, British shipbuilding was set on a course of decline which Geddes's measures could do nothing to reverse. One of the groups created as a result of his report, Upper Clyde Shipbuilders, collapsed in 1969. Those which survived were borne down in the 1970s by loss-making contracts and scarcity of orders.

Geddes's wisdom was constantly in demand: he declined invitations to stand as Conservative candidate for Marylebone and to become president of the CBI. He was a member of the Atomic

Energy Authority from 1960 to 1965, and deputy chairman of the Midland Bank from 1978 to 1984. He was also a director of Shell, and of the Rank Organisation during the boardroom battles of the late 1970s. He was president of the International Chamber of Commerce in 1980 and of the Charities Aid Foundation from 1991 to 1993.

Reay Geddes received the OBE for his wartime RAF service and was knighted in 1968.

He married, in 1938, Imogen Matthey; they had two sons and three daughters.

19 February 1998

Sir Peter Holmes

⊶⊜ 1932–2002 ⊜⊷

Unconventional Shell boss

Sir Peter Holmes was an unconventional chairman of Shell who pursued a deep cultural interest in many of the countries in which the giant oil company operated. As a young man, he won a Military Cross in Korea and climbed virgin peaks in the Himalayas.

A quick decision-maker with an open, light-hearted manner, Peter Holmes had little tolerance for what he called the 'tramlines' of corporate bureaucracy, seeing himself essentially as a 'downstream' marketing man in an organisation traditionally dominated by 'upstream' production engineers.

During his tenure from 1985 to 1993 as chairman of Shell Transport & Trading, the UK arm of the Royal Dutch/Shell group, Shell overtook Exxon in the league of oil giants and could claim to be one of the world's strongest and most profitable companies.

It was by no means an era of plain sailing, however. Shortly after Holmes took the helm, the abandonment of Opec production quotas caused the price of oil to collapse from over $30 a barrel to $10, temporarily wrecking the economics of many of Shell's exploration projects.

On the public-relations front, meanwhile, the company was under fierce attack from anti-apartheid protesters – who disrupted successive annual general meetings – for its decision to continue operating in South Africa when other British companies had bowed to pressure and withdrawn.

Holmes himself felt 'we could do more good by being there than by making an empty gesture and leaving'. Within South Africa, Shell was known for its overt opposition to apartheid and support for black aspirations, to the extent that in 1990 Nelson Mandela said, 'We're glad you stayed.' Holmes noted with satisfaction that at Shell's 1992 AGM, one vociferous protester from earlier years stood and congratulated him on what the company had done in South Africa.

Another moment of tension was the Iraqi invasion of Kuwait in 1990 and subsequent Gulf War, which caused a sharp spike in oil prices and placed Shell's staff, installations and tankers in the Gulf at risk. Throughout these events, Holmes remained cheerful and calm.

He believed that the strength of Shell lay in its collegiate management style, combined with a decentralised system that allowed managers on the ground to respond directly to changed circumstances. The corporate world, he said, drawing on his Himalayan experience, was 'a bit like rock climbing. When conditions get tough – a bit of snow and ice – then the people who are really fit will keep going. The role of the men at the top of a group like ours is simply to make sure the business stays fit.'

Peter Fenwick Holmes was born in Athens on 27 September 1932, and spent part of his childhood in Budapest, where his father had business interests. His grandfather and great-grandfather had served in the Levant Consular Service. The family had been based in Turkey until forced to leave when the Turks sided with Germany in the First World War. At the outbreak of the Second World War, Peter's American mother took her two sons first to the US and then to England, where Peter was sent to Malvern College. One of his teachers was the mountaineer Wilfrid Noyce, who inspired his love of climbing – and who was to be a member of Sir John Hunt's celebrated 1953 Everest expedition.

Before going to university, Holmes did national service as a second lieutenant in the Royal Leicestershire Regiment in Korea, distinguishing himself by leading a number of exploratory patrols deep into enemy-held territory. The first of these, in November 1951, took place close to a battlefield feature designated Point 217: Holmes was ordered to advance on two hills called Punch and Judy 'until you're shot at', in order to report on enemy defences. Finding Punch unexpectedly clear, he carried on up the steep slope of Judy towards earthworks which turned out to contain only dead and decomposing Chinese troops. In pine woods beyond, his patrol came unseen to within 50 yards of more Chinese – this time alive and busy brewing up. Camouflaged behind them was a self-propelled gun, a large artillery piece mounted on a tank chassis. Holmes radioed its position, and the regiment's Centurion tanks proceeded to destroy it. In all, Holmes went on 33 forward patrols, often in very dangerous territory. On one occasion, leading from the front, he set off a mine – which caused only a minor injury to his hand, while seriously injuring a man 30 yards behind him; on another, caught without cover in a paddy field, he was unscathed by Chinese machine-gun fire at 400 yards range. Commended for 'buoyancy, coolness and courage', he was awarded the Military Cross in 1952.

On demobilisation Holmes went up to Trinity College, Cambridge, to read history. His family remained scattered, so he spent winter vacations skiing, much of the summer playing golf and spring vacations climbing with Wilfrid Noyce. After graduating in 1955, Holmes and his new bride, also a keen mountaineer, set off to spend what was effectively to be a two-year honeymoon in the Himalayas. Taking a geologist with them to give the expedition scientific credibility, they climbed 14 virgin peaks, which Holmes described modestly as 'foothills compared to Everest – nothing higher than 22,000 feet'.

The trip was funded by a trust established by Hunt, but eventually money ran out and Holmes returned to England in 1956 to take the first international job he was offered, which was at Shell. He planned to work for four years then go back to the mountains, but found the job more than interesting enough to persuade him to stay. His first posting was to the Sudan, followed by a stint at the Foreign Office school in the Lebanon to learn Arabic and four years as a district manager in Libya, a country which he came to love. He steeped himself in the history and culture of the Arab world and made many friends there: such friendships, he said, were harder to make than in the West, 'but they last longer'.

He became general manager of Shell's marketing company in the Gulf in 1965, and chief representative in Libya in 1970, at a time when Colonel Gaddafi's revolutionary council was demanding steep oil price rises and production cuts, as well as threatening to block exports by Shell and other Western operators. Negotiations were long and tortuous, but Holmes would relax after a difficult day by scuba-diving to photograph algae in deep caves – 'the perfect way to unwind,' he said. His next appointment from 1977 to 1981 was as managing director of the joint Shell-BP operations in Nigeria – where again he spent every weekend up-country exploring tribal cultures and archeological sites.

He returned to London as president of Shell International Trading responsible for the group's retailing activities, becoming a managing director of Royal Dutch/Shell and a director of Shell Transport & Trading in 1982. At 52, he was unusually young to become chairman three years later; in the final year of his chairmanship, 1992–93, he was also chairman of the committee of managing directors of Royal Dutch/Shell, the most senior position in the combined group.

He was knighted in 1988. Holmes retired to live in the east wing of Wardour Castle in Wiltshire, determined to escape from business and to spend more time in remote places. He took on a role which bridged both worlds as president (succeeding the late Sir Fitzroy Maclean) of the Hakluyt Foundation, an organisation named after the 16th-century geographer Richard Hakluyt, which provided strategic intelligence on foreign markets for corporate clients. Holmes was fascinated by the writings of early travellers such as Hakluyt, and relished arduous journeys. Fiercely competitive, he was the wrong man to challenge to reach the top of a hill – not least because he loved betting, and usually won.

He was also a keen photographer and wrote three books based

on his explorations: *Mountains and a Monastery* (1958), *Nigeria: Giant of Africa* (1985) and *Turkey: A Timeless Bridge* (1988).

He was a trustee of the World Wildlife Fund for Nature (UK) and a fellow of the Royal Geographical Society.

Peter Holmes married first, in 1955, Judith Walker; they had three daughters. He married secondly, in 1999, Mary Snead, who had a daughter by an earlier marriage.

'I have tried to teach the girls,' he told an interviewer at the time of his retirement, 'whatever you do in life, enjoy it. Do it to the best of your ability, and remember the old adage: only two things in life really matter – friends and flowers.'

8 March 2002

Joe Hyman

⊷⇒ 1921–1999 ⇐⊷

Textile tycoon

Joe Hyman shook up the British textile industry of the 1960s by creating the Viyella International conglomerate through a series of bold acquisitions. He first made his mark in 1961 when his nylon company Gainsborough-Cornard achieved a reverse takeover of William Hollins of Nottingham, a long-established but under-performing business which owned the Viyella trademark for its wool-cotton pyjama fabric. Hyman revolutionised Hollins, slashed its costs and turned a £3 million overdraft into a credit balance within 15 months.

With Viyella as the new company name and £13 million of financial backing from ICI, he then set out to acquire a string of other businesses, including Amalgamated Cotton Mills – which owned the Van Heusen brand name – Combined English Mills and Bradford Dyers Association. Hyman wanted vertical integration, and created a group with strong positions in both synthetic and natural fibres and all stages of the manufacturing process from spinning and weaving to dyeing and finishing. Sales grew from

£6 million to £70 million, and profits multiplied tenfold. Rapid consolidation was triggered throughout the textile industry, as other groups formed up to compete with him.

A suave and cultured figure – more like a Mayfair antique dealer than a Lancashire textile man, according to one account – Hyman brimmed with zest and self-confidence. He was fiercely demanding to work for, but he also provoked great loyalty. 'While I was there it was terrible,' one of his lieutenants admitted. 'But it was one of the greatest experiences of my life.'

In his early forties Hyman was regarded as Britain's fastest-moving tycoon, and his buccaneering style brought admirers and critics in equal measure. As his advance continued, other takeover targets such as English Sewing Cotton resisted him, an American merger proved elusive and relations with ICI (which also held stakes in some of Hyman's leading competitors) deteriorated. Eventually, Viyella's takeover of the struggling carpet manu-facturer Cyril Lord provoked an internal crisis. Profits were declining, and Hyman's autocratic style had lost him the support of some of his key board members. In one of the most famous corporate rows of the era, he was ousted by his own colleagues in December 1969. Viyella was subsequently con-solidated into a larger group, Carrington-Viyella, with ICI as its major shareholder.

Joe Hyman was born on 14 October 1921 and educated at North Manchester Grammar School. His great-grandfather had been a textile merchant in Russia, and his father Solomon made a living buying up and reselling clearance lines from the Bradford Dyers Association. Young Joe left school at 16 to begin his career in the same line of business from a small office in Manchester. In 1945 he named his first company Gainsborough Fabrics 'to give the feeling of something old-fashioned'.

Hyman's first venture into manufacturing in the early 1950s was a failure that lost him £40,000. Undeterred, he looked for a way to take advantage of the coming nylon boom, and in 1957 he bought a small knitting firm in Suffolk called Melso Fabrics – based in the village where Gainsborough was born, which Joe thought a good omen. Renamed Gainsborough-Cornard, the business rapidly expanded and became the springboard for the creation of the Viyella empire.

Hyman's ousting from Viyella was a considerable blow to his self-esteem, and he never quite recovered the dynamism of earlier days. In 1971 he took control of a Huddersfield woollen business, John Crowther & Co – having outbid Courtaulds – but the growing problems of the woollen industry over the following decade put paid to any idea of building another conglomerate like Viyella. Hyman divided his time between London and Huddersfield and held out hopes for a public service appointment, perhaps to run a nationalised industry; but none came his way.

He stepped down from the chair of John Crowther in 1981, but re-emerged from retirement in the following year as an opponent of the merger between Carrington Viyella (in which he still held 5 per cent) and Vantona, the textile group headed by David Alliance. He was particularly incensed by ICI's willingness to commit its 49 per cent Carrington Viyella stake to Vantona. Showing flashes of his old style, Hyman described Carrington Viyella as 'an unwanted waif, an orphan of the storm' which needed 'a proper home where it can be loved'. Vantona prevailed, however.

Hyman was also briefly a player in the battle for ownership of Harrods: he was named as Tiny Rowland's candidate to become chairman of House of Fraser, Harrods' parent company, but Rowland's Lonrho group failed to win sufficient control to appoint him.

Joe Hyman was a trustee of the Pestalozzi Children's Village Trust and a governor of the LSE. He loved music, and in later years devoted much of his energy to the development of the garden and farm of his estate in Surrey.

He married first, in 1948, Corinne Abrahams; they had a son and a daughter. The marriage was dissolved and he married secondly, in 1963, Simone Duke, by whom he had another son and another daughter.

6 July 1999

Lord Kearton

⊷⇒ 1911–1992 ⇐⊷

Cantankerous Courtaulds chairman

Lord Kearton was a notably successful chairman of Courtaulds, but as head of the Industrial Reorganisation Corporation in the 1960s and of the British National Oil Corporation in the 1970s he cut a more controversial figure. Kearton transformed Courtaulds, of which he was chairman from 1964, from a slumbering company into the most efficient textile and fibre group in the world. The pillars of his stewardship were the takeover of more than fifty other companies, ambitious expansion overseas and diversification into such synthetic fibres as nylon and polyester.

These policies enabled Courtaulds to prosper in bad as well as good times. Though Kearton retired in 1975, in the middle of an acute recession in the textile business, at his last general meeting he was able to report exports of £285 million and net profits of £88.9 million.

Frank Kearton had long been recognised as the embodiment of Harold Wilson's hopes for 'the white heat of the technological revolution' – and he reciprocated this confidence, opining in October 1966 that Labour had a better appreciation than the Tories of business affairs. Earlier that year, George Brown had appointed him the first chairman of the Industrial Reorganisation Corporation (IRC), Labour's agency for promoting industrial rationalisation and mergers – a design viewed with misgivings in the City.

Although Kearton had resisted ICI's attempt to take over Courtaulds, at the IRC he was the apostle of the larger scale. The corporation played a crucial role in the amalgamation of English Electric, GEC and AEI, and in the merger of the British Motor Corporation with Leyland. In 1968 Anthony Wedgwood (later Tony) Benn, the minister of technology, noted that Kearton was 'certainly the one industrialist who has stuck loyally by the Government over the last three and a half years'. By way of corollary, the IRC was abolished by the Heath administration.

By that time Kearton had begun to express reservations about Labour's performance; in 1968 he warned Barbara Castle that she would have to make collective agreements binding, and in 1969 he criticised the management of nationalised industries. But in 1975 Benn, now Energy Secretary, appointed Kearton chairman of the British National Oil Corporation, where he proved himself an enthusiastic proponent of government participation in the North Sea oil bonanza.

'The more I see of this government', Kearton vouchsafed in 1978, 'the more I am impressed by it.' But when Mrs Thatcher began to loom, Kearton invited her to lunch.

'All on public money?' she sweetly inquired. After the Tories were returned at the 1979 election, Kearton resigned and took up a City directorship at Hill Samuel.

Tall and balding, in appearance more like a don than a tycoon, in his palmy years Kearton presented an affable figure on television, dispensing corporatist wisdom in a Staffordshire accent. But, while no one doubted his energy or mastery of detail, he was rarely inhibited by sensitivity when it came to enforcing his will. A colleague described his normal state as one of total dissatisfaction with everything in sight. Another, to whom Kearton bemoaned having come into the world with one skin too few, replied, 'Yes, and wearing hobnailed boots'.

The son of a builder in the Potteries, Christopher Frank Kearton was born on 17 February 1911 and educated at Hanley High School and St John's College, Oxford, where he took a first in chemical engineering. He began his career with ICI, for which he set up aviation petrol plants at Heysham and Billingham. During the Second World War he was seconded to work on the atomic bomb (both in Britain and America) and also helped to develop a special fuel for the Tempest fighter. In 1946 Kearton turned down Lord Hinton's pleas to remain in the nuclear industry and joined Courtaulds as head of chemical engineering research.

He was made a director in 1952 and deputy chairman nine years later. In 1961 and 1962 he played an important part in fighting off ICI's bid to take over Courtaulds, coming to the public eye for the first time as a result of scathing performances at press conferences.

But it was the terms and not the principle of the bid which aroused Kearton's ire; he was said to have dithered long before coming out against it. In 1962 he concluded an agreement whereby ICI handed over its 37.5 per cent share in Courtaulds and £10 million in cash in exchange for full control of British Nylon Spinners. Kearton was now in line for the chairmanship of Courtaulds. But there was still some resistance before Kearton attained his desire in 1964. Though he liked to insist in public that the management of Courtaulds was a team effort, some members of the board considered that they were often presented with *faits accomplis.*

Kearton's reaction to criticism could be prickly, as he showed in 1968 when the Takeover Panel judged that Courtaulds had offended the spirit of the code with its bid for International Paints. Kearton, furious, countered by demanding that the Bank of England undertake a public inquiry into the conduct of certain City institutions. This instinctively critical attitude towards the City may have been partly responsible for the most grievous error of Kearton's career when he was responsible for helping Robert Maxwell accomplish his takeover of the British Printing Corporation (BPC).

In 1971 the DTI had published a report in which it concluded that Maxwell was 'not in our opinion a person . . . to exercise proper stewardship of a public company'. So when Maxwell hovered over BPC in 1980, the City was hostile. Kearton, however, concluded that, 'Maxwell's wrongdoings were small compared to a lot of happenings in the City and the inspectors had been unfair on him'. His part in bestowing a vital respectability on Maxwell was rewarded by the chairmanship of BPC when Maxwell gained control in 1981.

Though Kearton moved into a non-executive role at BPC after five months, his opinion that Maxwell was 'a genius' did not change.

'If Britain had six more Maxwells,' he said in 1983, 'the country would have no more worries.' The circumstances of Maxwell's death in 1991 drew only a partial retraction. 'Maxwell was naughty,' Kearton summed up, 'but so were a lot of people.'

The Thatcherite years were not to Kearton's taste. Occasionally he gave apocalyptic warnings in the Lords about the decline of the manufacturing industry, and prophesied that the country would fall into the abyss when the North Sea oil money disappeared.

Kearton's numerous appointments included the chairmanship of the Electricity Supply Research Council; the presidency of the British Association for the Advancement of Science, of the Society of the Chemical Industry and of the Royal Society for the Prevention of Accidents. He was Chancellor of Bath University, a member of the Atomic Energy Authority, the Advisory Council on Technology and the National Economic Development Council.

Kearton was appointed OBE in 1945, elected a Fellow of the Royal Society in 1961 and an Honorary Fellow of St John's College, Oxford, in 1965; knighted in 1966, and created a life peer in 1970.

He married, in 1936, Agnes Kathleen Brander; they had two sons and two daughters.

2 July 1992

Sir Ian MacGregor

⤝⥤ 1912–1998 ⥤⥢

Controversial head of the Coal Board

Sir Ian MacGregor was the implacably tough National Coal Board chairman who defeated the miners' strike of 1984–5. Born and educated in Scotland, MacGregor had a long and successful career in the American mining industry before returning to Britain to take charge first of British Steel from 1980 to 1983, and then, at the age of almost 71, the NCB.

The belligerence of Arthur Scargill, president of the National Union of Mineworkers, signalled that a strike was only a matter of time. The Thatcher government had backed down in an earlier confrontation with the miners, but the Prime Minister was not of a mind to do so again, and massive stockpiling of coal had been in progress for some time. The NUM executive forced ahead with its strike plan in March 1984, in reaction to an announcement of pit closures. In the months that followed, waves of intimidatory picketing and clashes between miners and police became increasingly violent. MacGregor remained coldly resolute, despite his isolation both from the majority of his NCB colleagues – who, he said later, saw the coal industry as 'a social security enterprise' – and from Thatcher's Energy Secretary, Peter Walker.

Walker had inherited MacGregor from the previous energy minister, Nigel Lawson. Acutely conscious of the political reverberations of the dispute, Walker distanced himself from MacGregor's handling of it – and, by conducting his own discussions with key officials, seemed to MacGregor to be undermining him. When the pit deputies union, NACODS, also threatened action in autumn 1984, Walker persuaded the Cabinet to defuse the situation by dictating settlement terms to MacGregor.

Six months later, MacGregor's victory was overwhelming. The miners were routed and – with the formation of the Union of Democratic Mineworkers in Nottinghamshire – divided; Scargill was effectively silenced for the remainder of the decade. MacGregor was able to proceed with a programme of closures and voluntary redundancies, increasing productivity from 2.2 tons per man-shift to 3 tons. Losses were greatly reduced.

But he also attracted criticism in government circles for the weak presentation of his case to the public. Dour, impassive, sometimes curmudgeonly, MacGregor was once described as 'an armadillo with the jaws of a Staffordshire bull terrier'. He was an uncharismatic general on the bloodiest battlefield of the Thatcher era and although given a knighthood, he was distinctly cold-shouldered by Downing Street in his last months at the Coal Board. As his successor, the government appointed a more emollient figure, Robert Haslam, who had also followed him at British Steel. MacGregor clearly disapproved, and the choice was interpreted as a final snub.

MacGregor believed that Mrs Thatcher had got 'the results she paid for; in fact, much more than she paid for' from his stewardship of the Coal Board, and expressed some bitterness, particularly in Walker's direction, in *The Enemies Within*, a memoir published in 1986.

His fall from grace in the aftermath of the coal strike was in marked contrast to the success of his period at British Steel. MacGregor himself considered his resuscitation of the steel industry to be by far the more significant of the two assignments. His appointment there, announced by Sir Keith Joseph, Secretary of State for Industry in May 1980, had caused fury and scorn. The House of Commons received with incredulity the news that Lazard Frères (the Wall Street investment bank of which MacGregor was then a partner) would receive a 'transfer fee' of up to £1.8 million as part of the deal. In ignorance both of MacGregor's industrial record and of his Scottish origins, oppositionists trumpetted that Joseph had succeeded merely in replacing one 67-year-old banker, the outgoing steel chairman Sir Charles Villiers, with another – and an American to boot.

But MacGregor achieved a remarkable turnaround: in 1980, when he joined, the corporation made 14 million tons of steel with a workforce of 166,000, and lost £1.8 billion. By 1983 it was achieving almost the same production with only 71,000 staff, and losses of £256 million. By 1985, British Steel was in profit, acknowledged to be one of the most efficient steel companies in the western world, and on course for privatisation.

MacGregor was proud to have found at BSC a management of high technical calibre which, in his view, had in the past been badly led – by appointees who were administrators rather than real industrial managers. He was also pleased that drastic reductions in manning had been achieved entirely by voluntary redundancies. He often remarked that, unlike the attitude to life imbued by his own upbringing, 'the biggest ambition people have in this country is not to work'.

Ian Kinloch MacGregor was born on 21 September 1912 in Kinlochleven, Inverness-shire. His parents, a works accountant and a schoolteacher, brought up their four children in the strict Calvinist traditions of the United Free Church. His two elder brothers helped to break the General Strike as tram drivers in Glasgow.

Young Ian was educated at George Watson's College in Edinburgh and Hillhead High School in Glasgow. He went on to take a first in metallurgical engineering at Glasgow University and a diploma with distinction at the Royal College of Science & Technology, now part of the University of Strathclyde.

MacGregor later said that his engineering apprenticeship on pre-war Clydeside, under tough Scots industrialists like the shipbuilder Sir James Lithgow, taught him the two vital requirements of management: an understanding of technology, and an ability to get the best out of a workforce.

During the Second World War, MacGregor was drafted into the Ministry of Supply under Lord Beaverbrook. He became an adviser on tank design, and was dispatched to Washington to supervise the buying of armour to replace losses at Dunkirk. For the remainder of the hostilities he was involved in joint Anglo-American production of war materials. MacGregor's decision to stay in the United States after the war was partly influenced by his opposition to the Attlee government's decision to nationalise the British steel industry. But he had also come to admire American industrial techniques, and saw better prospects for his own advancement in the classless environment of American business.

His reputation for fearlessness in the face of industrial unrest had early beginnings. In 1949, workers protesting at his takeover of a factory in Connecticut attacked his car and turned it over with him in it. On another occasion he was threatened by the Mafia. Of an incident in 1983 when a hostile surge of Northumbrian miners knocked him to the ground, MacGregor said that he had 'seen it all a dozen times before'.

In 1956, the company for which MacGregor worked merged with another to form American Metal Climax, later Amax. He became chief executive of the group in 1966 and chairman in 1969, turning it from a small producer of molybdenum into a widely diversified international mining operation. In the early 1970s, aware of the dangers of over-dependence on oil as an energy source, he took the company into coal-mining, becoming America's third largest producer. MacGregor was a workaholic who believed that management was a quasi-religious calling, requiring 24-hour, seven-days-a-week devotion. He built a worldwide network of business interests and political contacts. A remarkable physical constitution allowed him to fly almost continuously between Australia, North

America and Europe for board meetings and public engagements. He was also president of the International Chamber of Commerce in Paris. The secrets of his boundless energy were, he said, 'a low threshold of concern' – a refusal to be upset by perpetual crises in business – and catnaps: he was noted for his ability to sleep soundly on intercontinental flights.

MacGregor's return to the British industrial scene began in 1977 with his appointment by the Callaghan government as deputy chairman of British Leyland (BL), the nationalised motor manufacturer. There he clashed with the chairman, Sir Michael Edwardes, over what MacGregor saw as feebleness in dealing with troublesome trade unions. MacGregor later claimed (although other accounts differ) that it was he, rather than the reluctant Edwardes, who initiated the sacking of Derek 'Red Robbo' Robinson, the communist convenor in BL's Longbridge plant.

At the end of six years of grappling with the problems of steel and coal, MacGregor showed no sign of wishing to retire from controversy. From time to time he made trenchant interventions on privatisation matters. In 1987, he was rebuffed in a bid to join the board of British Gas as a spokesman for disgruntled shareholders. His name was canvassed in the press as a possible 'efficiency manager' for the National Health Service or chairman of British Rail.

He believed that the programme of pit closures announced by Michael Heseltine in 1992 was inevitable, given the relative attraction of gas as a cheap source of power. But he also believed that the contraction of the coal industry would have been achieved more humanely, and less acrimoniously, if his own strategy had been followed through by his successor.

MacGregor's wisdom became much in demand as a company doctor. He rejoined Lazards as a non-executive director in London and took on a clutch of chairmanships: of Goldcrest Films; a North Sea oil venture; the troubled property group Mountleigh; an American security business, Holmes Protection; and a printing company, Hunterprint, where he vigorously challenged being eased out, at 78, on grounds of age.

MacGregor maintained his peripatetic habits well into his early eighties, allowing himself only occasional breaks at his Bermuda home and his mansion on the shores of Loch Fyne.

Ian MacGregor was knighted in 1986 and appointed Chevalier of the Legion d'Honneur in 1972.

He married in Washington, in 1942, Sibyl Spencer, a Welsh girl whom he met on a blind date on the eve of the bombing of Pearl Harbor. She died in 1996. They had a son and a daughter.

13 April 1998

Sir Nigel Mobbs

⇥⇒ 1937–2005 ⇐⇤

Steward of Slough Estates

Sir Nigel Mobbs was the long-serving chairman of Slough Estates, the property company founded by his grandfather, and a forceful non-executive director of several other major companies.

The Slough trading estate on which the Mobbs family fortunes were based was originally a tract of farmland to the west of the Berkshire town. It was purchased by the War Office in 1917 as a transport repair depot and by the end of the First World War it had become a dump for some 17,000 cars, trucks and motorcycles. In 1920, the 600-acre site and its contents were sold for £7 million to a consortium led by Sir Percival Perry, who later ran the Ford Motor Co's British operations, and Noel Mobbs – brother of Edgar, a pre-war hero of English rugby who had been killed at Passchendaele.

Mobbs, later knighted, had come from Northamptonshire and had made a career in the motor trade as chairman of a coachmaking company, Pytchley Autocar; he invested £20,000 in the Slough venture and became its sales director. The surplus vehicles were repaired and sold off, and from 1925 the vast covered workshops became the foundation of one of Britain's first industrial parks, with Citroën, Gillette Razor and the Hygenic Ice Company among the first tenants. By the time Nigel Mobbs joined the business in 1960, some 240 manufacturers were represented on the site. In modern

times the estate's position close to the M4 motorway and Heathrow
made it attractive to a wide range of business tenants, and it
acquired its own power station, shops and banking facilities.

Although Slough Estates was sometimes described as the
'sleeping giant' of British commercial property, Nigel Mobbs's
stewardship of it as chief executive through two decades of changing
market fortunes was much admired: he managed the estate's
properties directly, rather than through agents, invested shrewdly in
other real estate at home and abroad, and carried through a hostile
takeover of Bilton, a rival property group.

Immensely tall, with a lively sense of humour, he was compared
by one City journalist to 'a slightly lumbering but affectionate and
appealing Great Dane'. Behind the amiable manner, however, was a
willingness to be forthright and very decisive when necessary. His
firmness, common sense and commercial intelligence were much
valued in other companies' boardrooms. In 1995, as deputy
chairman of Kingfisher, the holding company of Woolworths and
B&Q, he resolved a clash over strategy between the chairman Sir
Geoff Mulcahy and chief executive Alan Smith by hastening Smith's
departure, moving Mulcahy to chief executive, and taking the chair
himself until a strong new chairman, Sir John Banham, could be
appointed.

As the senior non-executive director of Barclays Bank, he also
had a vital role to play in the ructions and recriminations which
surrounded the sudden resignation of Martin Taylor as chief
executive in November 1998. When the news broke, Mobbs had to
interrupt his public duties as Lord Lieutenant of Buckinghamshire
to rush to the bank's head office in Lombard Street and help steady
what appeared briefly to be a rudderless ship heading for the rocks,
though he was unable to persuade Taylor to change his mind. As the
story made front-page headlines day after day, Mobbs declared that
some of the reporting of it would have been 'more at home in a Tom
Wolfe novel'; it was, he said, no more than 'a serious hiccup' for the
bank.

Gerald Nigel Mobbs was born on 22 September 1937 and was
educated at Marlborough and Christ Church, Oxford, where he
spent three years but failed to obtain a degree – a lapse which he

attributed to a combination of the after-effects of a hunting accident and finding his subject, engineering, 'extremely boring'.

He went on to do a stint with the chartered surveying firm of Hilier Parker before joining Slough Estates, where his father had succeeded his grandfather at the helm. He joined the board in 1963 and became chairman and chief executive in 1976, relinquishing his management role to become nonexecutive chairman in 1999. He was also chairman of Bovis Homes, and a director of Howard de Walden Estates, which owns 120 acres of central London, and Cookson, the industrial materials group.

A notably robust proponent of free enterprise, Mobbs was chairman of the right-wing pressure group, Aims for Industry; treasurer of the Conservative Party, deputy chairman of the Airey Neave Trust, and chairman of the council of Britain's only private university at Buckingham. He chaired an advisory panel on deregulation for the DTI, the Groundwork Foundation – which promoted public, private and voluntary co-operation to improve the environment on the edges of sprawling towns – and the Association of British Chambers of Commerce. He was also a trustee of Historic Royal Palaces and the National Army Museum, a commissioner of the Royal Hospital, Chelsea and a member of the Commonwealth War Graves Commission. He was knighted in 1986.

Nigel Mobbs liked to keep business and public commitments very separate from the happy family life he enjoyed, comfortably surrounded by horses, dogs and sheep, on a small estate near Princes Risborough in Buckinghamshire. He was an enthusiastic foxhunter, skier and golfer – his grandfather having at one time owned the Stoke Poges course.

He married, in 1961, Jane Berry, whom he first met on horseback. She was the daughter of the 2nd Viscount Kemsley, whose family owned the *Sunday Times* and the *Daily Telegraph*; they had a son and twin daughters.

21 October 1995

Sir Alastair Morton

⤙⟶ 1938–2004 ⟵⤚

Combative Eurotunnel boss

Sir Alastair Morton was chief executive of the Channel Tunnel project, perhaps the greatest civil engineering feat of the 20th century. He went on to be the first chairman of the Labour government's Strategic Rail Authority, where his combative personality – and his belief in the need for massive long-term public investment, both public and private – put him at loggerheads with Labour ministers.

The tunnel, opened in 1994, was to be the first dry link between Britain and France since the Ice Age. The British government had halted two previous diggings, the first by Colonel Beaumont in 1880 for reasons of national security, and the second in the mid-1970s for fear of spiralling costs. The third attempt was encouraged by Margaret Thatcher as the ultimate demonstration of the power of private enterprise: the tunnel was to be built entirely without taxpayers' money.

This stipulation created special difficulties, and the project was in the doldrums even before tunnelling began in late 1987. Morton – an experienced project financier, known for his belligerence and stamina – had been drafted in by the Bank of England as co-chairman (with a French counterpart) earlier that year. As one associate remarked: 'God created Alastair to supervise the Eurotunnel project.'

The major problems of the tunnel were financial rather than technical. Morton's crucial task was to hold the balance between a consortium of ten contractors, Transmanche Link (TML), on one side and a syndicate of no less than 223 banks on the other. In the middle was Eurotunnel, a new company – initially no more than a blank sheet of paper – created to own and operate the tunnel. After its stock-market flotation, Eurotunnel had more than 660,000 shareholders, whose interests Morton had to defend in a series of increasingly acrimonious crises.

Inevitably, costs overran (the first estimate of £4.8 billion rose finally to almost £10 billion), and tunnelling fell behind schedule. The project came close to collapse in 1990, by which time Morton's personal relations with some of the contractors had become openly adversarial. He was accused of interfering with their operations and of refusing to pay for works already completed.

The banks rallied behind him, supporting his appointment as chief executive. TML agreed to bear part of the cost overruns, but a project manager was put in place under Morton to ease relations on the construction site. The twin tunnels – at 50 kilometres, the longest in Europe – were complete in their basic form by June 1991.

Much remained to be done, however, and another major confrontation with the contractors blew up in 1992. Delivery of special locomotives for the tunnel's vehicle-carrying trains was also delayed. The stalemate which followed forced deferral of the official opening, originally planned for mid-1993, first until December of that year (by which time, one disgruntled contractor remarked, 'The only thing you can guarantee will be open . . . is Morton's mouth'), and finally to May 1994.

Morton was by nature an interventionist rather than a free-marketeer, a preference formed by early experience with Harold Wilson's Industrial Reorganisation Corporation (IRC). He argued repeatedly for intelligent use of public money in combination with private finance and for long-term planning in infrastructure developments. In this he was in tune with the French taste for state-led *grands projets*, rather than the traditional English disdain for such ventures. He was particularly angered by the failure of the Conservative government to promote a fast rail link from Folkestone to London in time for the tunnel's completion – unlike the French, who had all the necessary links in place at the Calais end. It was ironic, therefore, that Morton of all people should have proved the Thatcherite proposition that such massive projects as the Channel Tunnel could be achieved by private enterprise. If his abrasiveness enraged many of the parties involved, his deter-mination, drive and clarity of focus won him many more admirers.

Not least of those admirers was a grateful Conservative government, despite Morton's frequent tirades at what he saw as the ineptitude and short-sightedness of Transport ministers and Treasury officials. In 1993, Chancellor Kenneth Clarke (describing Morton as 'a veritable warrior') appointed him to chair the Private Finance Working Group, charged with finding more fruitful ways of involving private capital in transport projects.

Conscious of his Celtic and Afrikaner roots, Morton often contrasted his own approach to that of typical Englishmen, represented by Sheffield steel men with whom he had dealings in the 1960s. 'There'll be trouble if you do that,' was their reaction to every new proposition he put to them. With the Channel Tunnel there was certainly trouble, but indubitably he deserved credit for the achievement of a formidable task.

Robert Alastair Newton Morton was born in Johannesburg on 11 January 1938. His father was a Scottish oil executive who had married into an Afrikaner family descended from early Cape settlers of the 1650s. The Morton parents divorced while Alastair was still a child. Young Alastair was a brilliant scholar, entering Witwatersrand University at the age of 16 to study Classics and Mathematics. He went on to read law at Worcester College, Oxford, and later to Massachusetts Institute of Technology.

Morton began his career with de Beers, the mining house, in Rhodesia. In due course he was posted back to South Africa, but he was fiercely opposed to apartheid and chose to go abroad again three months later. Had he stayed, he said, he would probably have ended up 'in jail, to no effect'.

In 1964 he moved to Washington to work for the International Finance Corporation, part of the World Bank, where he perfected his French while negotiating loans to Francophone African governments. Three years later he came to London to the IRC, the vehicle for the Labour government's interventionist approach to ailing industries. There he became a protégé of Lord Kearton, who thought him 'a very able young man'. Still under thirty, Morton began to develop a ferocious reputation, bolstered by unusually piercing blue eyes and a piratical beard.

'We worked like hell,' he said later. 'We weren't there to make friends for life. We aroused opposition and we aroused fears.'

After the change of government in 1970, Morton left IRC to

join the 117 Group, an investment trust business founded by the financier Harley Drayton. Morton became chairman of Draymont Securities, a joint venture with the merchant bank Samuel Montagu, and specialised in rescuing stricken engineering firms. It was at this period that he developed one of his best-known enmities – towards Philip Shelbourne, Drayton's chief executive, later chairman of Montagu, a feline City grandee who habitually provoked strong reactions. The loathing between the two men, well-matched in arrogance but radically opposed in style, deepened over the years.

Morton's next move, in 1976, was to rejoin Kearton at the fledgling British National Oil Corporation (BNOC), where he was responsible for arranging massive bank loans to finance new North Sea fields. He particularly relished the atmosphere of optimism among oilmen tackling exploration problems in deep seas and rough weather.

But BNOC was a prime target for break-up and privatisation by the incoming Thatcher government, a policy which both Kearton and Morton (by then managing director) vehemently opposed. When Kearton stood down and no suitable name could be found from the oil industry to replace him, the government's choice fell on the shimmering figure of Philip Shelbourne. Morton made his feelings clear – it was, he said, 'a bad appointment, badly made' – and had no choice but to resign. There followed two years in the City wilderness, although non-executive directorships at British Steel and elsewhere kept him well occupied.

In 1982, the Bank of England asked him to step in as chief executive of Guinness Peat, a finance house facing serious difficulties. Morton set about it with vigour, disposing of its saleable assets despite the opposition of its major shareholder and life president, Lord Kissin. The rescue was achieved, and Morton won the admiration of the Bank of England for his uncompromising handling of it.

Five years later, Guinness Peat was bid for by Equitycorp, a predatory investor from New Zealand. Morton put up a savage defence, comparing the bidder to 'a demented puppy chewing your trouser leg when you are trying to serve a customer', but lost the battle and resigned again. By then, however, he was also co-chairman of Eurotunnel, and the need to concentrate on the project was pressing.

After leaving Eurotunnel, Morton was a director of National Power and a number of other companies, as well as his work at the Treasury on private finance projects. In April 1999, he was appointed by John Prescott as chairman of the Strategic Rail Authority (SRA), a new body charged with formulating a long-term rescue plan for Britain's ailing rail network.

Morton declared that privatisation of the railways had been achieved only by 'fragmentation', and that his task was to draw the strands together again in a new form of 'public private partnership'; he also dismissed Railtrack's £27 billion investment plan as inadequate, citing his own figure of £40 billion, and made it clear that he would prefer to see fewer train operators on longer franchises to encourage investment. As time passed, however, he was increasingly at loggerheads with ministers, who he accused both of over-interference in day-to-day decision-making and of failing to listen to his advice. The Morton blueprint for the future of the railways was repeatedly delayed in the chaotic period that followed the Hatfield crash, and he was not consulted over what he described as Stephen Byers' 'massacre' of Railtrack and its replacement by the 'not-for-profit' Network Rail. Deeply disgruntled, he left the SRA at the end of 2001.

Morton was chairman of the National Youth Orchestra, but his appetite for work – he was often to be found in his office at 5.30 a.m. – left little time for other interests. His holidays were devoted to walking and sailing. He was knighted in 1992.

Alastair Morton married, in 1964, Sara Stephens, an English-woman whom he met in Rhodesia; they had a son and a daughter.

1 September 2004

Sir Antony Pilkington

⊶⇛ 1935–2000 ⇚⊷

Innovative glass-maker

Sir Antony Pilkington was the last family chairman of Pilkington Brothers, the Lancashire company that achieved world leadership in glass-making. Founded in 1826 by William Pilkington – later joined by his brother Richard – the company became the dominant employer of the town of St Helens.

Antony Pilkington represented the fifth generation of family management, and though his chairmanship from 1980 to 1995 was in many respects a period of radical change, the company preserved an element of Victorian paternalism in its relations with the local community, even extending to the provision of false teeth for company pensioners.

He wanted Pilkingtons to be 'a good company in the best sense', he told an interviewer in 1990, 'Not just a money machine'. His concern was reciprocated in a remarkable upsurge of local support for Pilkingtons when it became the target in 1986 of a hostile takeover bid by BTR, an industrial conglomerate known for its ruthless approach to cost-cutting.

In response to the industrial recession of the early 1980s, Pilkingtons had reduced its workforce from 11,500 to 6,700, but had done so on generous terms and with a considerable effort – through the pioneering Community of St Helens Trust, of which Sir Antony was founder chairman in 1978 – to create small-business opportunities for those made redundant. BTR, by contrast, was rumoured to have abruptly sacked many workers at Dunlop, one of its recent acquisitions, in the week before Christmas. Politicians and local councillors joined the Pilkingtons workforce in rallying to the board's support, and after an arduous nine-week battle BTR was forced to withdraw.

A diffident, gentlemanly figure, who disliked dealing with the press and the City, Sir Antony Pilkington was also a very effective moderniser. He reformed Pilkingtons' old-fashioned hierarchical management structure, reduced the size of its board and placed new emphasis on salesmanship. In former times, the company's market position had been so strong that customers simply queued up to do business with it. An attempt to diversify into spectacle and contact lenses, through the 1987 takeover of the US firm Visioncare, was problematic, but Antony Pilkington continued to search for ways to reshape the group in response to market conditions.

In 1992 – once again faced with a sharp recessionary fall in demand for glass – he was forced into another round of cost-cutting at St Helens and a rationalisation of operations in Europe. Recovery was slow, but Pilkingtons remains a world leader in glass technology.

Antony Richard Pilkington was born on 20 June 1935. He was educated at Ampleforth and did national service in the Coldstream Guards before going up to Trinity College, Cambridge, to read history.

He joined Pilkington Bros in 1959, working on export sales of flat glass. He became marketing manager of the flat-glass division in 1967 and joined the board in 1973. In 1979 he became deputy chairman to his distant cousin Sir Alastair Pilkington – the inventor of the float-glass process, whose relationship to the St Helens Pilkington dynasty was so remote that a special board decision had been called for in 1947 before offering him a 'family traineeship'.

The float-glass process, perfected in 1958, was one of the most important industrial innovations of its era, becoming the universal method of making flat glass for buildings and vehicles. Licensed all over the world, it produced handsome streams of royalties for Pilkingtons over the following decades – a factor which, according to some analysts, created the corporate complacency which Sir Antony did so much to correct.

Pilkington was also a director of GKN, National Westminster Bank and ICI. He was a governor of Liverpool John Moores University, a member of the Court of Manchester University, a Deputy Lieutenant of Merseyside and High Sheriff of Cheshire in 1996–97. He was knighted in 1990.

His modest manner hid a love of fast cars and motor-racing: he sometimes drove to work in a 1956 Maserati. He was also a devoted fan of P.G. Wodehouse.

He married, in 1960, Kirsty Dundas, daughter of Sir Thomas Dundas, 7th Bt; they had three sons and a daughter.

22 September 2000

Lord Riverdale

➶═ 1901–1998 ═☞

Sheffield steel man

The 2nd Lord Riverdale was the grand old man of Sheffield steel, and an enthusiast for vintage Sheffield Simplex motorcars. Riverdale was chairman and president of Balfour Darwins, an amalgamation of his family firm, Arthur Balfour & Co, with another local steel firm, Darwins. Balfour's, built up by Riverdale's father, was an archetypal Sheffield business producing special steels, forgings, magnets and hacksaw-blades – and exporting them through an extensive sales network in Asia and Australasia.

Having joined the business in 1918, Riverdale inherited the chairmanship of the company and the barony from his father in 1957. The merger with Darwins came four years later, and Riverdale was chairman of the group until 1969.

Riverdale's enthusiasm for business was primarily in its mechanical and scientific aspects rather than in the financial side. The profits, as with many traditional manufacturing industries, began to show signs of decline in the late 1960s. He enjoyed tinkering with engines, and among his proudest possessions was a 1910 'gearless' Sheffield Simplex car which he found in Australia and lovingly restored. The Darwins merger gave him incidental pleasure because Darwins owned the Fitzwilliam works at Tinsley where the Simplex was built. An early rival to Rolls-Royce, the car was capable of accelerating smoothly from 5mph to 60 in a single gear: like a cheerful Mr Toad, Riverdale liked nothing better than to take it for a spin – on one occasion from Land's End to John O'Groats.

Always a lateral thinker, he attacked the problem of giant icicles on his Sheffield mansion in the cold winter of 1947 by shooting them off the gutters with a deer rifle. He wrote two books about his pastimes: *Squeeze the Trigger Gently* and *A Life, A Sail, A Changing Sea.*

He was active in every aspect of Sheffield life and held many public offices, including, in 1946, the Mastership of the Cutlers' Company in Hallamshire, the steel-makers' guild; his father had been Master Cutler in 1911, and his son Mark (who also succeeded him as chairman of Balfour Darwins) held the post in 1969. Riverdale became by far the longest-lived Master, and was an avuncular presence at Cutlers' feasts for the last half century of his life.

Robert Arthur Balfour was born in Sheffield on 1 September 1901. His father, Arthur, acquired control of a steel business called Seebohm & Dichstahl, and built it at the turn of the century into a prosperous concern under his own name. In the era when Sheffield steel employed some 80,000 people (as opposed to perhaps 5,000 in the 1990s) Balfour's was one of its most celebrated names.

Having served on innumerable committees on industrial development and imperial trade, Arthur was created a baronet in 1929 and raised to the peerage, as Baron Riverdale, in 1935. Young Robert was educated at Oundle, and was slightly too young to see service in the First World War. He later joined the RNVR, and in his forties served as a lieutenant commander in the Second World War, seeing action in the aircraft carrier *Ark Royal* off Dakar in West Africa.

Returning to business, he became managing director of Balfour's in 1949 and eventually retired as president of Balfour Darwins in 1975. By then the business was suffering, threatened both by foreign competition and by new technology. It was to go through several more mergers and rationalisations, ending up under Australian ownership.

Riverdale was also a director of the National Provincial Bank and Yorkshire Television. He was president of the Association of British Chambers of Commerce, the National Federation of Engineers' Tool Manufacturers, the Milling Cutter and Reamer

Trade Association and the Twist Drill Traders Association, and a leading figure in export promotion. In Sheffield, he was president of the Chamber of Commerce, a governor of the local savings bank, Town Collector and Guardian of the Standards of Wrought Plate. He was a magistrate, and a deputy lieutenant of South Yorkshire. He was also, for more than fifty years, Belgian consul for Leeds and Nottingham, a post that, according to one account, chiefly involved 'persuading errant Belgian daughters to return home'; he was an officer of the order of Leopold II of Belgium.

In his spare time Riverdale was a talented naval architect, perfecting the design of the twin-keeled yacht – and becoming known to his yachting friends as 'Twin Keel' Balfour. He was commodore of the Royal Cruising Club. He was also a keen fly-fisherman, and a familiar figure on the grouse moors of the West Riding. As well as the Simplex, he owned a rotary-engined German DKW motorcycle, a 1932 Talbot and a variety of other vintage machines. In 1987 he was injured in an accident in a 1935 Lagonda, but he recovered to drive again.

Lord Riverdale married first, in 1926, Nancy Rundle, an admiral's daughter who died in 1928; and secondly, in 1933, Christian Hill, who died in 1991.

His son by the first marriage, Mark, died in 1995; he was survived by a son and a daughter of the second marriage. The barony and baronetcy passed to Mark's son, Anthony, born in 1960.

26 June 1998

Lord Trotman

1933–2005

British head of Ford in the US

Lord Trotman was the first British head of the Ford Motor Company, and was also briefly chairman of ICI. Alex Trotman advanced from running Ford of Europe to take charge of North American operations in 1989 and to become chairman and chief executive from 1993 to 1998. Ford had made heavy losses in the early 1990s, and Trotman set out to restructure the group's operations under a plan called Ford 2000.

Described as having 'a certain vigorous Scottishness about him' and a very clear idea of what he wanted to achieve, Trotman had built his career both at Dagenham and Dearborn, Ford's US headquarters, in the field of product planning, with a particular focus on the standardisation of model 'platforms' and components around the world. This approach became central to his strategy to reshape Ford for the new century. He put European managers and designers in global charge of small- and medium-sized cars (the Mondeo was a notable result) and their US counterparts in charge of larger cars, including the ubiquitous 'sports utility vehicle'.

The strategy generated billions of dollars worth of cost savings and restored Ford's profitability, but created fierce internal tensions which were only partially resolved when Trotman vacated the chair to make way for William Clay Ford, grandson of the company's founder, at the end of 1998. To the American motorist, however, Trotman was a hero for having rescued the Ford Mustang, the growling 4-litre 'muscle car' first launched in 1964. Its design had become outdated, but rather than see production cease, Trotman oversaw – for a relatively modest $700 million – a redesign which retained the side air vents and triple tail lights of the iconic original.

While still based in the US, Trotman became a non-executive director of ICI in 1997. Having returned to Britain, he was the chemical group's chairman from 2002 to 2003, and was a reassuringly strong presence for shareholders during a period of crisis caused by an excess of debt and a change of business direction. He was only the second of 15 chairmen in the history of ICI to come from outside its own senior management.

Alexander James Trotman was born at Isleworth on 22 July 1933, the son of an upholsterer, and was brought up in Edinburgh, where he was educated at Boroughmuir High School. After national service in the RAF as a navigator, he joined Ford at Dagenham as a trainee in the purchasing department and was given the task of chasing deliveries of radiators for the Consul model.

He went on to be chief product analyst on a new car project

codenamed Archbishop – which emerged in 1962 as the hugely successful Cortina, of which more than three million were eventually sold. This marked him for promotion, and in 1967 he was appointed the first product-planning director of Ford of Europe, which had been created chiefly to co-ordinate the previously disparate activities of the group's British and German factories.

Trotman was ambitious to gain experience at Dearborn and agitated for a posting there – but when he was offered one in 1969, it was at less than his British salary and he had to buy his own ticket across the Atlantic. He took the risk and continued his rise, becoming chief car-planning manager in 1975 and returning as vice-president of truck operations for Europe in 1979. Four years later he was posted as president of the Asia Pacific region in Melbourne, where he took on the Japanese competition and made Ford the Australian market-leader. He became chairman of Ford of Europe in 1988, and applied his skills to bringing productivity at Dagenham and Halewood up to the level of their sister factories in Germany.

During the 1990s he was also a director of IBM and the New York Stock Exchange. After returning to Britain he was president of the Hakluyt Foundation, which provides intelligence on foreign markets for corporate clients, and led a review of conditions for small businesses at the behest of Gordon Brown.

Trotman's understanding of car-making enabled him, as a hobby, to build a replica of the GT40, the classic Ford sports car which competed at Le Mans in the 1960s. He described himself as 'a North Atlantic person', holding dual US and UK nationality but retaining traces of a Scottish accent. At the height of his career he kept homes in Michigan and London as well as a log cabin in Canada and a cottage in North Yorkshire – whence he eventually retired. He was knighted in 1996 and was created a life peer in 1999.

He was twice married and was survived by his second wife Valerie and four children.

26 April 2005

Sir George Turnbull

1926–1992

Car industry leader

Sir George Turnbull was one of the most notable British executives in the modern mass-production car industry. He left Britain in 1974, after a row with Lord Stokes, the head of British Leyland, to help set up the first South Korean car plant. Often described as the best leader British Leyland never had, Turnbull returned to Britain to preside over the difficulties of the French-owned Chrysler company in the early 1980s, and was later chairman of Inchcape, an international trading group with extensive motor interests.

Turnbull was essentially a forceful production engineer, of exuberant energy and strong opinions. He was a man who got on well with other people and got things done, rather than a strategist and intellectual. He was perhaps unlucky that the peak years of his career coincided with a spectacular decline of the British motor industry which he and other able men steeped in its traditions could do little to reverse.

George Henry Turnbull was born on 17 October 1926 and educated at King Henry VIII School in Coventry. He joined Standard Motors from school and, as an indentured apprentice, went on to take an engineering degree at Birmingham University.

He rose rapidly through the ranks at Standard, becoming general manager at the age of 33 in 1959. Standard merged with Triumph in 1962 and in due course became part of the British Leyland group. By 1969, Turnbull was deputy chairman of Standard Triumph and a deputy managing director of BL. His responsibility at BL was the Austin-Morris range. He oversaw the introduction of the Allegro and Marina models, unlikely to be remembered as classics but typical, rear-wheel-drive, box designs of their era. It was a period when the trade unions were gaining the upper hand at Cowley and Longbridge. Management, including Turnbull, tended to appease rather than face up to them.

Turnbull had worked closely with the BL chairman Lord Stokes in their earlier days at Standard Triumph. But in October 1973 Stokes preferred another man, John Barber, for the managing directorship, after Turnbull had taken an outspoken stand against Stokes's policies of centralisation. Turnbull then surprised the motoring world by accepting a three-year contract with the Korean group, Hyundai, to set up a £36-million factory making the 'Pony' car, an early milestone in Korea's emergence as a new industrial force. 'You don't get the chance every day to build a whole motor industry from scratch,' he remarked as he left.

Turnbull recruited a team of British engineers to go with him to Korea and was able to direct substantial orders for parts and equipment to British exporters. The speed with which the Pony reached production provoked vivid comparisons between low-waged and ferociously diligent Korean workers and their British counterparts. With his Korean assignment successfully completed in 1977, there was talk of Turnbull returning to run BL. But the then National Enterprise Board chief, Leslie Murphy, could not offer him the freedom of action he wanted. The job went instead to Michael Edwardes, who endorsed and pursued Turnbull's earlier ideas on devolution of management power in what had become a hopelessly unwieldy organisation.

Turnbull chose to go abroad again, this time as adviser to the Iran National Motor Co, where – until shortly before the fall of the Shah – he presided over a plant assembling car kits based on the Hillman Hunter. He then accepted the chairmanship of Chrysler UK, owned by the Peugeot-Citroën group which had been involved in the Iranian project. Part of Chrysler's business depended on the export of kits to Iran and there were immediate difficulties as orders declined. It was a period of retrenchment for Chrysler, under pressure from its French owners, leading to the threat of closure of the Linwood plant and to cutbacks elsewhere.

Turnbull was obliged to be tougher with his workforce than he had been at BL. The Ryton factory in his native Coventry was, however, sustained for a time by the introduction of the Talbot Horizon model. But the designs were old-fashioned, and competition from Europe and Japan was increasingly aggressive and more stylish.

From 1982 to 1984 Turnbull was chairman of the Society of Motor Manufacturers, where he spoke out in vain against the 10 per cent tax on new cars and fought for tighter voluntary controls on Japanese imports. In 1984 he moved on to Inchcape, then a sprawling and loosely managed international trading group which included in its portfolio the lucrative Toyota dealership in Britain as well as Jaguar and Rolls-Royce concessions elsewhere. Turnbull took a firm grip of the management, increased the focus on the motor sector and revitalised Inchcape's interests in the growing markets of the Far East. He became chairman of Inchcape in 1986 and had planned to continue in that role until 1997. But declining health forced him to retire in 1991 at the age of 65.

From 1987 Turnbull was chairman of the Industrial Society, which worked for better communication in industry. He was knighted in 1989.

George Turnbull married, in 1950, Marion Wing. They had a son and two daughters.

22 December 1992

⋆⟾ PART SIX ⟽⋆

GLOBAL PLAYERS

HERMANN ABS – *German banker who led post-war reconstruction*
GIOVANNI AGNELLI – *Fiat heir and prince of playboys*
CHUNG MONG HUN – *Korean tycoon who committed suicide*
MARVIN DAVIS – *wildcat oilman turned Hollywood studio owner*
WIM DUISENBERG – *first head of the European Central Bank*
HAROLD GENEEN – *mastermind of the sinister multinational ITT*
EDMOND SAFRA – *murdered Lebanese banker*
LORD THOMSON OF FLEET – *Canadian newspaper billionaire*
MICHAEL VON CLEMM – *pioneer of the Euromarket*

Hermann Abs

✦═ 1901–1994 ═✦

German banker who led postwar reconstruction

Hermann Abs, the financier, played a central role in Germany's economic recovery after the Second World War. In his mid-30s Abs had been a *Wunderkind* of the pre-war German business community, head of the foreign department of the country's most powerful financial institution, Deutsche Bank, and a director of numerous industrial companies. He held important boardroom positions throughout the war, but survived accusations of complicity in war crimes and emerged as a key financial adviser to the British Military Government.

In 1948, Abs was asked to run the Reconstruction Loan Corporation, which had been set up to channel aid to industry under the Marshall Plan. He was scrupulous in avoiding any hint of favour in the distribution and his insistence, in concert with economics minister Ludwig Erhard, that heavy industry should be rebuilt first was later seen as a crucial factor in the German 'economic miracle'. He was also adamant that, in order to regain respectability in the international community, Germany should repay its pre-war debts.

Chancellor Konrad Adenauer accepted his advice and acknowledged Germany's liabilities in 1951. In the following year, Abs led the delegation to the London Debts Conference at Lancaster House, where he settled all outstanding claims at a cost of \$3.3 billion. The burden of repayments provoked criticism in Germany but before long, as the country's external trade improved, it was seen to be relatively modest.

The Deutsche Bank had been dismantled by the Allies, but Abs (who in the interim served as a director of one of its smaller successors, the Suddeutsche Bank) was able to revive it in 1957. Under his guidance it became one of the world's most respected commercial banks. He was spokesman of its management board until 1967, chairman of the supervisory board until 1976 and thereafter honorary chairman.

Hermann Josef Abs was born in Bonn on 15 October 1901. His father, Josef, was a lawyer and official interpreter, who had spent some years in England and instilled Anglophile tastes in his son. From an early age, Hermann was determined to enter the business world: in his final year at the Gymnasium in Bonn, he asked his teacher to note on his report that he had finished his studies 'in order to become a merchant'. He gave up studying law at Friedrich Wilhelm University after the first year to work for banking houses in Germany and Amsterdam, with training periods in London and New York, before joining Delbruck Schickler & Co, one-time bankers to Frederick the Great, in 1929. In 1935 he became a partner, but moved two years later to join the board of the Deutsche Bank.

After the war, American investigators demanded to know why Abs had moved from a lucrative private partnership to a lower-paid job at the politically important Deutsche Bank. Abs compared the choice to that of a well-paid church organist being offered the chance to play, for less money, in a great cathedral.

A devout Catholic, a democrat by inclination and a friend of many prominent Jewish businessmen, Abs was never an active Nazi. In 1942, having shown some disrespect for the party, he was forced to tender his resignation from the bank's board. But the board refused to accept it and Abs remained in his post throughout the war.

In November 1946, the Bulletin of the US Office of Military Government in Germany reported that 'Abs was the guiding spirit of the villainous Deutsche Bank which combined an unusual concentration of economic power with active collaboration in the criminal policies of the Nazi regime'. The bank was accused of looting financial institutions in Poland and other occupied territories.

Abs also served on the boards of a large number of industrial companies associated with the German war effort. These included Kontinentale Oel AG, which was formed to take control of Soviet and Eastern European oilfields, and IG Farben, the vast chemical conglomerate. But at the end of hostilities, Abs' expertise was immediately valuable to the British Military Government, which deemed him 'indispensible' and refused to hand him over to the Americans. The latter insisted that he should be detained – provoked, according to Abs, by the fact that his confident views on the reconstruction of the German currency differed from theirs. Abs was duly held and interrogated for 90 days in Bad Nenndorf detention centre. Although stripped of his business appointments he was released unconditionally, having been placed in 'Category 5' – the classification for those exonerated of active support for Hitler. A court in Zagreb took a different view, sentencing him *in absentia* to 15 years for war crimes.

Abs went on to build up considerable influence. He sat on the boards of 24 companies, including Lufthansa, Daimler-Benz and the Federal Railways. Although not affiliated to any party he frequently attended cabinet meetings and was known to have declined the post of foreign minister. He advised the International Finance Corporation in Washington, as well as a number of foreign governments, and – with Lord Shawcross – drafted a 'Magna Carta' for the protection of international lenders and investors. When Pope Pius XII died in 1958 German businessmen liked to joke that Abs was a candidate to succeed him.

Abs sported pointed moustaches and Savile Row suits, smoked fine cigars and generally suggested a German acting as an English gentleman. He spoke several languages, collected Impressionist paintings and played the piano.

His home, an estate at Remagen in the Rhineland, was noted for its dairy herd, vineyard and orchards. But Abs relaxed little and prided himself on his stamina, often swimming 600 yards before breakfast. His friend Sir Siegmund Warburg noted approvingly that Abs 'doesn't believe in holidays'.

Accusations against Abs were revived from time to time. On Armistice Day 1958, he was interrupted whilst addressing the Institute of Bankers in Lombard Street by a group of ex-servicemen waving a swastika on which was written: 'Go home Abs'. Also, in 1983, when he was appointed a special advisor to the Holy See in the aftermath of the Vatican Bank scandal, the Nazi-hunter Simon Weisenthal claimed to have documentary evidence that Abs had taken part in IG Farben board meetings at which the use of slave labour from Auschwitz had been discussed.

Abs was married to a cousin of the Schroder banking dynasty.

5 February 1994

Giovanni Agnelli

⤞⟾ 1921–2003 ⟾⤝

Fiat heir and prince of playboys

Giovanni Agnelli, the former chairman of Fiat, was one of Europe's most charismatic business leaders, and was often said to be the most powerful man in Italy. Agnelli was a princely figure in every sense. His family wealth was estimated at £3 billion and he controlled more than a quarter of the companies on the Milan stock exchange; little of significance happened in Italian corporate life without his say-so. Reversals in the Fiat group's fortunes before he died wiped much of that value from the stock exchange, but Agnelli himself remained an undisputed influence: stock prices rose and fell dramatically during his last years in direct response to news about the 'honorary chairman's' health. As an unelected statesman, a press baron and Italy's biggest private-sector employer, his pronouncements carried national and international weight.

Though the only public office he ever held was as mayor of the company town of Villar Perosa, Agnelli's position in Italy's fragile political structure was uniquely secure. The Soviet leader Nikita Krushchev once took him aside, among a gaggle of Italian cabinet ministers, and said, 'I want to talk to you because you will always be in power. That lot will never do more than just come and go.' Agnelli had the clout to veto public appointments which displeased him, and to ensure that Japanese car imports into Italy were kept to a minimum, preserving Fiat's 60 per cent domestic market share.

Agnelli looked and acted the patrician ruler. *Life* magazine described him in 1967 as having 'the sculptured bearing of an exquisitely tailored Julius Caesar'. Increasingly handsome as he grew older, he disdained personal danger, skiing and driving as though every day might be his last. He maintained a fine art collection, magnificent houses, yachts, private aircraft and – though his only marriage was contented and permanent – a roving eye for beautiful women.

He matured from the Riviera playboy of the early 1950s to become one of the world's most admired businessmen, but he remained the ultimate icon of Italian masculinity. Known universally as '*L'Avvocato*' (the lawyer) he was a law unto himself, both in the exercise of *strapotere* (all-embracing power) and in his personal style – he wore his wristwatch on top of his shirt cuff.

In business he was noted for his low boredom threshold, and was never a hands-on manager. He made notable mistakes, but was a shrewd deal-maker and a courageous leader, and in later years he willingly delegated to professionals. Having brought Fiat into the modern era, he steered it through the extreme difficulties of depression and terrorist threats of the 1970s to a golden era in the mid-1980s, when it was recognised as Europe's most successful car-maker.

Giovanni Agnelli (known as Gianni) was born in Turin on 12 March 1921, the eldest son of Edoardo Agnelli and Princess Virginia Bourbon del Monte di San Faustino – whose mother, a celebrated Roman hostess of her day, was American. Edoardo, who died in an air crash when Gianni was 14, was in turn the only son of Senator Giovanni Agnelli, the Piedmontese cavalry officer who founded Fabbrica Italiano Automobili Torino s.P.a. in 1899.

Brought up by English governesses, young Gianni learned to speak impeccable English and several other languages besides. After his father's death, he was groomed intensively for his future role as head of the family by his formidable grandfather, who fought a custody battle with Princess Virginia. When Gianni left school in 1939 he was despatched to Detroit – Henry Ford was a friend of the Senator – to study the workings of the American car industry. The Senator was also on terms with Mussolini, and the Agnelli empire prospered hugely throughout the pre-war era.

Gianni embarked on law studies at the University of Turin, but in 1941 – though he could have claimed exemption because Fiat factories were deemed essential to the war effort – he insisted on joining the army, in his grandfather's regiment. As a lieutenant on the Russian front in 1941, his armoured cars froze into the ice and he and his troops suffered appalling conditions without even the most basic winter equipment. Twice wounded, and having lost a finger to frostbite, he made his way home largely on foot. After a spell in hospital, he was sent to North Africa, where he won the Cross for Military Valour. Following the Italian surrender in 1943 he completed his doctorate at Turin then rejoined the army as a liaison officer with the Italian Legnano Group – which fought against the Germans alongside the US 5th Army – and was decorated again.

When Senator Agnelli died aged 79 in 1945, his fortune was divided into 12 parts. Gianni received two-twelfths, plus the family ball-bearing company RIV which he ran for some years, while each of his siblings and first cousins received one-twelfth.

Fiat itself was for the time being under the iron command of its second chairman, Vittorio Valetta. Though Gianni was given the title of vice-president and took a part-time interest, there was no real job for him. So he took his grandfather's advice to 'have a fling for a few years and get it out of your system'. With a reputed allowance of $1 million a year to spend, this was a pleasurable challenge. He threw legendary parties at the 28-room Villa Leopolda on the Côte d'Azur, and kept houses in New York and St Moritz as well as Turin. Among his girlfriends was the actress Anita Ekberg; among his companions were Prince Rainier, the young Kennedys and Errol Flynn.

But the years of self-indulgence came to an abrupt end in 1952. He had set up house with Pamela Churchill (née Digby, later Harriman), but she caught him *in flagrante* with a younger woman; a blood-curdling row ensued. As Agnelli drove the girl home, touching 140mph on the Corniche above Monte Carlo, his Ferrari slammed into a lorry. His right leg was broken in six places and permanently damaged, forcing him to wear a brace for skiing and to drive cars adapted for the use of the left leg only. The accident did not affect his nerve – the Formula One champion Niki Lauder later described being driven by Agnelli as one of the most terrifying experiences of his life – but it did make him reconsider his priorities. 'That jolt changed my life,' he said, 'I stopped playing and started thinking.'

From then on he took a more active part in Fiat, becoming managing director under Valetta in 1963. He was also chairman of Istituto Finanziario Industriale, the holding company established by his grandfather to control the family's widespread interests in shipping, oil-refining, armaments, banking, insurance, retailing and manufacturing. Also in the portfolio were two leading Italian newspapers, *La Stampa* and *Corriere del Serra*, Turin's football team Juventus, and Agnelli's private ski resort.

Agnelli finally took charge of Fiat in 1966, when Valetta retired. He immediately launched a massive reorganisation, introducing decentralised management systems to a group which had until then been controlled by autocrats. The model range at that time was dominated by the tiny, utilitarian Fiat 500, but the new chairman began a gradual shift upmarket.

Fiat rapidly overtook Volkswagen, its main competitor, in sales volume. Agnelli saw the whole of continental Europe as his marketplace (though he met some resistance to that idea in France) and by 1969 his company was producing 20 per cent of the EEC's cars and trucks. New factories were opened in Russia and Eastern Europe. Over the coming years, Fiat took over virtually the whole of the Italian motor industry, including Lancia, Alfa-Romeo and Ferrari.

In the mid-1970s however, Italy was afflicted by an economic slump and an upsurge of Red Brigade terrorism. Many Fiat executives were attacked, and the mother of Agnelli's son-in-law was kidnapped. Agnelli himself, the number one target, lived for some years under constant guard: his protectors had to be specially trained to keep up with his driving. But he refused to shift his base of operations outside Italy, and later shunned the elaborate security favoured by other Italian tycoons, which he said made it impossible for him to lead a normal life – though he carried a cyanide pill as the ultimate alternative to death in terrorist hands.

He also had no truck with state interference in his factories, and union militancy. In 1979, having lost production of 200,000 cars through strikes and indiscipline, Agnelli decided that enough was enough. He fired 61 militants and saboteurs, and laid off 23,000 others to make way for robots on the assembly lines. The vast Mirafiori plant in Turin was closed for 35 days, as left-wing ministers and even fellow industrialists pleaded with Agnelli to give way to strike demands. But he refused to budge.

Eventually, 40,000 workers marched silently through the city in opposition to their own strike leaders. The siege was at an end, the unions routed. Many Italians took the view that Agnelli had not only saved Fiat, but had saved Italy itself from communism and economic paralysis. But his strategic manoeuvres were not always admired. In 1976 Agnelli had attracted fierce criticism and some astonishment by selling 10 per cent of Fiat to the Libyan government, under Colonel Gaddafi. There were concerns that the Libyans were effectively underwriting expansion of Fiat factories in Russia in exchange for continued Soviet military support, though it was acknowledged that Agnelli had extracted a remarkably high price – $415 million – for the stake. The Libyans sold out ten years later for close to $3 billion.

By then, after twenty years of Agnelli's leadership, Fiat had prospered once more. The success of the Uno model helped take profits to more than $2 billion a year, though car production represented only half of the vast conglomerate's activities. Attention focussed increasingly on the problem of succession, but Agnelli was persuaded to remain in the chair until 1996, when he was 75, and to hand over to his long-time number two Cesare Romiti rather than his own brother Umberto.

After another difficult patch in the early 1990s, the group returned triumphantly to profit with the launch of the Punto, Bravo and Brava models in Agnelli's last years. Agnelli was also chairman of *Editrice la Stampa*, the newspaper group, and a director or adviser of several international companies, including Chase Manhattan Bank. He was chairman of the Italian equivalent of the CBI, and vice-chairman of the Association for Monetary Union of Europe.

Giovanni Agnelli married, in 1953, the tall and elegant Princess Marella Caracciolo di Castagneto. Reporting the engagement, the *Daily Telegraph* noted in Proustian terms that 'at the Marquis de Cuevas's ball in Biarritz last September, Princess Marella was regarded as the most beautiful woman present'. From an ancient Neapolitan family, she became a *Vogue* model and photographer, and in later years created a magnificent garden at the ancestral Agnelli estate in the Alpine foothills. They had two children: the only son Edoardo was, however, never a serious contender to take over the helm of Fiat. Known as 'Crazy Eddy', he became a drug addict and a devotee of mystic philosophies; in 2000, he died, apparently a suicide. It was Giovanni ('Giovannino') Alberto, son of Umberto, who emerged as the heir apparent – but in 1998, he died of cancer at the age of 33.

In 2000, Fiat struck a deal with General Motors, selling 20 per cent of its car manufacturing operation to the Detroit-based firm, with an option to sell the remaining share to GM by 2004. 'Our partnership with General Motors has given us the chance to return to America,' said Agnelli in 2001. But he turned down the role of honorary chairman of Mediobanca, a Milan investment bank in which Fiat had a 2 per cent stake, with the words, 'I'm too old for that.' Giovanni Agnelli was survived by his wife and their daughter, Margherita.

24 January 2003

Chung Mong Hun

◈⇒ 1948–2003 ⇐◈

Korean tycoon who committed suicide

Chung Mong Hun, who committed suicide by throwing himself from the 12th floor of his office building in Seoul, was the head of Hyundai, the once mighty but later deeply troubled South Korean industrial group. Founded by Chung's father in 1947, Hyundai had grown from a small construction business to become one of modern Korea's most powerful *chaebol* (conglomerates) with interests ranging from securities trading to shipbuilding, car-making and microchips, in which it was a global leader.

But a combination of crippling debt and internecine strife brought the group to a low ebb over the period from 2000 to 2003, while Chung Mong Hun was facing criminal charges for his part in a bizarre arrangement to bribe the North Korean leader, Kim Jong Il, into participating in what had been billed as an historic peace summit with South Korean president Kim Dae Jung in June 2000.

The encounter between the two Kims at Pyongyang earned Kim Dae Jung a Nobel Prize and produced a ground-breaking joint declaration on movement towards reunification of the two countries, which have maintained a heavily armed stand-off for the past half-century. For students of Korean body language, it also produced apparent evidence of personal rapprochement, as the two presidents were reported to have held hands in the back of their shared limousine; the Korean press waxed lyrical about 'a spark from heart to heart'.

But the new mood was not long sustained by the North Korean Kim, whose reactivation of his country's nuclear programme placed him high on President Bush's list of potential enemies. Meanwhile, South Korea's state auditors discovered that $186 million lent by the state-owned Korea Development Bank to Hyundai Merchant Marine – which ran cruise ships from South Korea to the North Korean resort of Mount Kumgang – had been passed to the North Koreans a week before the summit. Hyundai claimed the money was for 'development rights', but Chung Mong Hun was indicted in June 2003 on charges of doctoring company accounts to disguise the transfer.

Chung Mong Hun was born in Seoul on 14 September 1948, and graduated in Korean literature from Yonsei University, where his contemporaries nicknamed him 'country bride' for his excruciating shyness. He was the fifth of six sons of Chung Ju Yung, who had come to Seoul from the north as a teenager in the 1930s to find work in a rice mill, and bought an auto-repair shop in the city in 1940. After the Second World War, Chung senior ingratiated himself with the occupying US forces and began to win construction contracts both from the Americans and from the governments of Syngman Rhee and Park Chung Hee.

Ruthless and rough-edged, Chung slept and worked alongside the men he drove to phenomenal feats of labour on his construction sites. In the mid-1960s he bid a token price of one Korean *won* to rebuild the Han River Bridge, and completed it ahead of schedule. A 250-mile highway from Seoul to Pusan, which the World Bank had declared not to be feasible, was delivered under budget. With no prior experience of the shipbuilding industry, Chung went on to build the world's largest shipyard at Ulsan. At its peak his group encompassed 79 companies, with combined sales of $78 billion.

Chung Mong Hun joined Hyundai Heavy Industries in 1975, becoming president of the group's shipping interests in 1981. His methodical management style and filial loyalty impressed his father, who put the young man in charge of the group's electronics ventures – which were hugely successful until the downturn of global technology markets in the late 1990s.

As cracks began to appear in the structures which had sustained Korea's emergence as an Asian tiger economy, Kim Dae Jung's government called for the break-up of family-dominated *chaebol*. The octogenarian Chung Ju Yung's first response in December 1997 was to name Mong Hun as a co-chairman of the group alongside the eldest of the six sons, Chung Mong Koo – known as 'the bulldozer', and the head of the group's automotive businesses.

The two brothers fought for supremacy as the group sank deeper into financial trouble and faced continuing pressure for reform. After further interventions by Chung Ju Yung – at first announcing that both brothers should resign all their posts, which Mong Koo refused to do, and then that Mong Hun should become sole chairman – the group was finally broken up. Large parts of it were on the verge of bankruptcy at the time of his death.

Mong Hun retained as his principal role the chairmanship of Hyundai Asan, which was engaged in a variety of loss-making projects in North Korea, including a $5 billion industrial park at Kaesong; in this he remained loyal to the wishes of his father, who died in March 2001.

Chung Mong Hun was survived by his wife, a son and two daughters.

4 August 2003

Marvin Davis

◦◦▭ 1925–2004 ▭◦◦

Wildcat oilman turned Hollywood studio-owner

Marvin Davis was the billionaire oilman and media mogul who sold 20th Century Fox to Rupert Murdoch. Davis arrived on the Hollywood scene in 1981 as the new co-owner of the Fox studio – his partner in the deal was the controversial oil trader Marc Rich –

having made his first fortune from 'wildcat' oil and gas-drilling in the Rocky Mountains of Colorado.

Davis relished the glamour of the movie and television world – referring to Fox stars as 'my family' and expressing a desire to make a sequel to *The Sound of Music* – but was not a hands-on studio boss: for that role, in 1984, he brought in Barry Diller, the combative former head of Paramount, with whom he swiftly fell out as Fox's finances deteriorated.

By March 1985 Rich had become a fugitive from US justice (he was later to be pardoned by Bill Clinton). Davis arranged to sell Rich's stake in the studios to Rupert Murdoch; but Murdoch was not happy sharing power and bought out the other half later that year, for a total price of $575 million. Davis reportedly told friends he hoped Murdoch might fail to make the final payment, so that he could take back the studio and 'fire Diller'.

In later years, Davis owned New Jersey gambling interests and was a successful exponent of 'greenmail', profiting from threatened takeover bids which never actually came to pass. As he put it himself, 'All you have to do is look at the pretty girl and everyone thinks you're sleeping with her. You don't have to put up any money.' Among his rumoured targets at various times were Northwest Airlines, US Airways, CBS, NBC and Mesa, the oil company controlled by T. Boone Pickens. His last gambit, in 2002, was an unsolicited $15 billion bid for the entertainment assets of the French group Vivendi, which had acquired Universal Studios; but a major obstacle was Barry Diller, who held a stake in the businesses concerned, and the deal fell away.

Davis once remarked that 'as men get older, the toys get more expensive'. His wealth was estimated by *Forbes* magazine in 2004 at $4.9 billion. In his prime, he was in every sense larger than life, But in his last years he was reported to have lost 130lbs and to have become so enfeebled by illness that he had to be carried by his bodyguards.

Marvin Davis was born at Newark, New Jersey on 28 August 1925, and graduated from New York University in 1947. Having started his working life in New York's garment trade, he joined his father in building up Davis Oil in Denver. In the early 1980s, once he had taken over from his father, Davis moved his base of operations to California, where he bought the Beverly Hills Hotel and the Pebble Beach golf resort. A keen golfer himself, he described Pebble Beach as the asset he came closest to falling in love with – but later sold it to Japanese investors at enormous profit. He also had interests in Texas oil and Chicago real estate, and tried unsuccessfully to buy an NFL (American football) team franchise.

Davis and his wife Barbara were for some years major donors and fundraisers for the Democratic Party. They hosted a $25,000-a-head soirée for Bill Clinton – attended by the likes of Barbra Streisand and Steven Spielberg – and a similar event for Hillary Clinton during her senatorial election campaign. But when President Clinton subsequently sent a video-taped message rather than fulfilling a promise to appear personally as guest of honour at the Davis's annual Carousel of Hope ball to raise money to fight diabetes (which afflicted their daughter Dana), they took severe umbrage. 'There are 25 people in our family,' Barbara told an interviewer. 'I told the White House person, "You are now talking to 25 new Republicans."'

Marvin Davis was survived by his wife and four children; his son John became a Hollywood film producer.

25 September 2004

Wim Duisenberg

⊷ 1935–2005 ⊶

First head of the European Central Bank

Wim Duisenberg, who was found dead in the swimming pool of his French villa, presided over the launch of the euro as the first president of the European Central Bank.

A lanky chain-smoker, world-weary in appearance, Duisenberg never looked comfortable on public platforms and never matched the ability of his US counterpart, the long-serving Federal Reserve chairman Alan Greenspan, to appear omnisciently wise while saying nothing unequivocal enough to frighten the markets. Indeed Duisenberg attracted the nickname 'Euro-gaffeur' – or more unkindly, in the London foreign exchange markets, 'Dim Wim' – for his habit of making off-the-cuff remarks which caused the fragile new currency to totter. He became the target for much recrimination which might more sensibly have been aimed at the finance ministries of member countries for their failure to pursue economic reform and fiscal discipline.

His rough ride at the ECB was in contrast to the high reputation he had enjoyed among fellow central bankers during his tenure as governor of the Nederlandsche Bank, the Dutch central bank, from 1982 to 1997. There he was credited with playing a key role in turning the weak Dutch economy of the late 1970s into one of the strongest and most stable in Europe. He did so by aligning the guilder with the German deutschmark and taking the Bundesbank's monetary rigour as his guiding light, while encouraging a free-market approach by the Dutch government – in contrast to policies he had himself initially pursued as a left-leaning finance minister in the 1970s.

But his appointment as president of the European Monetary Institute in 1997 and of its successor, the European Central Bank, the following year, was dogged by political machinations. His candidacy had been strongly favoured by Germany, Chancellor Kohl having early recognised that a German nominee would not be acceptable to the French. But the French derided Duisenberg as Monsieur Cinq Secondes – for the time it supposedly took him to make up his mind to follow German interest-rate cuts – and at the Brussels summit in May 1998, Jacques Chirac nominated Jean-Claude Trichet, the governor of the Banque de France, as an alternative candidate. A furious row ensued, culminating in the announcement of a 'gentleman's agreement' that, in view of his age – he was in fact only 62 at the time – Duisenberg would step down halfway through the specified eight-year term for the job. Duisenberg himself never acknowledged that he had agreed to this and made it clear that he would decide the timing of his departure for himself – effectively guaranteeing that he would never have any support from Paris.

Though the introduction of the euro as a trading currency in 1999, and as notes and coins in 2002, was smoothly achieved, the

ECB failed to command international confidence in its early years, and the euro fell sharply against the dollar. Duisenberg was repeatedly criticised for being too cautious in cutting euro interest rates to stimulate the faltering Eurozone economy and for being high-handed with politicians. He was, for example, unwilling to meet requests from MEPs for the publication of ECB board minutes, suggesting that 16 years would be a suitable interval before they were made public.

The lowest point in both Duisenberg's and the euro's fortunes came in October 2000, when he was asked by a British journalist whether a currency crisis provoked by a Middle East war would justify central bank intervention in the foreign exchange markets. His unguarded reply – 'I wouldn't think so' – provoked a record low for the euro against the dollar. Shortly afterwards, French finance minister Laurent Fabius was asked three times in a press conference if he would like to endorse Duisenberg, and three times declined to reply.

There was much discussion as to how long the accident-prone Duisenberg could remain in his post. But meanwhile his intended successor, Jean-Claude Trichet, had been placed under investigation for matters relating to his earlier career as a senior executive of Credit Lyonnais, and was ordered to stand trial for fraud in 2002. Eventually Duisenberg announced that he would retire on his 68th birthday in July 2003 – by which time the euro had soared in value again and Duisenberg's standing had also somewhat recovered, though the Eurozone economy remained stagnant. Trichet was still busy defending himself in court and the handover was delayed until November 2003, after he had been acquitted.

Willem Frederik Duisenberg was born at Heerenveen on 9 July 1935, the son of a local official. He studied economics at the University of Groningen, completing his doctoral thesis on the subject of the economic results of disarmament, and remained at the university as a teaching assistant for some years until he joined the Europe division of the International Monetary Fund in Washington in 1965.

He returned home to become an adviser to Nederlandsche Bank, the Dutch central bank, in 1969 and professor of macroeconomics at the University of Amsterdam a year later. In 1973, still only 38, he was chosen as finance minister by the incoming centre-left Prime Minister Joop den Uyl. He initially favoured higher government spending to counteract recession – increasing the public-sector portion of Dutch GDP from 48 per cent to 55 per cent – but eventually switched to a policy of fiscal discipline which attracted criticism from his own former allies on the Left. He stood down from ministerial office in 1977 and sat as a Labour MP for a year before leaving politics to become vice-chairman of Rabobank, whose primary activity was agricultural lending. In 1981 he returned to Nederlandsche Bank.

Wim Duisenberg was a keen golfer – he once skipped a meeting with Dutch bankers during an IMF gathering in Madrid to play in a tournament organised by the Spanish hosts – and a fan of country and western music, with a particular liking for the ballads of Johnny Cash. He married first, in 1960, Tine Stelling, by whom he had a son and two daughters.

He married secondly, in 1987, Gretta Nienwenhuizen (née Bedier de Prairie), an outspoken left-wing activist. She was in the habit of denouncing the IMF even while her husband sat on its board, and caused embarrassment to him (and outrage among their Jewish neighbours) in 2002 by hanging a Palestinian flag from the balcony of their Amsterdam apartment in support of a demonstration against the Israeli government.

31 July 2005

Harold Geneen

→≡● 1910–1997 ●≡←

Mastermind of the sinister multinational ITT

Harold Geneen was the mastermind of ITT, one of America's most powerful – and to some observers, most sinister – multinational corporations. Geneen's conglomerate acquired the reputation of being, in the words of Anthony Sampson in his 'secret history' of

ITT, *The Sovereign State* (1973) 'accountable to no nation, any-where; and held together . . . by one man, against whom no one cared to argue'.

After a period of rapid expansion in the 1960s, when it grew to control 400 companies in 70 countries (including insurance and food interests in Britain), ITT overreached itself in the early 1970s and became enmeshed in scandal. It stood accused of tax-fiddling, bribery and trying to control governments, at home and abroad.

International Telephone & Telegraph had begun its existence in 1920 as a network of Caribbean telephone companies; as it expanded it encountered many governments that wanted to control their own telecommunications, and developed what Sampson called 'a web of corruption and compromise' to deal with the obstacles. When the British-born Geneen took over in 1959 it was a loose-knit empire producing modest profits: he removed the autonomy of its operating units and introduced a system of strict accountability.

At the core of the system were lengthy monthly meetings in New York and Brussels, of which Sampson provides a vivid account. 'On the last Monday of every month, a Boeing 727 takes off from New York to Brussels, with sixty ITT executives aboard – often including Geneen himself with a special office rigged up for him to work in. For four days they stay in Brussels, still insulated in their special ITT world: many of them keep their watches on New York time. A meeting is a weird spectacle, with more than a hint of Dr. Strangelove. The curtains are drawn against the daylight and a big screen displays endless tables of statistics. Round a big horseshoe table sit the top men of ITT from America and Europe, like diplomats at a conference. In the middle, swivelling and rocking to and fro in his armchair, is an owlish figure behind a label: "Harold S Geneen".'

The ordeal of being cross-questioned in these meetings could make managers physically sick, but Geneen liked to see their faces as well as read their reports. He believed that the highest art of management lay in being able to 'smell' the truth. In modern jargon he was a 'control freak'; his most famous dictum was 'I want no surprises'.

Harold Sydney Geneen was born in Bournemouth on 22 January 1910, the son of a Russian-Jewish concert manager and an

Italian mother. The family moved to the United States when he was still a baby, but his parents later separated. He was educated at Suffield Academy in Connecticut and New York University, where he studied accounting in the evenings while working as a runner on the stock exchange during the day.

In 1934 he joined an accounting firm and in due course he held financial posts with Bell and Howell, the Jones & Laughlin steel company and the electronics group Raytheon. As a controller of expenditure and collector of debts he was 'like a bloodhound on the trail of a wasted dollar', according to one early colleague. It was at Raytheon that he developed the techniques later perfected at ITT, including monthly management reviews and what he described as 'constant pressures and samplings to measure progress'. But his powers at Raytheon were limited, and in 1959 he resigned abruptly to become president of ITT.

As Latin American governments began nationalising local ITT telephone companies, Geneen bought a portfolio of other businesses, including the Sheraton hotel chain and interests in manufacturing, publishing and house-building. He liked consumer businesses but avoided anything to do with computers, making his decision on the briefest inspection of a company's books. His attempt to take over the American Broadcasting Corporation in 1966 was thwarted by the Department of Justice, but in 1970 he completed one of his most profitable acquisitions, the Hartford Fire Insurance Co. The Department of Justice again objected, but an out-of-court settlement allowed ITT to keep Hartford while disposing of other interests, including the Avis hire car company. Allegations followed that the settlement was connected with a $400,000 contribution to the Republican Party.

There were also accusations of tax evasion and stockmarket chicanery. It was rumoured that ITT had offered cash to the CIA to undermine the left-wing Allende regime in Chile, which was about to nationalise ITT's operation there – and it was later revealed that the company had funded illegal operations in Indonesia, Iran, the Philippines, Algeria, Mexico, Italy and Turkey. ITT became the subject of investigations by the Securities and Exchange Commission, the Internal Revenue Service, the Watergate special prosecutor, a Federal Grand Jury and the specially formed Senate Sub-Committee on Multinational Corporations, which threw light on Geneen's ruthless use of lobbyists to further ITT interests. The corporation's credibility was battered and its share price slumped, but Geneen was not to be easily unseated. He maintained his relentless, flinty management style, protected from press attention by the intense loyalty of his own staff.

He drew a salary of $1 million but lived across the street from his office as the modest accountant he was, preferring to be known as 'just plain Harold'. He finally stood down as chief executive in 1977, and as chairman two years later. His empire did not long survive his departure. His successors opted for consolidation rather than growth, much to Geneen's regret. What remained of ITT, after a period of poor performance in the 1980s, was eventually split into three separate companies.

In old age Geneen continued to work a ten-hour day, buying and selling businesses on his own account with considerable success. He was noted for aphorisms such as 'The worst disease which can afflict executives in their work is not alcoholism; it's egotism'. In 1997 he published a bestseller, *The Synergy Myth*, defending his own record and attacking fashionable management concepts, including that of the 'socially responsible corporation'.

For relaxation Geneen enjoyed fishing off Cape Cod, but his fishing trips were usually thinly disguised business meetings.

He was twice married, but had no children.

21 November 1997

Edmond Safra

⋆⟾ 1932–1994 ⟽⋆

Lebanese private banker

Edmond Safra, who died in an arson attack at his home in Monte Carlo, was one of the world's richest and most secretive private bankers. He founded banks in Brazil, Switzerland and the United

States, and inherited another in Beirut; his personal fortune was estimated at $4 billion and he was often referred to as a latterday Morgan or Rothschild. His success was built on the loyalty of some tens of thousands of wealthy clients – chiefly Sephardic Jews like himself – who were reassured by his total discretion and extremely conservative banking principles. A banker, he said, 'is the custodian of people's secrets'.

His businesses were unusually well capitalised, hoarding their customers' wealth in the form of deposits, ultra-safe securities and gold, rather than indulging in risky lending or speculative trading as other commercial banks did. Yet Safra also courted controversy, and – though he declared in 1997 that 'I want my banks to last ten thousand years' – not all his dealings were advantageous. In 1984 he sold his Swiss operation, Trade Development Bank, to American Express for $550 million – deeply superstitious, he often favoured the number 5. But relations swiftly soured once the deal was completed. Many of Safra's old clients took their business elsewhere, and Safra himself made it clear that he did not like the way they had been handled.

He was accused of poaching his own former staff to create a rival empire. After he severed all ties with American Express, rumours spread that he had been involved in the laundering of drug money and had links with, among others, the former Panamanian dictator Manuel Noriega, Mossad and the CIA. A legal battle ensued, in which American Express eventually admitted responsibility for a smear campaign, and made a seven-figure payment to charity in recompense.

Safra's New York bank, Republic National, was the 17th largest banking network in the United States and – despite loan write-offs in Latin America in the late 1980s – was widely viewed as one of the most risk-averse banks in the Western world. But the financial community was shocked to learn in 1998 that Republic had suffered trading losses of $190 million on Russian bonds. There was a feeling that Safra – who was suffering from Parkinson's disease – had lost his Midas touch; he agreed in May 1999 to sell Republic, and his Luxembourg-based private banking interests in Europe, to the British banking group HSBC for $10.3 billion. But a row over

Republic's role in the so-called 'Princeton affair' – an alleged defrauding of Japanese investors – held the deal back, and Safra had to agree to a $450 million cut in his share of the proceeds to keep it alive. He would still have collected $2.8 billion.

Not long before Safra's death, Republic was involved in uncovering the embezzlement of hundreds of millions of dollars of international loans and aid to Russia through another New York bank; Safra had ordered Republic to cease dealings with a number of Russian counterparties and to co-operate fully in investigations. Initial reports of his death speculated about a Russian involvement, but an American nurse, Ted Maher, was later convicted of arson.

Edmond Jacob Safra was born on 6 August 1932 in Beirut. He was the second son of Jacob Safra, a Sephardic Jew from Aleppo, Syria who had established a banking business in the Lebanese capital in 1920; the family had been bankers since the days of the Ottoman Empire, when they financed camel caravans between Aleppo, Constantinople and Alexandria.

Young Edmond joined his father at the age of 16, learning the rudiments of trade in precious metals and currencies in the souks of Beirut. One of the lessons Jacob taught his favoured son was always to look his customers in the eye, 'for eyes tell more than balance sheets'. Another, often quoted in annual calendars sent out to Edmond's clients, was 'Build your bank as you would your boat, with the strength to sail safely through any storm'.

When anti-Jewish riots in Beirut followed the establishment of the state of Israel in 1948, the Safra family looked for safer havens. Edmond moved first to Milan, where he made an early fortune of his own by arbitraging between Italian and British gold prices. In 1952 the family joined a wave of Jewish migrants to Brazil, where they founded the Banco Safra, which grew into a network of fifty branches. A decade later Edmond sold his interest in the Brazilian bank to his brothers, Joseph and Moise, and moved on.

In Geneva he founded the Trade Development Bank, catering for Middle Eastern clients disdained by traditional Swiss bankers. In New York he founded Republic National Bank; Robert Kennedy cut the ribbon at the opening ceremony in 1966. Republic was a full-scale retail operation, rather than an exclusive private bank, and

Safra showed a flair for attracting business off the street: he offered television sets as gifts to new customers and was briefly the largest distributor of colour televisions in the US.

Always dark-suited and solicitous, Safra combined ruthless charm with scrupulous integrity. His appetite for business was tireless; he used the telephone constantly, so much so that his wife once described going to bed with him as 'like a board meeting'. In his heyday, he was credited with an unerring instinct for market trends. He cultivated powerful friends, and hosted lavish parties at the annual World Bank meeting in Washington. He continued to own his father's original business in Beirut, now the Banque du Crédit National, and had a personal holding, thought to be worth £70 million, in the Canary Wharf property development in London.

He had homes in Paris, Villefranche-sur-Mer on the French Riviera, Geneva, London, New York and Beirut as well as Monaco. He was also a generous philanthropist: he endowed hospitals, schools and Jewish community centres in France and the city hall in Jerusalem, as well as an institute of Sephardic studies in New York and a chair in the same subject at Harvard. All his philanthropic projects were named after his father.

His Brazilian-born wife Lily Monteverdi, a wealthy heiress in her own right, was a patron of the arts and of environmental causes. The couple had no children.

3 December 1999

Lord Thomson of Fleet

⤙⟹ 1923–2006 ⟸⤚

Canadian newspaper billionaire

The 2nd Lord Thomson of Fleet was Canada's richest businessman, having inherited newspaper empires created by his father on both sides of the Atlantic; he was best known in Britain for having sold *The Times* to Rupert Murdoch in 1981.

The Thomson fortune was estimated at around £10 billion. The

Thomson Corporation of Toronto, of which Kenneth Thomson –
who rarely used his title – was chairman from 1976 to 2002, had
become an international publisher of legal, financial and educational material in electronic form, having gradually withdrawn
from the newspaper business which was its foundation. In Britain,
the family also had significant interests in travel, publishing and oil,
but the name of Thomson of Fleet will always be associated with
ownership of *The Times* and *Sunday Times* during a turbulent
period of Fleet Street history.

Kenneth Thomson's father Roy (created Lord Thomson of Fleet
in 1964) was by his own account 'a rough-neck Canadian' who had
prospered by building a chain of local newspapers and radio stations.
In 1954, aged 60, following the death of his wife and the failure of a
brief bid to launch himself in Canadian politics, he moved to
Edinburgh as the new proprietor of the *Scotsman*, leaving Kenneth in
charge in Toronto. Five years later Roy Thomson acquired the
Kemsley newspaper group, which included the *Sunday Times*; and in
1967 he bought *The Times* from the Astor family, bringing the two
titles together as Times Newspapers.

Thomson senior's brash, commercial approach made him an
unlikely and, in the Establishment view at the time, unsuitable
proprietor of *The Times*. But he was content to accept rigorous
editorial safeguards, and regarded the paper's restoration to
financial health as a worthy task, even if it would never repay his
investment. 'We conceived it our duty, Ken and I, to do a good and
unstinted job on this project,' he wrote in his memoirs. 'And I was
greatly moved that my son . . . wholeheartedly agreed with me in
pouring away all those millions to save an ideal.'

This was an uncharacteristic attitude for Ken, whose deep
pockets were matched by remarkably short arms. More millions were
poured away than either of them could have anticipated, however.
Kenneth became chairman of Times Newspapers in 1968 and joint
president of the company (with Gavin Astor) from 1971, but his
commitment was by no means as emotionally driven as his father's.
As losses mounted and production was disrupted by constant
disputes with the all-powerful Fleet Street print unions, Roy
Thomson told an interviewer in 1973 that 'my son . . . is even more

enthusiastic . . . than I am. If I was to suggest to him that we should close *The Times* and save the drain on our resources, I think he'd shoot me.' But, as the paper's historian put it, this was 'pure self-deception'. Ken's true loyalty was to his father, but not to *The Times* or to Britain: his own family life was firmly settled in Toronto.

Soon after Roy Thomson's death in 1976, Kenneth made clear that he would continue to sustain the papers' losses only if their staff co-operated in fundamental reforms – including the introduction of new technology to allow journalists to type their copy straight into the production system, rather than have it retyped by a member of the typesetters' union, the National Graphical Association. But the NGA fiercely opposed any change. After a series of stoppages, Thomson issued an ultimatum that *The Times* and *Sunday Times* would have to close until sensible agreement was reached on uninterrupted production. The closure began in November 1978 and lasted a year, at a cost of £40 million. Thomson – less resolute than some of his own senior managers – eventually backed down, and when publication recommenced it did so with almost no concessions from the unions, which rapidly reverted to form.

The *Sunday Times* was in reasonable health but *The Times*' losses (ultimately borne by the family, rather than by their British public company, International Thomson Organisation) were still running at more than £1 million a month.

A strike by *Times* journalists asking for a large pay rise in August 1980 came as the last straw for Thomson – who felt personally let down by journalists he had paid throughout the 1978–79 stoppage. In October he put Times Newspapers up for sale, on the understanding that *The Times* might have to shut down permanently if no sale had been agreed by the following March. There were plenty of potential buyers, however, including Lord Rothermere, Robert Maxwell, and consortia led by the editors, William Rees-Mogg of *The Times* and Harry Evans of the *Sunday Times*.

But Rupert Murdoch's reputation as a proprietor tough enough to ensure the papers' survival made him the front-runner, despite fears that he would interfere editorially and take the papers downmarket. Murdoch's final offer of £12 million was lower than Rothermere's £20 million, but without a guarantee as to the future of *The Times*, and was at least half covered by the value of the *Sunday Times* building in Gray's Inn Road. But Kenneth Thomson was content to accept it, having done his utmost to fulfil his promises to his father.

Kenneth Roy Thomson was born in Toronto on 1 September 1923. His father, whose ancestors had emigrated from Dumfriesshire, tried his hand as a young man at a variety of occupations, including farming in California, and at the time of Kenneth's birth was running an automotive parts business. When it fell on hard times in the late 1920s, Roy became a radio salesman, moving the family first to Ottawa and then to the bleak, provincial towns of North Bay and Timmins. In 1931, aiming to boost radio sales, he opened a radio station, and in 1934 he bought a newspaper, the Timmins Press. He gradually acquired more papers and radio stations across Ontario, and expanded into a variety of other businesses, including hairdressing salons.

Meanwhile, young Kenneth was educated at Upper Canada College and for a year at the University of Toronto before joining the Royal Canadian Air Force, in which he served from 1942 to 1945.

A late academic developer, he went on to gain a First in law at Cambridge before beginning his newspaper career in the editorial department of the *Timmins Daily Press* in 1947. He moved on to the *Galt Reporter* at Cambridge, Ontario, where he was general manager until 1953. After his father moved to Scotland, Kenneth returned to Toronto to take over the chairmanship of the North American interests, which grew to include local titles in Florida and the Caribbean as well as the largest group of newspapers in Canada. When *The Times* was acquired, it became the 138th title in the Thomson portfolio. By the late 1970s the group's American papers alone had a daily circulation of over a million, and in 1980 it acquired a leading Canadian national daily, the *Globe and Mail*.

On other fronts, meanwhile, Thomson Travel was established in Britain in 1965 to develop the emerging package-holiday market, and netted more than £1 billion for the family when it was sold off in 1998. And a speculative investment in North Sea oil in 1971 paid handsome dividends from the exploitation of the Piper and Claymore fields. In the 1990s the Thomson group followed fashion by selling off all its newspaper interests and investing heavily in electronic information and publishing businesses. Its last British regional newspaper interests were sold in 1995, and ownership of the *Globe and Mail* was exchanged in 2001 for a 20 per cent stake in Bell Globemedia, a multimedia venture.

Over four decades at the helm in Toronto, Kenneth Thomson proved himself a highly competent steward of a wide-ranging portfolio. He was a quiet, cultivated man, with none of his father's rumbustiousness. He did not renounce his peerage because he had promised his father he would keep it, but never used the title in Canada and admitted that it gave him 'a somewhat uneasy feeling'. He never took his seat in the House of Lords.

Besides his own companies, he was a director of Hudson's Bay Company, Toronto-Dominion Bank and IBM Canada. He was a member of the Baptist church, and a patron of art and music in Toronto. His private art collection, which included European sculpture, ivory portrait miniatures and Renaissance jewellery, was the finest in Canada, and much of it was expected to be donated to the Art Gallery of Ontario.

Ken Thomson married, in 1956, Nora Marilyn Lavis; they had two sons and a daughter. The heir to the barony is the elder son, David, born in 1957, who became chairman of the Thomson Corporation in 2002; that year he paid £49.5 million at auction for a recently rediscovered Rubens masterpiece, *The Massacre of the Innocents*, as a present for his father.

12 June 2006

Michael von Clemm

◦→═ 1935–1997 ═←◦

Pioneer of the Euromarket

Michael von Clemm was a pioneer of the international capital markets and a polymath of exceptional range. An anthropologist by discipline and an American by birth, von Clemm was one of a group of young London bankers of the 1960s who created the 'Euromarket': the fast-moving, largely unregulated network in which international borrowers (whether governments or large companies) were able to borrow US dollars held by banks and investors outside the United States. It was the growth of this market which consolidated London's position as the world's pre-eminent financial centre.

First at Citibank, then at Credit Suisse First Boston (CSFB) and lastly at Merrill Lynch, von Clemm was one of the City's most potent conceptual thinkers and one of its most successful business-getters. A complex, driven man, he was a perfectionist and a hard taskmaster to those who worked with him. But many of his disciples (such as the former White House budget director David Mulford) rose to great heights, and he remained intensely loyal to close friends and colleagues.

His contacts around the world were extraordinary. He had introductions at the highest level everywhere – though it was all discreetly done, without an excess of name-dropping. He was said to spend 200 days a year travelling, and was an early exponent of constant use of the mobile telephone. His expense account was immense: invitations were prized for his parties at the annual IMF and Asian Development Bank meetings, including one memorable reception in a private pavilion of Beijing's Forbidden City on the eve of the Tiananmen uprising.

But despite the pressures of his banking career, von Clemm maintained a broad hinterland of other interests. He helped the Roux brothers to create their restaurant empire, and conceived the Canary Wharf development in Docklands. He taught at business schools on both sides of the Atlantic, and supported numerous artistic and academic projects. His last appointment was as president of Templeton College, Oxford, the university's school of management studies.

He was also a sportsman who travelled the world in pursuit of exotic game. Asked once how it was that he maintained his ferocious enthusiasm for business, he replied simply, 'I'm a hunter. I like to bag things.'

Michael von Clemm was born in Long Island on 18 March

1935, the son of a Bavarian father, Werner Clemm von Hohenberg, and an English mother. He was educated at Exeter Academy, New Hampshire and Harvard, where he graduated cum laude in 1956. He went on to pursue postgraduate studies in Anthropology at Harvard and Corpus Christi College, Oxford. As fieldwork for his doctorate, he and his wife spent two years studying social change among the Wachagga tribe of Mount Kilimanjaro, in what was then Tanganyika: among his published work at that time were contributions to *Economic Botany*.

Von Clemm's first ambition was to be a journalist, and in an interval of his studies he spent a period as a night staff reporter on the *Boston Globe*, often covering crime stories. On leaving Oxford in 1962 he was about to join the *New York Times*, but the paper was on strike: instead he took a job in the London office of First National City Bank of New York (later Citibank), a pacesetter in international finance in that era.

There he was 'stuck in a corner and put to work on something the old-timers knew nothing about'. Several bankers have been credited with 'inventing' the Euromarkets (notably Siegmund Warburg, who launched the first Eurobond issue in 1963) but von Clemm's particular contribution was the development of Euro-dollar certificates of deposit. The first sample of this breed of instrument, which came to be traded between banks in huge volumes, was kept framed in his office, made out in the name of his elder daughter.

In 1967 von Clemm was invited to teach at Harvard Business School. He did so for four years, commuting from his home in London and at the same time developing his own strategic consultancy firm, with corporate clients on both sides of the Atlantic. It was in the late 1960s that he also began his association with Michel and Albert Roux. Von Clemm was frustrated by the dearth of good food in the City, but greatly admired the Roux brothers' cooking at Le Gavroche, then in Lower Sloane Street. The three of them formed what Michel called 'a fraternité'. He became chairman of Roux Restaurants, and together they expanded the empire to more than twenty outlets, including Le Poulbot in Cheapside, La Tante Claire in Chelsea and the Waterside Inn at

Bray. In restaurant service as in complex financings, von Clemm demanded the highest standards: though the Rouxs were exceptionally good at what they did, von Clemm was often 'able to make us think, to see details that might have escaped us', according to Michel.

Returning to the City in 1971, von Clemm became a partner in the investment banking firm of White Weld, as well as a visiting professor at the London Business School. White Weld in due course merged into a joint venture with Credit Suisse, and later became Credit Suisse First Boston – of which von Clemm was chairman and chief executive from 1978 to 1986. He kept the firm at the top of Eurobond market league tables for 15 years, acquiring a formidable reputation for winning new business from governments and large companies. As a diplomat and high-level salesman he was supreme, but he was also a brilliant and obsessive technician. In 1980 he and his colleague Hans-Jeorg Rudloff brought radical change to the Eurobond market – and raised the stakes for its leading participants – by launching the first 'bought deal', in which CSFB underwrote an entire bond issue on its own account rather than spreading the risk amongst a syndicate of banks. He also did much to develop (though he did not invent) the floating-rate note, an instrument which became a vital component of capital funding for international banks.

In 1984, von Clemm spotted an opportunity of a different kind. Visiting the undeveloped, semi-derelict Canary Wharf in search of small industrial space for a Roux Brothers catering venture, he saw the potential for office developments akin to those recently completed in the waterside area of Boston. He brought in an American developer, Ware Travelstead (who in turn brought in the Reichmann brothers of Olympia & York) and set out to persuade other bankers, and the Bank of England itself, that the project could become an extension of the City – which indeed it did, though only after a period of extreme financial difficulties. CSFB was one of the first trading firms to move there.

In 1986 von Clemm moved to become chairman of the capital market operations of Merrill Lynch, one of the giants of Wall Street, where he controlled 12,000 staff in more than sixty countries. His office was now in New York, but again he preferred to commute from London.

He retired from Merrill Lynch in 1993, but maintained a wide portfolio of international business interests ranging from director-ships and advisory roles in the United States, Norway, India, Indonesia and East Africa to a stake in the Berkeley Square florists which supplied table decorations to the Gavroche. His private holding company, Highmount Capital, held stakes in a number of merchant-banking businesses around the world.

In October 1996 he was elected president of Templeton College. He maintained strong connections with Harvard. In London he was an adviser to the Royal Academy, a trustee of the British Museum Development Trust and a vice-president of the City of London Archeological Trust. He was also a prime mover in the Compton Verney opera house project in Warwickshire.

Von Clemm described his hobbies as collecting Michelin stars with the Roux brothers and collecting airline boarding cards. But he also found time for fishing (preferrably in Iceland) and shooting – anything from duck-flighting in Pakistan to sand grouse on the fringes of the Kalahari Desert.

He married, in 1956, Louisa (Lisa) Honeywell, who made her own career as a bookbinder; they had two daughters.

6 November 1997

PART SEVEN

FORTUNES INHERITED

EARL CADOGAN – *Chelsea landlord*
VISCOUNT COWDRAY – *Polo-playing Pearson group chief*
SIR PAUL GETTY – *philanthropist and cricket fan*
LORD HAYTER – *last of the Chubb Lock dynasty*
LORD HOWARD DE WALDEN – *Marylebone landlord*
LORD LATYMER – *Coutts heir and expert on Mediterranean plants*
LORD MARKS OF BROUGHTON – *Marks & Spencer heir*
VISCOUNT ROTHERMERE – *Daily Mail proprietor*
LORD ROTHERWICK – *shipping heir*
BARON HANS HEINRICH THYSSEN BORNEMISZA – *art collector*
GARRY WESTON – *sliced-bread billionaire*

Earl Cadogan

⊰⇒ 1914–1997 ⇐⊱

Chelsea landlord

The 7th Earl Cadogan was a London landlord on the grandest scale. The Cadogan family originated from Radnorshire, claiming descent from Elystan Glodrydd, founder of the fourth Royal Tribe of Wales. The name means 'battle-keen' in Welsh. Their London estate covered more than 90 acres of Chelsea from Cadogan Place and Sloane Square in the east to Old Church Street in the west. The manor came into their possession through the marriage in 1717 of Charles Cadogan (younger brother of General Sir William Cadogan, the Duke of Marlborough's confidant and Quartermaster-General) to Elizabeth, daughter of the physicist and landowner Sir Hans Sloane. Sir William received an earldom in 1718, but died without an heir; the present Cadogan line descends from his brother's son, who became the 1st Earl of the second creation in 1800.

The estate was transformed by Cadogan's grandfather, the 5th Earl, in the last quarter of the 19th century. Until then the family were not so rich; where Cadogan Square now stands was a large cricket pitch. As leases fell in, tenants were evicted. They were followed into the street by their floorboards, torn up to discourage them from returning. Chelsea was redeveloped with a distinctive mix of red-brick architecture and stucco terraces. Many of its streets were named after family connections: Elystan Street after the legendary Welsh prince; Margaretta Terrace after William Cadogan's wife.

The 5th Earl was Lord Lieutenant of Ireland, particularly remembered for abolishing the kiss of fealty given by Irish debutants to the holder of that office. The 6th Earl was a less sober figure. A heavy drinker and spendthrift, he was the third son and unexpectedly inherited the title in 1915 when his young nephew died of appendicitis. A compulsive gambler, he was bankrupted three times, and in the 1920s confessed to losing £2000 in a single night at chemin-de-fer. He spent much of his time thereafter watching birds at Culford Hall, the family estate in Suffolk.

Like many of his forebears, the 7th Earl was essentially a soldier
and a sportsman – he was a senior figure on the Turf and in later life
he spent much of his time on his Perthshire estate Snaigow. But he
was also a shrewd steward of the Chelsea property, which had been
left in trust on the death of his grandfather (who was Lord
Lieutenant of Ireland) in 1915, so that little could be done in the
way of development until the ultimate heir, the 7th Earl's son
Viscount Chelsea, came of age in 1958.

Thereafter Cadogan promoted a number of striking projects,
including the Carlton Tower Hotel – adjacent to the site of Chelsea
House, the family mansion which burned down in 1933 – and Arne
Jacobsen's controversial Danish Embassy building in Sloane Street.
In the mid-1960s he was disappointed to be refused permission for
a housing complex in the area around Tedworth Square designed by
the architect Minoru Yamazaki. The original estate remained
largely intact, and new investments were added in Australia and
elsewhere. Cadogan handed over the management to his son in
1974; their portfolio was estimated in the mid-1990s to be worth
£500 million.

William Gerald Charles Cadogan was born in London on 13
February 1914. As a child, he and his sister Beatrix were fascinated
by the hair of his uncle Eddie, who had gone bald while still young
and painted his scalp with Clarkson's Blacking instead. Young Bill
used to wonder how his uncle made his parting. He was educated at
Eton and Sandhurst, where he hunted hares with his own pack of
Bassett hounds. He succeeded to the earldom (together with the
subsidiary titles of Viscount Chelsea, Baron Cadogan and Baron
Oakley) on the death of his father in 1933.

The following year he sold Culford. His uncle Eddie subsequently sold at auction some of the Chelsea china he had taken from
the house. Lord Cadogan bought it anonymously, and made sure to
use it the next time his uncle came to dine.

Though he was to remain on the Reserve of Officers until 1964,
he resigned his commission to marry in 1936, and devoted the
immediate pre-war years to foxhunting – as Master, first of the
Cricklade and then of the Grafton. In 1939 he rejoined the Army as
an officer of the Royal Wiltshire Yeomanry: his unit was one of the

last to take its horses to war, embarking at Marseilles for Palestine. Cadogan rose to command the Royal Wilts and fought throughout the war, winning a Military Cross at El Alamein and taking part in the Sicily landings, the fall of Palermo and the fall of Rome. The war, which had taken so many of his friends, had a profound effect on Cadogan, whose upbringing made it difficult for him to express his emotions. Seeking a period of quiet recuperation, he bought Snaigow, a 4000-acre sporting estate, where he devoted much of the rest of his life to improving the land and the forestry. The house was vast – the children's bedrooms were more than 120 yards from the front door – and badly in need of repair. When rainwater finally cascaded through the drawing room from a broken roof, Cadogan decided to rebuild, demolishing Edwardian wings to create a more practical home around the Victorian core.

Lord Cadogan was a Chelsea borough councillor, and was the last mayor of Chelsea before its merger with Kensington in 1964 – his grandfather, the 5th Earl, having been the first. He was never active in national politics; he withdrew his financial support for the Conservative Party in 1993 in protest at legislation designed to allow leaseholders (including most Cadogan Estate residents) to acquire freehold possession of their homes.

Freemasonry played a major part in Cadogan's life: from 1966 to 1984 he was Pro Grand Master (the Duke of Kent being titular Grand Master) of the United Grand Lodge of England, the governing body of more than 8000 lodges in England and Wales.

In later years he was very much in favour of greater openness about Masonic affairs, and he took the view that the Masonic brotherhood was never truly a secret society. But in 1981, as president of the Board of General Purposes, he felt it necessary – in reaction to journalistic intrusions – to issue to all Lodges a reminder of the wording of their 'antient charges ': '. . . be cautious in your words and carriage, that the most penetrating stranger shall not be able to discover or find out what is not proper to be intimated . . .'

In the racing world, Cadogan was best known as a former senior steward of the National Hunt Committee, and was closely involved in the subsequent merger of the National Hunt Committee with the Jockey Club, where he served as a disciplinary steward. Over the years he kept horses with many of the leading trainers of the day, both over jumps and on the Flat. Among his successful runners were Green Drill, which came third in the Grand National in 1958 and later Snaigow and Verono, which both won the Mildmay of Flete over two and a half miles at Cheltenham.

Cadogan was fiercely punctual and a firm but fair disciplinarian in every aspect of his life. He loved trees, horses and dogs and had a retentive memory for Gilbert and Sullivan, military marching songs and snippets of light poetry: his favourite was 'The Fox's Prophecy'. He was a devout churchman and a benefactor of the Salvation Army.

An expert sempster, he embroidered a hassock for Chelsea Old Church.

Cadogan married first, in 1936, Primrose Yarde-Buller, daughter of the 3rd Lord Churston; they had a son (the former merchant banker Viscount Chelsea, who succeeded to the titles) and two daughters. The marriage was dissolved in 1959 and he married secondly in 1961 Cecilia (Bunny) Hamilton-Wedderburn.

4 July 1997

Viscount Cowdray

⤙⟚ 1910–1995 ⟛⤚

Polo-playing Pearson group chief

The 3rd Viscount Cowdray was the head of the Pearson family and a shrewd and energetic guardian of its multifarious business interests; in addition he made his name synonymous with British polo.

He was born Weetman John Churchill Pearson on 27 February 1910. His father, the 2nd Viscount, was Liberal MP for Eye in Suffolk; his mother was a granddaughter of the 6th Duke of Marlborough and thus a first cousin once removed of Sir Winston Churchill.

The Pearson fortune had its origins in a humble 19th-century brick-making concern in the Spen Valley in West Yorkshire. Weetman Pearson, created a baronet in 1894, a baron in 1910 and 1st Viscount Cowdray in 1917, was the third generation in the brick business; which he developed into one of the great engineering companies of the late Victorian era and later into a broad portfolio of investments. He built the Blackwall Tunnel, the East River Tunnels in New York and Dover Harbour. He also opened up the Kent coalfields. In Mexico he solved the capital's drainage problems, and built railways from coast to coast. He established the Mexican Eagle Oil Co – which he sold to Shell in 1919 at vast profit. A Mexican peon was adopted as a supporter in the Cowdray arms.

His grandson, John Pearson, was an only son with five sisters, who included his twin, Angela, mother of the Duke of Atholl; she died in 1981. He was educated at Eton and Christ Church, Oxford. For the twins' coming of age in 1931, a pavilion was erected at Cowdray Park to seat 112 guests; 500 more came to dance after dinner.

John succeeded as 3rd Viscount after his father's death in 1933. Despite two slices of death duty in six years, his inheritance was still vast. It included the 17,000-acre Sussex estate, its cottages and farmhouses recognisable by distinctive yellow paintwork in a shade derived from the flaming torch in the Pearson crest (motto: *Do it with thy might*). There were also more than 60,000 acres at Dunecht in Aberdeenshire, and properties in Rhodesia.

In the 1930s, Lord Cowdray was a territorial officer in the Royal Artillery. As a captain with the Sussex Yeomanry in 1940, his vehicle came under heavy fire near Arras whilst he was being driven towards Dunkirk. His driver was seriously injured and his own left arm was mangled, but Cowdray took over the wheel and got through to the beaches, where he spent 48 hours before being rescued. When he awoke in an English hospital some days later to find that his arm had been amputated, his first reaction was reported to have been: 'Thank God, now I won't have to play golf any more.'

Invalided out of the Army, he served briefly (in 1941 and 1942) as PPS to Lord Sherwood, the Under-Secretary of State for Air – thus maintaining the family connection with the RAF, in the formation of which his grandfather had been highly influential.

For some years he followed family tradition by sitting as a Liberal in the House of Lords, but in 1950 he resigned the Whip to become an independent.

Cowdray added enviable assets to the family property. In 1951 he bought the 905,000-acre Matador Ranch in Texas, the second largest in the United States. In 1962 he paid £500,000 for 51 per cent of Chateau Latour. Later additions included Chessington Zoo and Madam Tussaud's waxworks.

He was chairman of S Pearson and Son from 1954 to 1977. In his time the group's main spheres of activity were merchant banking, through Lazard Brothers; publishing through Pearson Longman and Penguin; newspapers, including the *Financial Times*, the Westminster Press group of provincial titles, and stakes in *The Economist* and the *Investor's Chronicle*; Royal Doulton china; and oil interests in America and the North Sea. Another family company controlled power stations in Greece.

Ably supported by the former Conservative politician Lord Poole, and later by Lord Gibson, he encouraged his subsidiaries to run themselves while keeping a sharp eye on their finances. In 1969 he decided to float Pearson on the stockmarket, revealing the detail of its holdings for the first time. It was valued at £72 million. Although Cowdray's direct personal stake turned out to be relatively modest, some 100 Pearson family members and trusts were thought to own 45 per cent of the shares between them.

He eschewed proprietorial interference in the editorial tone of his newspapers. A shy man of unglamorous, almost bucolic, looks, he disliked press attention. Although convivial in private he could be peppery. He had plain tastes, favouring 'cottage pie and meat and potatoes'.

Cowdray's only great extravagance was polo, for which Cowdray Park became a mecca. As an undergraduate he had followed his father in captaining Oxford University. He was non-playing captain of a Great Britain team which competed in the West Chester Cup on Long Island in 1939 and toured Argentina ten years later. From 1947 to 1967 he was chairman of the Hurlingham Polo Association, the game's governing body. In the 1950s, he and Prince Philip, who played for the home team at Cowdray Park, brought increased popularity to the game as a spectacle for the general public. Despite his disability, Cowdray himself was a brave and competent player – his reins tied to a specially designed artificial hand.

He was equally undaunted in other pursuits. His shotguns were balanced to allow him to shoot one-armed. He wielded a full-length salmon-rod adapted so that he could both cast and manipulate the reel with his good hand.

Lord Cowdray married first, in 1939 (dissolved 1950) Lady Anne Bridgeman, daughter of the 5th Earl of Bradford; and secondly, in 1953, Elizabeth Jackson, a former secretary to the American Ambassador's wife in London and daughter of Sir Anthony Mather-Jackson, Bt. Each marriage produced a son and two daughters.

His elder son, Michael Pearson, born in 1944, succeeded as 4th Viscount Cowdray.

19 January 1995

Sir Paul Getty

◦═══◦ 1932–2003 ◦═══◦

Philanthropist and cricket fan

Sir Paul Getty, the American-born multimillionaire, was one of the most generous philanthropists Britain has ever seen. The third of five sons of the legendary oilman of the same name, J Paul Getty Jr passed in his middle years through the kind of nether world of family tragedy and self-inflicted ill-health to which limitless wealth is sometimes a passport. But he emerged, somewhat diffidently, in his late 50s to be acknowledged as a great benefactor of the arts, a connoisseur on an 18th-century scale, and – an unlikely attachment, but one which brought him deep satisfaction – a lover of cricket.

Getty once described philanthropy as 'my duty'; and his charitable gifts amounted to more than £100 million – perhaps much more, since he preferred them to be unpublicised. 'I am going to continue to give away all I can', he said on one occasion. 'Of course I am.' A single gift of £50 million went to the National

Gallery and another £50 million – reflecting Getty's special interest in cinema – to the British Film Institute. The Imperial War Museum received £2 million. Canova's statue of 'The Three Graces' was saved for the nation by a Getty donation – in competition against the Getty Museum, his father's foundation in California. He gave £5 million for the cleaning and restoration of the West Front of St Paul's Cathedral.

In 2001 he donated £5 million to the Conservative Party, in the wake of its second crushing election defeat, to defend what he called the 'British way of life'. Getty greatly valued British civility and self-effacement, and lamented what he saw as the erosion of traditional British values. He participated in the first Countryside March.

Many of his benefactions were more whimsical, and personal. He gave money to the SAS to buy exotic weaponry, and to striking miners' families. When he read that the pianist John Ogdon, in financial difficulties, had been forced to sell his piano, Getty issued a message that Ogdon should buy another and send him the bill. When Claus von Bulow (former assistant to Getty senior) was charged with the attempted murder of his heiress wife, Sunny, Getty arranged an open account on which von Bulow could draw to fund legal costs of millions of dollars.

Most of these donations came from Getty's own pocket. He also gave money through the medium of his J Paul Getty Jr Charitable Trust, the stated aim of which was to alleviate 'poverty and misery' by encouraging 'self-help, building esteem and enabling people to reach their potential'. Among those who benefited were the homeless, the unemployed, the mentally ill and those dependent on drugs.

Naturally, all this largesse prompted some unwelcome approaches. Getty once received a letter from an African claiming to have lost every job he had had because he suffered from sleeping sickness; would the philanthropist please send him £1 million? Getty disliked the attention which his generosity brought him – he failed to appear in public even to receive a 'Benefactor of the Year' award from the Prince of Wales. But he also hated to be called a recluse. In truth, he was a shy man, who had suffered many years of illness, and who preferred the private company of a small circle of friends. In later years, after his third marriage, he was seen about more often, particularly in connection with cricket.

At heart Getty was a scholar *manqué*. His greatest passion was his collection of rare books, which included a number of priceless medieval manuscripts, and not long before his death he paid Oriel College, Oxford, £3.5 million for a First Folio of Shakespeare's plays. He absorbed himself not only in the texts and their provenance, but also in the practical art of fine bookbinding. He was a cinema buff and an authority on the work of Howard Hawks and Charlie Chaplin; his video library was vast. He had a wide knowledge of music. At the other end of the scale, Getty was an inveterate watcher of television soap operas with a particular affection for the downmarket Australian series, *Neighbours*.

Getty's tastes found complete expression at Wormsley, the 3000-acre estate in the Chilterns, previously the seat of the Fane family, which he bought in 1984 for £4 million. Regardless of expense, Getty restored the estate's buildings and relandscaped its parkland, with new lakes, 90,000 new trees and an Arcadian cricket ground. He reintroduced the red kite to Wormsley, building breeding pens and hiring security guards to protect their nests. The centrepiece, disguised as a medieval castle, was a circular flint-clad library building to house the Getty collection in perfect atmospheric conditions. Elsewhere were grottoes and follies, one of which concealed four huge satellite dishes to feed the billionaire's television appetites. A hundred men worked on the reconstruction of Wormsley for seven years; Getty called it his Shangri-La.

Getty was appointed honorary KBE in 1986. Much as he loved Britain, he made it known that he preferred to make donations to his adopted country by his own choice, rather than through the Inland Revenue. Tax considerations therefore prevented him from taking up British citizenship. However, in 1997 he changed his mind, revoked his American nationality and acquired a British passport in the following year. Thus in 1998 he was able to receive his accolade from the Queen, who knighted him at Buckingham Palace.

John Paul Getty was born on 7 September 1932. His mother, Ann, was the daughter of Sam Rork, an early Hollywood producer who had launched the film career of Clara Bow. Ann had become the fourth wife of Getty senior in 1932, but the tycoon's relentless obsession with business, and his wandering eye, soon drove the marriage apart. By 1935 he had already taken up with his future fifth wife, 'Teddy' Lynch. Divorce came when Paul Jr was four.

Thereafter Paul Jr was brought up in California by his mother. Communication with his father – who would return his son's letters with the spelling mistakes underlined – was distant and cold. The two men came to know each other better only when Paul Jr, like his three surviving brothers, went to work in the family oil business. This followed a period of service with the US military in Korea.

Getty senior – said to be the author of the observation, 'The meek shall inherit the earth – but not the mineral rights' – insisted that each son should undergo rigorous on-the-job training, commencing with a period as a filling-station attendant and including experience in the oilfields of what was then the Middle Eastern Neutral Zone in Saudi Arabia. Although Paul later declared that he had hated his oil career – and would have preferred to be an oceanographer or a librarian – he showed promise in business and was an effective diplomat in dealings with Arab potentates.

His father thought well of him. In 1959, with his first wife Gail (a former water-polo champion, whom he had married three years earlier) Paul Jr moved to Rome as head of Getty Oil Italiana. But Paul Jr gradually lost interest in tycoonery – the Italian company functioned partly as an efficient tax-loss for the Getty group, and was never its most glamorous wing – and succumbed to the temptations of Rome in the 1960s.

In 1966, he divorced Gail. He became increasingly involved with the hippy movement, espoused radical anti-Vietnam views, and took to drugs, becoming addicted to heroin. In 1972 his beautiful second wife, the Dutch actress Talitha Pol (stepdaughter of Augustus John's daughter, Poppet), died of a drug overdose. Paul, under suspicion of contributory negligence of which he was later cleared, fled to London to avoid police questioning. He took up residence, in seclusion, in a house in Cheyne Walk in Chelsea.

The following year, tragedy struck again. Getty's rebellious 16-year-old son, Paul III, who was still living in Rome, was kidnapped. When the first ransom message arrived, the family suspected a ploy by the teenager to extract money from his miserly grandfather. A second demand was delayed by an Italian postal strike. Finally, Paul III's severed ear arrived at a newspaper office, with a threat of further mutilation unless $3.2 million was paid.

Paul Jr did not have access to funds on such a scale. He was obliged to borrow the money from his father, at 4 per cent interest, in order to secure the release of his son – who was permanently affected by the trauma, and himself became a drug addict. In 1981, Paul III was rendered speechless, blind and paralysed for the rest of his life by a disastrous cocktail of drugs and alcohol.

Getty senior, reputed in his day to be the richest man in the world, died in 1976. Paul Jr was the only son to attend the funeral, looking thin and pale behind dark glasses. It was virtually his last appearance of the 1970s. His father had left a large part of his $3 billion estate to his art museum in Malibu, but Paul Jr nevertheless received a substantial inheritance, chiefly in the form of Getty Oil shares, augmented by his grandmother Sara Getty's trust. It was not until 1984, when his brother Gordon negotiated the sale of Getty Oil to Texaco, that the inheritance turned into some £900 million of cash.

Although by then cured of addiction, Paul suffered debilitating after-effects. He underwent long periods of treatment for phlebitis, which had weakened his legs, and for cirrhosis of the liver. When he first bought Wormsley, it was thought that he might never be fit enough actually to live there, but a long stay at the London Clinic in 1985 did much to restore him. It also brought friendship with an elderly fellow patient, the pre-war English test captain Sir George 'Gubby' Allen, who inspired a fascination for cricket which brought mellow enjoyment to Getty's later life. Getty had first been introduced to the summer game on television some years earlier by his Chelsea neighbour, Mick Jagger of the Rolling Stones. Allen now tutored him in the rich complexities of cricketing lore.

Getty became a fanatic, amassing videos of important games and offering to buy a radio station on which to preserve *Test Match Special* when the BBC threatened to curtail it. He gave £2 million for the new Mound Stand at Lord's (where he was occasionally to be seen in his box, after the lunchtime edition of *Neighbours*), and lesser sums to a number of other grounds, including the Oval, where he was president of Surrey County Cricket Club. A believer that, in cricket as in art, the best things should be in the safest hands, he also became the owner of *Wisden Cricketers' Almanack.*

Getty's love of the game inspired the most remarkable new feature of Wormsley – a perfect oval cricket ground with a mock Tudor pavilion, exquisitely set against the wooded Chiltern ridge. Getty's eleven, of former test players and celebrities – he himself remained a spectator – played a season of fixtures in the truest village-green tradition, free of limited-over gimmickry or commercialism. Getty once said: 'Cricket is so much more than a game to me. It's the surroundings as well. I love it all. I think that's what sets cricket apart, really. There's a whole way of life about it which I adore – and I like cricketers.'

At the ground's inauguration in 1992, when both the Prime Minister, John Major, and the Queen Mother joined him for tea in his pavilion, Getty remarked that the game had given him 'the happiest summer since my boyhood'.

Paul Getty married thirdly in 1994, Victoria Holdsworth, the daughter of a Suffolk farmer who served with distinction in the Special Operations Executive; she was widely credited with aiding his gradual re-emergence into public life. She survived him, together with two sons and two daughters of his first marriage, and a son from his second.

17 April 2003

Lord Hayter

⟶ 1911–2003 ⟵

Last of the Chubb Lock dynasty

The 3rd Lord Hayter was the last family chairman of Chubb & Sons Lock & Safe Co, founded by his great-great-grandfather, Charles Chubb; he was also a deputy speaker of the House of Lords.

The brothers Charles and Jeremiah Chubb were ship's ironmongers at Portsea until Jeremiah was granted a patent in 1818 for his Detector Lock, and was awarded a prize of a hundred guineas by the government. The money was used to found a new business with workshops in Wolverhampton, where the best locksmiths were to be recruited: Jeremiah took charge of manufacturing, while Charles went to London to open a sales office.

It was said that the Detector Lock first achieved fame after the Prince Regent sat on one, with key protruding. The device was certainly recognised as a significant advance, and Chubb received a Special Licence (the precursor of a Royal Warrant) from George IV in 1823. Chubb became the sole supplier of postbox locks to the General Post Office, and found another growing market in Her Majesty's Prisons. The firm also patented a burglar-resistant safe and developed the first time-lock – products which sold well in the United States in the era when armed hold-ups were a constant threat for small-town banks.

As George Chubb, Lord Hayter joined the firm in 1931 and became managing director ten years later, playing a major part in its postwar expansion from a highly specialised family concern to a diversified international business. He travelled to Australia – initially by flying boat – and to Canada and South Africa to open new businesses, and during his chairmanship from 1957 to 1981 he oversaw acquisitions and expansion which took Chubb into a broad range of security products, including fire-protection equipment, in 17 countries. The group's workforce grew from 700 to 17,000, and profits multiplied.

Hayter was a wise and skilful chairman, in business and in a variety of public roles. In personality he was somewhat reserved – as befitted a manufacturer whose products guarded the Bank of England, the Crown Jewels and the Shah of Iran's treasure – describing himself as 'a Victorian at heart'. But he appreciated the irony of the fact that in a world without sin, there would have been no demand for locks and safes. Among his papers was a letter signed 'Yorkshire's ex-Burglar Bill' which concluded: 'You can take it from me that your lock is definitely invulnerable to light-fingered gentlemen of my profession and I congratulate you.'

George Charles Hayter Chubb was born on 25 April 1911. He

succeeded his father in 1967 in the barony and baronetcy created for his grandfather, George Hayter Chubb, who besides running the company was very active in charitable work establishing homes for sailors. He was said to have chosen to use his middle name for the baronial title, when it was conferred in 1927, after a family member suffered a burglary which provoked headlines, deeply embarrassing for the world's leading locksmith, along the lines of 'Chubb gems stolen'.

Hayter was educated at the Leys School and Trinity College, Cambridge, where he read history. His ambition was to be a barrister, but he was pressed into joining the family firm: his grandmother told him, 'The first three years you won't like it. The next three years you'll get used to it. After that it becomes part of you.'

He learned the intricacies of lock-making in the Wolver-hampton factory, and went on to work on the sales side in the firm's St James Street branch. Eventually he took over the running of the business from his uncle, Emory Chubb, who had served his own apprenticeship under an aged locksmith who recalled being reprimanded for taking time off to watch the Duke of Wellington's funeral procession in 1852. Wellington had been a Chubb customer and so was Winston Churchill: during the Second World War Hayter handled an order for a new set of secure fire-resistant cabinets to hold the Prime Minister's papers. The ones they replaced, bearing the initials WSC, sat in Chubb's St James Street's cellar for many years until they were bought by an American souvenir hunter.

During Hayter's chairmanship the firm was also asked to make a set of ornamental keys (there were no locks) for use in guard-mounting ceremonies at Buckingham Palace, the Tower of London and Windsor Castle, which had previously involved the handing of imaginary keys by the captain of the old guard to the new.

Meanwhile, the firm continued to develop a range of high-tech security devices for more practical purposes, and to acquire other lock brands such as Union. Expansion also meant dilution of family control, however, and Hayter was the last family member on the board, though his eldest son worked in the business overseas. After

Hayter's retirement the firm was several times taken over and restructured, its locks business ending up under Swedish ownership.

When he stepped down from Chubb in 1981, Hayter was asked what he planned to do next. 'There is a very good club', he replied, 'called the House of Lords.' Sitting as a cross-bencher, he emerged as a leader of a coalition of peers opposed to Margaret Thatcher's 1986 abolition of the Greater London Council. His objections were practical – to do with the future of emergency services and voluntary sector funding in the capital, for example – rather than ideological. Hayter admitted that he was relieved not to have achieved a historic defeat over the government (the bill passed in the end, but by a margin of only three votes) which would have dragged him into the political thicket. He was a deputy chairman (deputy speaker) of the House of Lords from 1981 to 1995, and continued to attend debates regularly until Labour's reforms removed his right to sit as a hereditary peer.

Hayter was chairman from 1965 to 1982 of the management committee of the King Edward's Hospital Fund for London – now the King's Fund, the healthcare research charity. He encouraged its efforts to promote a shift of emphasis in NHS policy towards patients' needs rather than doctors' priorities. He also championed the development of the 'King's Fund bed', a robust, adaptable design which became the standard in British hospitals.

Strongly interested in design issues, he also served as chairman of the Design Council and the Royal Society of Arts, where he encouraged the introduction of children's lectures. He was chairman of the Duke of Edinburgh's 'Countryside in 1970' committee and the British Security Industry Association, and president of the Royal Warrant Holders' Association, the Business Equipment Trades Association and the Canada-UK Chamber of Commerce. He served as upper bailiff of the Worshipful Company of Weavers, the City's oldest guild, where he pressed for the admission of women liverymen.

In his later years he enjoyed being president of his local cricket club at Ashtead in Surrey. He collected paintings by modern Australian and British artists, the work of British furniture-makers, and Staffordshire figurines.

He was appointed CBE in 1976 and KCVO in 1977.

He married, in 1940, Elizabeth Rumbold, who was appointed MBE in 1975; they had three sons (of whom the eldest, George William Michael Chubb, born in 1943, succeeded to the titles) and a daughter.

2 September 2003

Lord Howard de Walden

⊷⇛ 1912–1999 ⇚⊷

Marylebone landlord

The 9th Lord Howard de Walden was a prominent racehorse owner-breeder, a former Senior Steward of the Jockey Club and one of Britain's wealthiest landlords, owning more than 100 acres of Marylebone in central London. The Howard de Walden estate, the inheritance of Lord Howard's Cavendish-Bentinck great-grandmother, runs between Oxford Street and Marylebone Road, encompassing Cavendish Square as well as the medical districts of Harley Street, Wimpole Street and the Middlesex Hospital. Its value has been estimated conservatively at £250 million.

John Howard de Walden was a grandee of the Turf, and was popular throughout the racing industry. He became a steward of the Jockey Club in 1955, serving as Senior Steward in 1957, 1964 and 1976. Realistic and far-sighted, he presided over numerous innovations, from the introduction of starting stalls to the admission of lady members to the Club itself. In 1964 he supported the creation of the Turf Board, as a first move towards more professional management of the sport.

Some years earlier, he led the first delegation from the Jockey Club to visit its American counterparts, on the occasion of the Laurel Park International race, and was invited to meet President Eisenhower in the Oval Office. He gave the President a tip for the race – the Ali Khan's horse, Rose Royale – which, to his embarrassment, came nowhere.

Howard de Walden's horses were trained by Noel Murlees and Henry Cecil. Among his successes was Kris, whose dam Doubly Sure was, according to Lord Howard, 'quite useless' and whose sire Sharpen Up was 'cheap and fast ... standing at £200 down the road'; Kris won 14 of his 16 races and became a champion stallion, as did his full brother Diesis. In National Hunt racing, about which Howard de Walden claimed to have been 'quite ignorant', Lanzarote, trained by Fred Winter, won 26 races for him, including the Champion Hurdle. But the horse which brought him greatest satisfaction was Slip Anchor (sired by a former Derby winner, Shirley Heights, from a German mare called Sayonara, to produce an example of what he called 'hybrid vigour'), which won the 1985 Ever Ready Derby by seven lengths.

Though unassuming in manner, Howard de Walden had his share of adventures. In Munich as a language student in 1931, he motored round a corner and struck a pedestrian: the man got up and walked off, but Howard's German companion said: 'I don't suppose you know who that was? He is a politician with a party and he talks a lot. His name is Adolf Hitler.'

Some years later, finding himself in the box next to the Führer's at the Munich Opera, he was able to lean across and ask him if he remembered the incident. 'To my surprise,' Howard wrote in his memoirs, 'he did, and was quite charming to me for a few moments. We never met again.'

John Osmael Scott-Ellis was born, with his twin sister Bronwen, on 27 November 1912. He was the only son of Thomas, 8th Lord Howard de Walden and 4th Lord Seaford.

The Howard de Walden title was created in 1597 for the 4th Duke of Norfolk's younger son, Lord Thomas Howard (later Earl of Suffolk), who was instrumental in the discovery of the Gunpowder Plot. The barony was one of the last to be created by Writ of Summons: this means that it follows common law in devolving on a daughter rather than to collateral male heirs. Where there is no son but more than one daughter (as in the present case), the peerage goes into abeyance. The title was in abeyance between 1689 and 1734, but devolved through the female line to the Earls of Bristol. Thereafter it passed to the Ellis family, who were originally seated at

Wrexham but had become prominent public figures in 18th-century Jamaica.

Charles Ellis, an MP and later 1st Lord Seaford, married a granddaughter of the 4th Earl of Bristol (and Bishop of Derry) in 1798. The son of that marriage succeeded as 6th Lord Howard de Walden, and married Lady Lucy Cavendish-Bentinck, daughter of the 4th Duke of Portland, whose dowry included the Marylebone estate. Lady Lucy was also the heiress of General John Scott of Fife, and the 8th Lord Howard added Scott to the family surname in 1917.

The 8th Baron, who fought in the Boer War and at Gallipoli, was a man of exceptional range – a medievalist, champion fencer, power-boat racer, explorer, painter and author of opera libretti on Byzantine themes, as well as a shrewd international investor, man of the Turf and steward of the Jockey Club. In 1905 he won the Ascot Gold Cup with Zinfandel.

Despite his immense wealth the 8th Lord Howard de Walden lacked a country seat of his own, so he rented Chirk Castle, a 13th-century pile in his ancestral Welsh border territory. It was there his son John and five daughters were brought up, though their father, a stern Edwardian parent preoccupied with his many interests, showed them little warmth. Among the guests at Chirk during John's childhood was the painter Augustus John, who advised on the Howard de Walden racing colours – recommending apricot, which he said would look well against the green background of the Turf. Descending to breakfast one morning, the painter was surprised to find Lord Howard reading the newspaper while wearing a full suit of armour – yet another of his enthusiasms.

On other occasions, the children observed Hilaire Belloc retiring across the ancient courtyard with a bottle of port under each arm, to drink in bed. Rudyard Kipling also came to stay, and offered to sign young John's collection of his works.

John's mother, Margherita, was as colourful as her husband and as distant to her children. Descended from the wealthy Dutch Jewish family of Van Raalte – her father owned Brownsea Island in Poole Harbour – she was a talented singer and formidable organiser, setting up a hospital in Egypt during the First World War and founding the Queen Charlotte's Ball. In later life she was in the habit of performing cartwheels on the battlements at Chirk.

Young John was educated at Eton, where by his own account he was not a success – 'Try to shake the little brute up', his father wrote to his mother, having seen a school report – but where he was able to develop a precocious passion for racing. He went racing for the first time in 1926, and saw his father's filly Sundry win at Newmarket.

Between school and Magdalene College, Cambridge, he studied in Munich, and was despatched to visit the extensive farming interests his father had acquired in Kenya. There he encountered the denizens of Happy Valley, whose louche behaviour he put down to the altitude. Arriving to stay with new acquaintances, he was greeted by the butler with, 'Good evening, sir. And who will you be sleeping with tonight?'

'I have spent the years since wondering what a good reply would have been,' Lord Howard wrote. 'Perhaps "please show me the menu".'

Down from Cambridge, John worked briefly in the City and assisted his father, whose empire was by now extensive. Though parts of the London estate north of Regents Park had been sold off in the 1920s, there were still 8000 acres at Dean Castle in Ayrshire and the island of Shona on Loch Moidart. In Africa he owned newspapers as well as farms, publishing the *East African Standard* and the *Ugandan Argus*. He had extensive investments in North America. In 1936 the 8th Baron established the South American Saint shipping line, of which John followed him in due course as chairman.

John was commissioned in the Westminster Dragoons during the Second World War, and was attached to the Canadian Army staff college as an instructor. Shortly after he was demobilised, he succeeded to the titles and estates on his father's death in May 1946.

Since his father had sold most of his horses in the 1930s, the new Lord Howard de Walden had to start racing almost from scratch; his first winner was Jailbird, at Chepstow in 1949. He went on to become a well-respected breeder, owning the Plantation Stud at Newmarket, the Templeton Stud near Hungerford, and for a time the Thornton Stud at Thirsk. Prior to Slip Anchor his best hopes of a Derby success came with Oncidium, winner of the Lingfield Derby Trial in 1964.

The new Lord Howard de Walden lived first at Wonham Manor in Surrey, then at Ormeley Lodge on the edge of Richmond Park (sold to Sir James Goldsmith) and later at Avington Manor, on the Kennet near Hungerford. Seaford House, his parents' mansion in Belgrave Square, notable for its massive green onyx staircase, became the Royal College of Defence Studies. Lord Howard's last London home was in Eaton Square, on the Duke of Westminster's estate rather than his own: 'Why on earth I should pay *him* rent,' he mused, 'I simply don't know.'

Lord Howard de Walden published, in 1992, *Earls Have Peacocks*, a charming anecdotal memoir in which he revealed his only regrets: that he had never learned to dance well, to speak Spanish or to fly, and had never done a course in accounting.

He married first, in 1934, Countess Irene ('Nucci') Harrach, a German of aristocratic Viennese ancestry whom he had met as a teenager in Munich; on the first night of their honeymoon they shared a hotel with Rudolf Hess. She died in 1975, and he married secondly, in 1978, Gillian Viscountess Mountgarret.

There were four daughters of the first marriage. The barony of Howard de Walden went into abeyance between them. The heir to the barony of Seaford was a cousin, Colin Ellis, born in 1946.

9 July 1999

Lord Latymer

-•═◑ 1926–2003 ◐═•-

Coutts heir and expert on Mediterranean plants

The 8th Lord Latymer was a scion of the Coutts banking dynasty who broke away from City life to sail to Australia, help develop the Caribbean island of Mustique and became an expert in Mediterranean gardening.

Hugo Money-Coutts – as he was known before he inherited the ancient barony of Latymer in 1987 – did not follow his father and grandfather into the directors' room of Coutts & Co, the exclusive private bank in the Strand which traces its origins to 1692 and is best known for providing discreet overdraft facilities for members of the Royal Family. Instead, Hugo made his early career with the merchant banking house of Robert Fleming, where he specialised in investment business. At the age of 37 in 1963, however, he left both his job and his marriage to sail his 39-foot ketch *Heliousa* – with a young girlfriend, Jinty Calvert, who was a cousin of his first wife and subsequently became his second – first to Majorca and then via the Panama Canal to Australia.

'I suppose my friends will think I'm crazy,' he said at the time, 'but I'm tired of fighting my way across London's traffic and tussling with people in the Underground. Everything has come easy to me in life so far, now I want to try it the hard way. Perhaps my friends may envy me, but while they are lashing into large dinners at the Savoy in a year's time, I might be on the dole in Australia ...' Nothing so tiresome came to pass, however, and the couple flew back from the Antipodes (having abandoned the notion of a round-the-world voyage) to set up home on Majorca. There, Hugo began to develop his passion for horticulture and established in 1967, with a local partner, a flourishing plant-nursery venture called Vivero Hortus.

For some years he diverted a large part of his energies to Mustique where, as managing director and co-owner of the development company for the four-square-mile island, he helped his Eton contemporary Colin Tennant (Lord Glenconner) to turn it into an exclusive holiday paradise for the glitterati of the day, who included Princess Margaret and Mick Jagger.

The mercurial Tennant was not easy to work with, and in due course Money-Coutts returned to Majorca, where he became an acknowledged authority on the design and cultivation of gardens suited to the island's climate, with its hot, dry summers and mild winters. He published in 1999 *The Mediterranean Gardener*, a comprehensive, practical guide – illustrated with photographs by Niccolo Grassi – which describes more than three hundred plants, from Chinaberry trees to twisted carobs and climbing lilies.

Hugo Nevill Money-Coutts was born on 1 March 1926, the only son of the 7th Lord Latymer, who was a director of Coutts & Co for 45 years (though as a non-executive in the postwar period) and chairman of the London board of the Ottoman Bank.

The Latymer barony dated from 1431, when it was created for Sir George Nevill, a son of the first Earl of Westmorland, of whom *Burke's Peerage* recorded that he 'went mad by 11 June 1451, but remained only intermittently so since he went on being called to parliament for another 18 years'.

George's grandson, the second baron, helped suppress the revolts of Lambert Simnel and Perkin Warbeck, and fought at the battle of Flodden; the third baron was a leader of the Pilgrimage of Grace – though he claimed to have been so under duress, and was pardoned – and married as his third wife Catherine Parr, who went on (in her own third marriage) to be the sixth wife of Henry VIII.

The fourth baron died without a male heir in 1577 and the title was in abeyance until 1912, when the Committee of Privileges of the House of Lords ruled, in the absence of other claimants, that it had passed through one of the fourth baron's daughters to Francis Burdett Thomas Money-Coutts. Francis's father was the Rev. James Money and his mother was Clara Burdett, daughter of the radical politician Sir Francis Burdett and Sophia Coutts – who was in turn a daughter of Thomas Coutts, from whom the banking house took its name. Hence, by a roundabout route, the adoption in 1880 of the surname Money-Coutts.

Hugo Money-Coutts was educated at Eton and won an exhibition to read natural sciences at Trinity College, Oxford, which he never took up. Commissioned into the Grenadier Guards at the end of the Second World War, he was posted to Germany where he served as an intelligence officer and on one occasion commanded a firing squad.

On leaving the Army he trained as an accountant before entering Robert Fleming, a family partnership with close connections to Coutts; in his bachelor days he shared a flat with Timmy (later Sir Seymour) Egerton, a brother officer in the Grenadiers who joined Coutts and was subsequently its chairman.

Money-Coutts played a major part, on Flemings' behalf and

alongside Andrew Carnwath of Barings, in the development of Save & Prosper, a joint venture which became one of Britain's largest and most profitable unit trust businesses. He was also a director of a number of investment and insurance companies with Fleming or Coutts connections.

Had he not set sail elsewhere, Hugo Money-Coutts might have gone on to senior positions in the financial world: he was highly intelligent as well as charming, with an enquiring turn of mind but a low threshold of boredom. Even during his City years he found time to travel widely in search of rare plants, particularly of the Daphne family: the collection he built up was donated to the Royal Horticultural Society in 1962.

He was also a dashing sportsman. Having rowed in the VIII at Eton, he and his schoolfriend Alan Godsall trained for the Silver Goblets at Henley after the war – but withdrew (as did several other pairs) when they realised the strength of the Soviet team taking part in the regatta. Undismayed, the duo took up motor sport, entering the Monte Carlo Rally in an Allard saloon. As cheerful amateurs without even a third man in their car, they observed with envy the large teams of mechanics who cosseted top professional competitors such as Stirling Moss. Nevertheless the powerful V8 Allard succeeded in being the first car to reach Monte Carlo. Money-Coutts went out on the town to celebrate, and had to be kicked and hauled out of bed at 5 a.m. to take the wheel for the last stage of the rally, a gruelling circuit of the surrounding hills.

They finished, creditably enough, in sixth place overall, but had less success in the notoriously hair-raising Alpine Trial: hurtling through treacherous Dolomite hairpins they slid off a precipice – shortly to be followed by another car containing the motoring correspondent of the *Daily Telegraph*. Both crews survived to commiserate in a local hostelry that evening – and Money-Coutts later returned to the Alps to take up bobsleighing, in which he represented Great Britain in the Oertzen Cup on the Cresta Run in 1960, finishing second. He was also a member of the Royal Yacht Squadron. In later years he left Majorca to live in mainland northern Spain.

He married first, in 1951, Ann Emmet, whose mother, Baroness

Emmet of Amberley, was Conservative MP for East Grinstead and a delegate to the 1952 UN assembly. They had two sons – of whom the elder, Crispin Money-Coutts, born in 1955, succeeded to the barony – and a daughter. By his second marriage to Jinty Calvert in 1965, he had a son and two daughters.

10 November 2003

Lord Marks of Broughton

1920–1998

Marks & Spencer heir

The 2nd Lord Marks of Broughton was the heir to a Marks & Spencer fortune but played a minimal part in the family business, preferring a life of artistic pursuits and the company of a succession of exotic wives. Michael Marks once described himself as 'a fugitive from a chain-store'. He worked briefly under the shadow of his formidably autocratic father Simon, the first baron and chairman of the firm since 1917, who was credited with revolutionising British dress and shopping habits in the postwar era and who died in his office, aged 76, in 1964. It was said of Simon Marks that he did not like the idea of being succeeded by anyone, and certainly not by his son. As it happened, the firm already had an outstanding leader of the younger generation in Michael's cousin Marcus Sieff, who observed that Michael simply did not have 'the inclination or qualifications' for business.

Accordingly, Michael limited himself to impromptu visits to the company's Baker Street headquarters: he would drop in on senior executives or take lunch in the canteen, where he engaged anyone who happened to be there in amiable conversation and read his poems aloud from a spiral notebook carried in the pocket of his corduroy jacket. A gentle eccentric, widely read, passionately interested in nature and totally oblivious to the value of money, he lived quietly in St John's Wood, where he also wrote children's stories, painted, and collected oriental antiques.

Michael Marks was born on 27 August 1920 and educated at St Paul's School and Corpus Christi College, Cambridge. His father was raised to the peerage in 1961, but his grandfathers were both penniless immigrants from Poland. One of them, Ephraim Sieff, established a business in Manchester sorting and reselling cotton waste. The other, Michael Marks, borrowed £5 to buy goods to peddle in the villages around Leeds, and went on to establish a stall in Leeds market under the slogan 'Don't ask the price, it's a penny'.

Michael senior (to whom the trademark 'St Michael' was a tribute) established Marks & Spencer as a chain of 'penny bazaars' in 1894, his partner Tom Spencer being a Yorkshireman who had taken a half-interest in the business in return for a £300 stake. The Sieff and Marks families were neighbours in suburban Manchester. The second generation, Israel Sieff and Simon Marks, were schoolfriends who married each other's sisters. Their business partnership was cemented in 1917, when control of Marks & Spencer was bought back, after a falling out, from the successor of Tom Spencer, and the company went public in 1927. The precepts of quality and value which made Marks & Spencer so successful were developed by Simon and Israel as the shop chain expanded in the 1930s.

The family acquired substantial wealth, and Michael inherited at least £30 million-worth of Marks & Spencer shares. His own habits were frugal, but he gave large donations to chosen causes through his private charitable trust, and his generosity to his wives became a gossip-column legend. He married first, in 1949, Ann Pinto, a cousin of the Rothschild family and an heiress in her own right. They had a son and two daughters. The marriage was dissolved in 1957 and Michael married secondly, in 1960, Helene Fischer. The couple lived together for only two years and were divorced in 1965.

Lord Marks's third wife was Toshiko Shimura, from Japan, whom he married in 1976 (dissolved 1985). His fourth, in 1988, was Liying Zhang, from China, and his fifth in 1994, was Marina Collins née Sacalis, 34 years his junior, the daughter of an Athenian lawyer. His last marriage was celebrated with a blessing in the Palace of Westminster and a reception for 200 guests at Claridges. He went on to buy a Greek villa and to make his new wife joint owner of a large block of Marks & Spencer shares. One family friend noted that Marks 'has always adored female company. He takes great pleasure in feminine beauty and has greatly cared for all his wives.'

But his generosity was to cause difficulties when his health deteriorated and he was made a ward of the Court of Protection in 1996. His son Simon, the heir to the barony, brought a High Court action on Lord Marks's behalf against Lady Marks, alleging that she had used 'undue influence' to procure money, gifts and property from the ailing peer. There was said to be confusion as to which of his assets he had given away, and the allegations were unreservedly withdrawn in February 1997.

9 September 1998

Viscount Rothermere

⊶⊷ 1925–1998 ⊶⊷

Daily Mail *proprietor*

The 3rd Viscount Rothermere was a hereditary press baron in the grandest style, controlling three of Britain's most successful daily newspapers – the *Daily Mail*, the *Mail on Sunday* and the London *Evening Standard*. A great-nephew of Viscount Northcliffe – who founded the *Daily Mail* in 1896 – Vere Rothermere did not in youth display much potential for the task of running a newspaper empire. Even in his palmy days, when he divided his time between luxurious homes abroad, he gave the appearance of a benign and mildly eccentric absentee owner. In fact, he was a formidable businessman and a worthy occupant of Northcliffe's grandly panelled Victorian office, which he moved in its entirety from Carmelite House in Fleet Street to Associated Newspapers' modern headquarters in Kensington.

His protégé, Sir David English once said that Rothermere would have made 'an excellent chief sub-editor' – to which Rothermere himself riposted that he would have made 'an extremely good editor'. His ruddy, patrician appearance and hesitant manner – he classified himself as a 'nobleman', and punctuated all his conversation with long silences – were deceptive. He thought deeply, acted ruthlessly when necessary and trusted his own judgment. 'The chairman is twice as clever as he looks, but only half as clever as he thinks,' said another close colleague. But in the light of Rothermere's stewardship of Associated Newspapers, no one seemed stupider than those who had disparaged his intellect.

In 1970, when Vere Harmsworth (as Lord Rothermere was known before succeeding to the viscountcy in 1978) took over the chairmanship of Associated Newspapers, the *Daily Mail*'s circulation was half that of the *Daily Express*, and its management was locked in battle with trade unions over redundancies. With the 2nd Viscount Rothermere's encouragement, there had been talk of a merger with the *Daily Express*.

Vere's father abruptly retired, and Vere swiftly established his authority. In 1971 he made two changes which set the *Mail* on a new course to success: he appointed David English as editor, and reduced the paper from broadsheet format to tabloid. Over the next two decades, the *Mail* comprehensively overtook the *Express* and attracted a younger, more affluent, and often predominantly female, middle-class readership – which was highly attractive to advertisers.

Though Rothermere left English a free hand as editor, he was in daily touch with his managers by telephone from his home in Paris. In business affairs Rothermere rarely missed a trick. He was outbid by Rupert Murdoch for *The Times* and declined to bid for the *Observer*, but he succeeded in a long campaign to control London's lucrative evening newspaper market. The London *Evening News*, part of the Associated Press stable, was merged in 1980 into a joint venture with the Beaverbrook Group's *Evening Standard*, but Rothermere went on to acquire full ownership of the *Standard* in 1987. In the same year he briefly resurrected the *Evening News* as a 'spoiler' to beat an attempt by Robert Maxwell to launch the rival *London Daily News* – a gambit which cost Maxwell £50 million. 'Squashing Bob Maxwell gave one enormous pleasure,' Rothermere admitted.

The *Mail on Sunday* was created in 1982, Rothermere having sold his investments in North Sea oil and gas to fund the project. Though the Sunday paper struggled in its early months, it too emerged as a successful, well-targeted product. 'What you need', he told an interviewer gleefully in 1993, 'is a morning, an afternoon and a Sunday newspaper. This allows a degree of efficiency. Ours are all market leaders now. So in a way we've even outdone Lord Beaverbrook because the *Evening Standard* wasn't market leader when he was alive. But it is now!'

Descended from an old Hampshire family, Vere Harold Esmond Harmsworth was born on 27 August 1925, the son of Esmond, second viscount, by his first wife Margaret Hunam Redhead. Esmond was himself the third son (two older sons were killed in the First World War) of Harold Harmsworth, the financial genius of the newspaper empire created by his brother Northcliffe. During Esmond's era, Associated Newspapers acquired the *Sunday Dispatch*, the *Daily Sketch* and in 1960, from the Cadbury family, the *News Chronicle* and *Star*, the last of the Liberal-leaning 'cocoa press'. In addition, the family controlled provincial papers, such as the *Hull Daily Mail*, the *Western Morning News* and the *South Wales Evening Post*.

Vere was educated at Eton, where he made little impression, and at Kent School in Connecticut, which he greatly preferred. He then did four years' national service as a private soldier, having failed his commission. This experience, he said later, 'gave me quite an idea about what the real world is really like for the majority of people', sowing the seed for newspaper promotions like the 'Win a Pub' competitions he ran in the 1950s.

After leaving the army, Vere spent a period of idleness in London then crossed the Atlantic to work for Anglo-Canadian Paper Mills in Quebec. When he returned, he was given a humble and ill-defined job at Associated Newspapers, working in circulation and advertising – and beginning with a tour of North Devon to assess provincial circulation trends. Relations with his father were distant – Esmond did not attend Vere's wedding and made little secret of his low opinion of his son's ability. But Vere developed an intuitive feel for the business, and a liking for journalists – employing them, he once remarked, was like 'keeping a hyena as a pet'. Among his allies from earliest days in Fleet Street was David English, then a features editor on the *Daily Sketch*.

Rothermere rarely involved himself in public controversy, but he spoke out in favour of press freedom, and expressed concern over the way in which he felt the Prince and Princess of Wales had sought to manipulate newspaper coverage during the break-up of their marriage. He declared himself an opponent of the monarchy.

Though his papers were the voice of Thatcherite Middle England during the 1980s, and always Eurosceptic (notwithstanding the proprietor's own more open attitude), Rothermere gradually lost faith in the Tory party, and caused some astonishment shortly after the 1997 General Election by announcing his intention to move from the cross-benches to the Labour benches in the House of Lords.

In semi-retirement, Rothermere retained command of the empire through the chairmanship of holding companies, but owned few assets in his own name. His family wealth was estimated in 1997 at £1,200 million.

He married first, in 1957, Patricia Brooks (née Matthews), daughter of a Hertfordshire architect. Known in later life as 'Bubbles' in recognition of her effervescent style and indefatigable love of parties, she was once voted one of London's ten most beautiful women. In the early 1950s, as Beverley Brooks, she had been a minor film star – playing the part of Douglas Bader's girlfriend in *Reach for the Sky*. She had married a guards officer, Christopher Brooks who by her account, tired of Vere 'hanging around' their house and told him, 'Take your Daimler and yourself away from my wife!' Vere eventually took all three. The marriage produced two daughters and, belatedly – despite a doctor's warning that another pregnancy could threaten Pat's life – a son, Jonathan, born in 1967, who inherited his father's titles and the chairmanship of Associated Newspapers. Rothermere remained fond of her despite what he described as her 'tempestuous and exhausting' nature. But he found their family homes – in Eaton Square, St Jean Cap Ferrat, Sussex, Jamaica and New York – increasingly 'impossible' to live in.

In 1978, at the Dogs' Hospital Charity Ball in New York, he met the former model Maiko Joeong-shun Lee, a Japanese-born Korean 25 years his junior. Though Pat was still his consort on official occasions and they remained affectionate, Maiko became his constant companion and shared his elegant bachelor flat on the Ile St Louis in Paris – together with a Japanese guard-dog named Ryuma. Rothermere developed interests in Zen Buddhism and the paranormal, and the couple lived for part of each year in an ancient villa in Kyoto.

After Pat died of a heart attack, aged 63, in 1992, Vere delivered a passionate memorial tribute to her at St Bride's in Fleet Street. In December 1993 he married Maiko Lee.

1 September 1998

Lord Rotherwick

⊷⊷⇒ 1912–1996 ⇐⊷⊷

Shipping heir

The 2nd Lord Rotherwick was a former deputy chairman of British and Commonwealth Shipping, which was formed from the merger of Clan Line Steamers and the Union-Castle Line in 1960. Rotherwick was a grandson of Sir Charles Cayzer, the founder of Clan Line Steamers, whose ships with their distinctive funnels, black with two red lines, began to ply the route to India in the late 1870s.

In the modern era, the Cayzers were notably shrewd in diversifying out of shipping, which they recognised as a declining industry. In the 1960s and '70s, they reduced their fleet, reinvesting the proceeds in other businesses, including aviation and hotels, many of them overseas. The Cayzer headquarters in the City, where Rotherwick worked in partnership with his two cousins and a brother, nevertheless retained its maritime style.

Rotherwick himself was chiefly interested in the family's property and farming investments, as well as the shipping side in which he had worked as a young man. He had a keen nose for the fundamental value of a transaction from the family's point of view, but in other respects he took a relaxed view of business, once observing that he disliked Wednesday meetings as they interfered with two weekends.

In the 1970s British and Commonwealth entered the financial-services sector by developing a fund-management business, Gartmore, named after one of the family's Scottish estates. This brought them into contact with John Gunn, a successful money-broker, with whom the Cayzers invested profitably first in the Exco group, a conglomerate of broking businesses, and later in Telerate, which provided financial information. Consequently, the value of British and Commonwealth multiplied and in 1985 the Cayzers invited Gunn to join them in running the company, whose interests were in need of rationalisation. But British and Commonwealth then embarked on a series of acquisitions, including Exco, which caused the Cayzer shareholding to be diluted.

Concerned that this process might go too far, the family asked to be bought out, and secured a deal at a generous price, guaranteed by the company's bankers, only three days before the 'Black Monday' stock market collapse in October 1987. British and Commonwealth later fell into severe financial difficulties, but the Cayzer fortune (estimated at £300 million) was unscathed.

As part of his retirement terms in 1987, Rotherwick received the newest model of Rolls-Royce – which proved to have insufficient headroom for the peaked cap of his chauffeur, who wore Clan Line uniform. Arrangements were duly made to lower the driving seat so that dignity might be maintained.

Away from the boardroom Lord Rotherwick was an assiduous farmer, a keen huntsman – he was for a time Master of the Heythrop – and a successful owner and breeder of racehorses. But his outlook was practical, and his affection for the land was not sentimental. In 1968, he sold his Scottish estates on the borders of Ayrshire and Lanarkshire, including Lanfine, which had one of the best grouse moors in the west of Scotland.

The previous year he had sold the 3000-acre Bletchingdon Park estate near Oxford, and bought Cornbury Park, a 15th-century manor near Charlbury, in Oxfordshire, with 6000 acres, including the ancient Wychwood Forest. Cornbury was once the home of Queen Elizabeth I's favourite, the Earl of Leicester, who died there in 1588. Rotherwick expanded the farm, instituted a programme of woodland regeneration, and developed a first-class shoot and stud.

His racing ventures were strategic but daring. In the early 1980s his success in breeding Swiftfoot and Morcon, trained by the Queen's trainer Dick Hern, brought him to the forefront of the racing world. Swiftfoot beat the Irish 1000 Guineas winner Prince's Polly in the Irish Oaks in 1982.

Herbert Robin Cayzer was born on 5 December 1912, the elder son of Herbert Cayzer, who became a baronet in 1924, and was created Baron Rotherwick in 1939. After Eton and Christ Church, Oxford, young Cayzer joined Clan Line in 1936, working in the firm's offices in Liverpool, Hull, Glasgow and Durban, South Africa. On the Supplementary Reserve of the Royal Scots Greys, he served during the Second World War in the Middle East, North Africa and Greece, rising to the rank of major.

From 1945 to 1948 he worked as a manager in Clan Line's office at Glasgow, and then went to Liverpool. He moved to the London office in 1950, and four years later, on the death of his father, became deputy chairman of British and Commonwealth.

In 1972 Rotherwick applied for permission to demolish the chapel at Cornbury, a listed building that had been designed by the Restoration architect Hugh May. He argued that the building stopped light reaching the central passage of the house, but his application was rejected.

Rotherwick was determined to prevent the public entering the 1500-acre Wychwood Forest on his estate, one of the last great stretches of primeval woodland in southern England. Tradition decreed that anyone carrying a bottle and a piece of liquorice would be admitted to Wychwood on Palm Sunday; for centuries, local people had mixed liquorice with water from a well among the trees to cure anything from the pox to gout. The issue of access to the forest aroused strong feeling. When Rotherwick's gamekeepers hung up vermin on gibbets to discourage predators from taking game, ignorant local protestors claimed that the carcases had been set up to scare off strollers and children. But in 1988 the Department of the Environment finally granted an application by Oxfordshire County Council to open a path through the forest.

Once an office colleague told Rotherwick that he had bought a new home with an acre and a half of garden. With a puzzled look, Rotherwick inquired: 'Can one fit a house into an acre and a half?'

Lord Rotherwick married, in 1952, Sarah-Jane Slade, the only daughter of Sir Michael Slade, 6th Bt. She died in 1978. They had three sons and a daughter. The eldest son, Herbert Robin Cayzer, born in 1954, succeeded to the peerage.

11 June 1996

Baron Hans Heinrich Thyssen Bornemisza

⊷═◉ 1921–1997 ◉═⊶

Art collector

Baron Hans Heinrich Thyssen Bornemisza de Kaszon was one of the richest men in Europe and the owner of one of the world's great art collections. When 'Heini' Thyssen inherited from his father Heinrich a vast collection of Old Masters, he thought there were 'already too many . . . I felt sure I would never have to buy another as long as I lived.' But when Heinrich's will was challenged under Swiss law by his three other children, and the collection broken up, young Heini became obsessed with the urge to buy back pictures taken by his siblings, and to add more and more works of art to his portfolio. The original collection of 400 Old Masters grew to one of nearly 600, whilst Thyssen acquired another 900 modern works which were outside his father's range of taste. In later years he devoted the majority of his time, and up to £40 million per year, to art deals. His only rival in scale of possessions was the Queen. 'But', the baron observed drily, 'I think the Queen is not perhaps really a *collector*.'

In his bedroom at the Villa Favorita on Lake Lugano, his

father's old home, Thyssen would wake to be greeted by Renoir's *Young Woman with Parasol in Garden*. To either side were another Renoir, a Manet, a Morisot and a Pissarro. Elsewhere in the room were a Winslow Homer and three sketches by Toulouse-Lautrec. In his study overlooking the lake were a Monet, a Cezanne and a selection of his favourite Expressionists. Outside the gentlemen's cloakroom was an Edvard Munch. In the adjacent museum were Titians, Tintorettos, Dürers and El Grecos.

Thyssen was extraordinarily eclectic in his taste, buying Jackson Pollock one day, Holbein the next. He was genuinely passionate about art: 'It is universal, it is impossible to have a disagreeable conversation about it. It should be shared by everyone,' he observed. But he was also notably hard-headed about its financial value. He expected governments to pay for the privilege of public access to his collection, and often deployed loans from it to open doors on behalf of his various business interests.

By 1986, the collection had overwhelmed the Villa Favorita. Thyssen was concerned that the bulk of it should be kept together after his death and had secured an agreement with his children to that effect. He then asked the Swiss authorities to fund an enlargement of the museum, but they offered less than $3 million. Piqued, Thyssen embarked on a search for a new site outside Switzerland that would be worthy of his patronage. He greatly enjoyed the process of being courted ('Mmm, that was a very nice period,' he told one interviewer) but he offended the dignity of some bidders by playing them against each other. President Richard von Weizsacker of West Germany called at the Villa Favorita bearing a proposal from Stuttgart. Disney World offered to house the collection in Orlando. The Getty Museum in California capped all other offers, but Thyssen did not like the design of its proposed new building. Late in the bidding, Margaret Thatcher sent a series of handwritten letters, and an invitation to Downing Street, to press the case for a museum in Docklands which would have cost £150 million: the Prince of Wales followed up with a visit to Lugano. Thyssen seemed at first to encourage the British proposal, but shortly rejected it, saying that 'people would not make the decisions I required'.

The final choice fell on Spain, birthplace of Thyssen's fifth wife. The Villahermosa Palace, close to the Prado, was refurbished to become the Thyssen-Bornemisza Museum, and the Spanish government paid $50 million for a ten-year lease on some 830 works of art: the baron had reserved the right to move them elsewhere at the end of the term, an arrangement which provoked hostility from some quarters of the Spanish press.

In 1994, Thyssen gave £800,000 to help keep Canova's statue *The Three Graces* in Britain, announcing that 'it would be nice to help British art a little, partly in compensation for the fact that my paintings did not go there'. It was not pure altruism, however: he let it be known that he would expect the statue to be available to his Madrid museum on loan.

Hans Heinrich Thyssen Bornemisza de Kaszon was born at Scheveningen, near The Hague, on 13 April 1921. He was a grandson of August Thyssen, a Rhineland peasant who built a chicken-wire business into a vast iron, steel and armaments conglomerate to rival the house of Krupp, and became a friend of the Kaiser. August's eldest son, Fritz, was an ardent early supporter of Adolf Hitler. Though he later broke with the Nazis and was interned in a German concentration camp, he was also jailed by the Allies after the Second World War and ended his days in Argentina.

August's third son, Heinrich, Heini's father, left Germany as a young man and settled in Hungary, where he married the daughter of the royal chamberlain, Baron Bornemisza, and was made heir to his father-in-law's title. But he fell foul of Bela Kun, the communist leader who took power in 1919, and the family was forced to move to Holland, where Heinrich redoubled his fortune in banking and shipping.

Young Heini, though one of four children, endured an extremely lonely childhood. He was brought up by a German governess (who later committed suicide) and rarely saw his parents. They divorced when he was eight, but by his own account, no one told him of the break-up until three years later. His mother remarried, to a Hungarian diplomat, whilst his father had moved to the Villa Favorita in Lugano. One of Heini's wives was later to observe that because of this solitary upbringing, 'He never really learned to relate to other people. He hadn't learned to love properly; he hadn't learned to trust properly.'

Heini was educated at the Realgymnasium in The Hague, and began work in a Thyssen-owned bank in Rotterdam. But when the Germans invaded Holland in 1939 he was summoned by his father to Switzerland, where he studied law and economics at Fribourg and Bern. In his student days, Thyssen took no interest in art, preferring football and swimming.

When his father died in 1947, Thyssen inherited, besides the picture collection, a business conglomerate which had suffered extensive damage during the war. All 12 Thyssen ships had been sunk; their Ruhr mines, Bremen shipyards and Rotterdam dock-yards were all in ruins. The 26-year-old baron set about rebuilding the empire, moving away from iron and steel to concentrate on shipbuilding, banking and a stake in the Heineken brewery in Holland, manufacturing and real estate in North America and sheep-farming in Australia. The Thyssen Bornemisza Group, run from Monaco and still entirely controlled by the family, grew to employ some 14,000 people around the world.

The rhythms of international business, art-dealing and jet-set social life attuned with Thyssen's fundamentally restless nature. Though Dutch by birth, German and Hungarian by ancestry, Swiss by citizenship and a resident of Monaco for tax purposes, he lived most frequently in later years in Spain, where he had four homes. Besides the Villa Favorita in Switzerland he had a chalet in St Moritz. There was a villa in Jamaica and *pieds-à-terre* in Paris and New York. In England he kept a house in Chester Square and for a time owned Daylesford, a Regency mansion in Gloucestershire built for Warren Hastings and acquired by Thyssen from Lord Rothermere. Although his English was accented, his tailoring was pure Savile Row.

Thyssen collected beautiful women rather as he collected homes and works of art – though he once observed that 'unlike women, the pictures can't talk back' – and, as one newspaper put it, old mistresses tended to be more troublesome to him than Old Masters. He married first, in 1946, the Austrian Princess Theresa de Lippe, by whom he had a son Georg Heinrich ('Heini Jr').

In 1953 Heini began an affair with Nina Dyer, a bisexual English model, to whom he gave a Caribbean island, two sports cars with gold-plated ignition keys, a black panther and a fortune in jewellery. He divorced Theresa and married Nina in 1954. But it transpired that Nina loved an impoverished French actor, whom Thyssen punched in a Paris nightclub only three months after the wedding.

'It sounds silly,' Thyssen once remarked, 'but I hate to divorce. It's a most disagreeable operation.' Nevertheless he swiftly divested himself of Nina and, having declared that he intended 'to stay a bachelor for some time', married another English model, Fiona Campbell-Walter, in September 1956. His third wife gave him another son, Lorne, and a daughter, Francesca – who in 1993 married (despite opposition from her fiancé's family) Karl Habsburg, grandson and heir of the last Austro-Hungarian emperor.

Thyssen divorced Fiona in 1964, and took as his next wife Denise Shorto, a Brazilian banker's daughter, who was to remain with him for 17 years and bear him another son, Alexander. His fourth divorce was his most acrimonious. Denise brought a High Court action to prove that Thyssen's disposable wealth was at least three times the £400 million he had declared; he responded with criminal charges alleging that she had failed to return family heirlooms worth £77 million. After four years of wrangling the case was dismissed, Denise having proved that one disputed item – a faultless 107-carat diamond set in a £2 million necklace – had been specially created for her, with a note attached to it from Thyssen saying, 'Darling, sorry for all my faults.'

In 1981 Thyssen met his fifth wife, Carmen ('Tita') Cervera, whilst holidaying on his yacht on the Costa Smeralda in Sardinia. She had been crowned Miss Spain in 1962 and was the fifth wife and widow of Lex Barker, an American film actor who once played Tarzan. Marriage had to wait until 1985, when the legal battle with Denise was settled, but was to prove happy and enduring. Carmen, an amateur painter with flamboyant tastes in interior design, took a close interest in the refurbishment of the Villahermosa Palace, somewhat to the chagrin of the Spanish artistic establishment. She also helped her husband to recover from a stroke in 1994. The couple became an almost permanent feature of the pages of *Hola!*, the Spanish progenitor of *Hello!* magazine. Thyssen adopted as his fifth child Carmen's son Borja, whose natural father she never publicly named.

After his stroke, Thyssen handed over control of his business empire to his son Georg Heinrich. But in 1996 there was a falling-out over money. Legal papers were filed in 1997, and a settlement was finally reached shortly before Heini's death. The Thyssen fortune was estimated at more than £2 billion.

27 April 2002

Garry Weston

⤞⧖ 1927–2002 ⧗⤝

Sliced-bread billionaire

Garry Weston, the Anglo-Canadian businessman and philan-thropist was one of the wealthiest men in Britain, having inherited a bakery empire, Associated British Foods, of which the principal product was sliced, wrapped bread. The company was founded in 1935 by Garry Weston's father, Garfield, and became best known for brands such as Sunblest, Ryvita and Twinings Tea. Until 1986, it also owned Fine Fare supermarkets, and in the 1990s it developed the Primark clothing retail chain.

Garry took over the chairmanship from his father in 1967, and acquired a reputation as a tough and frugal boss – a man who would 'only pay 50p for a pound's worth of business', according to one observer. But he was also straightforward and amiable, and pointed out that a sharp eye for cash control was essential in a business based on 'selling ten loaves to make a penny'.

His first task was to rationalise a sprawling conglomerate after a period in which his father had made acquisitions at the rate of up to 60 a year; a rumbustious autocrat, the elder Weston had also arranged matters so that 180 managers reported directly to him. Having brought order to the group, Garry went on in the 1970s to fight a battle for dominance of the British bread market – from which one of ABF's chief rival, Spillers, eventually withdrew, leaving ABF with a 30 per cent market share. But he did not subscribe to the 1980s fashion for buying up brand names, preferring to develop his own businesses from within. He began to encounter disgruntlement from outsider shareholders over his reluctance to invest in ventures which might have been more exciting than bread, while holding £1 billion of cash. But his position was unchallengable since the family controlled 63 per cent of the company, and as he told its 50th-anniversary annual general meeting in 1985, ABF was 'not about short-term excitement'.

He entered the large-scale takeover market only once, when he launched a hostile bid in 1987 for the commodity trading group S&W Berisford with a view to gaining control of its British Sugar subsidiary, and with it the Silver Spoon sugar brand. The bid was called off after the Black Monday market crash, but Weston returned to buy British Sugar for £880 million in 1991.

During his 32-year tenure as chairman and chief executive – he retired from the latter role in 1999 – the value of ABF rose from £90 million to more than £3 billion, helping his family, which has extensive other interests in Canada and elsewhere, to become one of the wealthiest in the world.

An intensely shy man, Weston himself remained resolutely downbeat and self-effacing, but never lost his appetite for business: 'I go to one of our factories and I feel ten years younger,' he said in 1993.

His career had been creative as well as cautious: he took the group into China and Eastern Europe, made a number of smaller acquisitions in the United States, and in his earliest days at ABF, when one of its factories needed a new product, he put two plain Marie biscuits around a marshmallow filling and invented the Wagon Wheel. A major part of the family shareholding in ABF was placed in a charitable foundation, which distributed more than £8 million a year. Its beneficiaries included the Great Ormond Street Children's Hospital and St Paul's Cathedral. In 1999 it gave £20 million towards the Great Court project at the British Museum.

Garfield Harold Weston, always known as Garry, was born in Canada on 28 April 1927. His father William Garfield Weston was in turn a grandson of William Weston, a Londoner who emigrated to Toronto and whose son George started work there as a ten-year-old baker's boy in 1875. George opened his own bakery in 1882 and made his first fortune by mechanising the business and producing in quantity to meet demand from Toronto's rapidly growing immigrant population. A tough operator, he was quoted as saying, 'People will eat horseshit if it has enough icing on it.' By 1911 he had sold his first business for a million dollars and started another, making biscuits.

George's son Garfield was born in 1898. On leave from France during the First World War, he visited British biscuit factories and conceived the idea of returning to the old country. When the crash of 1929 diminished the prospects of the Canadian business, he set off across the Atlantic.

Garfield was a domineering father to his three sons and six daughters, and a flamboyant entrepreneur. Beginning with the acquisition of an Aberdeen biscuit maker, Mitchell & Muir, he bought up bakeries and mills across the country; Allied Bakeries – later Associated British Foods – became a public company in 1935. A fervent Anglophile, he gave money to pay for RAF planes during the war, and sat for a time as Conservative MP for Macclesfield. In 1951 he bought Fortnum & Mason, the Piccadilly grocery store.

Garry was educated at Sir William Borlase School at Marlow, New College, Oxford, where he read PPE, and at Harvard, where he studied economics. Shy, sensitive and academically inclined, he was very different in personality from both his father and his younger brother Galen, a polo-playing socialite who ran the family's Irish interests before taking charge of the Canadian side of the empire and turning to luxury real-estate development in Florida. (The eldest of the three brothers, Grainger, left the business to become a Texas rancher.)

Garry started work in ABF and was given his first executive role at 23 as managing director of Ryvita, the crispbread brand. His father, he said, 'was always firing people. It was because of that I got my first job. I was passing his office one day and a man came out who had just been fired. My father came out, saw me there and gave me the job. But he would have given it to anyone who was passing. I had to go to Australia to get away from him.'

He duly spent 14 relatively happy years in Australia, where he developed extensive ABF operations, met his wife, and enjoyed an informal family lifestyle reminiscent of his Canadian childhood. In 1967, however, his father decided to retire and summoned Garry back to London to take over as chairman of ABF. On his father's death in 1978, he also became chairman of the family's British master company, George Weston Holdings, which held North Sea oil interests as well the ownership of Fortnum & Mason. Garry Weston was known to be an admirer and financial supporter of Margaret Thatcher, and it was said that she prevailed on him not to sell Fortnums at a time when other prominent London stores, such as Harrods, were falling into foreign hands.

Weston lived quietly in London and Oxfordshire, maintaining an almost invisible social profile: 'Money only attracts envy and weird people,' he once said, partly in reference to a 1983 IRA attempt to kidnap his brother Galen. Though his family's private fortune was estimated shortly before his death at £800 million, he was happy to take the Tube to work and was said to drive a second-hand Mercedes. In later years, he might have been mistaken for a retired family doctor. He relaxed by gardening and playing tennis.

Garry Weston married, in 1959, Mary, daughter of a New Zealand soldier, Major General Sir Howard Kippenburger. They had three sons – Guy, George and Garth, who all went to work in ABF – and three daughters, two of whom worked for Fortnum & Mason.

15 February 2002

⇢⇒ PART EIGHT ⇐⇠

GURUS

MARVIN BOWER – *father of management consultancy*
SIR ALEC CAIRNCROSS – *Keynesian government adviser*
SIR JOHN COWPERTHWAITE – *financial secretary of Hong Kong*
W. EDWARDS DEMING – *guru of Japanese factory methods*
PETER DRUCKER – *pioneering management theorist*
J.K. GALBRAITH – *doyen of American liberal economists*
HENRY GRUNFELD – *Warburgs founder and guiding light*
MICHAEL IVENS – *anti-union campaigner and poet*
MERTON MILLER – *Nobel laureate 'game theory' economist*

Marvin Bower

⋆⇒ 1903–2002 ⇐⋆

Father of management consultancy

Marvin Bower was the guiding light of McKinsey & Co, and the father of the modern management consultancy profession. McKinsey dates its origins from 1925, but the firm was re-established by Bower in New York in 1939, and grew under his leadership into an international partnership of 7000 consultants advising 100 of the world's 150 largest companies, as well as many government entities. Its clients ranged from IBM, General Motors and the Bank of England to NASA, the American Roman Catholic Church and the German finance ministry after the fall of the Berlin Wall.

In the depression years of the 1930s, 'management engineering' – as it was known – was regarded with some scepticism: in one popular definition, consultants were people 'who borrowed your watch to tell you the time'. Bower's achievement in the postwar era was to turn consultancy into a profession rather than a business. His formidable standards set the path by which his own firm and others grew in respect and authority. His approach was based on searching examinations of the specific problems of each client company, rather than endorsement of the management's own solutions. He believed consultants should exercise a rigour similar to that of lawyers, placing the clients' interests ahead of their own and only taking on assignments that would lead to positive change. He turned away potential clients such as the reclusive industrialist Howard Hughes – who 'didn't seem to want to manage in an organised way' – and declined to help the US government devise a bail-out plan for American Motors.

'The fun of working at McKinsey,' one of his partners observed, 'was that you never felt the need to say anything that wasn't so.' Such high integrity sometimes led Bower to blunt conclusions. On one occasion, at the end of a detailed presentation to a client company, he bellowed at the chief executive: 'The real problem with this company, Mr Little, is you.' The assignment was terminated, but Bower was untroubled.

Bower preferred to hire brilliant young MBA graduates – many from Harvard – rather than seasoned executives, so that he could indoctrinate them in the special McKinsey ethos. A London office was opened in 1959, and the British McKinsey cadre came to include names such as Sir Howard Davis, Adair Turner and William Hague. Among the principles that McKinsey trainees absorbed from Bower were strict quality control and consistency of presentation. Dashes and ellipses were banned from reports to clients, for example, and until the early 1960s, all McKinsey men were expected to wear hats, because their chief executive clients did so. When Bower realised that fashion had changed and arrived at the office bare-headed, colleagues who knew his innate caution reacted warily. 'Should we all give up our hats?' asked one junior. 'I'd wait six weeks,' a partner told him. 'It may be a trap.'

Marvin Bower was born at Cincinnati, Ohio on 1 August 1903, and spent his childhood in Cleveland, where his father was deputy recorder of Cuyahoga County. He graduated from Brown University in 1925, and went on to study at Harvard Law School. Failing to achieve good enough grades to join the Cleveland law firm of Jones, Day on which he had set his sights, he took a further qualification at Harvard Business School. In 1930 Bower was at last accepted by Jones, Day, where he served as secretary to several committees of bondholders of troubled companies. It was this experience which inspired his interest in analysing management problems: 'No one asked why these companies had failed,' he observed.

Three years later, he went to work for James O. McKinsey, a former University of Chicago professor who had established a small consulting firm of accountants and engineers in 1925. Bower became manager of the New York office, but McKinsey himself left the firm to become chairman of a Chicago company, and died of pneumonia in 1937. Bower and another partner, A.T. Kearney, decided to divide the firm – Kearney keeping the Chicago practice under his own name, and Bower reconstituting the New York office as McKinsey & Co. He was managing director from 1950 to 1967, and remained a partner until 1992.

Long before his formal retirement, Bower sold his shares in McKinsey to other partners at book value, rather than at the substantial premium they might have commanded. He insisted that older partners sell shares to younger ones, in order to give them 'a sense of ownership'. He continued to advise clients until his mid-eighties, and remained an active and revered father figure for the firm until the end of his life. He published *The Will to Manage* in 1967 and *The Will to Lead* in 1997. A professorship was established in his name at Harvard Business School in 1995.

Marvin Bower married, in 1927, Helen McLaughlin, who died in 1985; they had three sons, of whom one predeceased him. He married secondly, in 1988, Clothilde de Vèze Stewart, who died in 1999.

22 January 2003

Sir Alec Cairncross

⊷══ 1911–1998 ══⊷

Keynesian government adviser

Sir Alec Cairncross was chief economic adviser to successive governments during the 1960s and his soft-spoken advice was always implicitly Keynesian. It was not until monetarist policies began to be implemented in Mrs Thatcher's first administration that Cairncross made his fundamental Keynesian objections more widely known.

In response to Chancellor Geoffrey Howe's 1981 budget, Cairncross and no less than 363 other economists signed a letter to *The Times* which claimed that there was 'no basis in economic theory' for the government's approach and that 'the time has come to reject monetarist policies'. In March 1987, on the eve of what was expected to be a 'giveaway' budget, Cairncross offered Nigel Lawson unsolicited advice in purest Keynesian terms. 'All studies,' Cairncross declared, 'show that higher public spending is a far more efficient way of increasing employment than cutting taxes.' The underlying assumptions of Cairncross's approach had been criticised two decades earlier, in 1963, when he had expressed pessimism about growth rates. His 'complete failure to understand the priorities of Britain's economic policy' came under attack from, among others, the young Nigel Lawson, then City editor of the *Sunday Telegraph*.

Until then, Cairncross had been known for his preference for the details of applied economics. This led critics to label him 'the tin tack economist', for he was in the habit of telling those wishing to know about economic growth to go and study the tin tack trade. He was known for his brisk appetite for work and his shrewd scepticism in questioning other people's policy proposals, rather than for his power to generate bold new ideas. In a 1954 essay, *On Being an Economic Adviser*, he explained that it was best to proffer advice via senior civil servants, rather than to badger ministers directly, and that the role was more often a matter of providing common sense on a wide variety of day-to-day problems than of applying economic theory to great issues of state.

Alexander Kirkland Cairncross was born on 11 February 1911, the son of a schoolmaster at Lesmahagow, Lanarkshire. His younger brother John, a former communist who served in the Foreign Office and Treasury from 1936 to 1951, was to achieve minor notoriety – although he was never prosecuted – as a protégé of Anthony Blunt and a source of secret material which was passed to the Russians by Guy Burgess.

Young Alec was educated at Hamilton Academy, Glasgow University and Cambridge – where he was taught by Maynard Keynes. In the pre-war years he lectured in economics, but in 1940 he joined the Civil Service and rose to become Director of Programmes in the Ministry of Aircraft Production. At the end of the Second World War he was sent to Berlin as a member of the Economic Advisory Panel.

Cairncross then spent a brief period as a journalist for *The Economist*, before re-entering public service as economic adviser first to the Board of Trade and later to the Organisation for European Economic Co-operation.

In 1951 he returned to academe as professor of applied economics at Glasgow, but he found himself in constant demand for public committees, ranging from the Crofting Commission and the Anthrax Committee to the 1957 Radcliffe inquiry into Britain's monetary and credit system – 'Sometimes I wish people would leave me alone,' he once remarked.

In 1956–57 he spent a sabbatical year in Washington as the first director of the Economic Development Institute, the World Bank's staff college for officials from underdeveloped countries. He was chosen as the government's senior economic adviser by Selwyn Lloyd, Harold Macmillan's Chancellor, in January 1961. It was a tribute to his durability and usefulness that he survived the change of administration from Conservative to Labour in 1964, providing advice to Harold Wilson's administration under the new title of head of the Government Economic Service. Though Cairncross left Whitehall in 1969, he took on several more public appointments, including a review of government aid for industry in Northern Ireland as the Troubles intensified in 1971.

In 1974 he was asked to chair a group of independent advisers to reassess the prospects of the Anglo-French Channel Tunnel, but without waiting for his report (and to the fury of their French counterparts) Labour ministers unilaterally abandoned the project. Five years later, Cairncross advised the incoming Conservative government on the same subject: though characteristically cautious, particularly in relation to competition from ferry services, he recommended in favour.

Cairncross's home in later years was Oxford, where he became Master of St Peter's College in 1969. His predecessors since St Peter's 1929 foundation were all clergymen; the college had a somewhat modest academic reputation, which Cairncross did much to raise. Retiring from the mastership in 1978, he became a supernumerary fellow of St Antony's.

In February 1981, his name appeared on a list of 100 notable supporters of the 'Gang of Four', the Labour rebels who broke away to found the SDP. In 1987 he played a prominent role in Lord Jenkins of Hillhead's successful campaign (against Sir Edward Heath) for the Chancellorship of Oxford. Cairncross himself had been elected Chancellor of Glasgow University in 1972, beating the chain-store magnate Sir Isaac Wolfson by 4201 votes to 3750. He remained in that post until a few days before his 85th birthday in 1996 – becoming the first of 39 incumbents in 300 years to resign rather than die in office.

A member of the Glasgow faculty described Cairncross as 'a kenspeckle figure ... with his ubiquitous cloth cap and unassuming manner – a friend and counsellor to all he encountered'.

Cairncross was a fellow of the British Association, serving in 1970–71 as its president, a rare distinction for a non-scientist – or, as a fellow economist put it at the time, 'an inexact scientist'. He caused some stir among the fellowship when he told them that applied technology had more to contribute to economic salvation than pure science. He was also president of the Royal Economic Society and the Scottish Economic Society.

Cairncross was a prolific author, particularly in old age. His *Introduction to Economics* (1944) ran to six editions, and he produced numerous other academic texts. From 1954 to 1961 he edited the *Scottish Journal of Political Economy*. His works on economic history included *The Price of War* (1986), an analysis of reparations policy at the end of the Second World War; *Managing the British Economy in the 1960s* (1996); and, with Kathleen Burk, *Goodbye, Great Britain* (1992), a trenchant account of the economic crises of the mid-1970s. He edited two volumes of the diaries of Sir Robert Hall, his predecessor as government adviser, and wrote a life of the Cambridge economist Austin Robinson (1993). He also published a book of poetry, *Snatches* (1981).

Alec Cairncross was appointed CMG in 1950 and KCMG in 1967. He married, in 1943, Mary Frances Glynn. They had three sons and two daughters; their elder daughter, Frances, became a noted economist and author.

21 October 1998

Sir John Cowperthwaite

⋅◦══◎ 1915–2006 ◎══◦⋅

Financial secretary of Hong Kong

Sir John Cowperthwaite was Financial Secretary of Hong Kong throughout the 1960s; his extreme laissez-faire economic policies created conditions for very rapid growth, laying the foundations of the colony's prosperity as an international business centre. Cowperthwaite was a classical free trader in the tradition which stretched from Adam Smith to Gladstone and John Stuart Mill, rather than a modern monetarist. He was also a seasoned colonial administrator, with a strong streak of common sense. But his achievement in Hong Kong was hailed by Milton Friedman and other free-market economists as a shining example of the potency of laissez-faire when carried through to its logical conclusions in almost every aspect of government. The right-wing American commentator P.J. O'Rourke called Cowperthwaite 'a master of simplicities'.

Cowperthwaite himself called his approach 'positive non-intervention'. Personal taxes were kept at a maximum of 15 per cent; government borrowing was wholly unacceptable; there were no tariffs or subsidies. Red tape was so reduced that a new company could be registered with a one-page form.

Cowperthwaite believed that government should concern itself only with minimal intervention on behalf of the most needy, and should not interfere in business. In his first budget speech in 1961, he said: 'In the long run, the aggregate of decisions of individual businessmen, exercising individual judgement in a free economy, even if often mistaken, is less likely to do harm than the centralised decisions of a government, and certainly the harm is likely to be counteracted faster.'

From 1961 to 1971, Cowperthwaite exercised almost complete control of the colony's finances under successive governors, Sir Robert Black and Sir David Trench, who were sympathetic to his policies and content to give him his head. Among his peers in the Hong Kong government, it was said that only Claude Burgess, the colonial secretary, could keep him in line. 'His brilliance and argumentation prevailed, and he thus made policy by ruling on all items of expenditure,' said one colleague. But Cowperthwaite summed up his part in the colony's success over the decade with some modesty: 'I did very little. All I did was to try to prevent some of the things that might undo it.'

The measure of that success was a 50 per cent rise in real wages, and a two-thirds fall in the number of households in acute poverty. Exports rose by 14 per cent a year, as Hong Kong evolved from a trading post to a major regional hub and manufacturing base.

Cowperthwaite's style was polished and amusing, but his intellect was razor sharp. Once his mind was made up on an issue, he was not to be shifted. His refusal to compromise was such that it was often said he would not have lasted five minutes in any equivalent post in the Home Civil Service. Denis Healey, as Labour's defence minister, tried several times to persuade him that Hong Kong taxpayers should contribute more towards the British military presence in the colony: 'I always retired hurt from my encounters with the redoutable Financial Secretary,' he later recalled.

Another aspect of Cowperthwaite's *modus operandi* was a habit of holding his cards very close to his chest: when Milton Friedman asked him in 1963 to explain the mechanism which kept the Hong Kong dollar pegged to the pound, Cowperthwaite remarked that even the management of the HongKong and Shanghai Bank (through which the peg was operated) did not understand it. 'Better they shouldn't. They would mess it up.' As for the paucity of economic statistics for the colony, Cowperthwaite explained that he resisted requests to provide any, lest they be used as ammunition by those who wanted more government intervention.

The only real constraint on him was the requirement that he should hold the colony's credit balances in sterling. The arrangement was to cost Hong Kong dear when the chronic weakness of the British economy – shaped, it might be said, by interventionist, high-tax policies diametrically opposite to Cowperthwaite's own – forced the devaluation of the pound in 1967, resulting in a loss of some £30 million to Hong Kong's reserves. The unfettered Hong Kong economy took that blow in its stride, however, just as it had recovered from a crisis of confidence in local banks in 1965 and withstood the destabilising impact of Mao's Cultural Revolution. In its annual report for 1971, the year of Cowperthwaite's retirement, the government was able to boast that Hong Kong had become a 'stable and increasingly affluent society comparable with the developed world in nearly every respect'.

If there were critics who doubted that claim, few were to be found within Hong Kong itself, where hundreds of thousands of industrious Chinese refugees were grateful for the opportunities such an open economy offered. Seen from the perspective of the British welfare state, however, Hong Kong's social provision looked harshly inadequate. There were those who argued that the colony's prosperity was driven by its inhabitants' undiluted dedication to moneymaking, rather than by its style of government, and that a little more expenditure on education and health might have generated an ever faster growth rate. Others pointed out that even the modest sums Cowperthwaite did allocate to these areas were regularly underspent by a wide margin: in 1970–71, for example, medical spending – budgeted at little more than a pound per head of population – undershot by more than a quarter. But statistics for mortality and disease showed steady improvement, and despite its parsimony the government maintained an ambitious refugee rehousing programme. Cowperthwaite himself had a Gladstonian sense of obligation towards the least fortunate: he rejected the notion of tax relief on mortgage interest because it would have benefited the better-off and might have prejudiced 'our maximum housing effort at the lower end of the scale'.

To the extent that he left stark gaps in Hong Kong's social provision, the balance was partially rectified during the inter-ventionist governorship of Sir Murray (later Lord) MacLehose in the 1970s. But Cowperthwaite's successors in the financial secretary's office adhered to his core principles, funding increased public expenditure through land sales rather than tax or borrowing.

John James Cowperthwaite was born on 25 April 1915, and was educated at Merchiston Castle School in Edinburgh. He went on to study economics at St Andrew's University and Christ's College, Cambridge, before joining the Colonial Administrative service in

Hong Kong in 1941. During the Japanese occupation he was seconded to Sierra Leone. Returning to Hong Kong in 1945, he was asked to find ways in which the government could boost postwar economic revival: but he found the economy recovering swiftly without intervention, and took the lesson to heart.

He was appointed OBE in 1960, CMG in 1964 and was knighted in 1968. After leaving the government, Cowperthwaite was international adviser to Jardine Fleming, the Hong Kong-based investment bank, until 1981. He retired to St Andrews, where he was a member of the Royal & Ancient.

He married, in 1941, Sheila Thomson, who came from Aberdeen. Their son predeceased him.

21 January 2006

W. Edwards Deming

1900–1993

Guru of Japanese factory methods

W. Edwards Deming was a management guru who made a vital contribution to the postwar Japanese recovery with his doctrine of quality control, but was long ignored by Western companies. The Japanese believed Deming to be teaching them techniques widely practised in the United States, whilst American industrialists believed Japan's supremacy in manufacturing to be the result of a unique and alien cultural heritage. Both were wrong: the Deming creed influenced every modern factory in Japan, but was virtually unheard of in his native land until he was 78 years old.

The essence of Deming's approach was the use of statistical methods to identify the cause of product defects and inefficiencies. He campaigned for a commitment to 'total quality' at every level of industrial companies; through quality would come greater productivity, lower costs, increased market share and long-term stability. He believed that shop-floor workers are naturally motivated to do well, but are thwarted by incompetent management.

'American management has a negative scrap value,' he once said. 'It's like an old refrigerator . . . You have to pay someone $25 to cart it off.' His '14 Points for management' included 'allow pride in workmanship' and 'improve constantly and forever the system of production and service'. Their effect in action helped to change the image of the words 'made in Japan' from one of cheapness and shoddiness at the beginning of the 1950s to one of near-faultless reliability in the 1980s. The fruits of Deming's evangelism could be seen in Japanese-owned factories all over the world.

When at last Deming was discovered by his fellow countrymen (his first American sponsor was the president of Nashua Corporation, a photocopier company in New Hampshire, who had been puzzled by the reverence accorded to Deming by Nashua's Japanese joint-venture partner) his fame rapidly spread. In 1980 a journalist interviewed him at his Washington home for a documentary called *If Japan Can, Why Can't We?*; their conversations lasted for 25 hours. 'Here is a man who has the answer and he's five miles from the White House and nobody will speak to him,' the journalist said later, having discovered that high officials of the Carter administration had never heard of Deming.

Thereafter, despite advancing age, Deming pursued a relentless mission to convert ailing industries to his way of thinking – 'trying to keep America from committing suicide' as he put it. The chairman of the Ford Motor Company declared himself 'proud to be called a Deming disciple', and one prominent management professor attributed Ford's continuing existence to Deming's influence. A multitude of other organisations, ranging from Campbell's Soups to the US Navy, began to take the aged doctor's advice.

For the remainder of his life, Deming conducted a tireless schedule of four-day seminars for managers, enlivened by his oracular speaking style and by theatrical demonstrations of his theories at work – using audience volunteers to 'process' thousands of red and white beads. Although confined to a wheelchair and reliant upon oxygen tanks to ease his breathing, Deming was still conducting seminars a month before his death.

William Edwards Deming was born in Sioux City, Iowa on 14

October 1900, the son of a part-time lawyer and land developer. He studied at the universities of Wyoming and Colorado before completing a doctorate in mathematical physics at Yale in 1928. He then joined the US Department of Agriculture, where his fascination with the power of statistics began to develop. He was much influenced by work done in the Bell telephone laboratories by Walter Shewhart, who had identified two types of problem in industrial processes: 'controlled' or 'common' variations, which are due to defects in the design and management of the process itself, and the 'uncontrolled' or 'special' ones, which are external to the process – such as errors by factory workers.

This distinction became central to the Deming philosophy: in his definitive estimation, 94 per cent of the scope for improvement in industrial processes lay in the area of controlled variations – that is, in the hands of management and only 6 per cent could ever be blamed on the workforce.

In 1939 Deming moved to the National Bureau of Census, where he applied his theories to such effect that productivity in some areas of census work improved by six times. During the Second World War Deming began teaching his ideas to managers and engineers, but with little response or recognition. The turning point in his career came in 1946, when General Douglas MacArthur invited him to Japan to advise on the Japanese census. There he made contact with the Union of Japanese Scientists and Engineers, who were impressed by what they were shown of his wartime work. In 1950 he was asked to lecture on statistical methods for industry, and over the next two years he addressed many of Japan's top executives. They embraced his philosophy with a dedication which surprised him, after so many years' fruitless preaching to their American counterparts. In 1960 (27 years before he was honoured in his own country), Dr Deming became the first American to be awarded the Order of the Sacred Treasure.

Deming was a prolific author. *Out of the Crisis* (1986) was considered his seminal work. His last book, *The New Economics*, was published in the year of his death.

Awareness of Deming's work was promoted after his death by groups of his followers throughout America and in Holland, France and New Zealand. The British Deming Association was formed in 1987.

Deming's first wife, Agnes Bell, died in 1930; his second, Lola Shupe, died in 1986. He lived modestly, giving much of the income from his seminars and writings to his local church and to medical charities.

20 December 1993

Peter Drucker

⟶⟩ 1909–2005 ⟨⟵

Pioneering management theorist

Peter Drucker was a social theorist who identified management as the essential organising requirement of 20th-century life. An Austrian-born exile from Nazi Germany, Drucker emerged as the first modern management guru as a result of a study of the structures and practices of General Motors, which he undertook in 1943. The resulting book, *Concept of the Corporation* (1946), looked at a large manufacturing company for the first time as a living social organism, and – though GM tried to ban its executives from reading it – became an international bestseller. It argued for treating workers as valued team members, rather than mere assembly-line fodder, and developed the idea of management as a specialised skill, the aim of which is to make people capable of joint performance – like players in an orchestra, under the baton of a conductor but each responsible for their own instrumental part. This was to become the core of Drucker's life's work.

He went on to write many more books and thousands of articles on similar themes: his interest was less in economic or political theories than in people, and how to get the best out of them, jointly and individually. One of his notions which was widely adopted by British companies from the late 1960s onwards was 'management by objectives', the process of agreeing, rather than imposing, per-formance targets to which each worker or team becomes committed.

Successful leaders, he said, are masters both of focusing on the right targets and of delegation: 'They don't tackle things they aren't good at. They make sure other necessities get done, but not by them.' They also check their own performance, as well as that of their subordinates. 'They put away their goals for six months and then come back and check ... They find out whether they picked the truly important things to do. I've seen a great many people who are exceedingly good at execution, but exceedingly poor at picking the important things. They are magnificent at getting the unimportant things done.'

Much of Drucker's wisdom in this vein was little more than common sense, expressed with great vigour and wit. Though often credited as the inventor of management theory, he believed it was better understood through practical experience than through college teaching, which he regarded as 'largely a waste of time' – better to study at the University of Scranton, the industrial town in Pennsylvania, he once said, than at Harvard Business School. Similarly, though he was hired to advise many companies and organisations, he was scathing about the explosive growth of the consultancy profession.

And although he was a brilliant platform speaker, he was also wary of charisma in business or politics: the American presidents he most admired were Harry Truman and Ronald Reagan. Truman, Drucker observed, 'was as bland as a dead mackerel' but was worshipped by those around him because he was absolutely trustworthy. 'If Truman said no, it was no, and if he said yes, it was yes.' As for Reagan, 'His great strength was not charisma, as is commonly thought, but that he knew exactly what he could do and what he could not do.' These were the qualities that made for good management, and in Drucker's world view, the best managers were the heroes of the modern age.

Peter Ferdinand Drucker was born on 19 November 1909 in Vienna, where his father was the head of the export department of the Austrian government. Peter began his working life as a clerk in a trading company in Hamburg, where he also studied law. He transferred to Frankfurt University, where he took a doctorate in international law in 1931 and found work as a journalist on a local paper – for which he interviewed Adolf Hitler. In 1933, after an essay he had written about Friedrich Julius Stahl, a 19th-century Jewish political thinker, was burned in the street by Nazis, Drucker left for England, where he worked in a bank and attended lectures by J.M. Keynes.

Four years later he moved to the United States, where he taught at Sarah Lawrence College in New York and began work on the first of his books on social and political themes, *The End of Economic Man: The Origins of Totalitarianism* – which drew praise from, among others, Winston Churchill. His next book, *Future of Industrial Man* (1942), identified management as a set of skills and principles quite different from the command mechanisms to be found alike in fascism and in the organisation of early mass-production factories such as those of Henry Ford.

Drucker taught business management at New York University until 1971, when he moved to Claremont Graduate University in California as professor of social science, a post which he held until 2002. He was also a columnist for the *Wall Street Journal*, and his 32 books were translated into many languages; he devoted some of the proceeds of his success to a foundation to teach management skills to non-profit organisations.

Peter Drucker was also a scholar and connoisseur of Japanese art. He married, in 1937, Doris Schmitz, whom he had first met in Frankfurt; they had a son and three daughters.

11 November 2005

Professor J.K. Galbraith

⊷⧫⊜ 1908–2006 ⊜⧫⊶

Doyen of American liberal economists

Professor John Kenneth Galbraith was the high priest of old-fashioned American liberalism. Galbraith once remarked that he would rather be remembered as a writer than as an economist 'or anything as dreary as that'. He was indeed much more renowned as a polemicist than as an interpreter of economic theory, but he was also a diplomat, a journalist, a novelist, a political campaigner, an inveterate television pundit and a globetrotting conference speaker – deploying craggy features (he was 6 feet 8 inches), a rich *basso profundo* and a sardonic wit, to powerful effect.

His views were formed by a rigorous Scots-Canadian upbringing in rural Ontario and by enthusiasm for Franklin Roosevelt's radical New Deal policies of the 1930s. He believed in 'the miracle of the modern mixed economy' – capitalism with substantial public investment and guidance.

For sixty years he made the case for more generous welfare spending: 'I see a choice', he said, 'between affirmative government on behalf of all the people or a negative approach to government, with the main objective of avoiding its cost. There are minor variations on that theme. But the basic point is unchangeable.'

His seminal work, a blast against the consumerist obsessions of 1950s America, was *The Affluent Society* (1958), which provided generations of speechwriters with the versatile phrase 'private affluence and public squalor'. The core of his argument was that 'we must find a way to remedy the poverty which afflicts us in public services and which is in increasingly bizarre contrast to our affluence in private goods. This is necessary to temper, and more hopefully to eliminate, the social disorders which are the counterpart of the present imbalance.'

In a much-quoted passage, he summoned the image of the family which takes its 'mauve and cerise, air-conditioned, power-steered and power-braked car' through blighted cities to picnic by a polluted stream 'and go on to spend the night in a park which is a menace to public health and morals . . . Amid the stench of decaying refuse, they may reflect vaguely on the curious unevenness of their blessings. Is this indeed, the American genius?'

The Galbraithian view – which included a limited defence of socialism as a mechanism for wealth-distribution and industrial organisation – was wholly at odds with the free-market orthodoxies of the 1980s, both in Britain and the United States. Galbraith's relationship with the Reagan administration was 'zero', and he railed against tax-cutting policies which destroyed welfare and created a massive budget deficit: it was 'the Mexicanisation of the American economy . . . carried far beyond anything yet achieved by Mexico'.

Unshakeable in his tenets, he evolved a theory in *The Culture of Contentment* (1992) to explain why the developed world had moved so decisively in the opposite ideological direction. This pessimistic thesis held that the New Deal and the British Welfare State had, by softening the inhumanities of raw capitalism, created a self-satisfied political consensus which now looked with contempt on the enlightened policies of the past, and was without compassion for 'the voiceless poor of the great cities' whom the system had failed. Conservative economics had become merely a rationalisation of vested interests, which allowed for no more than 'a minimum measure of social concern'.

Galbraith's certainty in his own rightness was part of his charm. He took satisfaction in having predicted, nine months before the event, the world stock-market crash of 1987 – which he saw as the product of 'the euphoria of self-conceit' among speculators with shorter memories than his own. He saw the thesis of *The Economies of Innocent Fraud*, published when he was 93, as having been vindicated by the Enron scandal, which broke shortly after.

Views with which he disagreed were dismissed as 'the conventional wisdom', a Galbraith coinage which entered everyday language. His own most contentious statements, on the other hand, were often presented as 'the all-but-universally-held view' – as in: 'that the market does not produce socially optimal results has, in fact, been long recognised by economists'.

A master of acid invective, he was particularly cruel to industrialists (who conducted much of their business 'under conditions of advanced intoxication'), bankers ('a profession where style, self-assurance and tailoring are much more important than intelligence') and the United States Congress, which 'uniquely among modern organs of public and private administration . . . rewards senility'.

But he feigned elegant surprise that opponents should find his grand New England scepticism offensive: he once remarked to President Kennedy that he did not see why the *New York Times* had to call him arrogant. 'I don't see why not,' the President replied, 'Everyone else does.'

Of Argyllshire ancestry, John Kenneth Galbraith was born at Iona Station in Ontario on 15 October 1908. His father, William, was an insurance executive, local dignitary, Baptist and breeder of Shorthorn cattle. Galbraith completed a first degree at Ontario Agricultural College in 1931 and a doctorate at the University of California in 1934. In the summer months that year, before moving on to lecture at Harvard, he served briefly in the Department of Agriculture in Washington.

In 1937, he crossed the Atlantic to Cambridge, where he absorbed in fuller measure the influence of John Maynard Keynes. In 1940 Galbraith returned to Washington to join the National Defence Advisory Committee (NDAC). His periods of public service never lacked for controversy: his first task at the NDAC, which he relished, was to direct the siting of munitions factories towards depressed areas of the country, rather than to those areas convenient to the military-industrial establishment.

His next project, as deputy head of the Office of Price Administration, was more provocative still: in seeking to control inflation, particularly in food prices, he incurred the wrath of the farm lobby and other influential groups. In 1943 he was obliged to resign. Roosevelt sent word that he should be given another senior job – but Galbraith chose instead to become a member of the editorial board of *Fortune* magazine.

Towards the end of the war he re-entered government service as director of the US Strategic Bombing Survey, charged with assessing the extent of economic damage accomplished by air strikes on Hitler's Reich. He arrived in Germany in the spring of 1945, and subsequently took part in interrogations of Speer, Goering, Ribbentrop, Keitel and Jodl. Speer aside, he found them to be an 'incredible collection of often deranged incompetents'. He then worked briefly for the State Department but, finding himself at odds with the prevailing view that US foreign policy should now focus on the Soviet military threat, he resigned once more, returning to *Fortune* and academe. In 1949, Galbraith was appointed Paul M Warburg Professor of Economics at Harvard, which was to be his base for the rest of his life. He became emeritus professor in 1975.

During the 1950s his career advanced both as an author and as a political activist. He was a member of Adlai Stevenson's campaign staff in the presidential campaigns of 1952 and 1956, and chairman of the economic committee of the Democratic Advisory Council.

From an early stage, he was an advisor to the then Senator John F Kennedy, whom he had first met at Harvard in the 1930s; he became one of the most loyal courtiers of the Kennedy clan. After JFK's election in 1960, Galbraith was rewarded with the post of ambassador to India, where he befriended Prime Minister Jawaharlal Nehru; Cambridge provided a common bond. Apart from a brief period of intense behind-the-scenes activity during the 1962 border conflict between India and China, Galbraith found that the diplomatic role demanded no more than an hour or two of his time each day.

While in Delhi, he found time to write *The Scotch*, a memoir of his boyhood and ancestry; a volume on economic development; a daily diary later published as *The Ambassador's Journal* and (under the pseudonym Mark Epernay) his first experiment in fiction, *The McLandress File*. He also collaborated in a book on Indian painting.

After Kennedy's assassination, Galbraith was a speech-writer for Lyndon Johnson, who once remarked to him: 'Did y'ever think, Ken, that making a speech on economics is a lot like pissing down your leg? It seems hot to you, but it never does to anyone else.'

Galbraith's opposition to the Vietnam War eventually estranged him from the White House, and he twice declined to run for the Senate. In later years he professed disenchantment with the Democratic Party in general. The thought of attending the 1992 convention in New York was, he said, 'something that would absolutely repel me'.

Galbraith spent a second period at Cambridge in the early 1970s and became an honorary fellow of Trinity College in 1987. In 1977 his resonant, lugubrious delivery became known to a wider British audience through the medium of a documentary series for the BBC, *The Age of Uncertainty*, which rehearsed his beliefs in the context of a discursive travelogue through the history of economic thought. He was fond of Britain for having declined 'rather gracefully' and as 'the only country where economic discussion is enjoyed'. He was also one of the few to emerge with credit from an interview with Ali

G, who asked Galbraith whether one could be a millionaire with £100,000. Having replied 'no', Galbraith was asked, 'In't that racist?' He did not rise to the bait. Galbraith was awarded the Medal of Freedom by President Truman. He was a past president of the American Economics Association and the first economist to be president of the American Academy of Arts and Letters. He published more than twenty books, notable among which were *The Great Crash, 1929* (1955), *The New Industrial State* (1967) and his autobiography, *A Life in Our Times* (1981).

He married, in 1937, Catherine 'Kitty' Atwater. They had three sons.

29 April 2006

Henry Grunfeld

⊰⥱ 1904–1999 ⥲⊱

Warburgs founder and guiding light

Henry Grunfeld was for 60 years the guiding light of the investment banking house S.G. Warburg & Co, in which he had been a founding partner with Sir Siegmund Warburg. Grunfeld was a discreet private banker in the German tradition, and a subtle and meticulous technician. Having joined Siegmund Warburg's nascent firm (then called the New Trading Co) as its third member in 1935, he became the guardian of its distinctively austere intellectual ethos and exacting professional standards, providing the perfect foil to the brilliant, volatile Warburg. His significance in the bank's history is said to be reflected in the choice by Siegmund Warburg of the name 'Mercury' for the group's holding company – the chemical symbol for mercury is *Hg*, Grunfeld's initials. Warburg described Grunfeld as 'not only my beloved friend but also a hard taskmaster to me'. Whilst Warburg was prone to fierce enthusiasms, rages and disappointments, Grunfeld was invariably calm, sceptical, and attentive to detail.

Grunfeld was pre-eminent among Warburgs' 'uncles', the small group of older men who guided the firm's younger practitioners and shaped its strategic decisions. In his heyday in the 1960s, Grunfeld would slip unannounced from meeting to meeting in the bank's unadorned Gresham Street building (which had no name plate at its entrance), steering each separate negotiation for a few minutes, maintaining an encyclopaedic grasp of the business in hand. In his eighties, he would apologise to younger colleagues if they found him leaving for the day as early as half-past five.

Grunfeld and Warburg developed between them a set of working practices which were first sneered at by the rest of the City as sinister and Prussian, but later widely envied. In an era when the aristocratic directors of other merchant banks arrived at ten and went home not long after a substantial lunch, Warburgs started at eight and was dubbed 'the nightclub' by competitors who saw its lights burn late into the evening. There were, famously, two sittings of lunch, of exactly one hour each, enabling the seniors to entertain twice in the same day. The table was frugal, but Warburgs' clients learned to acknowledge the obverse of the City dictum that 'the better the lunch, the worse the advice'.

The Warburg partners demanded fearsome standards of accuracy from their staff, right down to punctuation, and believed in rigorous self-criticism. They developed an elaborate internal monitoring system which recorded all significant correspondence and conversation throughout the firm. Courteous to a fault – he saw no distinction between his home and his office – Grunfeld was also capable of expressing icy displeasure when standards slipped. He and Siegmund would review each day's business as they were driven home together at night. The alignment of their ideas even extended to Siegmund's famous insistence on handwriting analysis as a guide to the character of potential recruits – having used graphology to identify an embezzler in his pre-war German firm, Grunfeld shared an enthusiasm for this abstruse science.

Sir Siegmund Warburg died, aged 80, in 1982. The business which he and Grunfeld built together grew to act for half of Britain's top 100 companies and to manage over £60 billion of investments. If it bore the more obvious imprint of Warburg's powerful personality, it was also very much the product of Grunfeld's cool intellect and high integrity. 'You couldn't have done it without me,' Warburg told him on one occasion, 'And I couldn't have done it without you.'

Henry Grunfeld was born in Upper Silesia on 1 June 1904, into a prominent Jewish family with steel and chemical interests. He trained as a lawyer before joining the family business, which included the Berlin metals trading house of Rawack & Grunfeld. As a young industrialist and financier, he spent most of his nights in railway sleeping cars, shuttling from one plant to the next. But in 1934 Grunfeld and his father were summoned to the Kaiserhof hotel in Berlin, crowded with Brownshirts, and invited to hand over their business to be Aryanised. Young Henry was arrested by the Gestapo. After his release, he and his family lived in hiding for some weeks in the Black Forest.

Having served as an honorary consul for Spain, he was eventually able to leave Germany under Spanish diplomatic protection and make a new life in England. Returning to Berlin airport on his last brief visit in 1937, Grunfeld noticed Heinrich Himmler's limousine pulled up beside his taxi; he never set foot in the city again. The Grunfeld fortune was plundered, and many family members were killed by the Nazis.

Grunfeld had never met Siegmund Warburg in Germany, but heard through mutual acquaintances that the recently established New Trading Co needed someone with industrial expertise to match Warburg's financial flair. In 1935 they joined forces, with empty desks and no particular plan in mind – but a burning ambition to regain the kind of position in the business world which they had been forced to abandon in Germany.

At the outbreak of war, Grunfeld was declared an enemy alien, and took to wandering in Hyde Park during the morning hours when German Jews were most at risk of arrest and internment. At the New Trading offices in King William Street, the émigré partners were constrained by a wartime ban from writing or speaking in their native tongue; as most of their British staff had been called away to the forces, the language of the firm became a heavily Germanicised form of English, typified by Grunfeld's exhortation: 'Then into action we must swing.'

In the early years, they were shunned as outsiders by the City establishment. Innovative ideas and specialised knowledge of the continental business scene helped them to capture corporate clients from other houses. But as lenders they were notably cautious: Grunfeld had learned from experience, having sat on the board of a failed German bank in the early 1930s. Many years later, it was he who guarded Warburgs' liquidity during the fringe bank crisis which rocked the City in 1974.

The great advance in the bank's reputation came with victory in 1959 in an acrimonious battle for control of British Aluminium, in which Warburgs acted for the bidders, Tube Investments and the American group Reynolds. Displaying equal measures of complacency, snobbery and xenophobia, the grandees of the City closed ranks against what was in effect the first truly contested takeover bid in the London market. But the combination of Warburg's aggressive determination and Grunfeld's mastery of tactics won the day. 'We just didn't make any mistakes and the other side did,' Grunfeld said later.

This coup attracted other prestigious clients, including the Canadian newspaper tycoon Roy Thomson, who Grunfeld advised on his ownership of Times Newspapers and in his later interests in North Sea oil. Another first for Warburgs was the launch, in 1963, of the first Eurobond issue, raising funds for the Italian Autostrade. Again Siegmund Warburg was the bold innovator, but it was Grunfeld who set his mind to the technical details – applying knowledge gained in the international bond markets of the 1920s and early '30s.

Grunfeld was chairman of Warburgs from 1964 to 1974. Thereafter he was president until his 90th birthday, when he became 'senior advisor'. He continued to attend the office daily 'because I enjoy it, because I think it's healthy for me and because I think I can still make a contribution'. His role was described as that of a constitutional monarch: to be consulted, to encourage and to warn. In the 'Big Bang' market reforms of the late 1980s, Grunfeld saw what had once been a family-sized firm sold to Swiss Bank, multiply in size and become a powerful force in international securities dealing. These developments were in many ways alien to the private banking ethos which he represented – an ethos in which confidential advisory work was regarded as a much higher calling than trading. But in an earlier era he had observed the fate of Warburgs' Wall Street associate firm, Kuhn Loeb, which, having failed to move with the times, had eventually faded away. 'Having seen all this as a necessity,' Grunfeld said of the new, flamboyant world of giant trading floors, 'I was very much in favour of it.' He believed that Siegmund Warburg would have come to the same conclusion.

Some outsiders saw the acquisition of Warburgs by Swiss Bank (later Union Bank of Switzerland) in 1995 as the end of the firm's glory days. Henry Grunfeld took the opposite view; he declared that Warburgs would be reinvigorated by the new alliance, as indeed it was.

He lived quietly, and seldom spoke to journalists or allowed his picture to be published.

Henry Grunfeld married, in 1931, Berta Lotte Oliven, who died in 1993. He was survived by a son; a daughter predeceased him.

10 June 1999

Michael Ivens

⁕≡◉ 1924–2001 ◉≡⁕

Anti-union campaigner and poet

Michael Ivens was an ardent campaigner for free enterprise and trade-union reform in the pre-Thatcher era when those causes were distinctly unfashionable. Ivens was director from 1971 to 1992 of Aims of Industry, a pressure group established during the Second World War by Lord Beaverbrook and other business leaders to combat the advance of socialism on the shop floor. The Aims organisation had campaigned against the postwar Labour government's nationalisation programme, and under the Wilson and Callaghan administrations it stood up both for employers and for individual workers against the might of the unions. Ivens was particularly associated with opposition to the National Dock

Labour Scheme, the closed-shop arrangement which kept casual workers out of the docks: Margaret Thatcher, who finally abolished it, called it 'that monument to modern Luddism'.

Ivens was also a founder, with Norris McWhirter and Viscount de L'Isle VC in 1975, of the National Association for Freedom (NAFF, later the Freedom Association) to campaign against all forms of abuse of individual freedom – particularly from overweening union power. The association established its name through its support of three railwaymen dismissed for refusing to join a union, and achieved a membership, at its peak, of 20,000. It went on to fight an action to prevent British post-office unions from boycotting mail to South Africa, and in 1977 it played a prominent role in the Grunwick dispute.

Grunwick was a photo-processing business in north London owned by an Anglo-Indian entrepreneur who had dismissed a number of immigrant workers after a walk-out. The APEX trade union signed up the sacked workers, demanded recognition at the plant, and organised mass pickets which rapidly turned violent. The majority of Grunwick workers – mostly veiled Asian women – who did not want to be unionised had to be bussed in each day through a hail of abuse. Grunwick's outgoing mail, containing the developed films on which the business depended, was 'blacked' by postal unions and had to be smuggled out and discreetly posted elsewhere by NAFF volunteers. Without NAFF, Grunwick would almost certainly have gone bankrupt. For his part in the campaign Ivens was condemned by the communist *Morning Star* newspaper as 'one of the three most dangerous men in Britain'– an accolade which he quoted with pride.

Ivens specialised in campaign tactics rather than academic argument, but he was also an accomplished writer – and far removed from the conventional image of a right-wing activist. On issues of immigration and law and order, he held relatively liberal views: he was a member of the Howard League for penal reform, and on one occasion gave both a job and a home to a former Broadmoor inmate. In one of his campaigns, in support of Stanley Adams, a 'whistleblower' employee of the drug company Hoffman La Roche, he gained as much support from the left as the right. He was also director for 25 years of the Foundation for Business Responsibilities, which promoted notions of corporate obligation towards employees and suppliers as well as shareholders.

Aggressive in debate but convivial and soft-spoken elsewhere – including favoured watering-holes such as El Vino and the Ritz – he maintained friendships across the political spectrum and beyond it, notably in the world of poetry. He was especially proud to have had one of his poems chosen by Philip Larkin for the *Oxford Book of Twentieth Century Verse*. It was titled *First Day at School*, and recalled 'the large boy' hurling Ivens's ball over a roof:

> *unstintingly*
> *I gave him*
> *my admiration*
> *As others have done*
> *when their respect*
> *money*
> *virginity*
> *honour hope and lives*
> *have been hurled*
> *triumphantly out of sight*

Michael William Ivens was born on 15 March 1924. His father, a salesman, came from Aston in Birmingham; his mother was Jewish. Part of his childhood was spent in Australia, but he returned to complete a shortened education at the Quinton School in London, associated with the Regent Street Polytechnic.

During the Second World War Ivens served in the East Surrey Regiment in Palestine in the British Mandate administration: his last duty as a captain was to supervise the return to Cyprus of former concentration-camp inmates arriving in Palestine with inadequate documents. He expressed his distaste for the task first by absenting himself without leave to stay on a kibbutz and later in a striking poem, *Haifa Bay in the Morning*.

As a young man, Ivens had flirted with anarchism, and he remained throughout his life a free-thinking outsider rather than an

Establishment figure. After demobilisation he went to work for a Soho magazine publisher called Kaplan, becoming editor and writer-in-chief of a magazine called *Sports Reporter*. There he recalled trying but failing to recruit Brian Glanville, then a reporter for a rival weekly and later the doyen of Fleet Street football correspondents; the 17-year-old Glanville had demanded two guineas an article, well in excess of Kaplan's rates.

Ivens moved on to work for Esso, where among other jobs he edited the staff magazine. In the 1960s he turned increasingly to writing, publishing a series of works on management and industrial communication, including *Case for Capitalism* in 1967 and *Industry and Values* in 1970. In that year he became joint founding editor and columnist of a literary and political magazine, *Twentieth Century*, and soon afterwards he went to work for Aims of Industry. He left to work for a year as a director of Standard Telephone, part of ITT, before returning as director of Aims (known in the mid-1970s as Aims for Freedom & Enterprise) in 1971.

As well as exposing trade-union abuses, he maintained a long-running Aims campaign against nationalisation: the scuppering of the Callaghan government's plan to nationalise the Bristol ship-repair yard was at least partly due to his lobbying. Later he espoused the cause of 'contracting out' of central and local government services to combat what he called 'the disease of direct labour'.

After retiring in 1992, Ivens redesignated himself as 'consultant' to Aims of Industry, and the organisation – having seen the victory of its free enterprise philosophy – withered away. In recent years, both Aims and the Freedom Association (of which Ivens was vice-president) were associated with campaigns against joining the euro and for renegotiation of Britain's EU membership.

Ivens was a founder, in 1969, of the Junior Hospital Doctors Association, formed to combat the closed-shop tendencies of the British Medical Association, and of the Foundation for the Study of Terrorism in 1986. He was a member of the advisory council of the Airey Neave Foundation. He was also treasurer of the Poetry Society from 1989 to 1991, helping to rescue it from financial difficulties. He published six volumes of poetry: *Another Sky* (1963), *Last Waltz* (1964), *Private and Public* (1968), *Born Early* (1975), *No Woman is*

an Island (1983), and *New Divine Comedy* (1990). A devout
Catholic, he developed an interest in later years in religious
mysticism.

Michael Ivens was appointed CBE in 1983.

He married first, in 1950, Rosalie Turnbull; they had three sons
– of whom one predeceased him – and a daughter. The marriage
was dissolved and he married secondly, in 1971, Katherine
Laurence, by whom he had two more sons.

4 November 2001

Merton Miller

1921–2000

'Nobel laureate 'game theory' economist

Professor Merton Miller was a free-market economist of the
Chicago school; his contributions to the theory of corporate finance
brought him the Nobel prize in 1990. Miller's work helped
companies to make better decisions about borrowing to finance
new projects. The so-called M&M Theorem, first developed by
Miller with fellow economist Franco Modigliani in 1958, said that
the mixture of debt and equity in a company had no effect on its
total market value, because the more debt it took on (by issuing
what came to be known as junk bonds, for example) the more the
stock market would discount its shares to take account of increased
risk.

What really mattered, on the other hand, was how much cash
the company could generate. In essence, therefore, companies
should focus on improving 'shareholder value': the question was
not how an activity should be financed but whether it was worth
doing at all. Nor was it worthwhile for corporate managers to
diversify their businesses in order to reduce risk and please
investors, because investors could always adjust their own risk by
altering their portfolios. Managers should just concentrate on
maximising earnings. Though now regarded as received wisdom,

this was revolutionary work in its day. Miller liked to explain the theorem by means of a joke about Yogi Berra, the celebrated baseball coach who was given to gnomic utterances. After a game, the pizza-delivery man says to him, 'Yogi, how do you want this pizza cut, into quarters or eighths?' And Yogi says, 'I'm hungry tonight, cut it into eighths.' The joke illustrated the idea that no matter how you divide up a company – no matter what the relative proportion of debt and equity – the total value of the various parts stays the same.

'Reporters would say, "You mean they gave you guys a Nobel prize for something as simple as that?"' Miller told an interviewer. 'And I'd say, "Yes, but remember we proved it rigorously."'

The son of a lawyer, Merton Miller was born in Boston on 16 May 1923 and graduated from Harvard in 1943. He did economic research work for the US Treasury and the Federal Reserve before returning to study for a doctorate at Johns Hopkins University in Baltimore. From 1952 to 1953 he was a visiting lecturer at the London School of Economics. His next appointment was at the Carnegie Institute of Technology (now Carnegie-Mellon University), one of a new wave of academically-oriented US business schools, where he teamed up with Modigliani. In 1961 Miller moved to the Graduate School of Business of the University of Chicago – where Milton Friedman presided over a powerhouse of laissez-faire thinking – and in due course he became Robert H. McCormick Distinguished Service Professor there.

His work continued to focus on corporate finance until the early 1980s, when he turned his attention to one of the most complex aspects of the modern financial world: the economics of securities and derivatives trading. He became a public director of the Chicago Board of Trade and the Chicago Mercantile Exchange, for which he chaired a special panel which conducted a post-mortem on the stock market crash of October 1987.

Part of the intellectual underpinning of the concept of derivatives – contracts which enable traders to fix future prices for commodities and financial instruments – had been developed out of Miller and Modigliani's earlier work by his former research assistant Myron Scholes (also to become a Nobel laureate) working with Fischer Black and Robert Merton. Miller was a stout defender of derivatives against assaults by nervous regulators and opponents of free markets. He believed that as instruments of risk control rather than speculation, they made markets safer rather than more dangerous. He also liked to point out that the world's banks had lost far more on bad property lending than they ever had on futures and options. *Merton Miller on Derivatives* (1997) was hailed by the chairman of the Chicago exchange for its brilliance in cutting through a fog of 'misunderstanding and nonsense' surrounding the topic.

Among his other widely read works were *Macroeconomics: A Neoclassical Introduction* (1986) and *Financial Innovations and Market Volatility* (1991). Miller once remarked of his own books that 'they're repeatedly given the best kind of flattery: imitation.'

Miller received the Nobel prize in 1990, five years after Modigliani. At the prize-giving ceremony in Stockholm, an audience member asked one of the other economics laureates if he agreed that computerised trading had caused the '87 crash. 'I really would have answered that differently,' Miller observed later. 'I would have climbed down off the stage and punched the guy.'

Miller was a good-humoured man who liked to drink beer and watch the Chicago Bears football team. His first wife, Eleanor, by whom he had three daughters, died in 1969. He was survived by his second wife, Katherine.

3 June 2000

PART NINE

COMMONWEALTH AND COLONIAL

SIR CECIL BURNEY – *Zambian car dealer and politician*
SIR COLIN CAMPBELL – *Kenyan tea trader*
MAJOR SIR RUPERT CLARKE – *Australian landowner*
SIR MICHAEL HERRIES – *model for James Clavell's Taipan*
LORD KADOORIE – *Hong Kong power-station magnate*
KERRY PACKER – *Australian media tycoon*
SIR Y.K. PAO – *shipping magnate*
SIR FRANCIS RENOUF – *colourful New Zealand banker*
SIR JOHN SAUNDERS – *war hero and Hong Kong banker*

Sir Cecil Burney

⊸⟳ 1923–2002 ⟳⊱

Zambian car dealer and politician

Sir Cecil Burney, 3rd Bt, was a successful businessman and one of the last white MPs in the Zambian parliament. Burney became a member of the Legislative Council of the British protectorate of Northern Rhodesia in 1959. He acted as deputy to John Roberts, leader of the Northern Rhodesia United Federal Party, in negotiations over the future of the Central African Federation – the union of Northern and Southern Rhodesia and Nyasaland which was seen by British governments of the 1950s as the blueprint for decolonisation of the region, but which was opposed by black leaders in all three territories. He briefed the colonial secretary Iain Macleod on his visit to Lusaka in 1960, and took part in the constitutional conference at Lancaster House in London in 1961 which tried unsuccessfully to devise a new legislative assembly for Northern Rhodesia balancing white and African interests. Over the following two years, the possibility of a multi-racial settlement for the Federation foundered as the Macmillan government failed to find common ground with Sir Roy Welensky, Federation Prime Minister and United Federal Party chief. Burney worked with Welensky but took a somewhat independent line, recognising the inevitable demise of the Federation and looking for ways to smooth the transition.

The Federation was duly dissolved at the end of 1963, and Northern Rhodesia became independent Zambia, with Kenneth Kaunda as its president, in October 1964. Burney was one of ten white former Legislative Councillors to sit in the new parliament on the 'reserved roll'. He was member for the northern town of Ndola until 1968, and was also chairman of the public-accounts committee, bringing his business acumen to bear on the fragile finances of the new country.

Burney could be very abrasive in his political dealings, but was respected for his integrity and intelligence. He made no secret of his concerns about Africa's future when he returned to England in 1970. But he remained on friendly terms with Kaunda, and proudly retained Zambian citizenship until the end of his life.

Cecil Denniston Burney was born on 8 January 1923, the only child of Sir Charles Burney, 2nd Bt, and his American wife Gladys. Sir Charles was in turn the son of Admiral of the Fleet Sir Cecil Burney, who was second in command of the grand fleet at the Battle of Jutland in his flagship *Marlborough*, and was created a baronet in 1921. Sir Charles was also a naval officer and subsequently Conservative MP for Uxbridge, but his chief distinction was to have invented the Paravane, a steel skirt which could be floated around the hull of a ship in order to deflect mines and cut their mooring cables. The design – which saved many thousands of lives – was bought from Burney by the armaments company Vickers for some £400,000, a substantial fortune in the 1920s.

Cecil was educated at Eton, and joined the Royal Navy in 1942. He served as a radar officer, and saw action in Russian convoys; at the end of the war he was present at the surrender of the German Atlantic U-boat fleet at Loch Eriboll. On demobilisation, he went up to Trinity College, Cambridge, to read engineering. He also rowed for Trinity, and later won the Four-oar Coxless Visitors Cup at Henley. In the 1930s his father had acquired a beautiful farm (called Little England) in Southern Rhodesia, and after graduation Cecil set out to make a life in Africa, joining the Anglo-American mining company to work in the copper belt of Northern Rhodesia. He fell out with his mine manager, however, and in 1951 he set up his own business, a car dealership called Northern Motors, of which he remained chairman until 1972.

Back in England, he had hopes of becoming a Conservative MP, but was told that in his late forties he was too old. He was, however, an active member of the political committee of the Carlton Club for many years, and became president of the West Berkshire Conservative Association, which he helped to revive after the loss of the Newbury seat to the Liberal Democrats in 1993.

In business, Burney took on the chairmanship in 1975 of Hampton Trust, a commercial property group then at a low ebb after the crash of 1973–74. The company acquired interests in the

Mount Martin gold mines in Western Australia, which were spun off as a separate public company, and in oil exploration. Hampton's shares recovered from a low of 3p at the time Burney became involved to 120p when the company was sold as the property market boomed again in 1987.

He was also a mentor and associate of Michael (later Lord) Ashcroft, during the years when the young Ashcroft was building up his Hawley Leisure (later ADT) group by a series of bold acquisitions. They invested together in Customagic, a maker of stretch covers for armchairs, of which Burney became chairman. Burney was also chairman, from 1988 to 1992, of Rhino Group plc, a computer software retailer.

Burney was a stylish figure, with a youthful spirit and a lively sense of humour. He enjoyed tennis and skiing in his prime, racing, shooting and fine wine in later life. He succeeded his father in the baronetcy in 1968. The family's Zimbabwean property was sold in the early 1990s – the name Little England being thought too provocative to avoid expropriation by the Mugabe regime.

Cecil Burney married, in 1957, Hazel Coleman; they had two sons, of whom the elder, Nigel, born in 1959, succeeded to the baronetcy.

19 April 2002

Sir Colin Campbell

⤙═ 1925–1997 ═⤚

Kenyan tea trader

Sir Colin Campbell, 8th Bt, of Aberuchill, was awarded an MC in 1945 and became a leader of the East African tea trade. Known affectionately as 'Sir Cumference', Campbell was a substantial figure in every sense. As the general manager in Nairobi of the Glasgow-based tea merchants James Finlay & Co, he was chairman for ten years of the Tea Board of Kenya, three times chairman of the East African Tea Trade Association and president of the Federation of Kenyan Employers.

An astute but idiosyncratic operator, Campbell was regarded by his own staff with a mixture of 'awe, fear, exasperation and affection, in that order', as one colleague put it. Never an enthusiast for modern management techniques, he addressed almost everyone by their surname only and peppered his memoranda with Latin, French and Hindi phrases. He drove like a maniac, claiming to have set a record for the fastest journey from Nairobi to Finlay's estates at Kericho in the Kenyan Highlands in his Humber Super Snipe.

The only son of the 7th baronet, Colin Moffat Campbell was born on 4 August 1925 and succeeded his father in 1960. The family descended from Lord Aberuchill, a Lord of Justiciary who sat as MP for Perthshire in the old Scottish parliament and was created a baronet in 1667 or 1668, the original patent having been lost. Young Colin was educated at Stowe where he conceived an ambition to join James Finlay, to become chairman, and from that position to devote his time and money to restoring the family's Scottish seat, Kilbryde Castle, at Dunblane. All of this he did.

The castle had not been lived in by his father or grandfather (it had been let to a girls' school) and was much neglected by the time Campbell and his wife moved in on their return from Africa. The gardens had become a wilderness, but they worked hard on them, transforming them into a work of art far surpassing the original. The castle itself, though notorious for its freezing temperatures, became known in Campbell's time for its abundant hospitality.

During the war, in 1943, Campbell joined the third battalion of the Scots Guards, and was involved in the final stages of the North West Europe campaign. On 8 March 1945, when the battalion was in the wooded and heavily mined area near Bonninghardt, Lieutenant Campbell led his platoon in the dark, captured the Romer Bridge and held it under sustained enemy mortar fire. Though wounded, Campbell stayed with his platoon, refusing to be evacuated until the next day. When, after a period in hospital, he felt he had recovered sufficiently, he discharged himself and rejoined his regiment – to the dismay of the hospital which, finding its patient missing, reported him as a deserter.

The next April, at Kircktimke, the area was so heavily mined that the left flank company in which Campbell was serving lost all but two tanks and most of its senior officers, who were either killed, wounded or incapacitated. Campbell, already wounded by shell splinters, found himself the senior officer in the village. He took control of his own and F company and co-ordinated the attack using the two remaining tanks. When the two new company commanders arrived, they found the position consolidated, the village clear of snipers, three self-propelled guns destroyed – one by a PIAT (Projector Infantry Anti-Tank) – under Campbell's personal direction, and all under control in spite of heavy shelling by the Germans.

On leaving the army in 1947, Campbell joined James Finlay and spent ten years in the firm's Calcutta office. There, his enormous, autocratic personality was quickly and firmly established in the commercial, social and sporting life of the city. In 1958, he moved to Nairobi, where he became chairman of the Kenya Tea Board. He found Kenya less congenial than Calcutta. His definition of perfect boredom was 'sitting in the car, keeping quiet, watching sleeping lions in a game park'. In Kenya his weight rose to 26 stone. When playing squash he would position himself in the centre of the court and, by playing ambidextrously, would make it impossible for an opponent to get past him to score a point. When serving on committees, his huge figure, wreathed in cigar smoke, dominated the proceedings. Of Campbell's management style, a friend wrote that 'whatever tactics he used for reigning supreme, furtiveness was not one of them. He was wont to announce his impending arrival by shouting at all and sundry as they came within range – a considerable distance.' Though forthright, Campbell was never overbearing towards his inferiors. He had a keen sense of humour and delighted in shocking colleagues with outrageous remarks. He was a keen race-goer and a first-rate bridge player.

Returning to Scotland in 1971, he joined the main board of James Finlay, and was chairman from 1975 to 1990. When in 1983 a *World in Action* programme reported that conditions on the company's Bangladesh plantations were the worst in the world, Campbell dismissed the allegations as 'absolute codswallop'. Though he defended the level of wages paid to tea-plantation workers, he was critical of company bosses who awarded themselves extravagant pay rises.

In 1981 he became a member of the Commonwealth Development Corporation (CDC was the government's vehicle for lending to Commonwealth projects) which he had helped to establish. He was deputy chairman from 1983 to 1989. To the horror of earnest development economists on CDC's staff, Campbell invariably referred to the corporation's clients as 'darkies', but his practical knowledge of Africa was invaluable, and it was recognised that, in terms of rudeness, he treated all races with complete equality.

In later life, Campbell showed utter disregard for the risks of his diabetic condition: he drank a concoction of gin, cointreau and bitter lemon before dinner, and never missed a chocolate pudding, declaring that he could always take another slug of insulin if things took a turn for the worse. His physical condition did not deter him from gruelling itineraries to visit CDC schemes.

Colin Campbell married, in 1952, Mary Bain, whom he described cheerfully as 'my most consistent and determined critic' whilst acknowledging equally cheerfully that no one else could have put up with him as a husband. They had a daughter and two sons, of whom the elder, James, born in 1956, succeeded to the baronetcy.

1 December 1997

Major Sir Rupert Clarke

╼═╾ 1919–2005 ═╾

Australian landowner

Major Sir Rupert Clarke, 3rd Bt, was a prominent Australian landowner, businessman, socialite and gentleman of the Turf. During the Second World War he was a valued ADC to Lieutenant General Sir Harold Alexander, later Earl Alexander of Tunis.

Rupert William John Clarke was born in Sydney on 5 November 1919. His great-grandfather William, known as 'Big Clarke', emigrated from Somerset to Van Dieman's Land (now Tasmania) as a stockman and butcher in 1829. A notorious miser, he prospered through moneylending and in due course amassed vast land holdings in the colony of Victoria. These properties and a £4 million fortune passed to Big Clarke's son, also William, who was created Australia's first and only baronet in 1882. Sir William had built himself a fifty-room mansion called Rupertswood (after his own eldest son) near Melbourne, which – also in 1882 – provided the venue for the original 'Ashes' cricket match.

That summer, as president of Melbourne Cricket Club, Sir William had watched an Australian team trounce England at the Oval – prompting the *Sporting Times* in London to publish an announcement of the death of English cricket: 'The body will be cremated and the ashes taken to Australia.'

Clarke returned to Australia on the same ship as the English touring party and invited them to spend Christmas at Rupertswood, where they beat the local side. As a congratulatory gesture, Lady Clarke burned the bails and presented the ashes in an urn to the English captain Ivo Bligh.

Rupert inherited the baronetcy in 1926 from his father, also Sir Rupert, whose achievements included leading expeditions to remote parts of Papua New Guinea. His widowed mother was remarried in 1928 to the 5th Marquess of Headfort, whose seat was in County Meath. The young baronet was educated at Eton and Magdalen College, Oxford, where he read law.

Clarke was commissioned into the Irish Guards in May 1940 and posted to the 1st Battalion. In April the next year he was appointed ADC to Lieutenant General Sir Harold Alexander, GOC Southern Command, whose HQ was at Wilton House, near Salisbury. When Alexander was appointed GOC Burma, Clarke accompanied him in the withdrawal to India. Shortly before Rangoon was evacuated, he and Alexander were having dinner with the governor at the residency when a number of dacoits invaded the garden, intent on looting the place. Clarke leaped through the French windows and routed them. He remained with Alexander in the campaign to push Rommel's forces out of North Africa and, subsequently, in the invasion of Sicily and the long slog up through Italy. There, King George VI visited the troops and Clarke was given the job of finding a bath for HM. Having 'liberated' one, he placed it under some trees near HM's caravan, fetched hot water from the cookhouse and, knocking on the door, said: 'Your Majesty, the bath is ready.'

Clarke thought he had done rather well, and was somewhat put out when the King gave him a rocket in the Mess, complaining that he had found olive leaves floating in his tub.

The two Irish Guards battalions in the Guards Armoured Division had suffered heavy casualties in the Ardennes, and Clarke felt that it was his duty to return to regimental service. Alexander was reluctant to lose him, but gave his permission; and Clarke considered himself fortunate when General Joe Cannon offered him a lift to Marseilles in his personal B-26 bomber. As they made their way across the Mediterranean, the plane lost an engine and rapidly descended to a few hundred feet. Clarke helped to jettison everything that could be thrown out: guns, ammunition – all went, including his personal kit and his parachute. The aircraft skimmed over the beach with a few feet to spare and landed on the airfield.

After attending the Senior Officers' Battle School, in April 1945 Clarke caught up with the 3rd Battalion in Germany and served as company commander of 2 Company until the end of the war. He returned to England in October 1945 and relinquished his commission the following year in the rank of major. He was appointed MBE (Military) in 1943. In 2000 he published a book of reminiscences, *With Alex at War*.

After the Second World War he returned to Australia. Rupertswood having been sold in the 1920s, he restored another family mansion, Bolinda Vale, where he entertained on the grandest of scales, welcoming visitors who ranged from Gregory Peck and Rex Harrison to the Emperor of Japan.

Among a portfolio of business interests acquired over the years, he was chairman of the Australian interests of P&O and United Distillers, and a director of Cadbury Schweppes. He was also a director for 36 years, and chairman from 1986 to 1992, of National Australia Bank, of which a constituent part, the Colonial Bank, had been founded by Big Clarke in 1856.

Sir Rupert was chairman of the Victoria Amateur Turf (now Melbourne Racing) Club from 1972 to 1988. He was one of the most influential and respected administrators in Australian racing as well as a successful owner and breeder in his own right. Though his Victorian landholdings were smaller than they had been in his grandfather's day, he also had an interest in a 3 million-acre ranch in Queensland.

He was president of the Royal Humane Society of Australia and honorary consul general for Monaco in Melbourne. He was appointed AM in 1999. Rupert Clarke married first, in 1947, Kathleen Grant Hay, by whom he had two sons (of whom the second predeceased him) and two daughters. Kathleen died in 1999, and he married secondly, in 2000, Gillian de Zoete. The heir to the baronetcy was his son Rupert, born in 1947.

4 February 2005

Sir Michael Herries

⊶≡⊙ 1923–1995 ⊙≡⊷

Model for James Clavell's 'Taipan'

Sir Michael Herries was a business leader and a respected public figure in Hong Kong, and later in his native Scotland. Having been Taipan of Jardine Matheson, the Far Eastern trading house, he went on to be chairman of the Royal Bank of Scotland. It was said that Herries provided the physical model for the Taipan in *Noble House* (1981), James Clavell's colourful novel about trading-house rivalries. Clavell's character – 'a big, ruddy, well-kept Scotsman with a slight paunch and white hair' – is advised by his successor to take up the post of deputy chairman of the 'First Central Bank of Edinburgh'.

In fact Herries returned to Britain to become chairman of the London end of Jardine Matheson, as was traditional. But his aim was always to return to his native Scotland, and in 1972 he joined the board of the Royal Bank, becoming deputy chairman in 1975 and executive chairman from 1976 to 1990. He was also chairman of the Scottish Widows Life Assurance Society.

Herries was a careful and determined businessman, with a head for figures and a meticulous eye for detail. Although not a banker by upbringing, he provided the Royal Bank with far-sighted strategic direction at a time of rapid change in the financial industry. He oversaw the merger of the bank with its English sister company, Williams & Glyns, and the broadening of its base by acquisition in America and by the development of the Direct Line insurance business.

The two strands of Herries's business career were briefly intertwined in 1981, when the Royal Bank was the subject of rival takeover bids from Standard Chartered and the HongKong & Shanghai Banking Corporation, of which Herries had been a director. HongKong Bank's bid was initially the higher of the two, but despite his former connection, Herries made clear to shareholders that he did not want the venerable Scottish institution (founded in 1727) to become a satellite of a business run from the Far East. In this he was in accord with the Governor of the Bank of England, Gordon Richardson, who had been offended by HongKong Bank's tactics. Herries's stance was in due course supported by the Monopolies Commission, which found against both bids on the grounds of potential damage to the Scottish economy. The Royal Bank retained its independence, and prospered under Herries' leadership.

Descended from Glasgow merchants and Edinburgh lawyers, Michael Alexander Robert Young-Herries of Spottes was born on 28 February 1923 at his ancestral home, Spottes, near Castle Douglas in the Stewartry of Kirkcudbright. He was educated at Eton and Trinity College, Cambridge, where his studies were interrupted by the outbreak of war in 1939.

Commissioned in the 5th (Dumfries & Galloway) Battalion of the Kings Own Scottish Borderers, which his father had commanded, he served in the northwest Europe campaign, and was awarded the Military Cross for his actions at Flushing in Holland in November 1944. Promoted acting major, he went on to be a battalion adjutant in the Middle East.

After the war he considered staying in the Army, but instead trained briefly with an Edinburgh accountancy firm before returning to Cambridge to finish his degree. A career with Jardine Matheson was in a way a natural choice for him since the Glenkiln estates of the Keswicks, descendants of Jardine Matheson's founder, lie not far from the Herries lands, although the families were unconnected; many young men from the area have found fortune in Hong Kong over the years.

Michael Herries joined Jardines in 1948 and – having first obtained his employers' permission to marry his fiancée – was posted to Hong Kong the next year. He also served in Tokyo and Singapore before becoming a director of Jardines in 1959 and Taipan in 1963. His early years with the firm saw much development of Jardines' China trade, including the controversial sale to the communist government of a fleet of Vickers Viscount aircraft. But with the advent of the Cultural Revolution the focus of growth shifted to South-East Asia and Australia. Herries spoke in later life of the 'great broadening' he had gained from his years in the East. Despite a background of turmoil in China, Herries was able to hand over a strong, well-ordered business to his successor, the young Henry Keswick, in 1970.

His many commitments outside business included the chairmanship of the Scottish Disability Foundation and the presidency of the Royal Highland Show. He was a member of the Royal Company of Archers, the Queen's Bodyguard for Scotland, and in 1989 was appointed Lord Lieutenant of the Stewartry District of Dumfries & Galloway.

A countryman at heart, Herries was deeply attached to his estate at Spottes, where he did much to modernise the house (built by his ancestor in 1784) and 350-acre farm. He was a magistrate, a pillar of both the Kirk and the Episcopal church, and patron of all manner of local causes and activities – ranging from Dumfries & Galloway Enterprise, of which he was founder chairman, to the Kirkcudbright & District pipe band, of which he was honorary president. He was a regimental trustee, and devoted supporter, of the KOSB.

Herries was appointed OBE in 1968 and knighted in 1975. He married, in 1949, Elizabeth Russell (née Smith). They had two sons and a daughter.

6 May 1995

Lord Kadoorie

⟶ 1899–1993 ⟵

Hong Kong power-station magnate

Lord Kadoorie was the last of Hong Kong's old-style Taipans, and a founder of the former British colony's modern economic miracle. Laurence Kadoorie's life spanned almost the entire modern history of Hong Kong – from shortly after the granting of the New Territories lease, to the period of debate over the return to Chinese rule when that lease was about to expire. In his untiring resourcefulness and optimism, Kadoorie embodied the unique character of Britain's last Asian colony. He was also powerfully representative of the political pragmatism which made Hong Kong what it is. He believed with Deng Xiaoping that 'in time the threads in the cloth will be so closely woven that capitalism and socialism will be as one', and that the territory would prosper in constructive co-operation with China without 'ill-considered interference by would-be politicians'.

Kadoorie himself had close ties with Chinese leaders. In 1984 he went so far as to hoist the Chinese flag over one of his power stations to welcome a visiting mainland official. In an interview with the *Daily Telegraph* in 1992, he said there was a good deal of conceit in Hong Kong. 'People seem to think that we are a country, but we are not and never have been. We are a free zone of China,' he observed.

Laurence's father, Sir Elly Kadoorie, came from a family of Jewish merchants in Baghdad. He had arrived in Hong Kong in 1880 to work for Sassoons, the trading company, which he represented in Shanghai and other Chinese cities – until he was dismissed, at Ningpo, for using disinfectant from the company's stores without authorisation. Returning to Hong Kong, Elly was given 500 dollars by a brother already established there, to enable him to start trading on his own. Under the surname Kelly (adopted by the family for some years) he set up the brokerage firm of Benjamin, Kelly & Potts, the foundation stone of the Kadoorie business empire.

Elly married into another old Jewish family, the Mocattas. Their son Laurence was born in Hong Kong on 2 June 1899. Educated at the Cathedral School in Shanghai and later at Clifton, he went on to read for the bar in Lincoln's Inn and served his pupilage in Shanghai before joining his father's business. That business had grown to encompass the China Light & Power Company, the sole supplier of electricity to Kowloon, the New Territories and Lantau Island; a string of hotels, of which the magnificent Peninsula on the Kowloon waterfront was the flagship; and extensive interests in Shanghai, then the Paris of the Orient, where the family lived in grand style in the 1920s and '30s.

The Second World War took a heavy toll on the Kadoories. The family was interned, and Sir Elly died in captivity. Japanese soldiers tore down China Light's main power station, and what they did not destroy in Shanghai was shortly to be confiscated by Chinese communists. But Laurence and his younger brother Horace set to rebuilding the Hong Kong businesses after the war, with outstanding success. Their style was conservative, with tight cost-control and low borrowing, despite the capital-hungry nature of the business.

China Light's position was consolidated in 1959 when Laurence outmanoeuvred a threat of nationalisation from Whitehall and obtained instead a favourable 'scheme of control', under which the company was allowed to earn profits in relation to the capital devoted to its plants. It continued to invest heavily in new capacity, and Kadoorie was frequently beseeched by politicians (including Margaret Thatcher) to buy British – which he did to the tune of some £600 million for the Castle Peak power complex in the early 1980s.

More controversial was China Light's participation in a £2 billion nuclear venture in China, the Daya Bay station in Shenzen. Kadoorie believed passionately in the value of such projects to cement triangular relations between Hong Kong, China and Britain, but fellow residents were deeply concerned by the safety risk of a Chinese nuclear plant only 50 miles from the border.

Kadoorie's experience gave him a philosophical view of Hong Kong's notoriously volatile economy and stock market. His father had told him not to worry about the colony 'as long as people keep digging holes', and there was rarely a time when the panorama from his office did not include massive construction works along the harbour front. During the communist riots of 1967, he ordered welders to keep working on his own sites so that the sparks in the night would show people he had confidence in the future. He was saddened, however, by the speculative short-termism of some of the colony's younger businessmen which, he said, 'destroys the past'. In 1987, with help from the colony's banking establishment, the Kadoories fought off an audacious bid by the Lau brothers for Hong Kong & Shanghai Hotels (the group which includes the Peninsula); the tussle seemed to symbolise the difference between business generations.

Kadoorie's other interests included the chairmanship of Hong Kong Carpet Manufacturers, Nanyang Cotton Mill and Schroders Asia (originally Schroders & Chartered) as well as joint proprietorship with Horace of the family holding company, Sir Elly Kadoorie & Sons. The two brothers worked closely in all their endeavours; it was even said that they shared a personal bank account, never querying each other's expenses.

Charitable work was also jointly initiated, and characteristically practical: through the Kadoorie Agricultural Aid Association and the New Territories Benevolent Society, they provided Chinese war widows and displaced farmers with goats, pigs and other necessities of peasant subsistence. By the mid-1950s, some 300,000 citizens had benefited.

Diminutive, sharp-eyed and sprightly, Kadoorie continued to attend his office daily at the end of his ninth decade. It was said that, whenever he was driven about Kowloon and the New Territories, he would telephone managers of China Light from his Rolls-Royce to tell them of street lights in need of repair.

In December 1992, he finally retired as chairman of China Light and Power, though he became honorary chairman and remained on the board.

'I think it's time for a little change,' he said, 'but the policy of the company remains the same. We are conservative, we are careful, and we think we have done a lot for the people of Hong Kong.'

Kadoorie was appointed CBE in 1970, knighted in 1974 and created a life peer in 1981.

In private Kadoorie had a passion for sports cars – he opened the colony's first Aston Martin agency 'so that I can own one myself'. He was also a connoisseur of Chinese art and the keeper of a fine family collection of jade.

Laurence Kadoorie married, in 1938, Muriel Gubbay. They had a son, Michael, who became chairman of the family hotel interests and a daughter, Rita.

25 August 1993

Kerry Packer

⊶⊷ 1937–2005 ⊷⊶

Australian media tycoon

The Australian media baron Kerry Packer proved himself one of the toughest and shrewdest business brains of his time, but his name will always be associated with a coup that irrevocably altered the character of international cricket. In May 1977 one of his magazines, the *Bulletin*, announced out of the blue that 35 of the world's best cricketers – including Imran Khan, Barry Richards, Graeme Pollock, Tony Greig, Greg Chappell, Clive Lloyd and Viv Richards – had signed lucrative contracts of between one and three years to play a series of one-day games in Australia that year.

The deal had been born of Packer's frustration at his failure to negotiate an arrangement with the Australian Cricket Board that would give Channel Nine – owned by Packer's Television Corporation – exclusive rights to televise first-class cricket in Australia. The board's obduracy was inexplicable to Packer, whose business philosophy was always robust. 'Come on,' he told them, 'we're all harlots – what's your price?'

This exchange set the tone for the subsequent struggle between a conservative cricket establishment, which was unwilling on any account to relinquish control of the game, and a ruthless, dynamic entrepreneur who had no desire whatever to be taken as a gentleman. Packer once expressed his regret that Australians had inherited the English mentality rather than the American. 'In business,' he philosophised, 'you don't tell your opponents what you are going to do; you do it and let them get on with it.'

In truth, the cricket authorities, taken completely by surprise, hardly knew what to do. Their initial reaction hardly went beyond outrage that Packer's organisation had, in total secrecy, managed to suborn players whose loyalty appeared beyond question. Tony Greig, who had not only signed for Packer himself, but actively canvassed other players to join him, was captain of England at the time; and Greg Chappell, the captain of Australia, had been serving on a sub-committee of the Australian board that had been designed to involve players more closely with the administration of the game. The cricket authorities' fears that cricket would be prostituted to the demands of television were to some extent justified by events; and there was no denying that the fixtures which Packer had arranged were in direct conflict with the official Test programme.

At first, it seemed that some compromise might be possible. A meeting at Lords on 23 June 1977 between the International Cricket Conference (ICC) and Packer (with Richie Benaud in attendance) appeared at first to be on the brink of success, only to founder on Packer's absolute insistence on exclusive television rights. 'Now it's every man for himself, and the devil take the hindmost,' was Packer's parting shot as he left the meeting.

For his part, the ICC chairman reflected that, 'Wars are not won by appeasement.' The ICC's determination not to be browbeaten, however, led it into grave error, for it issued a diktat that, after 1 October 1977, any player who made himself available to play in a match disapproved by the Conference would thereafter be banned from Test cricket. In the autumn the High Court decreed that the ban constituted an illegal attempt to interfere with the players' contracts with Packer's organisation.

The World Series Cricket, as the Packer matches were known, certainly represented a departure from traditional ideas of cricket. Many games were played under floodlights at night, with a white ball, black sightscreens, and teams attired in what appeared to be pyjamas – pink for the West Indies and yellow for Australia – in order to secure the largest possible television audience. But the matches were by no means an instant success; the cameras had to concentrate on the pitch to avoid showing the yawning spaces in the stands. Only during the second year's programme, in 1978–79, did the matches begin to attract a large following – mainly because the Australian crowds, notoriously intolerant of sporting failure, turned away in disgust from the contemporaneous spectacle of the official national side going down to humiliating defeat against Mike Brearley's England team.

Packer, ever the opportunist, offered the Australian board large sums of money to field a full Australian team, including 'his' players, in a 'deciding' fixture. This notion came to nothing, but the Australians were now ready to come to terms that appeared close to surrender. In April and May 1979 it was agreed that Kerry Packer should disband World Series Cricket. The board agreed what they had always previously rejected, that – in return for an unspecified amount of money – they should give Packer exclusive rights to the televising of first-class cricket in the country. In addition the board undertook to cancel the Australian tour of India scheduled for 1979–80, to allow a further series of one-day fixtures between Australia, England and the West Indies. PBL, one of Packer's companies, was to be in charge of selling the game to the Australian public. Packer also demanded that no player should be victimised for having signed a contract with him. The truce was ratified by the ICC at the end of June 1979.

Nevertheless, Packer's influence on cricket did not die with the World Series. Through the terms he had offered, and through the sponsorship which he had attracted into the game, the salaries of top players were more than doubled. It has been remarked, with justice, that players' pay was improving before the Packer revolution, and that the lesser players did not share in the bonanza; even so, the difference in the remuneration of Test cricketers before and after Packer remains startling. In the mid-1970s Bob Willis was earning £7,000 a year, or twice the average male salary; in 1987 Graham Dilley received some £45,000 – four times the average salary.

Packer's brash methods also left the authorities more conscious of the need to please crowds, while television coverage was greatly improved. Although the proliferation of one-day cricket might be counted on the debit side by purists, the jolt which Packer delivered cannot be reckoned either untimely or undeserved.

But the controversy over Packer's involvement with cricket, for all the heat that it generated, was only one incident in its protagonist's protean business career. With Rupert Murdoch he was the most successful of the new breed of international operators produced by Australia. Packer was Australia's richest man – thought to be worth A$6.9 billion (or nearly £3 billion). Television stations, magazines, films, cattle stations, engineering works, property and building, ski resorts, plantations, mines, chemicals, mineral water – he made or lost money on them all.

No deal was too big for his pocket, or too small to engage his interest. If Packer built no outstanding monuments, he nevertheless took the long view with some of his investments, particularly his cattle properties, which he invariably left in better shape than he found them.

He denied being interested in power – 'it doesn't keep you warm at nights' –and he convincingly repudiated any intellectual interests – 'the ultimate purgatory for me would be to go to the Opera House and hear Joan Sutherland sing; ugh!'

Everything, even his television empire, was for sale if the price was right. Packer's affairs had a kaleidoscopic quality – forever changing, never achieving final coherence. Nevertheless, supported by a small and expert management team, he never seemed in the least danger of joining the grim procession of those Australian contemporaries who overreached themselves. Detractors claimed he owed less to ability than to the good fortune of inheriting, in 1974, a publishing and broadcasting empire from his father, Sir Frank Packer. But if Kerry Packer was lucky in business, his luck endured. He managed to sell most of his stock market investments just before the crash of October 1987. Perhaps his most remarkable feat, though, was to obtain an absurd A$1,055 million from an eager Alan Bond in 1987 for two television stations in Sydney and Melbourne, and some radio interests – and then to buy the television interest back from the ruins of Bond's empire (after Bond had been disgraced) for a fifth of what Bond had paid him.

Apart from television, Packer's main business interest was in magazines – among them *Australian Business*, *Australian Women's Weekly*, *Cosmopolitan*, and the *Bulletin*. He also owned Valassis, the largest publisher of free-standing coupon inserts in the US. In addition he was one of Australia's biggest landowners, with vast rural properties in the Northern Territory, Queensland and New South Wales, and with interests in cattle, wool and cotton.

As an employer he adopted a patriarchal approach: all his employees would receive food-and-drink hampers at Christmas. He was always prepared to delegate – but he expected results, and those who failed to achieve them were liable to find themselves on the wrong side of his temper.

Socially Packer might have appeared to be shy, but his features, which suggested a bruiser, and his bear-like physique, which underscored the impression, did not deceive. 'When you see Kerry Packer,' Sir Les Patterson, Australia's cultural attaché (as created by Barry Humphries), advised, 'don't ask him why he's wearing a stocking over his face, he'll have heard that one before . . .'

Packer mixed with politicians and used them when he could, but had no loyalty to any party and, despite his friendship with various politicians, no one ever alleged corruption against him in relation to them. What did tarnish his reputation, though, was the Royal Commission conducted by Frank Costigan, QC, which began as an inquiry into union activities in Victoria, but burgeoned out to examine an enormous area of Australian society. Allegations arose that Packer had been involved in a tax offences, in smuggling drugs, in pornography, and in the death of a bank manager. In reporting these claims the *National Times* used the code name of 'the Goanna' (a large Australian lizard), whereupon Packer identified himself publicly as the person referred to, and came out fighting. He had the satisfaction of an unqualified clearance by the Federal Attorney General, and apologies in four newspapers published by the Fairfax Group. But the experience left him bitter towards the media.

Kerry Francis Bullmore Packer was born on 17 December 1937, the second of two sons of Sir Frank Packer, the Sydney media proprietor. In the 17th century the Packers, established in Berkshire, had been staunch Royalists; in the 18th century the family had shown a strong musical bent – Kerry's great-great-great-grandfather was the organist of St Mary's Minster in Reading; and his great-great-grandfather Frederick Alexander Packer, also a musician, married Augusta Gow, daughter of Neil Gow, one of Scotland's best-known composers.

Frederick Alexander emigrated to Tasmania in the middle of the 19th century. It was Kerry's grandfather, Robert Clyde Packer, who began the family's association with journalism, becoming editor of the Sydney *Sunday Times*, having moved from Tasmania after finding 10 shillings in the street and placing it on a horse. Frank, Kerry's father, once heavyweight boxing champion of New South Wales, built up a newspaper empire with a combination of hard work and devil-may-care bravado.

Life was tough for young Kerry. When he erred he would receive a summons from his father to don boxing gloves and meet him in one of the larger rooms of their Belvedere Hill mansion, a method of discipline that at least had the merit of making Kerry the school boxing champion. At Cranbrook School in Sydney and Geelong in Victoria, the boy devoted himself to games as an escape from schoolwork that was often beyond him. In later years it became clear that he had suffered a degree of dyslexia. On one occasion, when Kerry returned from Geelong to Sydney for the school holidays without his tennis racquet, his father, anxious to inculcate a sense of the value of possessions, sent him straight back by train – a 1,200-mile journey – to retrieve it. 'Arrived Melbourne safely,' the miscreant telegraphed, 'no love, Kerry.'

His elder brother Clyde was brought up as the future controller of Consolidated Press, parent company for the Packer newspapers, but departed after a fierce row with his father for Los Angeles, where he became a successful impresario. Kerry bought out his share in the business, and after Sir Frank died in 1974 assumed control of the television, radio and magazine interests. In 1983 he took the company private and accelerated the diversification and growth at a rate that astonished even his admirers. He came within an ace of merging his media interests with those of the *Herald* and *Weekly*

Times, which backed out at the last moment, only to be taken over soon afterwards by Rupert Murdoch.

In 1989 he acquired control of Australian National Industries, the country's largest engineering group, but his interests stretched far beyond his native land. 'I want to live in Australia,' he said, 'but you have to protect your organisation by going overseas and by being defensive when investing in Australia.' In 1987 he made a handsome profit by selling his holding in Hill Samuel to the Trustee Savings Bank, and in 1989 he linked up with Sir James Goldsmith and Jacob Rothschild to buy a 30 per cent share of Rank Hovis McDougall in Britain. Later the same trio made a £13 billion bid for BAT Industries, the tobacco conglomerate, but this venture came to nothing.

In 2004 he entered an agreement with the British betting exchange Betfair to help it enter the Australian market; he had been planning to build supercasinos in this country next year. Packer was an expert, and compulsive, gambler, both on the horses and at the tables. He told the Costigan Inquiry that at one stage he had withdrawn a million dollars in cash from a Sydney bank for betting purposes. In 1999 he was reported to have lost £11 million at Crockford's in London. He was, more remarkably, once reported to have won twenty hands of baccarat in a row at Las Vegas. There, a Texan oilman at Packer's table brashly announced he was worth $60 million. 'Toss you for it,' came the laconic reply.

In the summer of 1989 he was said to have won £7 million at Crockford's and Aspinall's in London; he later won a further £4.5 million, £2.4 million of it playing blackjack at the Clermont, betting £25,000 on each of the seven boxes on the table. With typical generosity he gave away much of his winnings – £100,000 to each of the seven members of his polo squad. Similar stories abounded. After a restaurant refused to open for him after hours, he proceeded to the next, where he tipped the waiter £10,000. 'Make sure your mate down the road gets to hear,' he said. When one waitress at a coffee shop, asked why she wasn't at home with her family, pointed out that she had a mortgage, she got home to find it had been paid off.

Other, less well-known, examples of his beneficence included his purchase of a von Guerard painting, said to be worth A$750,000, for the National Gallery of Victoria; a donation of A$500,000 for the Cambridge Commonwealth Trust for postgraduate study at Cambridge; finance for a theatre for the exclusive Ascham Girls School in Sydney; and a Disneyland holiday for a child suffering from cerebral palsy.

With the demise of World Series Cricket, polo became Packer's ruling passion. Failing health and increasing bulk (though he was a heavy smoker) never stood in his way; he took up the sport up on a grand scale in the 1980s, spending £15 million at Ellerston, his 75,000-acre estate in New South Wales, on a new house and seven polo grounds. He also laid out $1.5 million on ponies in Argentina, and in 1989 bought a 1000-acre estate, Fyning Hill Farm, at Rogate in West Sussex for £5 million – for the use of the players in his Australian team. Unsurprisingly, Packer's Ellerston White established itself as the most consistent team in England; and his contribution to the sport was recognised when the Queen invited him into the royal box to watch a polo match.

After a heart attack on the polo field in 1991, he was declared clinically dead, but returned with the news that there was no after-life. It was the first of a series of cardiac arrests; he also received a kidney (donated by his pilot) in 2000, when he was falsely reported dead. He was also reported as having suffered from cancer.

Packer was a Companion of the Order of Australia. In 1963 he married Roslyn Weedon; they had a daughter and a son, James, to whom Packer ceded control of some of the family businesses several years before he died.

26 December 2005

Sir Y. K. Pao

-+⇒ 1918–1991 ⇐+-

Shipping magnate

Sir Y.K. Pao was one of the ten richest men in the world, with a personal fortune estimated at £3.5 billion. A banker-turned-ship-owner, he was once dubbed 'the Chinese landlubber who came to rule the seas'.

He started his merchant fleet by investing what he called 'a few dollars' in a pre-war tramp steamer, bought in London and named by him *The Golden Alpha*. By the 1980s 'YK' had taken on and beaten the big Greek shipowners and had a fleet of some two hundred vessels, which at 19 million tons or so was equivalent to half the British merchant marine, and bigger than the Soviet Union's.

The landlubber then returned to the land, with control of six of Hong Kong's top two hundred companies, and humbled the great trading house Jardine Matheson (of which he then owned about 18 per cent) by beating 'the Princely Hong' in a battle for control of the Hong Kong and Kowloon and Godown Property company.

'Hong Kong,' went the old adage, 'is run by the Jockey Club, the HongKong Bank and the Governor – in that order.' Now Pao had to be added to this list, a role model to the millions of Hong Kong Chinese who, like him, had fled communist China.

Based in Hong Kong, he spent much of his time in Tokyo, Hong Kong and London, where he was said to be a generous contributor to the Conservative Party. Certainly he was friendly with Margaret Thatcher – she called him YK and he called her PM.

'Perhaps no other industry,' he told a United Nations committee in 1970, 'can enjoy such a high degree of leverage as is available to shipowners, partly due to assistance from the public or semi-public sectors in most shipbuilding countries.'

Despite his astonishing riches, Pao was on excellent terms with mainland China. Peking made him vice-chairman of the committee which drafted the Basic Law, the mini-constitution which will govern the territory after China takes back sovereignty in 1997.

Personable, urbane and effusive, Pao's chief disappointment in life was described as being second into the hotel swimming pool for his early morning dip. He was virtually teetotal and a non-smoker – examples he liked his employees to follow – but did allow himself some relaxation, particularly at the launching of his ships. In 1971, for example, in the festivities attending the launch of a tanker at Nagasaki, Pao could be seen at the city's premier geisha establishment, clad in Japanese 'happi' coat and headband leading a group of dignitaries (including Sir John Saunders, the then head of the HongKong and Shanghai Bank) in an impromptu dragon dance, complete with full-blown Banzai choruses.

Yue-Kong (the name means 'Silver Jade') Pao was born at Ningpo in Zhejiang Province in eastern China on 10 November 1918, the second of three sons in a trading family. He began his banking career at twenty in Shanghai, and by the end of the Second World War was the general manager of that city's municipal bank. In the immediate postwar period Pao's job was to grapple with the effects of inflation – an experience which stood him in good stead.

In 1949, with innumerable others, he fled the mainland ahead of the new regime and established himself in an import-export business in Hong Kong. Having acquired *The Golden Alpha*, he soon added three more ships to his fleet, and in 1956 he gained some impetus with the Egyptian seizure of the Suez Canal and its effect on international shipping. More important, in terms of his fleet's dramatic growth, was his policy of fixing ships on time charter – a strategy dating from his banking days – rather than involve his vessels in the vagaries of the spot market through single-voyage charters. And, much like a property developer with a tenant, he would arrange charters before his ships were built, borrowing 80 per cent of the cost.

During the 1950s Pao established himself as the key financial intermediary between the shipping lines on one hand and the bankers and builders on the other. In 1956, for example, he forged strong links with the HongKong and Shanghai Bank, and with the British concern of Wheelock Marden. In the 1960s he phased out the old ships and acquired a modern fleet, displaying the white 'W' (for Worldwide) emblem on a red background bordered in white and blue on the funnels.

The bulk of his fleet was built in Japanese yards. 'I will build anywhere if the price is right,' he explained. 'I would like to order more from Britain, but frankly it is very difficult for your yards to control delivery dates. Nor is the price competitive. And we worry about individual UK shipbuilders going bankrupt.' Similarly, Pao preferred flags of convenience, which meant that there was no legal requirement for senior officers to be British or Commonwealth nationals.

The fuel crisis of the mid-1970s brought the worst slump in shipping for more than forty years, in the midst of which 'YK' sat happy and secure, with a fleet of 135. He was building still more, and waited for bargains as the banks moved in on less prudent owners. His years of going for the thin profit margin had paid off handsomely. At that time, too, he moved into a new generation of very large crude carriers in the 400,000-ton class – just as in the 1980s he welcomed the new idea, robot ships, predicting vast convoys of them by the end of the century.

In 1986 Pao officially retired, but he continued to take an active role in the decisions of his companies. The same year, for instance, he helped thwart Lloyds Bank's bid for Standard Charter, by spending £180 million on a 15 per cent holding (which he sold three years later). In the late 1980s he bought the American Omni Hotels Group for $135 million cash, emerged as a large investor in British banks, and made an unsuccessful attempt to get into cable television in Hong Kong.

Pao controlled the Star Ferry, the upper deck of which offered the best view of the Hong Kong skyline. He also owned the Hong Kong Tramway Co, the only surviving builder of wooden double-deck street cars.

A local JP in Hong Kong, Pao was appointed CBE in 1976 and knighted in 1978. A benefactor of the British Film Institute's Museum of the Moving Image on London's South Bank, and the only Buddhist on the Westminster Abbey Trust, he was also a member of the Royal & Ancient and Sunningdale Golf Clubs, where he had a handicap of 18.

He married, in 1940, Sue-Ing Huang; they had four daughters. The control of his companies passed to his four sons-in-law – a Chinese banker, an Austrian lawyer, a Japanese architect and a Chinese cancer specialist. As one of them put it, thanks to the conservative approach of their father-in-law, 'We can stand on our own feet in Hong King come hell or high water.'

23 September 1991

Sir Francis Renouf

-··=◇ 1918–1998 ◇==··-

Colourful New Zealand banker

Sir Francis Renouf was a flamboyant New Zealand financier nicknamed Frank the Bank; most of his millions were destroyed in the 1987 stock market crash.

Renouf claimed to have 'created the New Zealand capital market'. He made his name as a stockbroker and merchant banker in the 1950s, introducing innovations such as share underwriting and a national share price index. He went on to acquire industrial and real-estate interests, building a £90 million empire.

Frank Renouf was a glamorous and commanding figure, with the physique of the tennis champion he had been in his youth. He maintained luxurious homes in London and Australia as well as in New Zealand, and a fleet of Rolls-Royces – he complained about an oil leak in one of them at Rolls's annual general meeting. But the world stock market crash of October 1987 caused a dramatic reversal in his fortunes. Having already resigned as chairman of his major company, Renouf Corporation, he watched its shares lose 90 per cent of their value.

His second wife, the former Susan Sangster, then launched a legal battle to recoup £1.2 million which she claimed he had lost on her account. 'Everything has collapsed around me,' he said. 'A life's work has vanished.' Renouf's finances were in due course partially restored – he was said to be 'down to his last £15 million', and still drove Rolls-Royces – but his domestic life was not. His marriage to Susan ended in one of the southern hemisphere's most spectacularly acrimonious divorces, and was followed by a third marriage, to a former model and self-styled countess, which lasted a matter of weeks.

Francis Henry Renouf was born into a family of Channel Island descent on 31 July 1918, and educated in his native city of Wellington. During the Second World War he served as a captain in the New Zealand Expeditionary Force and was taken prisoner, spending four years in a German POW camp – after which, he said, 'I never want to sit down again.'

Returning from the war, he qualified as an accountant and studied economics at Oxford, where he won two Blues for tennis, having already represented New Zealand Universities. In later life he was president of the New Zealand Lawn Tennis Association and gave a large sum for the building of a tennis centre in Wellington which was named after him. He was knighted for his services to the game in 1987.

Renouf married first, in 1954, Anne Marie Harkin, by whom he had a son and three daughters. The couple separated in 1978 and the marriage was dissolved in 1985. In that year he married secondly the 42-year-old Susan Sangster, daughter of an Australian diplomat and ex-wife of the pools heir and racehorse owner Robert Sangster. Before Sangster, she had been married to Andrew Peacock, a former foreign minister of Australia who later led the Liberal Party in opposition.

Though she had first caught Renouf's eye some years earlier, the romance was a whirlwind one, conducted partly at the Wimbledon tennis championships. Susan claimed to have succumbed only when Renouf proposed for the fifth time, while according to the bridegroom, it was Susan who proposed, in the discotheque at the Intercontinental Hotel at Hyde Park Corner. Known to the press as 'The Sheila' and often described as Australia's leading socialite, the new Mrs Renouf denied that she was marrying for money, while one of her friends told the press that she was looking for 'a stable, calm relationship built on friendship'. Shortly after the wedding, Renouf bought Robert Sangster's £4 million waterfront mansion at Point Piper near Sydney – the most expensive house in Australia at the time – and renamed it, perhaps ill-advisedly, Paradis-sur-Mer. When the crash came Renouf needed the house as collateral for his debts, but Susan immediately claimed that he had given it to her as a love token. She also claimed that his share-dealing had lost a substantial portion of her £3.5 million divorce settlement from Sangster, and had welshed on an agreement to reimburse the shortfall – though Renouf countered that he had merely lost what he had made for her and she was still 'well ahead of the game'.

They separated, and Renouf sued his wife for defamation. But after two months of legal wrangling she returned to Paradis-sur-Mer to claim possession, provoking a two-week stand-off, dubbed by the local press 'the Siege of Point Piper', which involved rival teams of hired security guards. Renouf sought unsuccessfully to have Susan removed by the police, while she shouted to reporters over the fence that he was trying to starve her out of the house. Reconciliation was briefly attempted, but they were divorced in 1989, and Paradis was sold for £8 million.

His third marriage, to Michele Ivan-Zadeh-Griaznoff at Chelsea register office in 1991, was if anything even more disastrous. Twenty-eight years his junior, Michele styled herself Countess – the title apparently descended from her ex-husband's Russian great-aunt – and claimed to be the daughter of a deceased hotelier. This came as a shock to retired Australian taxi-driver Arthur Mainwaring, her real father, when he read about the wedding in a newspaper. He had never been an hotelier, he told reporters, though he might have played the piano in one.

The couple parted after six weeks, and were divorced in 1996. 'I mistook his pressing marriage proposal as a need for long-term commitment,' Michele said, 'rather than a short-term modelling engagement to adorn his empty arm at the Melbourne Tennis Open.'

13 September 1998

Sir John Saunders

◆═══◎ 1917–2002 ◎═══◆

War hero and Hong Kong banker

Sir John Saunders was chairman of the HongKong and Shanghai Banking Corporation at a time of rapid but turbulent development of the Hong Kong economy. During the Second World War he had won an MC and a DSO in Italy.

As chief manager (effectively chief executive) from 1962, and chairman from 1967 to 1972, Saunders was at the helm of Hong Kong's most important financial institution at a time when the Crown Colony was rapidly changing from a trading post to a regional centre of manufacturing and finance. A fierce pace of economic growth was fuelled by an influx of industrious migrants from China and an administration dedicated to laissez-faire policies on tax and trade. From 1966, however, domestic business confidence and dealings with mainland China were severely disrupted by Mao Tsetung's Cultural Revolution. In 1967 the devaluation of sterling – to which the Hong Kong currency was then fixed – brought another sharp blow.

Tall and confident, with perfect manners, Saunders led the bank through these events with a calming hand. In its centenary year, 1965, HongKong Bank was offered a majority stake in Hang Seng, a local retail bank which had suffered a sudden run on deposits after rumours that it was in trouble. Saunders was out of the colony when the crisis arose, but returned to complete the negotiation. In the same period, he broadened HongKong Bank's own customer base to include a new generation of Chinese (often Shanghainese) entrepreneurs, and acquired an equity stake in the shipping empire of Sir Y.K. Pao, with whom Saunders formed a close friendship. The bank also invested in the Swire family's Cathay Pacific airline. Its branch network expanded, and it was a frontrunner in the computerisation of retail banking.

The son of a banker, John Anthony Holt Saunders, widely

known as Jake, was born at Uxbridge on 29 July 1917 and educated at Bromsgrove School. He joined the HongKong and Shanghai Banking Corporation in London in 1937 on the introduction of the Duke of Devonshire, to whom his maiden aunt Elsie was private secretary. As training for his first tour of duty in the Far East, he was posted to the bank's Lyon branch, where the principal business was financing the silk trade with Indo-China. He became a lifelong Francophile, acquiring a particular enthusiasm for champagne and oysters.

When war broke out he resigned and took the train back to England to enlist in the Army. He attended OCTU at Sandhurst where he was awarded the Belt of Honour. He was commissioned into the 1st Battalion, East Surrey Regiment and fought with the battalion in North Africa, first as a platoon commander and later as intelligence officer. After the campaign in Sicily, he disembarked at Taranto with his battalion in September 1943. Early in October the next year, the battalion travelled on a circuitous route that took them through Assisi, Perugia and Arezzo to San Apollinare in the Tuscan Appennines. It was a grim, mountainous area with narrow, winding tracks, pitted with shell holes which turned to slippery mud in the heavy rain. The task of 78 Division, of which the 1st Surreys formed part, was to join in the offensive to break through the mountains to the Lombardy plain. The battalion's role was to capture two objectives, Monte La Pieve and Monte Spaduro, which blocked the advance.

On the night of 15 October, the 1st Surreys' attack on Monte Pieve was only partly successful, but an attack in brigade strength two days later ended in anti-climax when the enemy was found to have gone. Monte Spaduro, a massive, razor-backed ridge running from south to north remained in German hands and on the night of 23 October the battalion took part in a brigade attack on the feature. The approach march to the brigade assembly area took the 1st Surreys along miles of winding mountain tracks with steep, muddy gradients. After a heavy artillery barrage, A Company, commanded by Major Saunders and D Company led the assault on Monte Spaduro with C Company bringing up the rear.

By one o'clock in the morning, after heavy fighting, the

battalion had achieved the objective, but persistent sniping and machine-gun fire from the cover of deep gullies pinned down A Company and prevented C Company from moving up to its correct position. The following afternoon, Saunders tried to flush out the Germans with 2-inch mortars but this failed. The use of heavier weapons was considered but dismissed; the enemy was too close. When two men in the 1st Surreys attempted to move their position, one was sniped in the head and killed; the other took a bullet in the arm. Saunders grabbed a rifle and bayonet and, taking two men with him, worked his way round to the gully. Reaching a point above where the enemy appeared to be, he charged down the gully towards them, yelling as he did so. Four German soldiers with two Spandau light machine-guns surrendered. Saunders was awarded an immediate MC.

In the spring of 1945, the 8th Army's objective was to break through the German defences on the River Senio and River Santerno and drive through the Argenta Gap, a strip of land between Lake Comacchio, and flooded land south of the River Reno, to destroy the German armies south of the River Po. On 14 April, the 1st Surreys and the 2nd Battalion, the Lancashire Fusiliers, as part of 11th British Infantry Brigade, moved up to a concentration area in readiness for an assault on the Argenta Gap. The Lancashire Fusiliers had suffered heavy casualties and Saunders was transferred from the 1st Surreys and appointed second-in-command.

The 11th Brigade crossed the River Reno and negotiated extensive minefields until it reached the outskirts of Argenta. On the approach to Fossa Marina, a canal running north-eastwards from Argenta across the entire width of the Gap, it ran into strong opposition. It was essential to press on to the Fossa Marina before the enemy could establish a firm defence there, and it was decided that a full-scale assault would be necessary.

On the evening of 16 April the 1st Surreys moved forward after dark and secured a base from which the Lancashire Fusiliers could cross the Fossa Marina and establish a limited bridgehead beyond it. At midnight, after a bitter struggle, a foothold had been secured across the canal when the commanding officer of the Lancashire

Fusiliers was wounded and the attack became stabilised on the line of the canal. At this critical moment, Major Saunders took command of the battalion and, under his leadership all the objectives were reached and held against determined counter-attacks the following morning. He was awarded an immediate DSO. He finished the war in Austria and left the Army in 1946.

After the war he rejoined the bank in Singapore and was posted to Hong Kong in the early 1950s. He became Chief Accountant in 1955 and held a series of appointments in Hong Kong and Singapore, before becoming Chief Manager. As head of the bank, Saunders was also an important civic figure: he was a member of the Executive Council, was much involved in the development of Hong Kong University, and was chairman of the stewards of the Royal Hong Kong Jockey Club, where he introduced a new level of professionalism. He was also a longstanding trustee of the Gurkha Welfare Trust. He was appointed CBE in 1970 and was knighted in 1972.

John Saunders married, in 1942, Enid Cassidy, who died in 1996. They had two daughters.

4 July 2002

⭑⟾ INDEX ⟾⭑